10-17-77

ROYAL ANTELOPE AND SPIDER

West African Mende Tales

Marion Kilson

ROYAL ANTELOPE AND SPIDER

West African Mende Tales

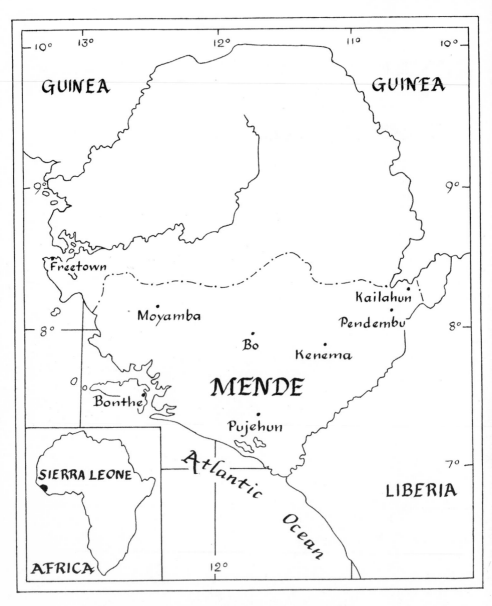

Map of SIERRA LEONE
showing MENDE Country

ROYAL ANTELOPE AND SPIDER

West African Mende Tales

Marion Kilson

The Press of The Langdon Associates
Cambridge, Massachusetts 1976

This is the second publication of
The Press of the Langdon Associates.
Langdon Associates was incorporated in
The Commonwealth of Massachusetts in March 1975
"to carry on any business, consulting, or other activity
related to publishing and/or acting as literary
agents or publishing consultants."

The Associates are men and women committed
to integrity, entertainment, and value in
publishing activities of all kinds. They
plan to collaborate at different times in
different projects according to their
talents, interests, and needs.

For Thomas O. Beidelman

ACKNOWLEDGMENTS

Anyone who does field research necessarily acquires a great many debts to individuals and institutions facilitating that research. When that research spans more than a decade, the indebtedness accrues proportionately.

My interest in collecting Mende tales led me to a course in the Mende language given by the Reverand A. Stott at the Institute of Commonwealth Studies, Oxford University in the fall of 1959. Late in 1959, my husband and I arrived in Sierra Leone where we enjoyed the hospitality of Fourah Bay College for fourteen months, thanks to then Principals Grant and Nicol. Throughout this period, my Mende studies were assisted by the Reverand Isaac M. Ndanema who graciously and generously helped me by finding narrators, transcribing and translating tales with me, and discussing Mende concepts. Others who were particulary helpful to me in 1960 included Madame Nancy Koroma, Mr. Kpanga Edwards, Miss Josephine Demby, Mr. Michael Alpha, Mr. J. Brima Konteh, and Mr. R. S. Burkett.

In the summer of 1972, I returned briefly to Sierra Leone under the auspices of a National Endowment for the Humanities Research Grant to enjoy the hospitality of Fourah Bay College, especially its Institute of African Studies, Mr. and Mrs. John Labor in Bumpe, and the Bunumbu Teacher Training College. Once again Mr. Ndanema was important to the success and enjoyment of my research. Mr. Samuel S. Lansana, as research assistant and interpreter, made an invaluable and essential contribution and to my work in Bumpe, Bunumbu, and Freetown. I am also appreciative of the generous help given to me by P. C. Mustapha and his staff in Bunumbu and the members of the local government authority in Bumpe.

Subsequently, I enjoyed the largesse of a National Endowment for the Humanities Faculty Summer Stipend while preparing this monograph. I also thank my family for their special contribution to my work. Martin Kilson has shared treasured parts of my two Sierra Leonean experiences. Jenny, Peter, and Hannah Kilson have let me travel afield and have entertained me at home; during my absences in Sierra Leone and at my New Hampshire desk Marion Greene, Edna Sargent, and Thomas Queenann have helped to amuse them.

Finally, I am grateful to Ann Orlov for embarking on this collaborative publishing venture with me and to Emily G. Dusser de Barenne for contributing her artistic skills to the creation of the cover, map, and title page of the book.

I thank you all!   M. K.
                                                    January 1976

CONTENTS

TABLES

INTRODUCTION: THE STUDY OF MENDE TALES

A renaissance of interest in African oral literature as
well as other art forms has occurred in social anthropology in
recent years.[1] Increasingly the value as well as the methodo-
logical limitations of oral literature for sociological understanding are stressed.[2] Moreover, whatever uses an analyst may
wish to make of oral literary forms, a renewed appreciation of
the necessity for vernacular textual materials has developed.
Without such data it is impossible for other students of an
oral tradition to reanalyze effectively their predecessors' interpretations. The study of Mende tales presented in this book
is intended as a contribution to the continuing tradition of
sociological concern with African oral literature.

From time to time during the twentieth century, articles
have appeared in various Sierra Leonean and European journals
recording and/or analyzing Mende songs, proverbs, and tales.[3]
Hitherto most scholarly attention has been given to Mende tales
both with respect to recording and to analysis.

Mende tales have been published in Mende, in English translation, and in summary form. Mende texts with and without
English translations are presented in Migeod's The Mende Language (1908), Sumner's A Handbook of the Mende Language (1917),
Eberl-Elber's "Two Mende Tales" (1940), and Stott's unpublished
manuscript "Mende Storytelling and Stories." In addition, several English texts or summaries of tales have been published by
Migeod, Harris, Little, Innes, Winch, and myself.[4] Not surprisingly a number of these tales are versions of one another.
I calculate that if the tales in this book are included in the
sample, Mende texts exist for 137 tales, while there are versions in Mende or English of 160 tales.[5]

Turning from the recording to the analysis of Mende tales,
several articles dealing with this issue have appeared in
Sierra Leonean journals over the past fifty years. Most of
these articles are concerned with issues of content rather than
of structure, but since certain articles have sparked debate in
others, it is useful to review this analytical literature
chronologically.

The first analytical article of which I know is J. S.
Fenton's "Characters in Mende Stories" (1929). Fenton main-
tains that Mende tales are amorphous, deriving their stability
from "the few characters, which have definite attributes, pos-
sibilities and limitations."[6] According to Fenton, such stock
characters include human beings, animals, and spirits. His
discussion of the behavior of twins and of three clever ani-
mals--Royal Antelope, Cat, and Spider, in stories are of continuing interest to contemporary scholars. Fenton does not
give any information about the corpus of tales on which his
analysis is based and his discussion is limited to a content

analysis of tales. Unfortunately, the patronizing tone of
Fenton's article and his employment of British rather than
Mende literary and cosmological categories seriously detract
from his pioneering commentary.

The second study of Mende stories is the Reverend A.
Stott's unpublished manuscript, "Mende Storytelling and
Stories." Stott, a Methodist missionary in Tikonko during
the 1940's, recorded tales while he was in Mendeland. In his
manuscript, Stott presents 26 Mende tales introduced with a
brief but comprehensive discussion of storytelling, tale categories, and characters. Stott concludes that "the characteristics of morality and humor as revealed in the folk-tales
seem to be borne out in real life--their portrayal in the tales,
it would seem, an objectifying of subjectivity."[7] Following
this preliminary discussion, Stott gives a schematic analysis
of the 26 tales in terms of such categories as kind of tale,
types of characters, ethical characteristics, types of humor,
and general critical comments. Additionally, English summaries
of the tales precede the presentation of the Mende texts.
Stott's effort to understand Mende categories of tale form,
discussion of Mende storytelling, and presentation of 26 texts
constitutes a significant, but relatively unknown, contribution
to Mende tale scholarship.

In 1960 and 1961, I published three short articles based
on my preliminary understanding of Mende tales. The first article, "Mende Folktales," noted briefly the role of storytelling
in Mende culture and the significance of tales for ethnographic
understanding; delineated four kinds of tales: origin tales,
fables, riddles, and proverb tales, and presented an example
of each "type" of tale in English. As is clear in Chapter 3, I
no longer support such a classification based on the structurally
incidental rather than the central features of Mende tales.
"Mende Folktales" was followed by "Supernatural Beings in Mende
Domeisia" and "Social Relationships in Mende Domeisia." As the
titles suggest, I was concerned with a content analysis of Mende
tales from variant perspectives. In the "Supernatural Beings"
article, I inquired about different types of beings and their
interactions in the tales; in the "Social Relationships" article, I explored ideas about relationships conveyed in the tales,
especially with reference to the sex of the narrator. Both
analyses are marred, I now believe, by an analytical emphasis
on affective issues rather than cognitive issues which I hope
to correct in this monograph.

In 1964 and 1965, Gordon Innes published "Some Features
of Theme and Style in Mende Folktales" and "The Function of
Song in Mende Folktales." In the first article Innes explored
aspects of Mende folktales within a West African context
focusing his discussion on types of tales as classified
initially by protagonist and secondarily by themes concluding

with a discussion of certain stylistic features of tales. In the second paper Innes made an innovative deductive analysis of the uses of song in Mende tales, arguing that songs were used as magical formulae, utterances of spirits, and climactic markers in tales.[8] A weakness with Innes' papers is their failure to establish and initially work with Mende categories concerning the content and structure of tales.

Finally, Julian M. Winch published "Religious Attitudes of the Mende Towards Land" in 1971. This paper is an inter-esting inquiry into relations between categories of being and spatial categories as these are revealed in tales. After a few caveats about methods of tale recording, Winch launches into a criticism of the categories of relations in Mende tales proposed in my 1961 articles on social relations and super-natural beings. Alternatively, Winch modifies my classifica-tion of relations into two major sets: those between human being and human being; those between human being and spirit. Winch discusses the relation of his scheme to certain spatial categories in tales as these pertain to anxiety about different kinds of relations in Mende society. Winch's deductive anal-ysis correlates in interesting ways with Jedrej's 1974 article on Sewa Mende spatial and spiritual values.[9] As implied by my earlier comment, I think that Winch's pursuit of the "anxiety" issue initially raised in my articles is unfortunate. With respect to his classification of relations between kinds of being, I have found his scheme and remarks useful in rethinking my data; but I have not adopted it in Chapter 4, as I do not consider that it is consistent with Mende ideas about the char-acters in their oral literature or the existential notions con-veyed in Mende tales.

In this current study of Mende tales, I present a collec-tion of Mende tales introduced by a sociological analysis of aspects of Mende oral literature. The research underlying this monograph falls into two distinct periods: the Mende tales were collected in 1960 and the Mende literary and cos-mological notions were recorded in 1972.

Notes

1. Compare J. Berry, Spoken Art in West Africa (London, 1961) and Ruth Finnegan, Oral Literature in Africa (Oxford, 1970).

2. For example, T. O. Beidelman, "Hyena and Rabbit: A Kaguru Representation of Matrilineal Relations," Africa 31 (1961) 61-74 and "Kaguru Folklore and the Concept of Reciprocity," Zeit-schrift fur Ethnologie 92 (1967) 74-88.

3. Mende songs are found in F. W. H. Migeod, "Mende Songs," Man 16 (1916) 184-191; F. W. H. Migeod, "A Mende Dance," Man

17 (1917) 153-156; Kenneth L. Little, "The Mende Rice Farm and
Its Cost," Zaire 5 (1951) 264; Gordon Innes, "The Function of
Song in Mende Folktales," Sierra Leone Language Review 4 (1965)
54-63. Proverbs appear in E. Harnetty, "Some Native Proverbs
Revised," Sierra Leone Studies o.s. 9 (1927) 55-60; M. Mary
Senior, "Some Mende Proverbs," Africa 17 (1947) 202-205; Mu
Jaleisia Leenga (Bo, 1955); Kenneth L. Little, "The Mende in
Sierra Leone," in African Worlds, n. 113.

4. F. W. Migeod, A View of Sierra Leone (London, 1926); W. T.
Harris, "Ceremonies and Stories Connected with Trees, Rivers,
and Hills in the Protectorate of Sierra Leone," Sierra Leone
Studies n.s. 2 (1954) 91-97; W. T. Harris and E. G. Parrinder,
The Christian Approach to the Animist (London, 1960); W. T.
Harris, "How the Mende People First Started to Pray to Ngewọ,"
Sierra Leone Bulletin of Religion 5 (1963) 61-63; W. T. Harris,
"Ngewọ and Leve," Sierra Leone Bulletin of Religion 5 (1963)
34-36; W. T. Harris and Harry Sawyerr, The Springs of Mende
Belief and Conduct (Freetown, 1968); Kenneth L. Little, "A
Mende Musician Sings of His Adventures," Man 48 (1948) 27-28;
Gordon Innes, "Some Features of Theme and Style in Mende Folk-
tales," Sierra Leone Language Review 3 (1964 6-19); Julian M.
Winch, "Religious Attitudes of the Mende Towards Land," Africana
Research Bulletin 2 (1971) 17-36; Marion D. de B. Kilson,
"Mende Folk Tales," West African Review (December 1960) 87-91
(January-February 1961) 45-48; Marion D. de B. Kilson, "Super-
natural Beings in Mende Dọmẹisia," Sierra Leone Bulletin of
Religion 3 (1961) 1-11.

5. Mende Texts: There are 100 Mende texts in Part II of this
book. Eberl-Elber (1940) published 2 Mende texts that differ
from my tales, but are versions of two appearing in Migeod's
The Mende Language (1908). Stott's "Mende Storytelling and
Stories" contains 26 Mende texts of which 8 are versions of
tales in this collection. Sumner's A Handbook of the Mende
Language (1917) contains 4 Mende texts which differ from those
presented by Eberl-Elber, Stott, Migeod, and myself. Migeod's
The Mende Language (1908) includes 17 texts of which 4 occur in
my collection, 2 in Eberl-Elber's article, and 2 in both Stott's
and my collections. Thus, of the 149 Mende texts of which I
know, 135 are texts of different tales.
    English Summaries or Texts: Harris has published at least
5 tales in English, Little has published 1 ("Musician," 1948),
and Migeod (1926) three that all differ from mine. Winch summarizes 4 tales of which 3 are from my Sierra Leone Bulletin
of Religion article; Innes (1964, 1965) summarizes 24 tales of
which 11 appear in this collection, 2 in this collection and
Stott's manuscript, 1 in Migeod's (1908) and my recordings,
and 1 in Migeod's (1908), Stott's and my collections. Of these
37 additional tales, 14 are versions of other recordings. Consequently, at least 160 different Mende tales are available in

some form in the Mende and English languages. The notes accompanying the tales in Part II include references to other recordings of tales.

6. J. S. Fenton, "Characters in Mende Stories," Sierra Leone Studies o.s. 15 (1929) 34; cf. Chapter 3 in this monograph.

7. The Reverend A. Stott, "Mende Storytelling and Stories," (ms., n.d.) 6.

8. Innes (1965) passim.

9. M. C. Jedrej, "An Analytical Note on the Land and Spirits of the Sewa Mende," Africa 44 (1974) 38-45.

PART I: ANALYSIS AND INTERPRETATION

Chapter 1: Mende Society and Culture

Before discussing the Mende tales, it is useful to sketch
briefly aspects of the Mende social system necessary for understanding the context within which oral literature is performed
for the enjoyment and edification of Mende folk. Much of the
amorphous quality and diversity within the traditional Mende
social system noted by certain scholars can be explained as a
consequence of flexibility in the application of social principles both necessitated and generated by the historical and eco-
logical experiences of Mende people.[1] These circumstances include the geographical mobility of Mende, their dependence upon
a harsh tropical environment for their livelihood, and the existence of both a set of pan-Mende social institutions and a
common cosmological orientation. These factors account for
the coherence and diversity within the traditional Mende social
system, as well as the responsiveness of Mende to Western institutions in recent years.

The Mende, who today number approximately 700,000 representing nearly one-third of the national population, are concentrated in the southern and eastern provinces of Sierra
Leone.[2] Available historical sources indicate that in precolonial times Mende were aggressively intruding into their present
territory; establishing and overthrowing chiefdoms; fighting,
raiding, and enslaving Mende and non-Mende adversaries; and as-
similating through slavery and marriage the people with whom
they came in contact.[3] Since the imposition of colonial rule
at the close of the nineteenth century, the process of Mende
territorial and cultural expansion has proceeded peacefully as
Mende communities have been established in non-Mende lands and
the Mende language has increasingly become the mother tongue
of people whose grandparents spoke languages such as Sherbro
and Vai.[4]

Some indication of the geographic mobility of earlier
Mende and the culturally heterogeneous sources of contemporary
Mende people is reflected in dialectical differences among
Mende speakers today. Conventionally three linguistic subdi-
visions are recognized: Kpa-Mende in Western Mendeland, Sewa-
Mende in the southeastern area, and Ko-Mende in the northeastern
Mende territory.[5] Additional discriminations may include
Sherbro-Mende, Ndama-Mende, and Kalo-Mende or Gallinas. Apart
from the linguistic variants underlying these differentiations,
scholars disagree on associated cultural implications.[6] It
seems probable that the fundamental principles and processes
of the Mende social system are quite uniform while certain
cultural variations unquestionably exist within the wider
pattern.[7]

Today as in the past Mende arduously cultivate their lands primarily for upland rice and their trees, especially the commercially valuable palm nut.[8] Mende perceive an intimate relationship between the cultivators of the past and their living descendants farming the same crops and lands. Each phase in the agricultural work cycle is preceded by ritual in which living farmers inform and seek the approval of ancestral spirits.[9] Within Mende communities, patrilineal descent groups composed of dead and living members own land for settlement and cultivation.

The living members of such patrilocal descent groups form a number of farming households. Ideally such households consist of a joint family including the household head, his younger male siblings, these men's wives, their married sons, and sons' wives and children.[10] According to Little, in order for a man to become head of such a household, he should have four wives.[11] Polygyny, therefore, is valued and frequent in Mende society; among co-wives, the senior wife has authority over the junior ones in their domestic and farming duties.[12]

Although land ownership resides in patrilineal groups forming the nuclei of local communities, usufruct land rights may be extended to cognates, affines, and even strangers who, in time, may be assimilated into the local kinship network.[13] Some members of the community may join it as sons-in-law. While polygynous unions are invariably virilocal, initial unions of young men unable to pay sufficient bridewealth may be uxorilocal.[14] Nevertheless, whether living virilocally or uxorilocally, a young man and his bride cultivate the farm of the spouse's mother with whom they reside; only later in life as they assume greater seniority within the household do they cultivate their own farm.[15] Another way of becoming a member of a community is as a matrilateral kinsman of some resident, often as a sister's son. While a youth frequently lives with his maternal uncle and matrilateral cross-cousin marriage, which is highly regarded, invariably involes uxorilocal residence, the authority of the maternal uncle (kenya) over his sister's children was considerably more extensive. It included control over their general well-being: his curse was greatly feared and he might sell them into slavery; at the same time, he served as protector of their interests among their patrikinsmen; he must approve their marriages and received part of his niece's brideprice while often contributing to his nephew's brideprice.[16] Consistent with these ideas about the relations between living matrikin are both the veneration given to matrilateral ancestral spirits and Mende notions of conception whereby the father's semen contributes to the baby's physical form, while the mother provides its spiritual aspects.[17] Thus, although Mende communities based upon a limited number of patrilocal descent groups have continuity in time and space, the residents of any community may be affiliated in diverse ways to its landowning members.

While members of a local community undoubtedly have diverse
reasons for residing in the community, the range of legitimate
social principles that Mende may utilize in making residential
choices implies an inherent flexibility in the social system
that individuals may use to maximize their options, especially
in gaining their livelihoods as tropical farmers.[18] Thus, individual mobility based on the utilization of variant social
principles occurs within the framework of a consistent ideology
about the nature of the local community uniting living and dead
patrikinsmen.

Throughout Mendeland, such local communities of towns and
dependent villages are grouped into chiefdoms under the
authority of paramount chiefs. Without question both the territorial integrity of chiefdoms and the role of chiefs have
been enhanced in the colonial and independence periods, when
chiefdoms became units within the local administrative structure of Sierra Leone.[19]

Although the chiefdom represented the highest level of
social integration in traditional Mende society, a set of
pan-Mende sodalities organized independently at the community
level facilitated both the integration of Mende culture and
the assimilation of strangers into communities, while serving
as mechanisms of internal community control. Within Mende
communities, a number of "secret societies" existed including
the Poro, the Sande, and the Humui throughout Mendeland, and
the Wunde and Njayei among the Kpa-Mende.[20] Although these
societies were organized independently in each community, their
structure was uniform throughout the regions in which they existed. Consequently, an individual moving from one community
to another could join the local lodge of a society at the same
grade to which he had belonged in his old village or town.
Little has suggested that within Mende communities, these societies were analogous to the mediaeval church in Europe. "Like
the medieval church, they lay down various rules of conduct,
prescribe certain forms of behavior, and are the sole agency
capable of remitting certain sins."[21]

Throughout Mendeland all adults necessarily belonged to
either the men's Poro society or the women's Sande society
which they joined in early adolescence. Both societies were
organized into grades; each of which had its own obligations
and privileges. Movement from lower to higher grades depended
upon increasing social maturity and the payment of fees. While
each society had authority over its members' conduct as sexually
responsible adults, the Poro society also regulated the life
of the general community insofar as it controlled certain economic activities such as fishing and palm nut harvesting and
certain political processes including the installation of
chiefs and the arbitration of disputes.[22] In more recent
times, the functions of both the Poro and Sande societies have

been adapted to serve new needs. The traditional economic reg-
ulation function of the Poro society has been employed to fix
prices of commodities on the modern market, while the traditional sex education function of the Sande society was used
to introduce information about modern standards of personal hy-
giene.[23] Further, the Poro society has played an important
direct and indirect role in the colonial and national politics
of Sierra Leone.[24]

In traditional Mende society, these pan-Mende institutions
served a variety of societal purposes. They provided the basis
for collective action beyond the community and chiefdom levels
of social integration, as the 1898 Mende Rising devastatingly
demonstrated. They also facilitated the control of local communities over old members and newcomers, while enabling
strangers to achieve meaningful social identities within a community. In short, these sodalities contributed to the coherence
of Mende culture within a society of scattered communities composed of variously affiliated and fluctuating membership.

As important to the integration of Mende society as the
pan-Mende sodalities was a cosmological orientation underlying
and validating Mende institutions. Basic to this cosmological
orientation is the notion of a hierarchy of beings headed by
a supreme being, Ngewo, the creatures (fuhani) of his creation
which include spirits (ngafanga) of various kinds, living
people, animals, and lesser forms of plant life (tuhani). In
the recent literature on Mende society, there has been consid-
erable debate about the composition of certain classes of being
and the relations between various classes; some disagreement
may result from differences in the quality of ethnographic
scholarship and some may be attributed to regional variations
within Mende culture, as well as to Mende disinterest in
dealing systematically with this kind of issue.[25] In this
brief outline, I do not enter this debate but merely attempt
to summarize what I consider to be the basic attributes of
this hierarchy of living beings and its relation to Mende social
life.

Scholars agree that the world and its creatures were
created by Ngewo, a transcendental being associated with the
sky.[26] Ngewo, who is variously referred to as "the one chief,"
"the great chief," and "the chief who created us," is said to
be the husband of the Earth (Ndoi).[27] The Mende conception
of Ngewo as the ultimate determiner of human fortunes is expressed in the following phrases: "God give you long life";
"God is judge"; "nothing happens unless God approves."[28] Mende
villagers to whom I talked invariably attributed famine despite
hard work in the fields, sudden infant death, and unexpected
prosperity to God. Although in an ultimate sense, Ngewo con-
trols all life and cosmic processes, he is removed from the
affairs of men. While there is no cult of Ngewo, living men

attempt to achieve contact with Ngewǫ through lesser spiritual beings or directly invoke him to witness some ritual, such as a cursing ceremony.[29]

Of more immediate concern in human lives than Ngewǫ are various spiritual beings (ngafanga) created by him including ancestral and non-ancestral spirits.[30] Generally speaking, ancestral spirits are associated with--and thereby through their cult groups differentiate--important social units in a Mende community. Thus, among the Sewa Mende, Jedrej differentiates between the village ancestors (ndowubla), spirits of village founders, who are worshipped collectively and the ancestors of local kin groups who are invoked by their descendants; additionally, Hofstra includes the ancestral spirits of secret societies within the category of Ko-Mende ancestral spirits.[31] Ancestral spirits serve as guardians of the welfare and the conduct of the members of the social groups with which they are associated. When ancestral spirits are well-tended and pleased with the moral rectitude of their descendants, they enable the living to prosper. Conversely, ancestral spirits may send sickness or some other disaster to show their displeasure at misconduct or their own neglect.[32] Moreover, ancestral spirits may communicate with their descendants in dreams or through birds and insects.[33] According to Hofstra, ancestral spirits are the most important spiritual beings to living Mende.

Non-ancestral spirits include not only spirits associated with natural phenomena such as the forest (ndǫgbǫ yosoi) and rivers (jina and tingǫi), but gregarious white-haired drawfs (temuisia) associated with deserted villages, village dancing spirits (ndoli yafanga), and secret society spirits (hale yafanga). Jedrej's analysis of the relations between these spirits and human society shows how the spirits range on a control of power continuum from controlled village spirits through deserted village spirits to uncontrolled forest spirits.[34] The unpredictable and arbitrary nature of forest and river spirits who may assist and destroy human beings differentiates them from ancestral spirits and village spirits; ancestral spirits may be asked to appease non-ancestral spirits.[35] Accordingly, nonancestral spirits articulate certain differentiations not only within human society, but more basically between the civilized settlement and the uncivilized wild forest.

Living men comprised of both spirit and flesh are destined to become ancestral spirits. In life, however, certain human beings have greater spiritual powers than others and may utilize these powers for diverse ends. Among these supernaturally endowed are the witch (hǫnamǫ) whose witch force is located in the pancreas but whose spirit leaves the body at night entering owls, cutting grasses, or cats; the twin whose anomalous birth gives him unusual powers, associates him with termites and their

mounds, and involves him in a cult; the hunter whose use of
various medicines enables him to transform himself into animals and such natural phenomena as rocks and trees.[36]

Another lower class of being important to living men is
that of animals. The existential differentiation of animals
and human beings for the Mende villagers to whom I talked was
based upon animals' inability to talk, lack of culture, and
utility to man. Animals variously enter human lives: as
domesticated creatures, as totems, as omens, and as familiars.
As ordinary domesticated creatures, animals serve utilitarian
and ritual purposes, especially chickens which are used in both
ancestral sacrifices and divination.[37] Wild animals may also
serve as totems of patrilineal groups. Usually the origin of
such a totemic relation is attributed to an animal's befriending
of a person which led the person's patrilineal descendants to
avoid killing or eating their animal brothers.[38] Finally, the
appearance of certain animals may presage the future; for example, the unexpected presence of a chameleon means that someone
will die.[39] Apart from these inter-class relations between
animals and humans, certain members of each class have the
ability to transform themselves into the other. For example,
the crested porcupine of the forest is said to assume human
form in its lair; people from eastern Mendeland were said to
become elephants in their old age; and professional hunters'
medicines enabled them to change their form of being.

Within the general parameters set by this cosmological
orientation, variant ideas about the individual personalities
comprising classes, such as ancestral spirits or non-ancestral
spirits could be incorporated in different parts of Mendeland
without destroying the basic structure of belief. Throughout
Mendeland, living people interpreted aspects of the vicissitudes
of their lives in terms of the relations between themselves
and other classes of being, especially ancestral spirits. Just
as the pan-Mende sodalities facilitated the movement of people
and the integration of communities, so the structure of common
belief provided a shared world view and explanation of human
existence.

Certain attributes of precolonial Mende society including
the geographical mobility of individuals associated with both
political instability and warfare and with diversity in the
social status and kinship composition of communities, as well
as the possibility of social mobility within community sodalities produced individuals who would be responsive to new ideas
and modes of achieving success. Not surprisingly, Mende were
receptive to the new educational and occupational opportunities
offered initially by missions and later also by government.
Thus, of the six mission schools established in the Sierra Leone
hinterland between 1840 and 1892, five were in Mende or Mende-
Sherbro territory.[40] The disproportionate number of educational

institutions in Mendeland persisted throughout the colonial period.[41] When the colonial government opened the Bo School in 1906 for the sons and nominees of chiefs, 54 percent of the first pupils were Mende; in 1915, 76 percent came from Mende districts and in 1938, 37 percent were Mende.[42] Such educational opportunity and achievement has meant that Mende have been disproportionately represented in the modern elite of Sierra Leone.[43] Nevertheless, most Mende today are not literate in any language.[44] Moreover, most Mende continue to live in small local communities as upland rice farmers whose lives are still shaped by time-honored ideas and expectations though touched by radically different assumptions about man in the universe.[45]

Notes

1. For example, Jedrej (1974) and Harris and Sawyerr (1968).

2. Mende population in 1911: 453,356; 1931: 578,146 or 32 percent of the national population; 1963: 672,831 or 31 percent of the national population. Distribution of Mende population in 1963, southern province, 365,001; eastern province, 280,378; northern province, 5,905; western area, 21,547 (Report and Summary of the Census of 1911, Colony of Sierra Leone /London: 1912/ I, 10; II, 27; Report of the Census of the Year 1931, Sierra Leone, I, 46; II, 84; 1963 Population Census of Sierra Leone /Freetown: 1965/ II, table 3).

3. For example, W. R. E. Clarke, "The Foundation of the Luawa Chiefdom," Sierra Leone Studies n.s. 8 (1957) 245-251; N. C. Hollins, "A Short History of Luawa Chiefdom," Sierra Leone Studies o.s. 14 (1929) 11-21; Max Gorvie, Our Peoples of the Sierra Leone Protectorate (Bristol, 1944) 21; J. M. Malcolm, "Mende Warfare," Sierra Leone Studies o.s. 21 (1939) 47; Kenneth L. Little, The Mende of Sierra Leone (London, 1967 ed.) 23-42; Kenneth L. Little, "The Mende Chiefdoms of Sierra Leone," in C. D. Forde and P. Kaberry, eds., West African Kingdoms in the Nineteenth Century, (London, 1967) 239-259; George Thompson, Thompson in Africa (Dayton, 1857) 200.

4. For example, William H. Fitzjohn, "A Village in Sierra Leone," Sierra Leone Studies n.s. 7 (1956) 147; Kenneth L. Little, "Mende Political Institutions in Transition," Africa 17 (1947) 8.

5. Kenneth L. Little (1967 ed.) 76; William L. Hommel, Art of the Mende (College Park, Md., 1974) 37. Little estimates that Kpa Mende constitute 20 percent, Sewa Mende 35 percent, and Ko Mende 45 percent of the Mende population (Little, 1967 ed.) 76.

6. William Vivian, "The Mendi Country, and Some of the Customs

and Characteristics of Its People," Journal of the Manchester Geographical Society 12 (1896) 16.

7. Harris and Sawyerr (1968) xii.

8. Vivian (1896) 18ff; Little (1951); Sjoerd Hofstra, "The Social Significance of the Oil Palm in the Life of the Mendi," Internationales Archiv fur Ethnographie 34 (1937) 105-118.

9. Sjoerd Hofstra, "The Ancestral Spirits of the Mende," Internationales Archiv fur Ethnographie 39 (1941) 177-196; Little (1951). Harris and Parrinder note that farmers appeal to ancestors in the cultivation of upland rice but not of swamp rice. "Our fathers never knew this rice, they did not use this seed, how can we pray?" (1960) 52.

10. Kenneth L. Little, "The Mende Farming Household," Sociological Review 40 (1948) 39-40.

11. Ibid, 42.

12. See K. H. Crosby, "Polygamy in Mende Country," Africa 10 (1937) 249-264; Little (1951) 241.

13. See Little (1967 ed.) 89, 98, 101; Kenneth L. Little, "Land and Labour Among the Mende," African Affairs (March 1948) 25; Little (1947) 9; Sjoerd Hofstra, "Personality and Differentiation in the Political Life of the Mende," Africa 10 (1937) 438; Jedrej (1974) 38-39.

14. For example, Hollins (1929) 11; Crosby (1937) 250, 253-254.

15. Crosby (1937) 253.

16. Little (1967, ed.) 110; Harris and Sawyerr (1968) 129; Harry Sawyerr, God: Ancestor or Creator? (London, 1970) 64.

17. Little (1967 ed.) 110, 111.

18. See D. Westermann, "Samba, un Mende de Sierra Leone, Paysan et Soldat," in Autobiographies d'Africains (Paris, 1943 ed.) 102-117.

19. See Martin Kilson, Political Change in a West African State (Cambridge, 1966).

20. Hommel (1974) passim; Max Gorvie, Old and New in Sierra Leone (London, 1945) 27-48; Little (1967, ed.) 240-253; Kenneth L. Little, "The Poro Society as an Arbiter of Culture," African Studies 7 (1948) 1-15; Kenneth L. Little, "The Role of the Secret Society in Cultural Specialization," American Anthropologist 51 (1949) 199-212; W. Addison, "The Wunde Society," Man 36 (1936) 207-208; C. B. Wallis, "The Poro of the Mende," Journal

of _African Society_ 4 (1905) 186-187; F. W. H. Migeod, "The Building of the Poro House," _Man_ 16 (1916) 102.

21. Little (1967 ed.) 240.

22. See Wallis (1905) 187; Little (1967 ed.) 249; Little (Arbiter 1948) 4; Kenneth L. Little, "The Political Functions of the Poro," _Africa_ 35 (1965) 350; Gorvie (1945) 37.

23. Little (Arbiter 1948) 4; M. A. S. Margai, "Welfare Work in a Secret Society," _African Affairs_ (March 1948) 227-230.

24. See Kilson (1966) 256-258.

25. For example, Jedrej (1974) and Winch (1971); cf., Mary Douglas, _Purity and Danger_ (New York, 1966) 88.

26. For example, Sawyerr (1970) 62-81; Harris and Sawyerr (1968) 6-10; Harris (Ngewọ 1963) 35-36; Kenneth L. Little, "The Function of 'Medicine' in Mende Society," _Man_ 48 (1948) 127; Little (1965) 354.

27. Harris and Sawyerr (1968) 6; Sawyerr (1970) 71-73.

28. Harris (Ngewọ 1963) 64-65.

29. Vivian (1896) 32; Little (Medicine 1948) 130; Isaac Ndanema, "The Rationale of Mende 'Swears,'" _Sierra Leone Bulletin of Religion_ 6 (1964) 21-25.

30. Hofstra (1941); Sjoerd Hofstra, "The Belief Among the Mendi in Non-Ancestral Spirits, and its Relation to a Case of Parricide," _Internationales Archiv fur Ethnographie_ 40 (1941-42) 175-182; Jedrej (1974); Winch (1971); Sawyerr (1970); Harris and Sawyerr (1968).

31. Hofstra (1941) 192.

32. _Ibid_; Sawyerr (1970) 14.

33. _Ibid_, 51; Hofstra (1941) 187.

34. Jedrej (1974) 39-43.

35. Hofstra (1941-42) 177; Harris and Sawyerr (1968) 44.

36. See notes to Tales 15, 96, and 3.

37. Sawyerr (1970) 79-80.

38. Harris and Parrinder (1960) 93-94.

39. _Ibid_, 44.

40. J. E. M'bayo, "The History of Bo Government School" (Ms., 1955) 12.

41. See Gorvie (1945) 51-62.

42. M'bayo (1955) 30; Kilson (1966) 77.

43. See Ibid.

44. 1963 Sierra Leone Census of the Population (Freetown, 1965), II, Tables 12 and 14.

45. Ibid., III, Table 7.

The story is a lie, we just arrange it.
Ḍọmẹi ndẹ le, gbama le ma nda tenga.

From a comprehensive perspective, Mende literature comprises many forms including prayers to the dead (ngo gbia),
ritual slogans addressed to dancing spirits, dream (kibalo)
narrations, fictitious tales (dọmẹ; njele), myths and legends
(njia wova; njẹpẹ wova), place puzzles (hoboi), proverbs and
riddles (sale), and songs (ngule). Among these diverse literary forms, the most popular secular forms are prose narratives, songs, proverbs, and place puzzles. The attributes and
interrelation of each form merits a brief review before considering storytelling in greater detail.

Mende differentiate three types of prose narrative: njia
wova (old talk), dọmẹ (tale), and mbaka lọwula (puzzle tale).
These three types differ with respect to content and performance. While njia wova and mbaka lọwula are believed to report
historical events, dọmẹ is thought to be fictitious, as Mende
say at the close of a storytelling session, "The tale is a lie,
we just arrange it." The historical tales, however, differ in
their mode of presentation, for njia wova is narrated in a
straightforward conversational manner by the raconteur, while
the performance of mbaka lọwula involes the recreation of a
historical tale through questions and answers between narrator
and audience. In performance, dọmẹ and mbaka lọwula both involve interactions between a narrator and an audience of several people during an evening, whereas njia wova can be told to
one person or to many people at any time. The Mende proverb
comprises both a form of short pithy statement of social
verity--the full comprehension of which often depends on an intimate knowledge of cultural values, and a form of statement
and response more akin to the Euroamerican riddle.[1] Such proverbs mark the speech of Mende sophisticated in the nuances of
their culture.[2] Finally, the place puzzle entails that the
narrator give the first syllable of a place name and the audience try to guess the full name.[3] The performance of the four
basic forms of secular oral literature are variously related;
songs often form part of a tale performance; some tales explain
the origin of proverbs by describing the situation purported
to have occasioned the proverb; finally, place puzzling frequently concludes a storytelling session.[4]

For Mende people the two most widely recognized categories
of prose narrative are njia wova and dọmẹ. These forms differ
with respect to content and performance. Njia wova recounts
actual events, dọmẹ tells about fictitious happenings; dọmẹ invariably incorporates a song, njia wova does not; njia wova may
be told to a single individual or to a group at any time, dọmẹ

is performed for groups only at night lest a spirit appear to punish the offenders. One Mende villager eloquently summarized the salient differences in content between the two forms:

> "If it is njia wova, it should turn out to be something true; what our forefathers saw or what happened is what they tell as njia wova. Your child also when you are alive, it is what you advise him about. But in the case of dǫmę, people sit down, they create it; they say 'this animal and this; this creature and this'; at that point, they make a plan /about events that/ never happened in order to make it fit together."

Despite the clarity of this statement, many Mende villagers said that there was no difference between the two forms, especially after we had talked about the attributes that they understood to differentiate one form from another. In conversation villagers sometimes used the terms dǫmę and njia wova interchangeably. Moreover, when villagers were asked to classify a particular story, they did so in various ways; thus, villagers as frequently classified the narrative about how Spider's waist became slender (Tale 30) as dǫmę as they classified it as njia wova.[5] I think that this apparent lack of differentiation between njia wova and dǫmę relates to the nature of "historical event," for one person's experience may become the basis for another's tale. Such a possibility was vividly articulated by an older Mende farmer who said,

> "Dǫmę, they tell it and sing it. They say 'Dǫmę-o Dǫmęisia;'[6] you start from there, then they know that it is a dǫmę. There are those who say that njia wova explains about the past; that is the origin of the name. They say, 'Tell njia wova,' and you tell njia wova. The distinction between them: the end of the farm is the end of the bush; you see the farm, you see the bush. The distinction between them is nonexistent."

When I collected the stories presented in this book I assumed that I was collecting fictional narratives (dǫmę). Clearly there are no cosmogonic myths or legends about historical personages among the tales that could be classified unequivocally as njia wova. Yet if njia wova is perceived to include aetiological explanations for such current realities as why Spider's waist is tiny or why bushfowl is in the bush and hen in the barnyard, as some Mende do, then there are several njia wovęisia in the collection. Such aetiological tales, I believe, create the confusion in Mende minds about how to classify a specific narrative even though the general differentiating criteria relating to content and performance are generally acknowledged.

When Mende villagers were asked why people tell stories, sixty-seven percent stressed the educational and thirty-three percent the diverting aspects of tales. Mende said that stories impart wisdom, give advice, and tell about the past. When villagers were asked specifically about what stories might teach a person, twenty-five percent said nothing, while the majority cited three factors with equal frequency: appropriate conduct, understanding of Mende culture, and stories themselves. One older villager summarized the educational value of tales with these words:

"The advice could be thus: /when/ people tell these stories, it is for us human beings, because it is not only animals that do those things. It is for ourselves that people tell these stories. When they are told, you yourself may think that if something you do should lead you to this /situation/, this is what you will encounter."

Most Mende villagers with whom I talked thought that members of an audience might learn something valuable for their personal lives from the content of the stories.

While Mende villagers most frequently mentioned the educational benefit to be gained from stories, the entertaining function of the tales was also clearly important. Some villagers said that people told stories to while away time, to exercise their imaginations, and because the stories were interesting. When asked about when stories are told, the association of tales with occasions when people feel contentedly relaxed became clearer. Such storytelling occasions occur after the day's work and the evening meal, especially during the dry season following the harvest. As one young woman explained, stories are told "just when the rice is ripe, but in these /June/ rains no Mende person can tell a story, because hunger eats his heart." For Mende people storytelling is a form of entertainment associated with leisure, feelings of well-being and good fellowship.

Although Mende villagers agreed that anyone may tell a story and that men and women tell the same tales, occasions for storytelling can be differentiated into three main types: the public performance of professional storytellers, the public village entertainment in which men perform as narrators and women as singers, and the private household performance in which peers or adults and children tell tales for their mutual enjoyment.[7] These occasions are differentiated not with respect to literary content but to roles in the storytelling performance; in other words, the same tales may be told on all three types of occasions, but who may participate in their performance and in what way varies between occasions.

In traditional Mende society but apparently to a lesser extent today, certain people earned their livelihood by travelling from village to village exchanging an evening's entertainment for board and lodging. Such professional storytellers (dǫmęgbuabla) began their careers as apprentices to established storytellers. As one villager said, "If you are an apprentice, you can learn all his little tricks; you yourself--when you leave him and go to a small village--those amusing things that your master used to do are what you yourself will do." Storytellers were appreciated for their creative skill, but were thought to be "foolish people who prefer to earn their living that way /rather/ than by doing ordinary work!"[8]

When a storyteller arrived in a village and announced his business to the chief, arrangements were made for his performance in the evening and for his lodging that night. In such public performances of a professional storyteller, all the people in the community may attend. The storyteller is the sole narrating performer, but the members of the audience participate as singers or react critically to the storyteller's performance.

The second type of occasion for storytelling is the public village entertainment. On such occasions people gather informally in the barre where men narrate stories in turn and women will sing the accompanying songs. Both men and women stated unequivocally that men alone could tell tales on such occasions. One old man acerbicly stated,

> "Women's place is to sing, I have not seen a woman tell
> a story. It is men that tell /stories/, because they
> are much more clever, and so they are able to fit in
> many lies."

The third type of storytelling occasion is the private household performance in which adults and children both may participate. Again narrating roles are differentiated by age and sex, insofar as adults tell tales to other adults and children, but children tell them to one another and men tell tales to men, women, and children, while women tell tales only to other women and children. Some of the situations in which such informal household performances may occur are depicted in the following remarks by Mende villagers. One farmer said,

> "At times when people have spent the whole day in the
> farm and have returned, those feeling well and happy
> will say, 'Friend, let us sit today and tell a little
> story.' They make a fire, they gather around, they
> tell these stories; little children are amongst them,
> so that they will get wisdom."

A young woman also said,

"For example, when you are living in the house with
old women. If one has eaten, she sits near the fire
and says, 'Children, come, let us tell stories.'"

An older woman commented,

"We used to tell our stories to our children in the
house and we would laugh at them. It was a means
of self-entertainment for an evening."

The informal household performances resemble the public village
entertainment in that "one person starts telling a story, then
interested people follow suit. As soon as you finish telling
yours then somebody else starts his own."

Although the three types of performance differ with respect
to the formality of the occasion and to the eligibility criteria
governing the narrator's role, certain aspects of the relation
between narrator and audience pertain to all storytelling performances. Narrator and audience both expect to participate
actively in the performance of a story and audiences are expected to respond critically to the story during its performance. As participants in the story performance, the audience
may respond to the direct questions of the narrator or sing
the choral refrains of the songs that are incorporated within
most Mende tales.[9] Additionally through cat calls, clapping,
and laughter, Mende audiences convey their spontaneous evaluations of narrators' performances. Consequently, narrators
use a variety of devices to make their performances entertaining
including costume, pantomine, dance, musical instrumentation,
and various stylistic devices. Innes describes these stylistic
devices as direct speech in which "a different manner of
speaking /is used/ for each protagonist," "the use of the per-
fect tense where the past tense would be used in ordinary conversation," and "a greater use of ideophones."[10] During the
story performance, the entertainment of the audience assumes
primary significance for the narrator and audience, even though
on reflection Mende stress the educational value of tales.

Several years ago when I asked the Reverend Isaac Ndanema
what he considered to be the characteristics of a good tale,
he responded that there were "four essentials of a good dọmẹ."
He rank ordered these from most important (1) to least important (4).

(1) A good dọmẹ is one that causes the greatest amount
     of laughter. A good laugh is what we expect dọmẹ
     to bring out in the audience. You listen to dọmẹ
     because you want to laugh loudly and long.

(2) A good dọmẹ is one that makes you see with the
     mind's eye--very vividly the impossible happen

with conviction. The more wonderful incidents
a dọmẹ can bring before the audience the greater
will be the appreciation of the dọmẹ.

(3) A good dọmẹ is one that makes you hear good
     singing and if you can sing, one that gives
     you the opportunity to sing and shout to your
     heart's desire.

(4) A good dọmẹ is one that makes you go away with
     a proverb on your lips holding up one virtue or
     another. If a dọmẹ can make you see some form
     of wickedness or evil defeated and a fitting
     proverb thereby demonstrated or called to mind
     then you have a good dọmẹ.[11]

Ndanema went on to say that

"It will be very exceptional for any one dọmẹ to bring
out all these elements. The skill of the narrator is
displayed in the number of these essentials he can put
effectively in one dọmẹ. Two, that is laughter (fun)
and any other is the normal combination expected."[12]

A decade later when I asked Mende villagers what made one
story better than another, they mentioned the same four attributes, albeit with a different cumulative ranking: songs and
dances (67 percent), the art of fitting lies (42 percent), funny
incidents and jokes (25 percent), and the amount of information
(12 percent). In his excellent discussion of the use of song
in Mende stories, Innes has suggested that "to many audiences
the songs are more important than the narrative."[13] The
response of Mende villagers to my inquiries indicate that
audiences enjoy singing songs in tales, but the skillful construction of the plot is also important in evaluating a story
performance.

In conclusion, it is appropriate to consider how Mende
perceive this oral tradition to be evolving. When I asked
Mende villagers how storytelling had changed since their youth,
almost half (45 percent) said that storytelling had not changed
in any way. The majority, however, noted some form of change--
either that tales were told less frequently (45 percent) or
that stories were presented differently and were different in
content (10 percent). Quite probably the tradition is de-
clining as a result of the introduction of new forms of entertainment and new modes of education.

Notes

1. **Proverb**: If you do not know how to dance, you should not dance in your mother-in-law's house. **Riddle**: (statement) He climbs on the house and comes down; (response) it is his father's house.

2. See Senior (1947) and Harnetty (1927).

3. "They call it **hoboi**, like you think of a town, then you say, 'There is a town among towns, they call it 'Bu.' Then the person searches for it trying to get the answer for some time; he might say, 'Buuwah?" 'Buuma?" They only name towns; if he is unable /to guess it/, then he says, 'I am unable.' Then you name the town and say, 'It is Bumpe.' That is **hoboi**."

4. This discussion of Mende storytelling is based primarily on open-ended interviews with twenty-four men and women of various ages in Bumpe and Bunumbu in June 1972. These interviews on Mende literary conceptions were tape-recorded in Mende and later transcribed and translated into English with the assistance of Samuel S. Lansana.

5. Both Herskovits and Innes have discussed this problem. See Melville J. and Frances S. Herskovits, Dahomean Narrative (Evanston, 1958) 13-16 and Innes (1964) 7.

6. This is the conventional opening of a storytelling session.

7. Compare Chapter 4.

8. Stott (n.d.) 4.

9. Innes (1964) 18; Innes (1965) 54.

10. Innes (1964) 18.

11. Personal communication, October 5, 1961.

12. Ibid.

13. Innes (1965) 54.

Mende tales relate how a man discovered which of his wives truly loved him; why bushfowl and chickens are unfriendly; how a little twin killed a large troublesome spirit; why spiders are found in the eaves of houses; how a bushyam became a barren woman's child; and many other dramatic incidents. The tales depict activities and interactions of spirits and men, mothers and children, animals and people, chiefs and subjects, diviners and clients. Some tales concern a single dramatic incident; others are built upon the interweaving of several events involving the same situation or the same set of characters. Some tales revolve around the means by which ignoble wishes are defeated, others around the clever ruses by which difficult tasks are accomplished and still others around the ways in which supernatural powers and beings facilitate and sometimes complicate the solution of problematic human situations. Whatever the dramatic sequence of events or whatever the concatenation of characters of variant moral orders, the outcomes of Mende tales invariably uphold such basic moral percepts as the value of generosity among kinsfolk and friends, the desirability of moderation rather than excess in human life, and the ascendance of wit over brawn as well as over seniority in years and social status.

How are these tales generated? Are patterns of plot construction present in every tale despite the variability in the content of each tale? Can a syntagmatic model of Mende tales be developed which describes and predicts how activities will be interwoven irrespective of the activities themselves? A search for such underlying morphological patterns in Mende tales reveals several recurrent forms and processes operating at different levels of generality and specificity. Moreover, it is possible to describe the morphology of individual tales and to construct a syntagmatic model to account for the generation of any Mende tale.

As I noted, Mende tales concern social activities and interactions. The structurally simplest Mende tale depicts one situation of activity and interaction or one episode. Since more complex forms of tales involve the interconnection of two or more episodes, the analysis of the construction of single episode tales is necessarily preliminary to a consideration of tales composed of multiple episodes.[1]

Examining the structure of single episode tales, I have found that the action of the tale is segmented into three successive phases. The initial phase introduces the situation and the protagonists: a man sets out to gain a wife; Spider wants to get more food than his appropriate share; or a man wants to discover which of his bickering wives loves him.

The final phase of the episode concerns the outcome of the situation: the man succeeds in gaining his wife; Spider fails to get extra food; the man, finding that his beloved wife loves him least and his less loved wife loves him more, punishes and rewards each accordingly. The outcome of the plot depends upon the development or complication of the situation during the medial episodic phase: the man gains a wife after successfully completing a difficult task; Spider fails to get extra food after his ignoble ruse of disguising himself as his own brother is revealed; the man discovers which wife loves him by pretending to die and then observing the sincerity with which each wife mourns his death. Thus, the medial phase of the episode concerns the means by which a task is accomplished or not achieved, a desire is realized or left unsatisfied; the medial phase may depict the violation of one interdiction leading to some form of punishment or the upholding of another resulting in some reward in the final phase.

As I have mentioned, the outcomes of Mende tales invariably uphold Mende moral norms and values. Since certain tales end with punishments, others with rewards, some with tasks achieved, and others with desires unfulfilled, positive and negative evaluations may be assigned to the final phase of Mende tales. An analysis of Mende tales reveals that the evaluation of the final phase of a tale depends upon comparable evaluations of the two preceding phases in such a way that if both these phases are positively evaluated, the final phase will be positive and that if either the initial or medial phase is negatively evaluated, the final phase will be negative. These generative rules account for the evaluative pattern of episodic phases represented in my collection of Mende tales.[2] Every episodic phase, therefore, involves a negatively or positively evaluated action sequence.

Further examination of Mende episodes shows that the action sequences of different phases comprise a limited number of action patterns. These action patterns constitute the minimal structural units within which specific substantive actions, such as those I noted in describing the content of various episodic phases, operate. The sequential ordering of action patterns is such that four basic episodic forms occur in Mende tales. In order to facilitate the clarity of my exposition, I defer the discussion of specific action patterns to my subsequent analysis of episodic forms. Here I wish to note that I have now derived the basis for a structural model of Mende episodes; this model is presented schematically in Table 1.

As is clear from my discussion, I regard Mende tales as essentially triadic in structure. In presenting such a view of the morphology of Mende tales, I am departing from recent structural analyses of Amerindian and African tales which rely upon a binary model of tale morphology operating consistently

Table 1. Syntagmatic Model of Mende Tales

1. Mende Tale ———→ Episode (s)

2. Episode ————→ Initial Phase + Medial Phase + Final Phase

3. Initial Phase ———→ (Positive Initial Action Sequence
                      (Negative Initial Action Sequence

a) Positive Initial Action Sequence ———→ (Legitimate Deception
                                         (Interdiction
                                         (Task
                                         (Lack

b) Negative Initial Action Sequence ———→ (Deception
                                         (Illicit Interdiction
                                         (Illicit Task
                                         (Illicit Lack

4. Medial Phase ————————→ (Positive Medial Action Sequence
                          (Negative Medial Action Sequence

a) Positive Medial Action Sequence ———→ (Deception Revealed
                                        (Interdiction Observed
                                        (Legitimate Deception
                                        (Task Accomplished

b) Negative Medial Action Sequence ———→ (Deception Not Revealed
                                        (Violation
                                        (Illicit Lack
                                        (Illicit Task
                                        (Deception

5. Final Phase ————————→ (Positive Final Action Sequence
                         (Negative Final Action Sequence

a) Positive Final Action Sequence ———→ (Reward
                                       (Task Accomplished
                                       (Lack Liquidated

b) Negative Final Action Sequence ———→ (Punishment
                                       (Task Not Accomplished
                                       (Lack Not Liquidated

Key: + = and   ———→ = consists of   { = or

from the most general structural level to the most specific.[3]
I find, however, that such a binary conception of tale structure distorts the dynamic processes involved in the creation
of Mende tales. It is not that Mende tales could not be analyzed in terms of a binary model, but that such a binary analysis
would mask the basic proceses involved in Mende tale formation.

The action patterns of Mende tales are not only finite in
number but restricted in combination. An examination of the
content of Mende tales shows that any specific substantive
action can be classified within one of fifteen action patterns.
The fifteen action patterns involved in Mende episodes may be
combined in various but limited ways to produce four episodic
forms which I term Deception Episode, Interdiction Episode,
Task Episode, and Lack Episode. Given the evaluative generation rule previously discussed, within each episodic form at
least two alternative action patterns exist for each phase.[4]
The initial phase of a Task Episode may involve a licit or illegitimate task; the medial phase of an Interdiction Episode
may concern the observation or the violation of the interdiction of the initial phase; the final phase of a Lack Episode
may recount the liquidation of or the failure to liquidate the
lack. Although the initial and final phases of all episodic
forms and the medial phase of Deception and Interdiction Episodes involve only two alternative action patterns, the medial
phase of Task and Lack Episodes have five alternative action
patterns. The possible distribution of action patterns within
the phases of variant forms of episodes are summarized in Table
2.

Among the 35 single episode tales in this collection,
the following combination of action patterns occur (1) Deception Episode: D + DR + P; (2) Interdiction Episode: II + V +
P and I + V + P; (3) Task Episode: T + IO/LD + TA and IT +
IL/V/D + T $\neq$ A; and Lack Episode: IL + V/D/IT + L $\neq$ L, IL +
TA/LD + L $\neq$ L, L + IT + L $\neq$ L, and L + TA/LD + LL. If these
combinations of action patterns are expressed in terms of
positively and negatively evaluated action patterns, the following combinations occur in single episode tales: the patterns for lack tales are (1) + + +, (2) + - -, (3) - + -, and
(4) - - -; for task tales (1) + + +, (2) + - -; for interdiction tales (1) + - - and (2) - - -; and for deception
tales (1) - + -.[5] The importance of the evaluative patterning
of episodes and the formal diversity of action patterns within
the medial phase of Lack and Task Episodes have led me to consider that Mende tales are best analyzed as triadic in structure for a binary model of such tales fails to convey the sequential structure of Mende tale episodes as explicitly and
precisely as a triadic model.

Since all Mende episodes are constructed in the same way,
the four forms of episode constitute the basic units comprising

multiple episode tales. Within such complex tales, episodes are combined by means of two basic generative processes: chaining and embedding. Chaining involves a sequence of individual episodes (E) which may be expressed formally as $E_1 + E_2 + E_3...+E_n$. The following chaining patterns are included within the collection of tales in Part II: $DE_1 + DE_2$; $LE_1 + LE_2$; $LE + TE$; $IE + LE$; and $TE_1 + TE_2 + IE$.[6] Embedding involves the segmentation and interspersing of episodes in such a way that the first episode is completed only after the introduction of one or more episodes; this process may be schematically represented as $E_1 + E_2 + E_1 + E_3 + E_n + E_1 + E_n + E_3$. Among the embedding patterns represented in this collection of tales are $LE_1 + TE_1 + LE_1 + TE_1$; $LE_1 + DE_1 + LE_1 + DE_1$; and $TE_1 + TE_2 + TE_1 + TE_2 + TE_1$. Both processes may operate within a single tale in such a way that certain episodes are chained and others embedded; such a pattern is expressed by the following formulation: $E_1 + E_2 + E_3 + E_2 + E_3 + E_n$. Among the patterns of embedding and chaining in this corpus of Mende

Table 2: Action Patterns of Episodes

Form of Episode		Action Sequence		
		Initial	Medial	Final
Deception:	+	LD	DR	R
	-	D	D$\neq$R	P
Interdiction:	+	I	IO	R
	-	II	V	P
Task:	+	T	IO/LD	TA
	-	IT	IL/V/D	T$\neq$A
Lack:	+	L	TA/LD	LL
	-	IL	IT/V/D	L$\neq$L

Key: + = positive evaluation
      - = negative evaluation
      / = or
      $\neq$ = not
      D = deception
      DR = deception revealed
      I = interdiction
      II = illicit interdiction
      IL = illicit lack
      IO = interdiction observed

IT = illicit task
L = lack
LD = legitimate deception
LL = lack liquidated
P = punishment
R = reward
T = task
TA = task accomplished
V = violation

tales are $LE_1 + LE_2 + TE_1 + TE_2 + LE_2$; $TE_1 + DE_1 + TE_1 + TE_2 + DE_1 + TE_2$; and $LE_1 + TE_1 + TE_2 + TE_3 + TE_4 + TE_5 + LE_1$.[7]

Hitherto I have discussed several aspects of the forms and processes whereby Mende tales are generated, one final topic pertaining to the morphology of Mende tales remains to be mentioned: how these tales begin and end. Are there recurrent formal patterns for introducing and concluding Mende tales? Although the beginning and endings of tales are non-syntagmatic aspects of tales insofar as they do not contribute directly to the development of dramatic activity and consequently do not form part of the episodic structure per se, there are a limited number of ways by which Mende tales begin and end. Mende tales begin by naming the main characters involved in the tale (N:57), by introducing the initial action of the tale (N:29), by making an aetiological statement (N:11), or by stating a proverb (N:2) or a moral (N:1). They conclude without comment after the completion of the final episodic phase (N:44), with an aetiological statement (N:25), with a moral statement (N:21), a summary of the tale (N:4), a proverb (N:3), or a riddle (N:3). Most Mende tales in this collection, therefore, start with statements introducing the principal protagonists, such as "This tale is about Spider and Bat"; others begin with such statements of initial activity as "At one time a man met a bush spirit"; and less frequently tales commence aetiologically, "How Spider's waist became very slender at one time." While a great many tales conclude without specific comment or with a statement like "The story is ended," almost one-quarter of the tales conclude with aetiological statements such as "That is why Dog and Fly are not friendly, because Fly mocks Dog"; and another quarter end with moral comments such as "That is why jealousy is bad." Such prefatory and concluding elements serve as nonstructural aspects of tales which nevertheless deserve some comment in any discussion of Mende tale construction.

Considered as a totality, a Mende tale combines certain non-structural and structural features. The obvious nonstructural elements occur at the beginning and ending of the tale, while the structural aspects occur within the context of episodes. Alhtough each episode is built upon the same triadic structure, the action patterns of Mende tales combine to produce four episodic forms: deception, interdiction, task, and lack episodes. These episodes represent the basic units of all Mende tales. Some tales consist of a single episode, others of multiple episodes that are generated by embedding and/or chaining processes.

Notes

1. In the Mende tales presented in Part II, 65 consist of multiple episodes and 35 of single episodes. Of the 14 tales

narrated in one of four group session, 13 (93 percent) are multi-episodic, whereas 52 (61 percent) of the 86 tales narrated by individuals are composed of multiple episodes.

2. The four evaluative patterns of episodic phases in Mende tales are + + +; + - -; - + -; - - -.

3. Inspired primarily by Propp's classic morphological analysis of Russian fairy tales and by the development of transformational grammatical analysis in linguistics, several recent structural studies demonstrate with varying degrees of elegance the existence of finite patterns of tale construction and the operations generating these patterns in certain Amerindian and African cultures. Among these syntagmatic studies, I have found Robert A. Georges' "Structure in Folktales: A Generative-Transformational Approach," (Conch II, 2 /1970/ 4-17) especially stimulating methodologically. Since Georges' analysis relies on a binary model of tale morphology, my analysis of Mende tale structure uses a different structural terminology, while addressing itself to some comparable issues concerning the structure and generation of tales.

4. See Tables 1 and 2.

5. In the 35 single episode tales, the + + + pattern occurs in 17 tales, the - - - pattern in 7 tales, the - + - in 6 tales, and the + - - in 5 tales.

6. Capital letters refer to the form of episode (that is, DE: deception episode; IE: interdiction episode; LE: lack episode; TE: task episode) and subscripts refer to the sequence of episodes of the same form.

7. Of the 65 tales composed of multiple episodes, 33 (50 percent) are based on chaining; 12 (19 percent) on embedding, and 20 (31 percent) on chaining and embedding processes. There is some indication that the generative processes used by one narrator may influence another, for of the 13 multiple episode tales narrated within group contexts, 4 (31 percent) are based on chaining and 2 (16 percent) on chaining and embedding, but 7 (53 percent) are based on embedding.

Kasilo numu wiehinda
Spider is human behavior

In turning to an analysis of the content of Mende tales, two fundamental issues concern me: the relation between fiction and society, and the relation between a narrator and his story. In particular, I explore what Mende tales reveal and also fail to disclose about Mende society, and how a storyteller's situation may influence his tales. In approaching these issues I again use the tales in Part II. By considering the tale protagonists with respect to their natures, activities, and relations, I ultimately can discuss certain thematic values expressed in the tales.

In developing my analysis, I am mindful of Beidelman's cogent enumeration of some major limitations in the content analysis of oral literature.

Beidelman writes "1. Folklore texts may be valuable illustrations of the ways of thought and the nature of the values of a people, but by themselves, they can never provide the keys for deciphering their full significance or for understanding the basic social and ideological principles which underlie a particular society. 2. The forms of folklore are too concentrated, ambiguous and subtle to provide safe ground even for cautious conjecture, even though any thorough analysis eventually leads to such dangerous attempts. 3. Many years of experience with a particular people may still not yield sufficient information and insight to a researcher to enable him to clarify all the implications involved in each of the texts he has collected or even, much less, to 'see the point' at all in some of the most difficult and intractable of his material."[1]

I have attempted to confront the first of these issues by making it an analytical focus in my discussion of Mende tale content; the second and third present intrinsically unresolvable problems.

Although the protagonists of Mende tales include men and women, elephants and mice, twins and witches, leopards and monkeys, bush spirits and ancestral spirits, for the Mende two actors characterize tales: Spider (Kasilo) and Royal Antelope (Hagbe).[2] Without these characters storytelling could not exist, for they are the prototypical protagonists of Mende tales.

Ndamema writes: "To the Mende man Kasilo is dọmẹi and dọmẹi is Kasilo. You may use any characters you like in your form of dọmẹ, but whether you call the main character Kasilo

or not, to Mende listeners at least one of those major characters in your dǫmɛ is certainly Kasilo given another name
by you."[3]

When Mende villagers were asked why Spider and Royal
Antelope appear in stories, most (75 percent) said it is because they are tricky just as people are tricky. A Mende
proverb articulates the importance of Spider's role: Spider
is human behavior. Thus, through Spider's activities, Mende
people talk about human behavior. As several villagers said,
"It is our behavior that we call Spider's behavior." Ndanema
suggests that "when we say Kasilo numu wiehinda in proverb,
we also mean dǫmɛ numu wiehinda /tale is human behavior/.
Therefore, dǫmɛ is a picture of human behavior as seen by the
storyteller or as the storyteller would like the audience to
see it."[4]

Invariably Spider and Royal Antelope behave characteris-
tically. Both utilize deception, but Spider's deceit is associated with greed that leads him to some inevitable disaster,
while Royal Antelope's deceit involves some rational plan to
achieve a moderate goal that he attains successfully.[5] When
Spider and Royal Antelope interact in tales, Spider calls Royal
Antelope "uncle (kenya)."[6] Mende villagers said that Spider
calls Royal Antelope "uncle," because Royal Antelope is
cleverer or trickier than Spider. When asked in what way Royal
Antelope is cleverer than Spider, several villagers described
the following situation: "When he is in the bush, when a
leopard runs after him, if he is running down a hill, he breaks
an ant hill, then he holds the leaves with his hands; then the
leopard runs after the ant hill. While the leopard goes after
the ant hill, he /Royal Antelope/ gets up and goes back to
where he was." As one Mende villager observed, "The reason
why we say Royal Antelope and Spider are very tricky is that
they fool bigger animals; they fool them with the wisdom that
they have."

While the protagonists of all Mende tales may include
Spider and Royal Antelope figures, often they are identified
as members of differing classes of being of variant sexes and
ages. Initially I wish to note the kinds of activities engaging characters of different ages and sexes. In these tales,
both men and women are occupied primarily with food getting
and preparing activities: men farm, search for food in the
bush, hunt, tap palm wine, and fish, while women primarily
prepare food for their husbands, children, and visitors in
many tales but also harvest rice, search for food or fish.[7]
Other domestic chores such as housebuilding for men and
fetching water, chopping firewood, washing clothes, dying
cloth, or sweeping the house for women and performing ceremonial
obligations, such as mourning, paying bridewealth, or thanking
midwives are also mentioned in the tales. Finally in several

tales, recreational activities are noted for men but not for woman, such as visiting in other villages, dancing, and playing tops. Children in these tales are described as performing tasks for their parents: girls fetch water, sweep, and take food to visitors for their mothers, while boys perform tasks for both parents, fetching water and hunting for their mothers, and fetching fire, driving birds away from farms, carrying firewood, and hunting for their fathers. Even from an enumeration of these activities, it is clear that the focus of female activity centers around the domestic unit, while male activity includes both domestic and community orientations.

Although the activities that individuals perform may provide a situational context for a tale, the primary focus of interest in Mende tales is on the interaction of protagonists. Such protagonists have identified relations with one another and through their interaction reveal some Mende ideas about these relations. Characters are defined not only by sex and relative age but by kind of being--as spirit, animal, or person.

In Chapter 1 I discussed the Mende hierarchy of being noting that at the apex of his hierarchy is a supreme being, Ngewǫ. Mende believe that Ngewǫ created the world and its creatures, but is now largely removed from the affairs of men. In the tales in Part II, Ngewǫ does not appear as a protagonist. There are, however, a very few scattered references to him in the tales. In these references Ngewǫ is mentioned either to rationalize an otherwise inexplicable occurence or to avoid betraying a secret. Such references to Ngewǫ in the tales correspond to the attributions to him that Mende villagers made in response to questions about the causes of unusual cataclysmic or propitious events in human experience.

Although Ngewǫ does not appear as a protagonist in any of these tales, representatives of the spirit, human, and animal classes of being do. Thus, spirits figure in 28 percent of the tales, human beings in 54 percent, and animals in 52 percent. In the tales members of different classes tend to interact primarily with other members of their own class and to a lesser extent with members of other classes.[8] In each tale two principal protagonists are involved in a pivotal relationship around which the plot of the tale develops. In this collection, pivotal relations involve two animal protagonists in 48 percent of the tales, two human beings in 32 percent of the tales, and a human being and a spirit in 20 percent of the tales.[9] These pivotal relations fall into three main classes: (1) domestic relations of husbands and wives, parents and children, siblings, and affines; (2) community relations of uncles and nephews, leaders and followers, insiders and outsiders, and friends; (3) relations between human beings and spirits.[10] An examination of the kinds of beings involved in different categories of pivotal relations shows that in the

39 tales with domestic pivotal relations, 54 percent concern
human beings, 36 percent animals, and 10 percent human beings
and spirits, while in the 46 tales with community pivotal
relations 72 percent concern animals, 24 percent human beings,
and 4 percent humans and spirits.[11] Various explanations may
be offered for the predominance of human beings in the domestic
pivotal relations and the great majority of animals in the
community pivotal relations from fortuitous sampling factors
to Mende ideas about the association between tales and animal
protagonists. I think, however, that animals are disporpor-
tionately represented in tales about community relations in
part because many of these tales are aetiological in that they
explain existential antipathies or physical attributes of different animal species and in part because through the differentiation inherent in animal speculation, aspects of the relations
between non-kin within communities can be discussed readily.

In addition to such generic differentiations, pivotal relations among protagonists are influenced by the narrator's
sex.[12] Unfortunately women narrated only eight of the tales
in Part II. Nevertheless, the pivotal relations in women's
tales are distinctly different from those in tales told by
men.[13] All the protagonists in women's tales are involved in
domestic relations, while in men's tales 34 percent of the
principal protagonists are involved in domestic relations,
50 percent in community relations, 14 percent in relations
between spirits and human beings, and 2 percent concern isolated
individuals. This analysis of the pivotal relations of protagonists in tales told by men and women reinforces the

Table 3: Pivotal Relations by Protagonists' Classes of Being

Pivotal Relations	Protagonists' Classes of Being		
	Animal-Animal	Human Being-Human Being	Human Being-Spirit
Domestic:			
Husbands-Wives	6	6	--
Co-Wives	--	2	1
Parents-Children	2	9	3
Siblings	--	2	--
Affines	6	2	--
Community:			
Uncles-Nephews	7	--	--
Leaders-Followers	1	3	--
Insiders-Outsiders	6	1	2
Friends	19	7	--
Human Being-Spirit	--	--	13

Table 4:   Pivotal Relations by Sex of Narrator

Pivotal Relations	Female	Male
Individual:		2
Domestic:	8	31 (34 percent)
Husbands-Wives	2	10
Co-Wives	3	--
Parents-Children	3	11
Siblings	--	2
Affines	--	8
Community:	--	46 (50 percent)
Uncles-Nephews	--	7
Leaders-Followers	--	4
Insiders-Outsiders	--	9
Friends	--	26
Human Being-Spirit	--	13 (14 percent)
	(N=8)	(N=92)

the association between feminity and domesticity and between masculinity and a more diversified social context for men noted in discussing the activities of tale protagonists.

Narrators of different sexes also are concerned with different kinds of domestic relations. Both men and women narrate tales about spouses and about parents and children. Women raconteurs are concerned also with tales involving co-wives (37½ percent) and a woman and her co-wife's child (12½ percent). Male narrators disregard such relations for affinal relations (26 percent) and relations between siblings (6 percent). In the pivotal domestic relations of tales narrated by men and women, the raconteur never treats a relation with which he cannot identify. Men always tell tales involving some male character; women narrate tales concerned with some female protagonist. This association between the sex of the narrator and the sex of at least one principal protagonist in a tale pertains not only to the tales involving domestic relations told by men and women, but to the tales concerned with community relations and relations between spirits and human beings narrated by men.[14]

Turning to the content of the relations in tales, I consider only relations involving interaction in the tales and

do not treat relations mentioned merely to provide a context
for the interaction of protagonists. I begin by discussing
salient features of various domestic and community relations
and relations between human beings and spirits in the tales.
I conclude with a statement of general principles governing
interpersonal relations in Mende society as these are expressed
in the tales and a consideration of the relation between
these tale relations and Mende social life.

All the domestic relations in the tales are asymmetrical
ones in which it is expected minimally that the authoritative
superordinate role demands respectful deference from the subordinate role. Of course, the failure to adhere to such normative role expectations often constitutes the basis of tale plots.
Moreover, the substantive dimensions of asymmetry differ from
one relation to another.

The asymmetrical relation between husband and wife is
predicated on the notion that the husband is the authoritative
decisionmaker within the relations and that the wife should
defer to his decisions. Thus in tales, husbands instruct
wives about tasks, may use the threat of force to achieve their
wives' compliance, and may punish or reward their wives' conduct. If this dimension of the husband's role is reversed
with the wife acting as decisionmaker for the couple, disaster
is the consequence in the tales, perhaps suggesting the incom-
petence of women to make decisions as well as the inappropriate-
ness of such behavior within a conjugal relation. At the same
time, the decisionmaking right of husbands obligates them to
make wise decisions lest their ill-advised judgments endanger
their wives and children. Moreover, the husband as the superordinate partner is responsible for the well-being of his wife
to her kinsmen and in a polygynous marriage, he ought to treat
all his wives equally, lest jealousy arise from his differen-
tial demonstration of affection. Within the context of the
marital economy, husbands are expected to provide food which
women prepare for consumption. While it is possible for husbands and wives to have genuine affection and loyalty for one
another, several tales disclose a basic mistrust between spouses
based on an expectation of disloyalty and sexual infidelity.
Although husbands and wives should be honest with one another
and certain deceptive ruses to obtain more food or to conceal
a love affair are not condoned, deception in order to determine
the nature of a situation may be legitimate, such as a husband
pretending to die to discover which of his bickering wives
loves him, or a wife and friends playing a trick to disclose
the husband's greed. In conflicts between husbands and wives,
outsiders may be called upon to arbitrate or to intercede and
charges against an erring wife may be made in the presence of
her kinsmen, who are both responsibile for her conduct and
inextricably bound to her. In these tales, the relation between
husbands and wives emerges as an asymmetrical economically

interdependent one in which wives are expected to defer to
their husbands' decisions and in which reciprocal expectations
of affection and loyalty often are replaced by jealousy and infidelity.

While the asymmetry within the husband and wife relation
derives from the social superordination of masculinity in
Mende life, the asymmetry between co-wives results from seniority in the marital relation which usually is associated with
seniority in age. The senior wife has authority over her junior
ones insofar as she may set tasks for the junior wife, even
when these are shared tasks. While the relation between senior
co-wife and junior co-wife should be as mother to daughter,
harmonious interdependence is frequently marred by jealousy
about the husband's greater affection for one or another wife.
In a number of tales, jealous co-wives attempt to humiliate,
to destroy the property, and even to kill beloved co-wives.
Disapproval of such conduct is conveyed clearly in the dis-
asterous consequences befalling jealous wives.

The asymmetry within the relation between parents and
children necessarily derives from the generational difference
between them. As revealed in the tales, the relation may be
divided into three categories: father and son, mother and
child, woman and co-wife's child. In the father and son relation, the superordinate status of the father is expressed
through his setting tasks for the son, punishing the son, and
advising the son about his occupational choices. The right of
the father, like that of the husband, to make decisions for his
son implies the reciprocal obligation to make wise decisions
for his dependents. While fathers clearly are superordinate
and sons subordinate, nevertheless, they mutually assist one
another. Fathers give sons gifts and act to protect their
lives; sons help their fathers to provide food, obey their
fathers' instructions, and care for parents in old age. Just
as a son's occupational role is taught or arranged for by his
father, so a daughter's domestic duties should be learned
from her mother. For children of both sexes, the mother's
nurturant and protective role and the importance of obedience
to her advice are stressed in the tales. Sons are described
as helping their mothers with household chores and bringing
riches to them. Nevertheless, a foolish mother who permits
her immature son to determine her behavior or a disloyal woman
whose son knows of her infidelity may be killed. Although a
woman should treat her co-wife's child as her own and the child
should respect her father's wife as her mother, a woman may
vent her jealousy of her co-wife on that woman's child; such
illicit behavior leads to the offending woman's death in tales.
Consequently, the relation between parents and children rests
upon the expectations that the senior generation wisely in-
structs and protects the junior generation who reciprocate
with obedience and respect; violations of the first set of

expectations may lead to the legitimate violation of the second set.

Although relations between siblings are infrequently mentioned in the tales, their asymmetry derives from differences in age and from sexual differentiation. The elder brother should be in charge of his younger brothers and the sibling set should work together for their mutual advantage. Analogously, a brother is expected to be superordinate to his sister; his protective authority should be rewarded with her respectful obedience.

Finally in these tales, the relation between affines emerges with wife-givers superordinate to wife-takers. Wife-givers set the tasks necessary for a young man to gain his bride. Once the marriage is contracted, a mother-in-law is expected to be hospitable and generous to her deferential, hard-working son-in-law who may be living uxorilocally with her and who should mourn her death wherever he may be residing.

Although all the domestic relations in the tales are asymmetrical, community relations are both asymmetrical and symmetrical. The inegalitarian relations differ in certain basic attributes: the relation between uncle and nephew is nurturant and dependent; between leader and follower it is authoritative and dependent; and between insider and outsider it is competitive. Such inegalitarian relations contrast sharply with the reciprocal egalitarianism of friendship, the basis of many pivotal relations in tales told by Mende men.

As I have mentioned, in Mende tales Spider calls Royal Antelope his mother's brother. Other creatures also define their relation as that between uncles and nephews in a number of tales. The uncle has authority over his nephew, and he is expected to give his nephew wise counsel, while his nephew who should behave with respectful deference toward him may ask for his assistance. From various tales in this collection, it appears that the relation between mother's brother and sister's son represents the model of close asymmetrical relations between different species of creatures or different human kin groups. Further, its acknowledgement constitutes the mechanism whereby potentially dangerous relations are transformed into beneficial ones.

The nurturant responsiveness of the uncle to his nephew differentiates this relation from that between leader and follower. In Mende tales, the relation between chief and subject is prototypical of other relations between leaders and followers, such as master and apprentice and employer and employee. The leader is revealed as a decisionmaker for his followers, who are expected to adhere to his instructions even if they are unreasonable. A leader who is unable to make decisions courts social chaos. While a leader should make decisions on behalf of his followers, he should consult his elders in arriving at such decisions and should be generous to his subjects. Thus the authoritativeness of the leader is tempered by his munificence in the tales.

The mutuality of the relations between uncles and nephews and of leaders and followers contrasts with the hostility of relations between insiders and outsiders. In several stories a group of creatures, such as a herd of elephants, a pack of rats, or a flock of palm birds, formulate a plan to outwit or subdue an individual creature. If the group cooperates together to execute the plan, they will be successful; if, however, they fail to cooperate or if an individual reveals the plan to the outsider, the plan fails and the group's aim is not realized. Hostile competition, therefore, defines the relations between insiders and outsiders.

More frequently in Mende tales, the plot focuses not on the hostile competition of an outsider and a group of insiders but on the egalitarian reciprocity between individual male friends. Relations between friends, who often belong to different animal species and sometimes to different communities, should be characterized by mutual assistance and sharing. Friends who help one another in obtaining food or in performing some ceremonial duty expect to be rewarded for their contribution. A basic assumption underlying the relations between friends is that friends' capabilities are usually complementary and not identical. Moreover, a man should be aware of his friends' abilities so that he will be neither harmed nor deceived. Friends with complementary abilities should assist one another and act openly, but a person must be wary lest his friend violate these behavioral norms.

A major concern in tales told by Mende men is the range of relations between characters belonging to different animal species or different social units within communities. Most relations are asymmetrical, but friendship is a symmetrical relation; most of these relations are contractual, though uncles and nephews have an ascribed relation; most of these relations depend on a reciprocal exchange of services, but relations between outsiders and insiders are hostilely competitive. All these relations are threatened by failure to adhere to normative role expectations; such failure often constitutes the situational occasion for a tale.

In approaching the final set of relations described through these tales--those between immortal spirits and mortal men--I initially consider the nature of the spirits revealed in the tales. The spirits of the tales fall into two main categories: spirits of the dead and non-ancestral spirits comprising both river and bush spirits. The spirits have

anthropomorphic attributes in that their physical needs for
food, sleep, and sex correspond to those of human beings and
their domestic and community structures are similar to those
of human beings in certain tales. Spirits interact with human
beings either in dreams or in diurnal life, when they often
appear as animals, human beings, or even plants. In their
initial interaction with human beings, spirits may be hostile
or benevolent. Hostile spirits, who invariably are described
as eating people, may be legitimately destroyed by human beings
or they may seduce and kill unwary mortals. Such evil spirits'
powers can be overcome most readily by people who themselves
have some unusual powers such as twins, northerners, and medicine owners. Beneficient spirits, on the other hand, give
special help to people either in return for some good deed or
out of fondness for the person who may be their child. Among
the gifts that reciprocating spirits give to people are money,
special powers, and the spirit's transformation into a person.
Affectionate spirits may perform some task such as ritual
scarifying, doing farm work, providing nourishment, and sharing
the use of some utensil. Underlying all interactions between
beneficient spirits and human beings is the notion of trust
involving primarily secrecy about the relationship. If this
trust is violated, the person may be physically harmed or the
spirit may withdraw and resume its initial form, unless the
person is able to demonstrate a reasonable cause for violating
the norm of secrecy to the spirit. Thus, the relation between
spirit and human being, which is existentially asymmetrical
insofar as immortal spirits constitute a higher order of being
than living persons, involves individual members of each class
of being and is determined largely by the attitude of the spirit
toward the human being. If the spirit is hostile, a person
legitimately may respond with overt hostility; if the spirit
is benevolent, the person should be covertly appreciative of
the spirit's generosity.

The preceding discussion suggests that in Mende tales
most relations are asymmetrical implying minimally the
authority of the superordinate partner and the deference of
the subordinate partner. The sources of asymmetry in these
relations derive from several existential biosocial sources
including class of being, age, and sex. Accordingly, all
spirits are superordinate to all human beings; all older people
are superior to all younger individuals; all males outrank all
females. The interplay of these variables within a particular
context makes for more complex classifications that establish
certain existential principles as having greater salience
than others in such a way that an older woman or a female
spirit may be superior to a young boy or a human man, re-
spectively. Moreover, egalitarian relations based upon similar
values for each of these existential variables are relatively
rare in this collection of tales. Nevertheless, each relation
whether asymmetrical or symmetrical is premised upon certain

normative behavioral expectations involving complementary obligations. Should these normative expectations be violated
through either their abrogration or their excessive application
by one partner, the other partner is no longer bound by the
norms governing the relationship and legitimately may attempt
to punish or outwit the offending partner. As might be expected, punishment is usually the form of sanction utilized by
superordinate partners and clever deception the form employed
by subordinate partners. As my analysis of the structure of
Mende tales indicates, such violations of relational norms frequently constitute the basis of a plot.

Given the ethnographic analyses available on Mende society,
it is difficult to assess with any precision the relation between these tales and the social experience of most Mende villagers. Nevertheless, some general observations may be made.
Tales told by Mende men and women suggest that women's relations
have a more domestic orientation than those of men. While such
a deduction is probably valid in a general sense, Mende women
do have a rich communal life through their participation in
the Sande society and other communal sodalities. In fact, the
relation between Sande co-initiates is said to be especially
solidary in Mende society though it is mentioned rarely in
these tales. Analogously, the relation between brothers, which
is said to be a close one for Mende men, figures in very few
tales. Rather relations within Mende tales appear to concen-
trate on those that are important for the continuity of Mende
social life but are likely to be problematical.

When the situations and relations depicted in these Mende
tales are considered as a totality, two thematic values recur:
greed and rationality. Greed, which is negatively evaluated in
social life, centers around food and money in the tales. In
fact, activities relating to food whether to its procurement,
preparation, or consumption occur in 75 tales. Clearly then
food is a primary focus of concern in these tales relating
partly to the near-famine that Mende may experience before
the rice harvest and to the nature of Spider. Actually, most
of the tales concerning greed about food are stories about
Spider. Greed is negatively evaluated in Mende tales as the
consequence of Spider's and other protagonists' avaricious
behavior indicate. Moreover, Royal Antelope's moderate conduct provides a foil for Spider's greed suggesting how a mean
of moderation is positively valued in Mende culture. Consequently, in this collection of tales, a recurrent thematic
issue is associated with the negative evaluation of greed as
this is prototypically expressed in Spider's avarice for food.

The other central value conveyed through these tales is
the positive evaluation of rationality, as it is expressed
through the rewards and positive results accruing to cleverness,
forethought, and the comprehensive consideration of issues.

Such rationality enables protagonists to outwit and triumph over those who would harm them. At the same time, cleverness and deception in pursuit of some avaricious goal is not positively valued. Characters employing such negatively evaluated cleverness are so ashamed when their deception is discovered that they flee. Moreover, the value of rationality is positively evaluated only when it is used for legitimate ends that are not associated with greed.

Greed and rationality then constitute the two principal values expressed in the thematic contexts of Mende tales. In a sense, these values are most succinctly represented in the behavior of Spider and Royal Antelope. Representing the prototype of Mende protagonists, Spider and Royal Antelope also symbolize two basic and contradictory value orientations conveyed in Mende tales: illegitimate cleverness in pursuit of selfish ends and legitimate rationality for social goals. The Mende recognition of the threat that the former poses to social well-being is suggested by the proverb "Spider is human behavior."

Notes

1. Beidelman (1967) 84.

2. Royal antelope (neotragus pygmaeus) is a "tiny delicate antelope (the smallest of all the African ungulates), the size of a rabbit." See Jean Dorst and Pierre Dandelot, A Field Guide to the Larger Mammals of Africa (London:1970) 260. It lives in the dense high forest.

3. Personal communication from the Reverend Isaac M. Ndanema, October 30, 1961.

4. Ibid.

5. For example, Tales 44-46.

6. Mother's brother, kenya. I discuss the relation between mother's brother and sister's son below.

7. Activities of men: food getting and preparing 70 percent, other domestic 5 percent, recreational 18 percent, ceremonial 7 percent (n=57); activities of women: food getting and preparing 65 percent, other domestic 27 percent, ceremonial 8 percent (n=34).

8. Classification of all protagonists mentioned in tales: animal-animal (44 percent); human being-human being (20 percent); human being-spirit (16 percent); human being-human being and human being-animal (4 percent); animal-animal and

animal-human being (2 percent); human being-human being and human being-spirit (13 percent); animal-animal and animal natural phenomenon (1 percent).

9. Tales with animal-animal protagonists may be classified as aetiological or as allegorical.

10. These differentiations among pivotal relations constitute the basis for ordering tales in Part II. See Table 3.

11. Of course, human beings and spirits necessarily are the principal protagonists in all pivotal relations involving such beings. Ideas about such relations are discussed below.

12. I first discussed this issue in "Social Relationships in Mende Dọmẹisia," (Sierra Leone Studies, December 1961, 168-172).

13. See Table 4.

14. In the four group storytelling sessions, the relations between the narrators did not appear to be associated with the relations between protagonists, except in the case of two co-wives whose tales focused on this relationship. In a tale-telling session of two brothers and the wife of one brother, the tales were concerned with domestic relations; in a session in which three friends told five tales, three tales concerned friendship and two domestic relations; another group of four friends told tales involving relations between human beings and spirits and domestic relations. In the storytelling ses-sions, however, there was a tendency for the protagonists to be of the same class of being; in one session all five tales concerned animals; in another session all four tales were about human beings; in a third, half of the tales were about humans and the other half about human beings and spirits; while in the fourth session, two tales involved humans and one was an animal allegory.

PART II: WEST AFRICAN MENDE TALES

The tales in this book were collected during nine months
in 1960. They were recorded on tape in the Mende language by
people whose mother tongue and sometimes only language was
Mende. Some recording sessions involved single individuals,
others groups. Many of the recordings were made in Freetown,
others were made in the provincial towns of Bo and Kailahun.
While recording took place in a limited number of places, the
narrators' home-towns were located throughout Mendeland in Kpa-
Mende, Ko-Mende, Sewa-Mende, and Sherbro-Mende villages and
towns. Their occupations ranged widely including a sailor who
in his youth had been a professional story-teller, a tailor
who was seeking employment in Freetown, a nurse who had received her medical training in Europe, a provincial school boy
who was visiting his brother in the city, a petty trader whose
husband was a clerk, and a watchman who had travelled widely
but spoke only Mende with ease.

In asking narrators to tell stories, I did not ask for
stories of any particular type. The material presented here,
therefore, suggests what raconteurs considered of interest
and also suitable for me to hear. In the final months I did
ask three informants for "proverb" stories, but only one was
able to recall two (tales 25 and 65). Although none of the
narrators had used recording equipment before, they were not
inhibited by the machine and all displayed genuine delight in
hearing their stories replayed.

While transcribing and translating the taped tales, I enjoyed for many hours the patient and good-humored assistance
of Reverend Isaac M. Ndanema, Mr. James B. Konte, and Mr.
Michael Alpha who were variously affiliated with Fourah Bay
College in 1960. All three men were familiar with the phonetic
writing of their natal language. Following recording sessions,
I made preliminary and extremely inadequate transcriptions of
the stories which were painstakingly corrected from the tapes
with a Mende assistant. I then made a preliminary translation
into English of the text. In the early period of my work,
translation was hindered not only by my lack of familiarity
with the Mende language but also by the lack of an adequate
Mende-English dictionary, for Innes' fine dictionary has only
become available subsequently. The preliminary translations
were reworked with an assistant with the aim of achieving a
literal verbatim translation of the texts. Finally, in com-
piling the texts and translations for this volume, I have reworked the translations once more, assuming--of course--
responsibility for all inaccuracies.

In the following pages, tales are grouped according to the
relationship between the principal protagonists. Each tale is
annotated to identify its narrator and date of recording, to
note previous published recordings--if any, and to include

some ethnographic commentary. I do not include information
on tale types, though that might be an interesting exercise.

Table 5. Narrators' Attributes

Sex & Age	Home-Town	Occupation	Town Where Tales Recorded
Male c.40	Bo	Sailor	Freetown
Male c.20	Pujehun	Tailor	Freetown
Male c.29	Bunumbu	Clerk	Freetown
Male c.16	Bunumbu	Student	Freetown
Male c.30	Bunumbu	Clerk	Freetown
Male c.60	Mattru Jong	Watchman	Freetown
Male c.40	Bunumbu	Teacher	Kailahun
Male c.60	Kailahun	Translator	Bo
Male c.60	Bumpe	?	Bo
Male c.26	Mano	?	Bo
Male c.35	Tikonko	?	Bo
Male c.35	Bo	?	Bo
Male c.35	Bo	?	Bo
Female c.22	Bo	Trader	Freetown
Female c.35	Rotifunk	Housewife	Freetown
Female 26	Bo	Nurse	Bo
Female c.20	Bo	Housewife	Bo
Female c.30	Bo	Housewife	Bo

TALE 1:   A CLEVER MAN[1]

At one time a man went walking with three things: a goat,
a leopard, and a hamper of cassava.[2]   They journeyed for three
days.   During this journey neither the man nor the animals ate
anything; they all became extremely hungry.   They continued to
travel until they reached a large river.

There was a law about crossing this river: a person
could take only one load at a time across the river.

The man reached the river crossing with the goat, the
leopard, and the hamper of cassava.   If the man crossed the
river with the hamper of cassava, he would leave the goat and
the leopard together, and the leopard would eat the goat.   If
he crossed the river with the leopard, the cassava and the
goat would remain together, and the goat would eat the cassava.

What did he do?

When the man reached the river crossing and the law was
explained to him, he first crossed the river with the goat and
tied it up on the far side of the river before returning for
the leopard.   When the man had crossed the river with the
leopard, he untied the goat, recrossed the river with it, and
tied it up again.   Then he took the hamper of cassava, crossed
the river with it, and placed it near the leopard which would
not eat the cassava.   The man then recrossed the river, untied
the goat, and brought it across the river.   Then the man continued his journey with his three possessions.

This man showed cleverness by preventing the creatures
from eating one another.   He safely reached his destination
with his three possessions.

That is why cleverness is desirable.

Kenei wọ i yẹ jiama a haka sawẹi.   Haka sawẹi ji tia lọ
wọ a ye ji: nje,kọli, kẹ tanga gahẹi.   Kenẹi ji i lewe lọ, i
luvani wọ jiama kpeing lọwọ sawa; ẹẹ mẹhẹi mẹ; fuhani jisia
gbi ti ngi yeya ti kpẹlẹ ti galahu bẹ ndọlẹi ji gbọwongọ na ti
la.   Kẹ ti ya ti li ti fo nja wai yila ma.

Njẹi ji la jawẹi ye wọ a ji lo lọ: numu yila kẹ hakẹi
wua mia wa njẹi lewe wati ma.

Kẹ ti ya ti li ti fo njẹi ji la.   Njei ji lọ ngi yeya ta
kọli ji kẹ tanga gahẹi ji.   I njẹi lewenga a tanga gahẹi ji,

i njei ji ta koli ji ti longa; koli ji a njei ji me. I yama
gboma i njei lewenga a koli ji, tangei ji be gboma ta njei ji
ti longa hinda yila; njei a tangei ji melo.

Ta be i gboo wieni lo?

Kia i foni njei la ke ti sawei ji genga a ngie, ke i njei
leweni a njei yese ke i ya, i li i njei ji gbulo mia njei woma,
ke i yama koli woma. Kia i li koli woma, i lima i ye i li i
njei ji lewe na a koli; i li i njei fuloilo, i wa i kpulo gboma
mbei njei woma. I wani na, i tanga gahei lo wumbuni, i li i
ndo koli gblanga, koli ta ii tanga mema, ke i wa. Kia na i
wani ndii ye kelemangei na na i ye piema i wani na le i njei
wumbuni i lilo a ti jaango.

Nemahu le na wo i kpuani; naa wo i wie fuhani nasia, tii
ti nyonyou meni. I jia a hakei nasia kpele; i fo a tie. Hinda
gbi ii ti wieni.

Na va mia nemahu le manengo.

---

1. Recorded by a young man from Pujehun in Freetown on May 30,
1960.
2. Goat (nje) is also a protagonist in Tale 48 and mentioned
in Tales 22 and 54. Leopard (koli) also figures in Tales 45-
48, 57, 78, 82, and 94; in the mid-nineteenth century,
Thompson says that man-eating leopards were numerous in
Mendeland (Thompson:79-80). A hamper (kaha) is a container
made of leaves. Cassava (tanga) is a primary staple during
the rainy season and before the rice harvest (Little, 1967 ed. :
77).

TALE 2: CHIMPANZEE AND THE KOLA NUTS[1]

Why the chimpanzee became angry with the kola nuts.[2] At
one time, the chimpanzee did not eat any other food except
kola nuts. Once the chimpanzee was travelling for eighty
days without seeing a single kola nut to eat. He was extremely hungry. He kept travelling until he found a big kola
nut tree. He climbed up the tree; he searched and searched
for kola nuts, but he did not see any and he was extremely
hungry.

He said,"The night is coming on, so I will sleep here.[3]
Tomorrow I will look for another kola tree."

The chimpanzee sat down on the kola tree where the branches were thick not realizing that a big bunch of kola nuts

hung above him. His head touched the bunch of kola nuts, but he did not see it. He slept through the night.

In the morning the chimpanzee awoke and turned to climb down the kola tree. As he turned, he saw the big bunch of kola nuts. He said that the kola nuts had lied to him and that in the future, he would not eat kola nuts. He climbed down the tree; he was angry.

That is why the chimpanzee eats other foods; the chimpanzee does not eat kola nuts, because the kola nuts lied to him.

This story is ended.

Na wọ wieni ngolo lileni wọ tolo ma.

Ngolo ẹẹ mẹhẹ weka gbi mẹ wọ kẹ tolei. A tolei yakpe lọ wọ mẹ mẹhẹ gbi ndunya ẹẹ mẹ. I loni wọ lewema lọ i gu a lọ wayakpa ẹẹ tolo gbi lọ mẹ va. Ndọlẹi ji gbọwongọ wa ngi ma, hindẹi ji miningọ na ngi ma. I loni lewe ma lọ kẹ i ya kẹ i tolo wulu wai ji malenga kẹ i lẹnga hu. I tolei ji gọkọle, i lewe haa ii tolo gbi lọni. Ah, hindẹi ji miningọ ngi ma.

Yẹ "Ngii yaa lima" yẹ "kpena." Yẹ "Kpindi hu leke nga wa na," yẹ "fale" yẹ "ngi yima na mbeilọ. Sina ngi li ngi tolo weka lọndọ."

Ngi li ngi tolo weka lọndọ. Ke i ya kẹ i heinga tolei ji hu miando kpọvọi na kẹ i ya. Na mia wọ i lini i heini na mẹma tolo disa wai mia. Ngi wui ji i helẹni ngi wumba, ngi wui a họma ii tọni. I yini wọ na lọ gbuu. Ndọlẹi ji miningọ ngi ma.

Ngele wonga na gbalan ngi longọ i hitẹ i li. A yema i wotenga kẹ i tolo disa wai ji lọnga. "Kua, ah" yẹ "tolei i ndẹ gulanga ngi wẹ." Kuna ẹẹ yaa tolo mẹ. Kẹ i hitẹnga tolei ji hu a ye ndilewe.

Ang na lọ wọ wieni ngolo mẹhẹ weka mẹni wọ ẹẹ tolo mẹ, jifa tolei i ndẹ gula wẹ.

Na mia dọmẹi ji ye kẹlẹmangẹi le.

---

1. Recorded by man from Bo on January 7, 1960 in Freetown.
2. In the midnineteenth century, Thompson noted that chimpanzees (ngolo) were "plentiful in these regions of Africa" (Thompson:282). The chimpanzee is also a protagonist in Tales 54 and 71; in the former Royal Antelope outwits him and in the

latter he beats Spider. Kola (tolo) nuts are used as stimu-
lants and as small gifts; the first installment in a marriage
payment is called tolo la.
3. A Mende day is divided into a number of periods on the
basis of both the amount of sunlight and human activities.
Since various times of day are mentioned in the tales, it is
useful to note some of the major Mende differentiations:
kpindi, night; kpindilia, midnight; ngele wohu, last darkness
before dawn when deaths are announced; ngenda, dawn; ngenda
volo, morning when sun is hot; folo ngundia, mid-day; folo
lekpengoi, early afternoon or slanting sun; kpɔkɔ volo, late
afternoon or evening sun; fitii, first darkness or early
evening; heilenga, late evening or time for sitting face to
face; and ndagbele, bed-time.

Husbands and Wives

TALE 3: A HUNTER, HIS WIFE, AND THE BUSHCOWS[1]

This story is about a hunter who was a great magician.[2]
This hunter used to hunt bushcows, but the bushcows were unable to kill him, because he hid himself from them.[3] If he
simply said "I will jump into my magical hiding place," he
disappeared. Sometimes he turned into a big tree stump;
sometimes he turned into a big stone; sometimes he turned into
a big hill; sometimes he turned into a crab.[4] So every time
the hunter went hunting, the bushcows were unable to kill him.

Then the bushcows turned into human beings and came to
this hunter's wife. They said,"Explain something to us. Your
husband is very clever; he is very skillful. What does he do
so that the bushcows are unable to kill him?"

One day the hunter's wife said to the hunter, "Tell me
what do you do so that the bushcows are unable to kill you?"

Now the hunter began to tell her. He said,"If I simply
say 'I will jump into my magical hiding place,' I turn into a
big tree stump; the bushcows encircle me, they meet me, but
they do not see me. Sometimes I say 'I will turn into a stone,'
they keep going around me, they look at the stone, they do not
touch it. Sometimes I turn into a big hill, they do not touch
me." He said "sometimes I turn into a cra..."

As soon as he said 'I turn into a cra...,' his mother who
was in the house said "No." She said "Stop, do not tell your
secrets to a woman. Do not finish what you are saying."

And so the hunter stopped speaking.

At dawn the next day, the bushcows again turned into human
beings and came to the woman.[5] They said,"How does he do it?"

The woman said,"He told me everything; he named everything except the very last one; he did not complete it, he
just said 'cra...'"

Then the bushcows left.

When the hunter went hunting bushcows in the bush, he
shot a bushcow 'kpuu'; the other bushcows ran after him. As
soon as the hunter turned into a tree stump, the bushcows
started to pound on the tree stump. The hunter quickly
changed into a stone; the bushcows turned to beat the stone.

The hunter changed into a hill; the bushcows turned to beat the hill. As soon as the hunter said,"I will turn into a crab," the bushcows did not know that he had now turned into a crab. That is how he saved himself.

That is the end of our story.

Domei ji ndalongo kamaso lo na hi josomo wa mia wo a ngie. I ya wo tewuisia gbemei. Tewuisia tee gu ngi ma ngi wa va. A lowu lo i ndenga lo leke ye "Ngi wilinga so." Ke i longa hu a wotelo a ngulu wukpe wa, lo tenga ma a wotelo a kotu wa, lo tenga ma a wotelo a ngiye wa, lo tenga ma a wotelo a ngaku. Wati gbi na hi i yalo kpemei ji tewui jisia lolo ti ngi wa, ke te gu ngi ma.

Ke tewusia ti wotenga a numu vunga ke ti wanga kamasoi ji ngi nyahei gama. Te "Huge a mue, bi hini ji kasongo wa le tawao ngi belingo. Gbe lo na hi a pie na hi tewuisia tee gu ngi ma?"

Lo yila ma ke kamasoi ji ngi nyahei ji ndenga ye "Huge a nge vuli ba ye pie na hi tewuisia tee gu bi ma."

Ke ta lo na totoma a huge la ye "Ngi ndenga lo leke nge 'ngi wilinga so,' ke ngi wotenga a ngulu wukpe wa; ta nya gala ta nya gome ke tee nya lo. Lo tenga ma ke ngi ndenga nge 'ngi wote le a kotu,' ta nya galalo haa ta koti na gbe te jala. Lo tenga ma nga wote a ngiye wa lo tee ja a nge." Ye "Lo tenga ma nga woteoa nga..."

Kia leke i ndeni ye "Nga wote a nga...' ke ngi nje longa mia pelei bu ke i ndenga ye "Eeh," ye "gbe-o, baa bi ngai huge a nyaha, baa ngakpia."

Ke i gelenga mia.

Ngele woilo leke ke tewuisia ti wotenga gboma a numu vunga ke ti wanga nyapoi gama. Te "I ye na-o?"

Ye "I hugenga a nge kpele, ke i boisia kpele bi yenga ke ye kelema nge ta ii ko i ndeilo leke ye 'nga...' ii yaa na nga kpuani."

Ke ti yamanga-o.

Ke kamasoi ji ya ndogboi hu tewuisia, ke i kpandewilinga tewui ma 'kpuu,' ke tewuisia ti hitenga poma. Kia leke i woteni a ngulu wukpe, ke ti totonga a ngulu wukpei na ma hijala. Ke i gbuanga na fulo ke i wotenga a kotu ke ti wotenga kotui be lenga. Ke i gbuanga na fulo ke i wotenga a kotu ke ti wotenga kotui be lenga. Ke i wotenga a ngiye ke ti wotenga

ngiyei lenga. Kia leke wǫ i ndeni na yę "Ngi wote a ngaku,"
tii yaa na hungǫ i wonteni wǫ na a ngakui. Na lǫ na lǫwǫ ngi
ma na a bawoni.

Dǫmęi ji mu gbuani ngi gęlęmęi mia.

---

1. Recorded by young man from Pujehun in Freetown on February
16, 1960. A summary reference to a version of this tale
occurs in Innes 1964.
2. Hunters (kamasǫ; kpandęwilimǫ) are believed to possess protective medicines enabling them to transform themselves into
other kinds of being. Hunters also figure as protagonists in
Tales 17, 18, 29, 56, 80, 82, and 97.
3. The bushcow (tewu) also appears in Tales 29, 32, and 77.
This story is the only one in which the bushcow assumes human
form; in Tale 32 a spirit is said to assume the form of a
bushcow.
4. The crab (ngaku) also appears in Tales 40 and 44.
5. In this sentence, the woman is referred to as nyapoi or
young woman. Mende differentiate the human life cycle into a
number of categories; in early years and in older age, sexual
differentiations need not be made. Thus, the major life cycle
categories are: ndola, baby from birth to age of creeping;
jialo, young child from age that can walk until 5-7 years old;
hiilopo, boy, or nyalo, girl, for those years between seven
and initiation into Poro or Sande societies; hajo, newly initiated society members; ndakpaloi, young man, and nyapoi,
young woman; hindo kpakoi, middle-aged man and nyaha kpakoi,
middle-aged woman; kpakoi or nu wova, old person; haamǫ, recently dead person; ndemǫ, ancestor.

TALE 4: A HUNTER AND HIS ADULTEROUS WIFE[1]

The hunter and his wife.

At one time there was a big hunter who killed many animals. Whenever he went hunting his gun never sounded in vain;
every time he went hunting, he killed many animals. But his
wife was not very truthful with him; in fact, she was very
wicked. The hunter used to bring the animals that he killed
for the woman to cook; she used to cook all the best parts
for her lovers and to cook the feet, the hands, and the
little parts for her husband.[2]

When her husband asked her about the other meat, she
would say, "Oh, I am drying my meat." If her husband pressed
her, they quarrelled. She continued to behave in this way.

When her husband mentioned some of the things which she did in order to stop her infidelity, she continued to behave as before.

The hunter and his wife had one son.

One day the small child saw how his mother was deceiving his father. He saw that she loved above all a monkey who lived on top of a hill.[3] This monkey would change into a person and come to see the woman. The monkey and the woman were lovers. The little child used to observe how his mother called this monkey.

One evening when his father came, the boy said to him, "Mother's lover," he said, "I know the way to his place."

The hunter said, "Stop! Do not explain that."

When morning came, the hunter said to his wife, "My friend, the animals that I killed which are drying are many. The smell in the house is over-powering. Tomorrow, therefore, we will sell the meat."

The woman agreed with her husband.

The next morning, the woman gathered all the dried meat together and went to sell it.

When the woman had gone, the hunter and his son set out for the monkey's place. Before leaving the hunter loaded his gun; he and his little child went where the child used to go with his mother. They travelled until they reached the monkey's place. As soon as they arrived there, the little boy called the monkey. The monkey then changed into a person and came.

As soon as the monkey had greeted them, the hunter took his gun, placed it on the monkey's chest, and fired 'kpu.' The monkey fell.

Very quickly the hunter and his son carried the monkey home where the hunter skinned it. The hunter then hid the skin from his wife. Then the hunter cooked the intestines, the heart, and the other fine internal organs before his wife returned.

That evening when the woman returned from selling the meat, the hunter said, "My friend, I killed a small animal today." He said, "Look at your share over there."

The woman got up and went over to the meat. Of course that day she had left her sweetheart of whom she had been thinking throughout the day. Hastily the woman took all the best parts of the meat, put them in a pan, and prepared to carry it out.

As the woman was preparing to leave, the little child came. She saw that he was laughing, but she did not know why he was laughing.

The child ran to his father. He said,"Mother is putting the meat in a package!"

As soon as the man heard that, he took out the monkey skin, went to his wife, and put the skin in front of her.

When the woman saw the monkey skin, the hunter said, "It is the person to whom you took my food; I killed him today."

The woman got up.

There was a spirit's town called Folakunde. The woman decided that she wanted that spirit to eat her.

When the woman got up, she set out for the spirit's town. She walked a long way. When her breath reached the spirit, he began to wash his rusty pot in which he ate human flesh. As he washed the pot, the water sounded "kpu-gbu-ma-yembe." As the woman came to the spirit's town, this smell came to her; she became afraid and turned back. Then the spirit himself came running after her. Not long after she reached home, she died.

That is how the woman continually deceived her husband and that is what her husband did.

The story is finished.

Kpandẹwilimọ ta ngi nyaha. Kpandẹwilimọ yila wọ na i yẹ na a kpandẹ wili wa a huanga wa kpotongọ wa. Kpema gbi va i ya wọ kpandẹwilimẹi ji ngi gbandẹi ji ẹẹ yia gbama. I ye gbi lini a wa a hua gbotolọ. Kẹ ngi nyahẹi ji ii yẹ lọnyani wa a ngie ngi ngavango wa yẹla. I wa wọ a huẹi ji nyapoi ji hu i ji yinga lee; ye hakẹi ye kpekpemẹi na gbi a ngili wọ ngi lakpaoisia we ngi ndiamọisia. I ngilinga lee, ye kọwẹi jisia-a kẹ ye tokoi jisia ye kpagbani nasia ta mia a pu kenẹi wẹ. Gbema gbi va hi mia i yẹ a pie a kenẹi ji.

Kenẹi ngi mọlia. "Kuo" yẹ "nya huẹi nasia" yẹ "nya mbema." I gbọndanga ngi ma kẹ ta ta ti yia. I loni haa ji lọ wiema kẹ kenẹi bẹ tẹnga na i pienga wọ a ndelọ ngi ma. I ngi yama lalahu kọwẹi i gbe ye hindẹi na ma kẹ na hu gbi ẹẹ gbema. I ji wie haa a ngie.

Wati yila kẹ ngi lo wuloi ye nyapoi ji ngi lo wuloi ye na ta kenẹi ji ti nɖeni hindolo yila.

Ti yẹ na ke ndopo wuloi ji i hindẹi ji hu lọa gbọ nyapoi ji a pie a ngi kẹkẹ. Kẹ pẹing i ndoma kua yila mia i yẹ mia ngiyẹi wumbua; ye kua ji mia a maluve wọ a numui a wa ta mia ta nyapoi ji ti ndomẹi hu. Ndopo wuloi i yẹ wọ ti gbema, a yẹ ngi gbema kia a ye kua ji loli.

Kia le ndopoloi ji kpọkọ yila ngi kẹkẹ wẹile kẹ i hungẹnga a ngie yẹ "Ye" yẹ "ngi maloma yila na" yẹ "ngi lingama ndọlọ."

Kenẹi bẹ ndea yẹ "Inle, baa hungẹ lẹ."

Kẹ ngele wonga kẹ i ndea yẹ "Nyande," i ndea ngi nyahẹi ma yẹ "Nyande, huẹi ji ngi pa" yẹ "mbei ji gbotongọ wa le" yẹ "ngi longọi na ye kui ji i wẹlẹ muma, falọ sina mu hu i majia."

Kẹ nyapoi lumanga.

Kia ngele woni kẹ i houa mbei na gbi liama, i ya majiama.
Kia le i lini kẹ kenẹi bẹ i ngi loi wumbua kẹ ti ya hindẹi ji kua ji gama. Ti yẹ lima i ngi gbandẹi na jọsọi lọ ndei, i mbumbu kẹ ta ngi lo wuloi ji ti ya. Ngi lo wuloi ji i li ti li lọ wọ i pie na lua wo a ngie miando gẹ ta li na ta ngi nje. Kẹ ti ya ti li ti fo kua ji ma. Kia le ti foni kua ji ma kẹ ngi lo wuloi ji kua ji lolia kẹ i wa i maluvea a numui ji kẹ i wa.

Kia le ti njẹpẹi ji lei haa kẹ kenẹi ji bẹ i ngi gbandẹi ji wumbua i pu kua na lima, i mbola "kpu" ngi limẹi na, kẹ kua na gula.

Ta bẹ kia ti lini a kua ji fulo, fulo, fulo, fulo, kẹ i kọ gbua. Kia i kọ gbọe kẹ i ye kọẹi ha lọwua ngi nyahẹi na. Ti yi nyẹnẹi nasia-o, ye ndi na-o, ye kohu hakẹi nasia, ye nyande nyande na le keni, kẹ i ngi li ngi ngi nyahẹi gulọ.

Kẹ i gbua hua majiamẹi, kẹ i wa kpọkọi. Yẹ "Nyande," yẹ "ngi hua wulo wa ha-o" yẹ "bi ndẹi gbe mia."

Kẹ i hiyia. Kia le i hei huẹi ji ngọbu ingẹ ngi ndiamọi ji i lọa ha ngi hinda mia i yẹ ngi li hu foloi na kpẹing. Huẹi na i kẹilọ le yamu yamu yamu i ye kpekpei jisia kpẹlẹ wumbua, kẹ i punga pani hu, ngi longọ i lila.

Kia i ye lima kẹ ndopo wuloi ji wa na kẹ i tọnga a ngẹlẹi ji wielee. Ii hungọ gbọ a ye ngẹlẹi ji wie.

Kẹ i yamanga i li i nde ngi kẹkẹ ma yẹ "Ye lọ gbọma ha huẹi wuma hakẹi hu."

Kia le kenẹi i na humẹni le kẹ i wa tabẹ i wailọ le kẹ i
hua gọlọi ji gbua, ye kua gọlọi ji kẹ i punga ngi nyahẹi ji
gulọ.

Kia le i kua ji gọlọi ji lọi lee. "A yẹ numu gẹ ba li a
nya mẹhẹi jisia ngi gama, a yẹ ta lọ ha ngi pa."

Kuo, kẹ i hiyia.

Hani wa yetahu lọ wọ na la a Folakonde, yẹ i mania hani
wa i ngi mẹ. I hiyia ta lima na. I jia haa kia le ngi vẹvẹi
na wuni hani na ma kẹ hani wa tọtoa ngi numu mẹ fẹi ji wọ a
numu huẹi ji mẹ hu ngayia wọ wo. Kẹ ta na wuama. I ye wuama
njẹi na yia woi na mia na i yẹ a pie kpugbuma yẹmbẹ a mẹ gbou
njẹi wotea. Kia na i li haa hani wai ji ma, vẹvẹi ji wui ngi
ma kẹ i luwa i yaa li, kẹ i wotea i yama. Hani wai ji bẹ i
wa na a ngi gbẹ. Kia le wọ i yamẹi hu ii lẹmbi kẹ i ha.

So i kavẹi na wie lọ wọ haa a ngi hini hi wọ ngi hini bẹ
pieni.

Dọmẹi ji gbọyọa.

---

1. Recorded by young man from Pujehun in Freetown on February
16, 1960.
2. The relationship between a mature woman and her lover
(ndiamọ) is treated in Tale 25.
3. Monkeys (kuala) are also protagonists in Tales 47, 54, 66.

TALE 5: KPANA, HIS WIFE, AND A BUSH SPIRIT[1]

At one time a stranger came to a town. There he made
friends with one of the townspeople, a woman. They were together for a while until the time for farm work came.

Then the woman said to the man, "Friend, make me a farm."

The man agreed.

The woman went and begged for a place to make a farm.[2]
When they gave her a place, she went and showed the place to
the man. But he said that he would not make a farm there.
There was a forest near the town and the man said that he
would make the farm there.

The woman said, "Friend, never since my childhood have I
seen a farm made in that bush." She said, "Do not work there."

"Oh," the man said,"it is there that I will work." He said,"If you say that I should not clear that bush, then you are saying that I should not do any farm work."

All the townspeople said to the man, "Do not clear that place."

The man said that he would clear there.

One day the man arose and went to clear the bush (just as a person arises and says that he is going to lay a mark in the farm). The man went and worked; when the sun reached the middle of the sky, his wife brought his food. As soon as the man sat down before the food, an animal came; the man invited the animal to eat some food. The man and the animal ate the food. After they finished the food, the animal took some water in his mouth; he rinsed his mouth--suku-suku-suku; he spat the water into a basin and it turned into a lot of money. Then the animal rose and went away. Twice the animal did this.

In the evening of the third day, the man went to the town.

Then the man's wife said to him, "Friend," she said, "you mean that an animal eats food; then he washes out his mouth and the water turns into a lot of money!" She said,"If you kill the animal, you will see that we will get more money than anyone else in the world. You will see that you and I will bring wealth into the world." She said "Therefore, be very certain to kill that animal."

The man said,"All right."

You know that there are some men who listen a lot to women's advice.

In the morning the man got up and went to the farm. Although he worked continuously, he did not work as well as he had at other times. He kept sharpening his matchet; he sharpened the matchet until it was very sharp. When the sun reached the middle of the sky, the man's wife came with food. As soon as the woman left and entered the forest, the animal immediately came again. The man and the animal ate the food. When they had finished eating, the animal took some water into his mouth in order to wash it out; the animal was sitting with his back turned toward the man in a dog-like position.

Then the woman whispered to the man, "It would be good to kill the animal."

The man took his matchet. As the man prepared to kill the animal, he split his own knee with his matchet. While the man remained in the farm, his wife went to the town.

But before the man's wife went into the town, the animal sang this song to the man:

"Kpana split his knee; he wounded himself.
"He split his knee.
"Such is a woman's advice.
"Kpana split his knee; he wounded himself.
"He split his knee."

Then the man's wife got up and went into the town. There she said,"Kpana has wounded himself badly." She said,"My relatives, come with me to help me. We will bring him."

The townspeople arose and took a hammock. They carried the man in the hammock and brought him to the town. They put a lot of medicine on him. When the people brought the man into town, they laid Kpana in his own sleeping house.

When night came, the woman called all the townspeople. When all the townspeople gathered, she reported to them that "Kpana wounded himself today."

When all the townspeople gathered that night, they went to look for medicine. There is a tree in the bush called mbeli that has red sap.[3] If a farmer wounds himself in the bush, people will cut this tree and bring its sap to put on the wound, for the sap stops the flow of blood. People used the sap of this tree, because formerly they did not have European medicine.

In this forest was a sacred place where all the spirits gathered at night. That particular night, the spirits came to sing an important song in the town:

"Kpana split his knee; he wounded himself.
"He split his knee.
"Such is woman's advice.
"Kpana split his knee; he wounded himself.
"He split his knee."

While these spirits sang this song continuously for Kpana, Kpana's own breath went far to many people; Kpana was dying.

Then Kpana's wife came out weeping. She returned to the place in the forest where Kpana had split his knee. There she met the animal sitting.

The animal questioned her. He said,"I came to your husband when he was cutting the brush recently. I like you. When you brought food, your husband and I ate it; afterwards I would wash my mouth and put down money." He said,"You took the money away. When I washed my mouth, you got money to buy

things." He said,"Recently you told your husband that he
should kill me so that he could take the money out of my
stomach." The animal said,"Now you have come yourself. Do
you want to kill me?"

The woman fell down before the animal. She said that she
had come not to kill the animal but to beg him not to allow
her husband to die.

Then the animal took out a leaf and gave it to the woman.
He said,"If you take this leaf, grind it, and rub it on Kpana's
knee, he will be cured."

The woman ran back to the town carrying the leaf. She
ground the leaf very quickly on a stone; she rubbed the leaf
on Kpana's knee. As soon as the woman rubbed the leaf on
Kpana's knee, Kpana got up--his knee was cured.

Afterwards Kpana refused to farm again that bush. Moreover, whenever Kpana said that he was going to do something
and someone said,"Kpana do not do that," Kpana would agree
not to do it.

This is the end of this story.

Hotẹi ji gbe wọ i wani tẹi ji hu hoe. Kẹ i ndoma gbatẹnga
a tali yila nyaha mia yela a ngie. Ti loni na haani na kẹ
ngenge kpelei ji hitinga.

Kẹ nyapoi ji ndenga ngi ma yẹ "Nyande," yẹ "kpa la mbẹ-o."

Ke ta bẹ i lumanga hindẹi ji ma. Kẹ nyapoi ji kẹ i kpala
lama vẹlinga. Kẹ ti fenga ngi wẹ. Kẹ i ya i na gẹ a kenẹi ji.
Kẹ kenẹi ji ndenga yẹ ii kpalẹi lama na. Kẹ ngola lọ yẹ tẹi ji
gbla kẹ i ndenga yẹ na mia a kpalẹi ji la na.

Kẹ i ndenga ngi ma yẹ "Nyande," yẹ "kia wọ gba" yẹ "i
hihia" yẹ "nya yama wonga ndọgboi na ma" ye "tii yaa kpalẹi
na" ye "fale" yẹ "baa yenge na."

"Kuo," yẹ "na mia nga yenge na-o," yẹ "bi ndenga bẹ nga
ndọgboi na lue" yẹ "kẹ ba ndelọ bẹ nga kpala yengei wie."

Talinga gbi tẹi-na-hu-bla gbi ti nde ngi ma tẹ "A nduwe
wie hindẹi na."

Yẹ "A pielọ na."

Ke i hijea na folo yila ma kẹ i ya ndoei ji wiemẹi ji.
(Kia numu ba hiye bẹ bia lima tifa gulama kpa hu.) Kẹ i ya.
I yenge lọ haani kẹ foloi ji hitia ngundia kẹ ngi nyahẹi ji ya

kǫndǫi ji. Kia le i heini le męhęi ji gǫ bu kę huęi ji wa kę
i ngi lolia męhęi ji ma, kę kenęi ji huęi ji lolia męhęi ji ma.
Kę ta bę ti męhęi ji męa. Ti męhęi ji męngǫi ji gbǫyǫngǫi
ji kę huęi ji kę i njęi ji wua la kę i kęnga suku suku suku
suku kę i pua kaloi ji hu kę i wotea kǫpǫ gboto kę i hiyea kę
i ya.

I ji wieni heima fele yę sawa voloi ji a kpindi na kę ti
ya tęi hu.

Kę kenęi ji kę ngi nyahęi ndea ngi ma yę "Nyande" ye "bi
tǫ" yę "hua i męhę mę" ye "i ngi la wa" ye "i wotea a kǫpǫ
gboto" yę "ǫ ji ba ngi wa" yę "bi tǫnga bę mua kǫpǫ majǫlǫ
ndunyęi ji bu," yę "fale" yę "pie lę vuli bi na wie bi huęi
na wa."

Ta bę yę "Eye."

Bi kǫlǫ hininga tęnga lo na ta wolo lǫ wa nyahangęisia ti
layęi ji ma.

Kę i hiyea na kę i ya kpalęi ji hu a ngendei ji. I lini
i yengei lǫ haani kę ii yengeni vuli panda, kia a yenge la-o
wati ye pekęisia ma. I mbogbęi ji lǫ le yakpani kaka kaka
kaka. I ngakpalǫ vuli i yę ngęngęngę; i hou wa. Kę foloi ji
hitia na ngundia kę ngi nyahęi ji wa na a kǫndǫi ji. Ngi wa
ngolęi ji leke kę huęi ji wa gbǫma yakpe, kę ti męhęi ji
męnga; ti gbǫyǫa sęng. Kę huęi ji męhę męa gę a njęi ji wulo
la i ngi la wa kę wati ji ma na ta i ya ngi lo wani gulo bę
va, kę i heia kę i wovia i ngi gbulę gbulę gbulęi ji hu gę
vuli a kenęi ji.

Kę nyapoi ji kę i ndenga na kenęi ji ma ndondo yia hu yę
"Nyandengǫ na vuli" yę "bi huęi ji wa."

Kę kenęi ji kę i mbogbęi ji wumbua. Kia wǫ le yę i huęi
ji wa kę i ngi wombi bla fa. I loni na wǫ na haa kę ngi nyahęi
ji kę i hiyea kę i ya tęi hu.

Kę pęing ngi nyahęi ji a ya li tęi hu, kę huęi ji i ngulei
ji gbuani ngi ma yę:

"Ngombi bla Kpana ngi nęmua
"Ngombi bla
"Nyaha layia
"Ngombi bla Kpana ngi nęmua
"Ngombi bla."

Kę ngi nyahęi ji i hiyenga na i ya tęi ji hu kę i ya yę "Kpana
ngi nęmua wa" yę "fale" yę "nya bonda" yę "a wa wu li wu gbǫ
nya ma. Mu wa a ngie."

Kę nunga ti hiyea ke ti ya a mbomęi ji kę ti ngi la hu kę ti wa a ngie. Ti halenga gboto mawulǫ wǫ ngi ma. Ji na ti wa a ngie tęi ji hu kę ti ya ngi la pęlęi ji bu, ta ngi Kpana nyinyi węlęi ji bu.

Kę kpǫkǫ węlia na ngi nyahęi ji ya na i ndea nunga kpęlę kę ti tabla kpęlę kama kę ti ndenga ti ma tę "Kpana ngi nęmua ha."

Kę nunga kpęlę kę ti liama kę ti heia kpindi ji ti ya halenga goima. Ngulu yila lǫ na ndǫgbǫi hu ta toli a mbęli ye njęi ji kpǫugbǫungǫ ta mia numu ngi ngua ina kpala-lamǫ le i ya ndǫgbǫi ji hu ngi ngua ta li ti ye ngului ji lee ti wa ye njęi ji ti pu na ta mia a ngamęi ji hu le. Ti wa ngului ji ti ye njęi ji wuma kaka jifa wati na hu pu hale wa ii na.

Kpǫkǫi ji ti ya na le ti la kę ndǫgbǫi ji hu bi kǫlǫ ngolęi ji hu hęma mia wǫ i na ye jinęi jisia kpęlę kę ti liama a kpǫkǫi ji kę ti wa kpǫkǫi ji kę ti ngule wa gula tęi ji hu:

"Ngombi bla Kpana ngi nęmua
"Ngombi bla
"Nyaha layia
"Ngombi bla Kpana ngi nęmua
"Ngombi bla."

Ji na ngafęi jisia ti ngulei ji ya na haa Kpana ma. Kpǫkǫi ji welia na Kpana kę ngi lęvui vuli ji i ya na pulong nunga gbi gboto ma kę Kpana ji i hama.

Kę ngi nyahęi ji kę i gbua i li a ngǫęi ji wie. Kę i ya gbǫma lǫ ngolęi ji hu mbeindo haa Kpana ji ngi wombi ji bla na. I lini i malelǫ hu i ji hei gbǫma.

Kę huęi ji ngi mǫlia yę "Ji na bia lǫ gę bi ndea bi hini ma jifa nya ngi waa gę a wue wǫgba numu i ya kpalęi hindęi ji" yę "nya longǫ gę a wue" yę "wu wa" yę "mua bi hini mu męhę menga" yę "ngi la wa" yę "ngi kǫpǫi na wua" yę "wu ye kǫpǫi na wumbu wu li la ngi la wua bę wa ya ngeya a wu ma haka wulo." Yę "Bia lǫ gę bi ndea ngi ma bę i nya wa i kǫpǫi gbua nya ngohu." Yę "Bia bę bi wa" yę "bi longǫ bi nya wa?"

Kę nyapoi ji bę i ya kę i gula huęi ji gǫbu yę "ii lini hu i ji wa va" yę "i walǫ i ngi manęnę" yę "kǫ wǫi i pie" yę "ngi hini a ha."

Kę huęi ji bę kę i ya kę i tifęi ji gbua kę i fenga ngi wę kę i ndea nyapoi ma yę "Bi ya a tifęi ji" yę "bi kpongbo" yę "bi sia Kpana wombi ji ma" yę "a bawolǫ."

Kę nyapoi ji bę yama gbǫma a pimę tęi ji hu kę i wa tifęi ji i li i kpongbo fulo fulo fulo fulo kǫtui ji ma kę ti wa kę

ti sia Kpana wombi ma. Kia le nyapoi tifẹi ji jiani Kpana
wombi ma kẹ Kpana hiyea wombi na bawonga.

Kẹ i ya na wọ lumani a kpala la. Tao hinda gbi Kpana i
yẹ na wọ pie numu ndea ngi ma yẹ "Kpana baa ji wie," i yaa
luma a pie.

Jeli ji ye kẹlẹmẹi mia.

---

1. Recorded by young woman from Bo and her brother-in-law
from Bunumbu in Freetown on July 11, 1960.
2. It is appropriate that in an uxorilocal marriage, farmland
should be granted to the woman who belongs to the landowning
group (see p. 8). The different stages of activity in rice
farming are described in Tales 85 and 95. Aspects of the di-
vision of labor in a farming household are also noted in Tales
15, 67, 71, and 79.
3. Mbẹli (Piptadeniastrum Africanum).

TALE 6: KPANA, WASP, AND SNAIL[1]

Long ago there was a young man. He had two wives: one was
named Wasp; the other was named Snail. Wasp was the beloved
wife; her husband loved her very much. Those who do not tell
lies say that the box that he bought for her was bigger than
the whole world.

(Don't tell lies!)

If I am lying then the little fishes are lying.

(How do they lie?)

When the sun rises, go stand near the river. The fishes
sing a song.

(How do they sing?)

Kpang-gba, it has gone through my head;
Kpang-gba, it has gone through my head;
Kpang-gba, it has gone through my head;
Kpang-gba, it has gone through my head;
Kọndọ, it has gone through my head.

Ah, so it was that at that time the young man loved very
much his wife, Wasp. There was the other wife called Snail;
she was the one doing the slave work in the house.

One day the young man said, "In order to discover if these women love me, I am going to pretend that I am dead."[2]

In any Mende house if a person dies, his wives will come to sit in a mourning house; they will weep.[3] Through their weeping, they will show whether or not they love the dead person.

Then the young man, who was called Kpana, went to a farmhouse. There he lay down in such a way that if you saw him, you would say that he was dead.

Some people came to the town, they said to Kpana's wives, "We found your husband lying in the farmhouse; he is dead!"

The women got up and went to weep. Of the two wives, the beloved wife was named Wasp and the unloved wife was called Snail. When the corpse had been washed, it was brought from the farmhouse into the house. Then the wives came weeping.

First Wasp, the beloved wife, was called. The people said,"Come to weep for your husband."

The woman came; she sat on the ground weeping. What did she say?

"I, Wasp, am very slender;
"I have no dress to cover a corpse.
"Vengo yama vengo;
"Vengo yama vengo;
"Vengo yama vengo.
"I have no dress to cover a corpse.
"Vengo yama vengo;
"Vengo yama vengo;
"Vengo yama vengo.
"I, Wasp, am very thin;
"I have no headtie to put on a corpse.
"Vengo yama vengo;
"Vengo yama vengo;
"Vengo yama vengo.
"I have no headtie to put on a corpse.
"Vengo yama vengo;
"Vengo yama vengo;
"Vengo yama vengo."

That was how she kept weeping.

Then the people said,"Small wife, come here to weep for your husband."

How did she weep?

"My husband Kpana-o,
"Dovo dava, dava dovo;
"My husband Kpana is dead,
"Dovo dava, dava dovo;
"My husband Kpana-o,
"Dovo dava, dava dovo;
"My husband Kpana is dead,
"Dovo dava, dava dovo."

That was how the little wife wept.

The corpse that was lying there was looking at the women.
He looked continuously at his big wife; in his mind he said,"So
the woman whom I really loved has come to disgrace me in this
mourning house."

Then all the people dispersed.

When the wives were going to the farmhouse, the corpse
got up very quickly and reached the farmhouse before them.
When the women arrived at the farmhouse, their husband said,
"Ah, I did not die just now. I only pretended to die in order
to know which of you loves me." Then he said to the beloved
wife, Wasp, "Since you shamed my face in that mourning house,
disrepute will pursue you forever." He said,"As soon as you
come inside a house, the people will drive you away; they will
take brooms and they will slap you." Then he turned to the
little wife and said,"Ah, Snail, since you have not shamed my
face, I will give you such riches that whenever people will
see you they will jump."

Is that not so?

(It is.)

If the wasp enters a house, what do people do?

(They beat it; they hit it.)

When the rains come and you see a snail, what do you do?

(Oh, we shout a big shout!)

Ndakpaloi ji gbe wọ hoe. Nyahanga ti ngi yeya fele.
Yela la a higbọ, yela la a kole. Higbọ mia ndoma nyahẹi le
ngi hini longọ wa a ngie; nasia tẹ ndẹ gula tẹ kangai i ngeyani
ngi wẹ ta kpẹlẹ le, ngẹẹ ndẹ gula, ngẹ tewengọ ndoloi kpẹlẹma.

(Baa ndẹ gula!)

Ina ndẹ mia nga kula kẹ ndẹ mia tekuisia ta kula.

(Ta ye kula?)

Ji folei gbuanga lọ, bi li bi lo njẹi gblanga, nja lowẹi gblanga ngole mia tekuisia ta nge.

(Ta ye nga?)

Kpanggba nya wui ngele vonga,
Kpanggba nya wui ngele vonga,
Kpanggba nya wui ngele vonga,
Kpanggba nya wui ngele vonga,
Kọndọ nya wui ngele vonga.

Ah, hi mia ndakpaloi ndongọ wa yela a ngi nyahẹi. Nyahẹi ye ji lo na ta toli a Kole, ta i na lọ leke a nduwọi yengei ji wie pẹlẹ bu.

Folo yila kẹ ndakpaloi ji lọ ndema yẹ "Kọ ngi kọ nyahangẹi ye jisia ti longọ a nge ngi limalọ ngi pie bi tọngalọ bẹ ngi hanga."

A Mẹnde wẹlẹ bu ta numu hangalọ ngi nyahanga ta wa lọ ti hei pẹlẹ bu ngọwẹlẹ bu ti ngọẹ wie. A ngọẹi na ta pie ta kọlọma na ti lọngọi a numui ji hanga.

Kẹ ndakpaloi ji, ta toli a Kpana, kẹ i ya kpuẹla i li i la bi tọngalọ bẹ ngi hangọi.

Ke nunga ti wanga tẹi hu ti nde ngi nyahanga ma tẹ "Wu hini gbe mia mu ngi malenga lani gbuẹila ngi hangọ."

Nyahangẹi jisia lẹ ti wanga ngọlẹmẹi hu. O nyaha felei jisia ndoma nyahẹi ji ta ngi loli a Highbọ kẹ nyapoi ji ta ii loni a ngie ta ngi loli a Kole. Kia na ti pomẹi ji wani fo ti kpua kpuẹla ti wa la pẹlẹ bu kẹ nyahanga ti wanga na ngọmẹi.

Ndoma nyahẹi Higbọ yese ti ngi lolini tẹ "Wa bi bi hini wọ wo."

Kẹ i wanga i hei ndọlọmẹi. Ngọẹi ye gbẹlọ i pieni?

"Nya nya Higbo nya ya lengi lengi kula gbi nya ma nga pẹ poma.
"Vẹngo yama vẹngo,
"Vẹngo yama vẹngo,
"Vẹngo yama vẹngo.
"Kula ii nya ma ngaa pẹ poma ma.
"Vẹngo yama vẹngo,
"Vẹngo yama vẹngo,
"Vẹngo yama vẹngo.
"Nya nya Higbọ nya ya lengi lengi kpaya gbi nya ma ngaa pẹ poma.

"Vẹngo yama vẹngo,
"Vẹngo yama vengo,
"Vẹngo yama vẹngo.
"Kpaya ii nya ma ngaa pẹ poma ma.
"Vẹngo yama vẹngo,
"Vẹngo yama vẹngo,
"Vẹngo yama vẹngo."

I ngọẹi ji wie, i ngọẹi ji wie, i ngọẹi ji wie.

Kẹ ti ndenga na tẹ "Nyaha woi wa lẹ bi bi hini wọ wo."

Ngọẹi ye gbẹlọ i pieni?

"Nya hini Kpana-o
"Dovo dava dava dovo
"Nya hini Kpana hanga
"Dovo dava dava dovo.
"Nya hini Kpana-o
"Dovo dava dava dovo
"Nya hini Kpana hanga
"Dovo dava dava dovo."

Kẹ nyaha woi ji ngi nda wọẹi ji wienga.

Pomẹi ji lani a ti gbe. I nyaha wai ji gbe haa njẹpẹ hu
wie a nde ngi nẹmahu yẹ "A nyahẹi wọ vuli nya longọ la" yẹ "ta
lọ hi wa i nya ya wufenga ngọ wẹlẹi ji bu."

Kẹ nunga kpẹlẹ ti vayanga.

Kia na nyahẹi jisia ti lini kpuẹla kẹ pomẹi ji i hijenga
sa i hu lewe ti gulọ kẹ i ya kpuẹi ji la kẹ nyahẹi jisia ti
fonga ngi ma kẹ i ndenga ti ma yẹ "Ah ba ngi hani ye gẹ; ngi
ji wielọ leke kọ ngi kọ wu felei ji wu ma yelọ ngi longa a
nge." Kẹ i ndenga ndoma nyahẹi ma Higbọ "Kia bi nya ya
wufeni" yẹ "ngọwẹlẹi na bu" yẹ "kunafọ sọlẹma mia a yẹ bia bi
woma;" yẹ "bi fonga bi fonga leke pẹlẹ bu nunga ta bi gbelọ ta
kpankpa wumbulọ ti kpaji bi ma." Kẹ i wotenga nyaha woi lenga
kẹ i ndenga yẹ "A kole bia" yẹ kia bii pieni nya ya wufe" yẹ
"kunafọ" yẹ "ngi bi ma kpatẹmalọ vuli" yẹ "nunga ti bi longa
lọ leke ta windẹ a famia."

Hi ya na?

(Ta mia.)

Ji fọi a wa pẹlẹ bu ta ya pie nunga ta ye pie?

(Ta nde lọ; ta fogbalọ.)

A jina njẹi ji a wa wa kole lọ wa yẹ gbe?

(Kuo, yele wa mia ma kula!)

----

1. Recorded by woman in Bo on April 16, 1960. This story was
recorded in a group session, as indicated by the question and
response pattern that begins and ends the tale. The responses
of the audience are placed in parentheses.
2. For other simulated deaths, see Tales 7, 11, and 79.
3. The funeral rite of "crossing the river" occurs three days
after a woman's death and four days after a man's demise
(Harry Sawyerr and S. K. Todd, "The Significance of Numbers
Three and Four among the Mende of Sierra Leone," Sierra Leone
Studies, n.s. 26 (1970):30). The association of females with
four and males with three is an important aspect of Mende
culture expressed in the timing of personal life crisis rit-
uals such as naming, secret society initiation, and funerary
rites, the performance of ritual acts, and the symbolism of
Sande masks (Sawyerr and Todd:30-32; Hommel:3).

TALE 7:   MR. FONJA AND HIS THREE WIVES[1]

Mr. Fonja married three women: one was named Frog,
another Rat, and the other Hen.[2] He loved Frog very much.
Mr. Fonja was a farmer. Whenever he made farms for these
women, he made Frog's near the town, Rat's farther from the
town, and Hen's farthest from the town.

At one time these women used to grumble continuously
about their husband to people. Their grumbling disturbed the
man's heart a lot. So he said, "I will know which one of
these women truly loves me."

One day all three women went to the farm. The man lay
down in the house and pretended to be dead.[3]

Just then an old woman came to visit him. She found him
lying down; he was very still. Also she did not investigate
further. She returned to the people in the other house, crying "Mr. Fonja has died!"

Then everyone came and the sound of weeping filled the
town. The town chief called the young men.[4] He sent them to
the man's wives--one by one.

The young men went to Frog. Frog, whose farm was nearest
the town, came with this lament:

"Is Kpana dead? I don't care.
"Is Kpana dead? I don't care.
"Let me do my rice pounding; I don't care.
"Let me do my rice cooking; I don't care.
"Let me do my rice eating; I don't care.
"Mẹnọm mẹnọm kpọ;
"Mẹnọm mẹnọm kpọ."

The second messenger went to Rat and informed her. Rat clapped her hands; she put her hands on her head weeping. As she came to the town, she wept on the road:

"No more to be seen, no more seen;
"Kpana, his father-o, Kpana-o.
"No more to be seen, no more seen;
"I am not going to eat rice in Kpana's absence.
"No more to be seen, no more seen;
"I am not going to tie cloth in Kpana's absence.
"No more to be seen, no more seen;
"Kpana, his father-o, Kpana-o.
"No more to be seen, no more seen;
"I am not going to eat rice in Kpana's absence.
"No more to be seen, no more seen;
"I am not going to tie cloth in Kpana's absence.
"No more to be seen, no more seen;
"I am not going to drink wine in Kpana's absence.
"No more to be seen, no more seen."

She kept weeping until she reached the town; she was rolling; she was crying.

The other messenger reached Hen. Hen also came weeping:

"Kokole Ko,
"It is I myself; my honor is spoilt, in truth.
"Kokole ko,
"It is I myself; my honor is spoilt, in truth.
"Kokole ko."

Hen was particularly concerned about the death of the man who owned them all. Hen used to hunt with divining charms; she also made sacrifices; she wore charms; she put charms inside the house and under the beds. Hen thought that perhaps her charms had killed the man. That was why she wept that way; she said that she had disgraced herself. She came weeping; her mind was very confused.

Hen and rat gathered together weeping loudly. They made an arrangement: they bought the shroud; they sewed the shroud; they wrapped the man in the shroud for his burial. In all that they honored him well.

Frog only wandered about; she wept;

"Is Kpana dead? I don't care.
"Is Kpana not dead? I don't care.
"Let me do my rice pounding; I don't care.
"Let me do my rice cooking; I don't care.
"Let me do my rice eating; I don't care.
"Menọm menọm kpọ;
"Menọm menọm kpọ."

After the man had been wrapped in the cloth and lain
there for a while, he awoke and called Frog. He had water set
on the fire; when the water boiled, he put it on Frog and he
dropped her under the verandah wall. He said,"Forever you
shall be under the verandah wall." And also when the hot
water was poured on Frog, swellings came out all over her and
pus came out on her. For this reason, even today if you handle Frog, water will remain in your palm.

The man called Rat. He prayed for her; he lifted her into
the granary. He said,"Your mouth will never be troubled about
food; you will have food to eat; everywhere you go there will
be food for you to eat."

The man called Hen also. He prayed for her; he dressed
her well; he put her on her feet in the town. He said,"Going
to the farm is not for you unless it is easy on you; people
will carry you to the farm; you will have food to eat."

That is what happened to Mr. Fonja and his wives. Even
today it is a warning to us all that we should love each other.
Also as Hen thought that she had killed Mr. Fonja, it shows us
that we should not wear charms, not divine, not sacrifice.
This old word shows all that.

Kenei Fonja i nyaha sawanga jọe lọ ye na la a Ndovo, na
be la a Nyina, na la a Tę. Kę i yę loi lọ gbong a Ndovo. Tao
Kenei Fonja i yeni wọ a kpalamalọ i ya wọ kpaę ji lama
nyahangei jisia wę. A Ndovo ndęi la tęi gblanga lọ i li a
Nyina ndęi polong tęi ma guhama pọ i li a Tę ndęi poma pọ.

Wati yila ma nyahangei jisia ti yę lọ a ngi gbonyę wiema
nunga ma wati gbi kę hindęi ji i ngi li mọnęnga wa kę i ndenga
yę "Ngi kọma vuli nyahangei jisia ti nya yeya ye na vuli
ndongọ a nge."

Folo yila ma nyahangei jisia kpęlę ti lilọ kpaę hu kę i
langa pęlęi bu i ha a kęwę.

Kę mama wova yila wanga famamęi ngi ma. I wa i ngi
maleni lani lọ ngi ma ya long ta bę ii hugbęni kę i yamanga a

yele nunga gama pẹlẹ wekẹi bu yẹ "Kenẹi Fonja hanga!"

Kẹ nunga gbi kẹ ti yeinga na kẹ ngọwui gunga na tẹi hu ta
mahẹi na yẹ na kẹ i kọnga lolinga i tọtọ a ti lola kenẹi ji
ngi nyahangẹisia gama a ngila ngla.

Kẹ ti ya Ndovo gama. Ndovo ta ta ngi gbaẹ yẹ tẹi gblanga
kẹ i wanga a ngọẹ ji:

"Kpana hailọ kpọ,
"Kpana ii hani kpọ,
"Ngi nya ba hija kpọ,
"Ngi nya ba yili kpọ,
"Ngi nya ba mẹ kpọ,
"Mẹnọm mẹnọm kpọ,
"Mẹnọm mẹnọm kpọ."

Tomọi ye pekẹi na kẹi ya Nyina gama kẹ Nyina bẹ ti ngoi ji
hugẹnga a ngie. Kẹ i kpajinga i loko la wumba a ngọẹ a wa a
wọ pelei hu:

"Ki yeing yeing
"Kpana ngi kẹ-o Kpana-o,
"Ki yeing yeing
"Ngẹẹ yaa mba mẹ Kpana woma.
"Ki yeing yeing
"Ngẹẹ yaa kula yili Kpana woma.
"Ki yeing yeing
"Kpana ngi kẹ-o Kpana-o
"Ki yeing yeing
"Ngẹẹ yaa mba mẹ Kpana woma.
"Ki yeing yeing
"Ngẹẹ yaa kula yili Kpana woma.
"Ki yeing yeing
"Ngẹẹ yaa ndọ gbọi Kpana woma.
"Ki yeing yeing."

I loni haa ngoẹ ji wiema lọ i wa i fo fa tẹi hu a gedembe a
wọ. Tomọi ye pekẹi ji kẹ i fonga Tẹ ma kẹ Tẹ bẹ ta wama a
ngọẹ ji:

"Kokole ko
"Nya yekpe mia ngi nya bẹ nyaninga-o.
"Kokole ko
"Nya yekpe mia ngi nya bẹ nyaninga-o.
"Kokole ko
"Nya yekpe mia ngi nya bẹ nyaninga-o.
"Kokole ko
"Nya yekpe mia ngi nya bẹ nyaninga-o.
"Kokole ko."

Tẹ ta i ye gilii lọ la jifa hindoi ji ti yẹ ngi yeya ti
kpẹlẹ. Tẹ ta i yẹlọ a tọtọnga gbẹ a yama a saanga gbia a yama

a lasimǫnga yili a ngua pęlęi bu a ngua kpukęisia bu ta ngilii
lǫ la yę kęnga lasimǫi jisia i wama a tie pęlęi bu ta mia ti
kenęi ji waanga famia i yę a ngǫę ji wie yę ta yekpe mia i ngi
bę nyaninga. Kę męma sao na ii le i wai lǫ a ngǫę ji ta bę
ngi nęmahu gilingǫ wa.

Ti ngǫę ji wielǫ ka taa Nyina ti lęilǫ ma hinda yila. Ti
hugbatę wie ti li ti kasangei yeya ti wa ti fe ti hǫ ti li ti
kenęi ji bembe hu ngi gbǫova ti ngi bęlę houi lǫ panda na hu
gbi.

Ndovo ta ta ta leke lewema a ngǫę yę:

"Kpana hailǫ kpǫ,
"Kpana ii hani kpǫ,
"Ngi nya ba hija kpǫ,
"Ngi nya ba yili kpǫ,
"Ngi nya ba mę kpǫ,
"Męnǫm męnǫm kpǫ,
"Męnǫm męnǫm kpǫ."

Kę ti kenęi ji bembenga kulęi ji hu kę ti langa haa wati
hu guhangǫ wulǫ va kę kenęi ji yamanga i wu kę i Ndovo ji
lolinga. I pie ti njęi heinga; njęi ji i nę i pu ndovo ma i
yama i kpuja kakei bu. Yę "Bia kunafǫ bi kake bu lǫ." Tao
kia wǫ nja gbandi na wuni Ndovo ma ngi ma ve fei lǫ fǫnyinga
ta gbua ngi ma famia folei ji bę bi Ndovo hounga lǫ njęi a
lolǫ bi yeya. Fǫnyi a gbua lǫ ngi ma.

I Nyina loli i hęi ka ngi va i mbumbu i tę pęlęi hu kpui
hu yę "Bia" yę "Bęę mǫnę bi la męhę va" yę "Kę ba sǫlǫ bi mę
mia-o-mia bi lini na męhę ya lǫ na" yę "ba męlǫ" yę "mǫnę gbii
bi ma fa."

I Tę bę loli i hęi ngi va i ngi mayili panda i kpuja ta
hu yę "Bia kpama li la ii bi ma kę leke i nę bi wę numu i bi
wumbu i li a bie" yę "kę ba męhę jǫlǫ bi mę."

Kę hi hǫ i Kenęi Fonja maleni ta ngi nyahangęisia, fale
folei ji bę i yęni a ndahi lǫ mu kpęlę gama kę ma a houlǫ mu
lo a mu nyǫnyǫ tao kia bę Tę yę gili la yę kę ta i Kenęi Fonja
wani kę sao ta ii gę la tao kę na a kę lǫ a mue kę ma ii houni
mua bę lasimǫ yili va ǫ tǫto gbę va saa gbua va. Kę njępę ji
a mu ga a ji lǫ.

---

1. Recorded by man from Mano in Bo on April 16, 1960.
2. Frog (ndovo) is a protagonist in Tale 62; rat (nyina, Nile
rat) also appears in Tales 53 and 87, while chicken (tę) figures in Tales 14, 72, and 73. As in many other African societies, chickens are used for devination and sacrifice (Sawyerr

1970 :79, 80); Ndanema has written that "among the Mende, chicken is the commonest but most valuable domestic animal, that binds friends and relations (Ndanema:ns. 24-25)."
3. For other simulated deaths, see Tales 6 and 11.
4. Further aspects of a chief's (maha) role are expressed in Tales 12, 16, 17, 20, 31, 33, 38, 49, 51, 53, 55, 62, 86, and 93.

TALE 8: SPIDER AND HIS BROTHER[1]

At one time Spider and his wife were at a farmhouse.[2] They cooked some food.

Spider said, "Do you know something?"

She said, "Yes?"

Spider said, "You should cook more food." He was very concerned. He said to his wife, "I have a brother who looks just like me, except he has one sightless eye. Every day when you cook food, save some for him. Be sure to do as I say, please."

She said, "All right."

While they were sitting there, he got up and went to hide another shirt under a nearby tree. When the woman had cooked the food, Spider ate his share.

Then he said to her, "I am going to go to the farm."

She said, "All right."

When he went to the farm, he returned very quickly and went to the tree where the other shirt was. He ripped off his shirt; he put on the other shirt. As he returned to the house, he bandaged one eye. At the house he met his wife.

"Where is Tou?" he asked.

"Oh," she said, "your brother has gone out."

When he sat down, she said, "Your meal is prepared."

Then Spider ate the food. Soon afterward he left the house, went to change his shirt, and returned.

Spider continued to do this for some time.

One day his wife saw him. She had decided to fetch some water. When she went out, she met Spider just as he was

changing his shirt in order to return to eat his second meal.
As soon as Spider's wife approached him, Spider ran away and
hid himself from her.

Do you understand the little story that I have told?

Kasilo ji ta ngi nyahẹi ji mia wọ. Ti na kpuẹi ji la. Kẹ
ti mẹhẹi ji yilinga.

Yẹ "Na?"

Yẹ "E?"

Yẹ "A mahoungọ bi ya mẹhẹ yili saha." Ngi li lọ hẹma
wa kẹlẹma ii ma. Ta bẹ i ya wọ kẹ i ndenga ngi nyahẹi ma yẹ
"Nya ndewei lọ na" yẹ "mua ta mu yilakpe" yẹ "mu gbuangọ a
yee wa kẹlẹma ii ma. A" yẹ "folo gbi bi mẹhẹ i yilia" yẹ "bi
ya ngi nde i lọ" yẹ "kẹ ta" yẹ "ngi yamẹi mia ngolongọhu kaka
yila" yẹ "famia" yẹ "ngi ndema bi ma" yẹ "baa njẹi na gbua hu
hoe."

Yẹ "Eye."

Ta ta ti ya le heini kẹ i ya kẹ ndoma weka lọwua mia
ngului bu i na. Nyapoi ji mẹhẹi yilia i ngi ndẹi ji mẹnga
i kpọyọnga seng.

Kẹ yẹ ngi ma "Ngi ya kpa ji wukọ hoe."

Yẹ "Eye."

Kia wọ i ya na ngi lingọi ji na leke i wa fulo fulo kẹ i
ya kẹ i ndomẹi ji bla kẹ i kpọyọnga i ndomẹi ji bla i kpọyọnga.
Nya kẹ, kẹ i ndoma weka wunga i ya wama kẹ i ngi yamẹi ji
yilia kaka yila. Kẹ i wa fo ngi nyahẹi ji ma.

Yẹ "Ọ Tọu?"

"Kuo," yẹ "bi ndewe gbua."

"Sia ngi hei, yẹ "Mẹhẹ bi ndẹi mia loi."

"Kẹ i na mẹa. Ngi yamangọ hu ii guha i ya kẹ i ya i
ndomẹi maluve kẹ i wa.

I loni wọ ji lọ ma i loni ji lọ ma haa.

Folo yila ma ngi nyahẹi ji kia le ngi lọni. Ngi nyahẹi
ii gọni yẹ i lima nja hu lọ. I li i maleni kini i ngi ma
gbuama a ndomẹi ji maluve kẹ i wa i yama i wa i mẹhẹi ji yẹ

pekęi mę. A męi kula ngi nyahęi gbuanga a męi va i lewenga a
pimę i lǫwua fǫ ngi nyahęi ma.

Ba na wuloi męni nga hugę?

---

1. Recorded by man from Bo in Freetown on January 27, 1960.
2. This is the first of many stories about Spider's greed;
see also Tales 9-11, 30, 35-37, 42-44, 51, 55, 62-71, and the
discussion on pp. 41-42.

TALE 9: SPIDER, HIS WIFE, AND THE CASSAVA

At one time a big rain fell. One day Spider and his wife
got up and decided to go to look for food. At that time it
was raining a lot. They walked around in the bush for some
time; they did not see anything to eat. They continued to
walk until they came to a cassava farm. They dug up a lot of
cassava and brought it to their house. Spider wanted to eat
the cassava; the woman decided that she would find a sauce to
go with the dish of cassava that she was preparing.

Spider said, "Give me my cassava. I am going to eat my
share raw."

"Oh, Sama," she said, "I am looking for a sauce for this
cassava and the children are under foot. I will prepare the
meal, then we will all eat."

He said, "I am going to eat my share raw; I am not going
to eat any cooked cassava!"

Spider and his wife talked for a while; he became annoyed
with her. Then the woman divided the cassava secretly. She
gave Spider's share to him.

Spider said, "Now, go away." Spider ate some raw cassava
very quickly; he drank some water. Then he decided to find a
place to put the remainder of the cassava; he hid the cassava,
but afterward he was still hungry; so he uncovered the remaining cassava and ate it.

Meanwhile his wife went to cut firewood; she returned to
cook the sauce well; she removed the sauce from the fire and
set it aside. Then she began to slice the cassava; she sliced
it; she cooked it; she removed it from the fire. That night
the woman and all her children gathered; she divided the food
and they ate it; they set the remaining food aside. Now

Spider thought that remainder was for him, but the others ate it themselves.

Now at that time the moon was shining a lot. The moon was shining as it shines brightly during the Mende dry season. The woman and her children came outside the house to see the moonshine. They did not know that Spider was greatly annoyed that they had eaten all their cassava. He was looking for a way to quarrel with his wife, but he could not find a way.

When the woman came outside, she said, "Oh, the moon is shining brightly just like a dry season moon!"

Spider, who had stayed in the house, heard his wife say that the moon was shining like a dry season moon. He came out; he said, "If the moon is not shining like a dry season moon, may I beat you?"

Then all his children laughed at him. They knew that their father was saying this, because they had eaten the cassava and had not given it to him.

Spider came out and began to fight with his wife. They fought until the woman ran away from him.

"You," she said, "saw the cassava which we ate without giving you any; you are angry, so you are taking revenge on me."

Spider began to beat his wife. Then his wife went and appealed to some very important people.

My story is about Spider's well-known greediness. At one time he did not allow his wife to cook his share of the cassava. When the woman cooked her own share, he wanted her to give it to him, but the woman and her children ate it themselves.

Kasilo ta ngi nyahẹi. Hama wa i gulẹi lọ wọ. Folo yila kẹ Kasilo ta ngi nyahẹi kẹ ti hiyẹa tẹ ti li ti mehẹ gọli. Na hu njẹi a wa wa. Kẹ ti ya ndọgbọi ji ma, kẹ ti li le haa ndọgbọi ji ma tii hani lọi. Kẹ ti lewenga ti li ti li tanga yọpọi ji hu. Kẹ ti ya. Ti tangẹi ji gbua gboto kẹ ti wa ḻa. Ngi longọ a tangẹi ji-o. Kia nyapoi ji yẹ i tangẹi ji hinda hugbatẹ i bete gọkọi ma kẹ Kasilo ta ndenga bẹ.

Yẹ "Nya nda tangẹi ve. Nya ngi nya ndẹi ji mẹma ngundu lọ."

Yẹ "Kuo, Sama," yẹ "tangẹi ji ngẹ ngi bete gọi bẹ na ndopoisia mu gọbu mua ti mu bẹ gbatẹ mu mẹ ta bẹ bi mẹ."

Yẹ "Ngi nya ndẹi mẹma a ngundu lọ. Nya ngi tanga yiingọ
mẹma."

Kuo nyapoi bẹ ti njẹpẹi ji le gulo kẹ i gbalẹnga nyapoi
ma kẹ i tangẹi ji lọa hu gọlẹnga. I Kasilo ndẹi ji venga.

Yẹ "Eh gbe ji-o." Kasilo heia i tanga wundui na mẹnga
gbata gbata gbata i njẹi gbọlinga ye mọnui na yẹ i lima i
ndama gbatẹ. I li i ndọwu, kẹ i ndọwunga kẹ ngii lẹlini. Kẹ
gbọma i ngi wenga i mẹ. I mẹa i gbọyọ a gbẹlẹ.

Na hu nyapoi i ya i kọwui yale i wa i hakpẹ i na yi panda
i kpuanga i to kẹ i tọtonga a tangẹi na jẹjẹ la. I sẹsẹ i ngi
kẹ i kpuanga. Kpọkọi na kẹ ta ngi lenga kpẹlẹ kẹ ti lia ma; i
kọlẹ kọlẹ kẹ ti mẹa; kẹ ti ye mọni na heia. Ha ii lẹmbi haa
Kasilo a tọ yẹ ti ji heia ta wẹ kẹ ti ta bẹ mẹa.

Mẹngọ-o na hu na ngawui ji lọ voma wa. Ngawui ji voma ta
wa voma kia vui ngawui ji a vo panda-da Mẹnde ngele voloi ji.
Nyapoi ji tia kẹ ti gbua ngi ti ji ya ngawu foloi ji lọma,
ndọlọi numui ji ngi lenga ta pie, mẹma tangẹi ji ha ti mẹnga
gbalẹngọ wa le Kasilo ma ta pele gọi ma nyapoi ji ma kẹ ii
ya pele gọẹ.

Kẹ nyapoi ji gbua kẹ i ndea yẹ "Eh" yẹ "Ẹẹ ngawui woma
kpa kia ngele vo yawu."

Kasilo i longa pẹlẹi bu i njẹpẹi ji mẹnia nyapoi yẹ ngawui
lọ voma kia nge vo yawu. Kẹ i wa "Ọ ngawui ji ẹẹ voma kia
nge vo yawu ngi bi le? Ọ ngawui ji ẹẹ voma kia nge vo yawu
ngi nde le?"

Kẹ ngi lenga kpẹlẹ ti gula a ngi yẹlẹ la; ti kọlọlọ jifa
ti tangẹi ji mẹa tii ti kẹkẹ gọi kẹ fa i lema a ji wie.

Kẹ i ya i tọtonga a lapila a nyapoi na. Ti ndapi na gọ
haa kẹ nyapoi bẹ i gbua ngi yeya.

"Bi" yẹ "male tangẹi ji mu mẹa muii bi gọi bi ye kaplẹ
la bi wa bi kpua nya ma."

I tọtonga a nyapoi ji lewe la i nde. Kẹ nyapoi i ya i
li i wa nunga wa wa gọbu.

Na wọ i wieni Kasilo mẹhẹ hindẹi ye nasia wọ i yẹ
ngatiyẹi nga kpuamẹi mia yila. Ii lumani wọ ta tangẹi yi.
Nyapoi ngi ndẹi yii na ngi longọ yẹ la i ngi kẹ na lewengọ
nyapoi bẹ ta ngi lenga le lọ ti mẹni.

---

1. Recorded by young man from Pujehun in Freetown on February 16, 1960.

TALE 10: SPIDER, HIS WIFE, AND ROYAL ANTELOPE[1]

At one time Spider and his wife made a big farm. They had this farm. When the rainy season came, the famine was worse than it had ever been. When the famine came, the food problem worried Spider; he decided to hide. When Spider was alone in the bush, he cooked food and ate it there, so that his children would not bother him; he remained in the bush for three weeks.

Spider's wife's situation was very serious; she remained waiting until Royal Antelope came.

As soon as Royal Antelope came, he greeted her. He said, "Lusia, good afternoon. Where is your husband?"

She said, "The famine became too great for my husband. Some time ago he went searching for food." She said, "It is now three weeks since we had any food to eat; now the children need it."

Royal Antelope said, "It would be a good idea to set a big fire, put a big pot on it, fill it completely with water." He said, "When the pot boils, smoke will come out. If you agree to do this, your husband will see the smoke, he will come, he will think that you are cooking food. While you are doing this, you say, "The trap that Spider once set has just caught a big deer. Since my husband is not here, go to call your uncle in the town to come to carve our animal.'"

/Spider's wife did as Royal Antelope instructed./

Then Spider heard her and he said, "Why I set the trap that has caught an animal! She is sending someone to another person in the town to come to carve the animal or to take the animal out of the trap. Such a thing would happen if I remain away but it will not happen if I do not stay away."

So little by little Spider came; he reached the farm house; at once he looked into the pot and saw only water boiling. He said, "Where is the animal you are carving?"

When Spider discovered his wife's lie, they quarrelled. He said that his wife had lied to him.

You have heard the small story I have told about what Spider did to his wife at one time.

Kasilo mia wọ ta ngi nyahẹi ji kẹ ti kpa wa la. Kpai ji
lọ na ti yeya kẹ hamẹi ji wa ndọlẹi gbọwonga kẹlẹma gbi ma
Ji na ndọlẹi ji gula mẹhẹ hindẹi ji a ngi li hẹlẹ ngi longọ
i lọwu. Ji ta yakpe yẹ ndọgbọi ji hu a mẹhẹ yiliva a mẹ,
kọwọi ngi lenga taa ngi vawọi. I longa ndọgbọi ji hu lọ. Wati
sawa mis i kpọyọnga ndọgbọi ji hu.

Nyapoi ji hindẹi gbọwonga ta bẹ i longa hei lọ kẹ Hagbe
gbuanga.

Kia Hagbe gbuanga wọ kẹ i bẹ i vanga ngi ma yẹ "Lusia bia
na." Yẹ "A bi hini?"

Yẹ "Nya hini ndọlẹi gbọwoa gẹ i ya yẹ mẹhẹ gọima." Yẹ
"Wuki sawa lọ na." Yẹ "Mẹhẹ gbii mu yeya mẹ va" yẹ "kia hu
na ndengẹisia ti gbe lẹ."

Yẹ "Na nyandengọ," yẹ "ngọmbu wa yatẹ, bi fẹ wa lẹnga,"
yẹ "bi njẹi wu hu fendangọ kpa." Yẹ "Fẹi na ya nẹma, ndulii
na a gbua, i yẹ bẹ lumanga a tọlọ, a wa lọ, a nde lọ yẹ 'mẹhẹ
mia bi ngilima.'" Yẹ "Bi ya na wiema ba ya gbọma a nde bẹ
"Mani ji wọ Kasilo ngatẹnga, kia hu na kpẹlẹ manii ji a gọnga
a ndọpa wa nya hini ji-o ii mbei, li bi nde bi kenya ma tẹi
hu i wa mu huẹi ji hawa.'"

Kasilo na lọ mẹnini, kẹ i ndenga yẹ "Gbẹ eva nya nga mani
yatẹ, ye hua a gọ ta nu lo a nu weka gama tẹi hu kẹ i wa i ye
hua hawa ọ i ye huẹi ji gbua mani ya. Ang na bonda wienga kẹ
ba gbuama mia. Ngẹ lo poma na a wie."

Kẹ ta wama kulo kulo. I longa wama kulo kulo kẹ i fonga
kpuẹ ji la. A yẹ ma i fẹi ji hu gbenga, njẹi leke nẹma. Kẹ
i ndenga yẹ "A huẹi ji ha bi hawama?"

Kẹ na wotenga a ndẹ, kẹ ta ngi nyahẹi ji ti yianga. Yẹ
ngi nyahẹi ndẹ gula ngi wẹ.

Bi va woi na humẹni wọ ngi hugẹ. Na mia wọ Kasilo pieni
a ngi nyahẹi.

---

1. Recorded by man from Bo in Freetown on January 7, 1960.
Royal Antelope also is a major protagonist in Tales 38, 41-45,
54, and 57-59.

TALE 11: SPIDER AND THE STICK WOMAN[1]

A long time ago there was Spider and his wife. Spider
said that they should work and they made a farm. They put

all the little money that they had, all their property, into
the farm. The rice was drying during the rainy season; at 2
that time people wanted rice very much; people were hungry.
Spider did not want to give his rice to anyone.

Spider said to his wife, "I am going to be very sick.
When I become sick, I will die. When I die, do not bury me
in any other place except the rubbish heap near my farm house."

That very day Spider pretended to get sick. In the
afternoon he died. As soon as Spider died, his wife fulfilled
his instructions. She and her children went and dug a hole in
the rubbish heap; they laid Spider in it; they pushed rubbish
over him; they buried him.

Every evening Spider's wife would go to the farm house,
just as if one were taking food to a worker who had not eaten.
She would go, put a lot of raw rice in a mortar, and leave.
In the middle of the night, Spider would get up from his
grave, he would cook the rice, and eat it all. He ate all the
salt in the farm house. He did not leave anything. In the
morning the woman would come, she would not find anything in
the farm house. Every night Spider did this.

One day Spider's wife went to the town. She explained,
"My husband died in my farm house. When I come to the farm
house, I put raw rice in the mortar, I leave it there. When
I return, I do not find the rice in the mortar; I do not find
my salt or my oil in the farm house. I do not know who is
doing this to me."

One man was there who knew Spider. He said, "Where is
your husband?"

"Oh," she said, "my husband died."

"Ah, do not be concerned, he is the person who is doing
this. It is Spider." Then the man said, "I will help you to
catch the person that is eating your foods." He said, "I
know for certain that it is your husband. Your husband is
not dead; he is the one."

Then Spider's wife and the man went. He made a stick into
a person--not a real person--but just like a recently matured
woman whose breasts have just developed; he rubbed a lot of
wax on the stick; he stood it in the farm house. That night
they put a lot of raw rice in the mortar.

As soon as evening came, Spider felt very hungry; he got
up. He began to cook the rice; he was stooping and standing.
At first he did not see the stick; he cooked the rice. While
he was setting the rice on the coals and preparing to take out
the rice, he turned and saw the stick standing there. He
thought it was a person.

"Oh, friend," said Spider, "have you been here before now? Why didn't you greet me?" The woman remained silent. Come, greet me now. Come take out this rice; we will eat." The woman remained silent; Spider became annoyed; the woman did not respond. Then Spider said, "Let me touch you."

As soon as Spider touched the top of the stick, his hand stuck to it. He said, "Let go of my hand! If you do not let go of my hand, I will hit you with my head." Then he hit her with his head, and his head also got stuck. He said, "Let go of my head! If you do not let go of my head, I will strike you with my foot." As soon as he hit her with his foot, his foot also got stuck; he could not move away at all. He said, "Friend, I beg you to let go of me; let go of me; you take out the rice, we will eat." She did not let go of him; he remained standing there until morning.

Spider's wife called everyone. They came; they found her husband standing stuck to the stick because of greediness.

At one time Spider completely disgraced himself over his own rice. Because of his desire for food, he died. Afterward, he stole; he ate like a thief until they removed him from that stick; they took him into the town. That is why excessive greediness is bad.

Kasilo ta ngi nyahẹi. Kpema lenga lengọ woma wọ Kasilo ji ta ngi nyahẹi. I lilọ i nde ti ma yẹ ti yenge kẹ ta ta ti kpa ji la. Navo wọlẹi ji gbi ti yeya ti mahakẹi ji gbi ti ngua lọ kpalẹ yenge na hu kẹ mbẹi ji i bẹli, kine a hamẹi ji lọ kpemẹi na mbẹi ma maningọ wa. Nunga gbi ti longọ wa bẹ tao ndolẹi ti ma; ye wati ji mia ti mbẹi ji i bẹli. Kasilo ji ii loni i nu gbi gọ mbẹi ji hu.

Kẹ i ndenga ngi nyahẹi ji ma yẹ "Nya wama higbe wa tawao ngi higbe ngaa nga halọ kẹ hei ngi piema baa nya gbọwo hinda yeka gbi kẹ kawẹi hu nga gbuẹi gblanga."

Ye foli na hu ii leni kẹ Kasilo higbenga-bẹ a kaso. Kpọkọvolẹi kẹ i ha. Kia leke i hani ngi nyahẹi bẹ ingẹ i ngowili longa kẹ i pienga lọ taa ngi lenga ti li ti kawẹi na hubọ, ti kawẹi na hubọ kẹ ti Kasilo la na ti kei na lukpe ngi mahu ti ngi gbọwo.

Kẹ kpọkọ gbi nyapoi ji i ya lima. Kia wọ wa numu wa yenge i ya ye mẹhẹi ji mẹni i ya lima a mbagbalei ji wu lo kondẹi ji hu kpoto i ndo na i li. Ji le kpindi foma ndia kẹ Kasilo hiyenga kambẹi na hu. I li i mbẹi na yili i gbi mẹ; kpoloi na a ye kpuẹi na la a mẹ ẹẹ hani gbi lo na. Ngele wonga nyapoi ji wa ẹẹ hani gbi male gbuẹi ji la kpẹlẹma gbi lo Kasilo i ye ji lọ wie kpema gbi va a ji wie.

Ke folo yila ke nyapoi ji ya i li i huge tẹi ji hu yẹ
"Nya yẹ kpuala nya hini ha kẹ ngi ya wama nga mba gbale wulọ
kondẹi hu ngi ndo na kẹ ngi ya ngẹẹ mbẹi ji male hu tawao nva
gbolo-o ngulo-o kpẹlẹ ngẹẹ male gbuẹi ji la. Ngii kọ yọ wuli
ji wiema a nge."

Kena yila i ye na i Kasilo gọngọ kẹ i ndenga yẹ "Ọ bi
hini?"

"Kuo" yẹ "nya hini ha."

"Ọ ya ye baa bi mọnẹ numu yeka ya na a ye ji wiema.
Kasilo mia." Kẹ i ndenga yẹ "Nga gbọ bi ma numui na i mẹhẹi
nasia mẹma bi yeya mu ngi hou" yẹ "ngi kọlọ nya ngeke bi hini
mia" yẹ "bi hini na ya haa" yẹ "ta mia."

Kẹ ti ya i ngului ji ma i kpatẹ panda a numui i kpatẹ ẹẹ
numui ji panda. Kia leke nyahẹi ji a hiye a nina a gbela le
kine ngi nyini nasia heingo; i pie giwi ji i siama tẹleng. I
li i towu kpuẹi na la. Ye kpindi na ti mbagbale wuli lọ
kondẹi hu gboto.

Kia le kpọkọ wieni Kasilo mẹhẹ hinda wai ji ngi ma i
hiyenga. I tọtonga a mbẹi ji yila a wẹlẹ lẹ bau a hiye ii
humbui a ngului ji lọ o i mbẹi ji wyili wọ. Kia leke i mbẹi
ji heini tẹkẹi hu na ngi magbatẹngọ mbẹi ji gbua va hu kẹ i
wotenga kẹ i ngului ji lọnga loni kua a tọyẹi numui mia.

"Kuo, Nyande, gbẹ bi mbeindo lọ haa bi nya lọnga ha leke
pẹing gbẹ ha bẹ va nya ma." I loni ẹẹ lalima. "Wa bi va nya
ma na-o, wa na bi mbẹi ji gbua hu mu mẹ." I loni ti ndili ẹẹ
lalima kẹ i ya gbẹlẹ vuli. "Ngi wa ngi janga a bie."

Kia leke i li i ngi lokoi i ja le a ngului na venine hu
kẹ ngi lokoi gbama, yẹ "Gbẹ nya lokoli ma-o bi gbẹlọ nya lokoli
ma ngi bi le ma a wu." Kẹ i ngi lewenga a wu kẹ ngi wui bẹ
kẹ i gbaa na yẹ "Gbẹ nya wuli ma bi gbẹi lọ nya wuima hẹ ngi
bi lewema gbọng a gọu." Kia leke wọ i ngi leweni a gọwọ kẹ
ngi gọwọ i bẹ kpe ẹẹ gbama ẹẹ ya gbua hu ma a ndelona le yẹ
"Nyande, gbẹ nyama bi lemungọ vuli gbẹ nya ma li bi mbẹi gbua
hu mu mẹ." Ẹẹ gbẹma i loni wọ loni na haa ngele i wo.

Numui gbi nyapoi na i ti loli wọ ti wa ti ngi hini na
malelọ i loni ngului na ya mẹhẹ hinda woma.

Kasilo i ta yekpe ngniboniḷọ wọ fo ngi gbọgbọ mbaa ye
ngi wiengọ i mani mẹhẹ hinda ma a haa poma a ya huma a mẹ a
huma wohu wie ti wa wọfọ ti ngi gbua ngului na ya ti li a ngie
tẹi hu. Na va mia mẹhẹ hinda hulingọ ii nyandeni.

1. Recorded by young man from Pujehun in Freetown on May 30,
1960.
2. Rice (mba) is the staple of the Mende diet, without which
many do not feel satisfied at a meal. The importance of rice
to Mende people is suggested by the number of times it is mentioned in these tales.

TALE 12: A JEALOUS HUSBAND[1]

At one time there was a man and his wife. The man was
very jealous. Before he left the house, he would swear his
wife: "I am going out of the house and leaving you in it. Do
not put your foot outside in my absence; I will swear that."[2]
Also whenever the man went anywhere, he would lock the door
and take the key with him.

Now all the young men in the town loved the man's wife
very much, because she was very beautiful.

One day the man was going out; he locked the house; he
took the key. The woman went to the window; she looked outside.

One of the young men in the town saw her. He greeted
her, "Look, friend, come here and see something."

"Oh, my husband will swear me," she said. "When he goes
out, he swears me lest I go outside, lest I jump down in his
absence."

"Oh, is that all?"

She said, "Yes."

The young man said, "I will make it possible for you to
jump outside but your foot will not touch the ground until
you return."

She said, "Then do it."

Then the young man came and climbed to the window. He
said, "Get on my back."

The woman jumped on his back; her foot did not touch the
ground; he carried her on his back. They went out; they
stayed for a long time.

When the young man and the woman returned, they found
that the man had returned first. He had come; he had entered
the door; he had looked in the house, but he had not seen the

woman. He had looked at the bed; he had not found the woman there.

Then the man had gone to the chief to explain the matter to him. When he went to the chief, all the people in the town gathered to hear.

As soon as the man returned to his house, he found the woman lying on the bed. Then he asked her, "Where did you go today? I returned; I looked everywhere in the house; I did not see you. Where did you go today?"

Then the townspeople also helped him; they questioned the woman. Everyone pressed her for an answer.

Finally, the woman said, "He asked me where I went today; I thought he believed in the swear he placed on me. Because of his swear, I disappeared today so that he would know that if I ever die, it will not be due to that swear."

Kenẹi na wọ ta ngi nyahẹi. Kenẹi yila mia wọ. I ye na? Kenei ji tolongọ wa. Kenẹi ji pẹing i ya gbua ngi ye pẹlẹ bu a ngi nyahẹi ji jondu lọ kpo yẹ: "Pẹlẹi ji bu ngi gbuama na ngi bi loma na. Bii bi gọ hitẹ ngitiiya nya woma nga na jondu lọ." I yama i ya wọ gbuama i yẹ lima hinda gbi a pẹlẹ gbọwu lọ i yama i li a ye jiwi.

Folo yila kẹ i ya gbuama kẹ i pẹlẹi ji gbọwunga i li a ye jiwi.

Tawao foninge lakpaloisia gbi le ti tẹi ji hu ti longọ wa le a nyapoi ji jifa ngi nyahẹi ji nyandengọ wa.

Nyapoi ji wilinga le windẹi ji la a ngitiiya gbe.

Kẹ kena yila kenẹi jisia ti tẹi hu ye ngila kẹ i ngi lọnga kẹ i famẹi wie ngi ma yẹ "Gbe, nyande bi wẹ mbeindo" yẹ "wa le."

"Kuo! nya hini a nya jondulọ kpo" yẹ "ji a gbua ngi hitẹnga ngitiiya, ngi nya gọ gbuja ngitiiya ngi woma i sondua."

"Kuo! Ye na le le?"

Yẹ "M."

Yẹ "Nga pielọ bi gbuja ngitiiya kẹ na hi bi go ẹẹ gbuja ndoma i lohu bẹ bi yama."

Yẹ "Kẹ pie le."

Kẹ ta bẹ i wa i lẹ wundẹi la i lo kẹ i ndenga yẹ "Wẹlẹ nya woma."

Kẹ i wilinga ngi woma; nyapoi na gọ ii gbuja ndoma kẹ i ngi woponga. Ti gbua ti li ti lẹmbi hu ka."

Ta hi wati na na ti wani ti wie na ti maleni kenẹi ji i wanga i wa na i pẹlẹi ji la wua i wa i pẹlẹi ji bu gbe ii nyapoi ji maleni na, i kpukọi ji ma kpẹlẹ gbe ii nyapoi ji maleni na.

Kuo kẹ i ya mahẹi gama i hindẹi ji hugẹ a ngie. Ji na i li mahẹi yo, nungẹi nasia ti tẹi hu yo ti gbi lo na ti we ti wẹ na.

Kia le i pẹlẹi ji la wie i nyapoi maleni na pẹlẹi bu lo i lani kpukọi ma. Kẹ i ngi mọlinga "Bi ye ha ya? Ngi wa ngi pẹlẹi ji bu kpẹlẹ gbenga ngii bi lọni. Bi ye ha ya?"

Kẹ nunga bẹ ti gbọnga ngi ma na ti nyapoi mọli. Ti gbi ti nọna ngi ma.

Kẹ nyapoi ndenga yẹ "A nya mọli yẹ ngi ye ha ya nga tọ ngi langọi a sondui na a ngua sondui na fa a ngua na va ha ngi longa hu i kọye kẹ nya hala gbi kẹ sondui na ii le."

---

1. Recorded by young man from Pujehun on May 30, 1960 in Freetown.
2. See Ndanema (1964):21-25.

TALE 13: THE WATCHMAN'S BRIDE[1]

Oh the events of the world! How it happened that at one time a very beautiful girl and a watchman married.

At one time a law was made in the country that no one could fish in a certain river.[2] If anyone fished in that river, he would be killed. Then a girl, who did not know about the law, went to fish in the river.

When the watchman went to the river, he found her there. He said to her, "What are you doing here? Are you taking fish out of this river?"

She said, "No."

"Where did you get those fish?"

She said, "That river yonder is where I fished."

He said, "You are lying. You did not catch the fish there. Or shall I get a diviner who will tell the truth?" He said, "So you fished in this river. Will you marry me?

Then the girl was afraid. She knew after he had explained the law to her that if a person fished in the river, he would be killed. She said, "Yes, I will marry you."

Then the watchman and the girl went to her family. He said, "I have seen this girl; she is beautiful; I love her."

Then her relatives asked the girl.

She said, "I love him."

She said that so that she would not be killed.

That was how it happened that a watchman and a very beautiful girl married at one time.

Ah ya ndunyama hinda! Hinda mia wọ wieni ndopo nyande nyandi wa ta watchman ti heini wọ.

Ti sawa wie lọ wọ ndọlẹi hu tẹ njẹi na numu gbi ẹẹ kpẹ numu gbi bi njẹi na gbẹnga ta bi walọ. Kẹ ndopoi ji i hijenga ii hugọ kẹ i yanyẹ gbẹmẹi njei ji hu.

Kia watchman lini na kẹ i malenga na yẹ "A gbọ bi wa piema mbei? Bi nyẹi gbia njẹi ji hu lọ?"

Yẹ "Aaa."

"Bi nyẹi gbẹi mi lọ?"

Yẹ "Njẹi na miando pomẹi na na mia ngi nyẹi gbẹi na."

Yẹ "Bi lengọ bia" yẹ "bii nyẹi gbẹni na" yẹ "ọ nga wa hu kpekpe i nde a tọnya" yẹ "kẹ bi nyẹi gbẹni njei ji hu lọ. Ma bie mu hei?"

Ndopoi bẹ kẹ i luwa tao i kọlọ na i hugọnga na kẹ njẹi ji hu numu bi nyẹ gbẹnga na ta bi wa lọ. Ta bẹ yẹ "Aa."

Kẹ ti ya ngi bonda gama. Yẹ "Ndopoi ji mia ngi tọnga nyandengọ ngẹ nya longọ la."

Kẹ mbondẹisia ti punga ndopoi gulọ ndopoi bẹ.

Yẹ "Ngi longọi la."

Ta yẹpẹi hugẹ wẹi kẹ tii ngi wanga i lumani lọwọ.

Na wọ wieni watchman ta ndopo nyande nyandi ti hei wọ.

---

1. Recorded by man from Bo in Freetown on January 20, 1960.
2. Undoubtedly a reference to Poro prohibition on fishing
(see Chapter 1); a similar prohibition is mentioned in Tale 16.

TALE 14:   THE COCK'S ADVICE[1]

At one time there was a very rich man. He was so
wealthy that the word of his wealth reached all the world.
When the man had acquired his wealth, he decided to raise domestic animals. When he raised any animal, he raised two: a cock
and his mate, a horse and a mare, a pig and his mate, a dog
and his mate, a cat and his mate.[2] He owned at one time all
the animals of which a person can think.

His town was the biggest in the world. When he had acquired his wealth, he paid bridewealth for many wives; then he
returned to his town and built many houses. His houses filled
one half of his town.[3] Why the man paid bridewealth for so
many women, nobody knew.

Before long the man became very poor. Then word of his
poverty reached all the world. When he became poor, he sold
all his property and his wives left him. He kept only his
first wife.

As soon as the man had sold all his houses, he went and
built a little hut on the edge of the bush. The man and his
wife remained in this hut until the remainder of his money was
spent. When the money was spent, the man hid from his wife
in a big forest. The man remained in the forest until he was
completely covered with dirt. While the man was in the forest, he went far into the bush looking for bush yams every
morning.[4]

Once when the man went searching for bush yams, he saw a
large snake in the middle of a big fire.[5] When he saw the
snake, he cut a big stick; he took the stick and took the
snake out of the fire.

When the snake was saved, she turned to the man. She
said, "Since you have saved me, I am going to tell my father
that whenever you meet, he should ask if he can give you anything. Whatever he offers, say that you do not want it. Tell

him that you want him to give you some medicine. When he puts
the medicine in your ear, you will be able to understand the
speech of animals."

When the snake said this, the man immediately agreed to
her plan. Afterward the man was able to sleep a lot.

As soon as the man went again to look for bush yams, he
saw a big snake lying in a tree. As he ran past it, the snake
said to him, "Do not run away. It was my daughter whom you recently saved." When the snake had thanked the man heartily
for his help, the snake scattered many bags of money near the
man; the snake said that the man should take the money, but
the man said that he did not want it. Then the snake asked
the man, "Since you say that you do not want these bags of
money, by all means tell me what I can give you."

The man said to him, "The only thing that I want is this:
I want you to put medicine in my ear so that I will be able to
understand the speech of animals."

The snake replied that the man should show him his ear;
the man put his ear near the snake; the snake put medicine inside his ear.

When the man had received this medicine, he took his bush
yam. As soon as he arrived /at his camp/, the man quickly
went for water to cook his bush yam. As soon as he brought
the water (he had filled his pot completely), he prepared the
fire, and set the pot on the fire.

When the man bent over to blow the fire, a little bird
in the tree said "Isn't this man stupid! The kind of money
that he set the fire on! Why don't you take the pot off the
fire, dig a hole, take out the money, and take the money into
your own town!"

When the man heard this, he put out the fire; he took
away the firewood; he started to dig a hole. After he had
dug twice with his matchet, he hit the money with his third
blow. The man spent the entire day taking the money out of
the ground; it was night before he finished. As soon as the
man finished taking the money out of the ground, he began to
carry it into the town. He was carrying the money into the
town throughout the night until morning. When he finished,
he washed himself well; he went to buy new clothes and put
them on. As soon as the man finished preparing himself then
he took a lot of money in order to redeem his houses; he redeemed them all. Then he began to carry the money sacks into
one house; they filled the house completely.

When he finally completed his duties, he decided to walk
in the town. He passed along the edge of the bush and he saw

his wife sitting in the hut where they had lived. He ran to her; he caught her around the waist. Then he asked if she had not left the hut.

The woman said to him, "Friend, I have been waiting since you went out."

Then the man said, "Come, we will go into the town. I have redeemed all my houses."

When they went into the town, the man gave all the money to this woman, saying: "You are in charge of all these things."

Then the man was so wealthy that again word of his wealth reached all the world.

Once the man told his wife that they should go for a ride. Then he gave the woman's own horse to her and he sat on his own horse.

They rode until the horse on which the woman was sitting said, "This woman is heavy!"

The horse on which the man was sitting said, "This man is light. I do not even know that a person is sitting on me."

When the horses spoke, the man laughed. When the man laughed, the woman became angry. She told the man to tell her why he was laughing, but he refused for the snake had told him never to tell anyone what an animal said or he would be destroyed and desert his wife forever. The woman kept pressing the man for an answer; the man refused to answer her.

At last the woman said, "If you do not tell me, I am going home."

The man said, "Let's go home."

When they returned, the woman gathered together all of her relatives; she explained what had happened to them. She said, "Force this man to explain. If he does not explain, I will leave him."

Now at this time the man was sitting with his animals. The hens were very happy; they were laughing; some of them were singing.

A cat was sitting near the man, he said, "Hens, don't be so happy! This man may die today; you don't know what you may eat."

And a dog said, "If they were clever, they would not be making merry as they are."

When the dog said that, a cock standing nearby said, "Leave us alone! He is the one who wants to die."

Then the dog asked the cock, "Why did you say such a pompous thing?"

The cock said, "When I quarrel with my wife, I do not plead with her. Even if I knew that I was at fault and even if she gathered all her relatives, I would move sideways and hit her. Ah, if I come now, you will see that she runs away."

When the cock said this, the man got up; he seized the woman; he slapped her cheek once. When he was preparing to slap her again, the other people caught him. When the woman saw the man approaching her, she ran away. After a while she returned and told her relatives that they should plead with the man.

Because of the cock, the man did not die.

That is why even to this day, when cocks go to strike their wives, they move toward them sideways.

Kena gbatẹngọ wa yila i ye lọ wọ na. Kenẹi ji i gbatẹi lọ haa ngi gbatẹi ma lọwọ i ndọlọi gbi volo. Kpatẹi ji wiengọi ji hu kẹ ye kenẹi ji i gilinga a tohaninga lola. Kẹ kia wọ a tohani ji lola ta lọ wọ: ti gbi ti yẹ fele fele ma. I yaa wọ a tẹ hinẹi, ta ye hẹi le, so hinẹi ta sohẹi, ndonda hinẹi ta ye hei, ngila hinẹi ta ye hẹi, gọnẹ hinẹi kẹ ye hẹi. Tohani gbi le numu a gilila i ye wọ ngi yeya.

Tẹi na hu i yeni na wọi ye leni ta gbi ma le i ndunyẹi ji hu. Kpatẹi ji wiengọ-o, kẹ i nyaha gbotoa gọinga kẹ i yama i pẹlẹ gbotoa lo. Pẹlẹi nasia le i ye toni i ye lei ta loko yila ma. Gbọ wọ i wieni nyahangẹi jisia gọi gọi ji hu, numu gbi ii hugọni.

Hinda hu gutungọ kẹ ndakpaoi ji i nyaninga waa. Nyani ji bẹ-o kẹ ngi ma lọwọi i gbọma ndọlọi gbi volonga. Ngi nyaningọ kẹ i hakẹi gbẹlẹ majiaa. Nyahangẹi jisia bẹ-o, kẹ ti gbi tẹi hu vayaa ngi ma. Ngi nyahẹi ye haala ye yakpe mia wọ i loni ngi yeya.

Kia le wọ kenẹi ji i kpọyọni a pẹlẹi jisia majiala kẹ i ya i bafa wulo yila lo ndọgboi la. Bafẹi ji bu mia ta ngi nyahẹi ji ti loi na haa kẹ navo wuloi na i ye ngi yeya gbi i gbọyọa. Navo ji gbọyọngọi ji hu kẹ i lọwunga ngi nyahẹi ji ma i li ngola wa yila hu. Ngolẹi ji hu mia wọ i loni na haa

kẹ ngi ma gbi i gbitia. Ji i ye ngolẹi ji hu, ngele i wonga
wọ i yẹ a li ndọgbọi hu lọ polong ngawu gọkọimẹi.

Wati yila kia kenẹi ji i li ngawu gbuamẹi ji kẹ i kali
wa yila lọnga ngọmbui waa lia. Kali ji lọngọ kẹ i ngulu wa
lewenga. Ngului ji mia wọ i ngeweni kẹ i kali na gbua ngọmbui
na hu.

Kali ji bawongọi ji hu, kẹ i wotenga kenẹi gama i nde
ngi ma yẹ "Kia bi nya bawoa, ngi ya nya kẹkẹ gama, nga hugẹlọ
a ngie. Taa, ngi hugẹnga a ngie kpemẹi na lee gbi wa ta wa
lọ, i bi mọlia ọ i hani gbi venga bi wẹ bi nde ngi ma bẹ bii
loni la. Gbọ ba nde ngi ma bẹ bi longọ la taa a ji: bi nde
ngi ma bẹ bi longọ a halei lo i pu bi woli hu na a pie ba
fuhanisia wo mẹni.

Ji lengọ kẹ kenẹi ji bẹ i luma ngama. Na wọ ma, i guilọ
a nji gboto.

Kia lee wọ gbọma ndakpoi ji i lini ngawu gbuamẹi, kẹ i
kali waa lọa i la ngului hu. Kia ye i lewe a pimẹ kẹ kali
i ndea ngi ma yẹ "Baa wime. Nya nyaloi mia gẹ bi ngi baoni."
Kẹ kali ji i sie gbua pandaa ngi ma. Kia i gbọyọni kẹ i navo
hakẹi ji vaya ngi gbla kpẹlẹ; kẹ i ndenga ngi ma yẹ i ngewe,
ngi wo mia. Kẹ ndakpaoi ji bẹ i ndenga ngi ma yẹ ii loni la.
I kpatẹma hakanga gbi ve ngi wẹ yẹ ii loni la. Kẹ kali ji bẹ
i ngi mọlia yẹ "Ji naa bẹ bii loni a hakẹi jisia gbi, kẹ hugẹ
naa họ a nge gbọ nga fe bi wẹ."

Ji lengọ kẹ kenẹi ji i ndenga ngi ma yẹ "Na lee nya longọ
la ta lọa ji: nya longọ bi halei hitẹ nya woli hu nahi a pie
ka fuhaninga womẹni."

Ji lengọ kẹ kali ji i ndea ngi ma yẹ i ngi woli hugẹ a
ngie. Kẹ kenẹi ji bẹ i ngi woli lukpenga ngi gbla. Kẹ kali
ji i halei hitia hu.

Halei ji majọngọi ji-o kẹ ndakpaoi ji i ngi yawui ji
wumbua. Kia le wọ i foni kẹ i ya fulo njẹi hu kọ i wa i ngi
yawui yii. Kia le wọ i wani a njẹi ji kẹ i ngi vẹi na i ye
ngi yeya hu waa fọ, i ngọmbui hugbatẹ kẹ i fẹi heinga.

Kia i mawẹni ngọmbui ji yavo va, kẹ ngọni wulo yila i
longa ngului hu i nde yẹ "Ẹẹ kenẹi ji bẹ i gbowani kpa! Navo
bondẹi na i ngọmbu yatẹimẹi na, bei fẹi na gbuanga, bi ndomẹi
bo, bi kpua, bi li la bi ye ta hu bi wẹ."

Ji humeningọ kẹ kenẹi ji bẹ i ngọmbui ji lufia. I kọtui
gbi lufe kẹ i tatonga a ndomẹi na bola. Kia le wọ i mbogbẹi
hitẹni fele ye sawẹi na kẹ i kani malea. I luvani wọ kpẹing
kanii na gbuama, kpindi mia wọ i kpọyọni. Kia le i kpọyọni
kẹ i tatonga a mabelẹ la tẹi hu. I yii wo mabelẹma pi ngele

i wo ngi ma. Ngi kpǫyǫngǫ kę i ya i mua panda. Kę i ya i
kulanga yeya i pu. Kia le wǫ i kpǫyǫni a ngi ma kpatęla kę
i navo saha wumbua, livaala kǫ i ngi węisia wumawo. Kia i
lini kę i kpęlę wumawonga. Kpǫyǫngǫ a ji wie la-o, kę i
tatonga a navo hakęi jisia belęla ye pęlęi yila bu. Ti navoi
na belę i pęlęi ye ngila lave kpang.

Kia foloi hu ye gbama, kę i ndenga yę "Gbę ngi jęsia gulo
tęi hu." I loi wǫ lema ndǫgbǫi la lǫ kę i ngi nyahęi lǫnga
mia i hei foloi ye bafęi na bu wǫ ti yęna. Kę i ya ngi gama a
pimę. I hou ngi lia. Kę i ngi mǫlia yę ina i yaa wǫ a gbuani
le bafęi na bu.

Kę nyapoi bę i ndea ngi ma yę "Nyande, ba gbia wǫ
mawulomae."

Ke kenęi ji bę i ndea ngi ma yę "Wa mu li tęi hu. Ngi
nya węlęisia gbi wumawonga."

Kia ti lini kę i navoi ji gbi majǫnga nyapoi ji ma. Ke
i ndenga ngi ma yę "Bia bi hakęi ji gbi mahu."

Kenęi na gbǫma gbatęi iǫ haa ngi ma lǫwǫ i gbǫma ndǫlęi
na gbi volo.

Wati yila ma kę i ndenga ngi nyahęi ma yę ti li jęsiamęi.
Kę i nyapoi nda joi venga ngi wę kę i heia ngi nda joi ji ma.

Kia wǫ ti kani haa kę soi ye na nyapoi ji i ye heima
ndenga yę "Nyapoi ji ta ngi miningǫ."

Kę soi ye na i ye loni kulǫ i ndea yę "Kenęi ji ta i yaa
powo. Ngę kǫ bę kę numu lǫ hei nya ma."

Ji lengo kę ndakpoi ji i yęlęnga. Ngęę ji wiengǫ-o kę
nyapoi ji i lilenga. Kę i ndenga kenęi ji ma yę i hugę a
ngie gbǫ i ye ngęlę wiema. Kę kenęi ji ii lumani a hugę, kę
nyapoi ndenga yę ti yama. Kenęi ji bę i lumaa. Kę kali ji
i ndeilǫ wǫ ngi ma yę vuhani gbi i yępęnga baa hugę a numu
gbi. Bi hugęa ba nyanilǫ. Taa gbǫma, kunafǫ a gbęlę ngi
nyahęi ji ma. Nyapoi ji gbodeilǫ ngi ma haa kenęi ji ii
lumani a njępęi ji hugęla a ngie.

Nyapoi ji bę kę i ndenga yę "Bii hugęilǫ nga yama."

Kenęi ji bę yę "Mu yama."

Ke ti yama. Ti yamangǫi ji hu, kę nyapoi ji i ngi bonda
gbi liama i njępęi ji hugę a tie, yę "Vaa kenęi ji ii hugęilǫ,
a gbelelǫ ngi ma."

Na ye kpemęi ji kenęi ji lǫ heini a ngi vuhanisia. Tęngęi
jisia ti gohunęngǫ yela waa. Ta ngę wie; ti tęnga ta ngolei ya.

Ngọnẹi ji i ye heini kenẹi ji gbla i ndenga yẹ "Tẹngẹi jisia wa gohunẹ wu! Kenẹi ji i hama ha: wa kọlọ gbọ wa ya a mẹ."

Kẹ ngilẹi ji bẹ i ndenga yẹ "Nẹmahu lewe a ye tima tẹẹ na gbele wie ti piema."

Ji lengọ kẹ tẹ hinẹi ji ngi mọlia yẹ "Gbẹva lọ bi jẹmbẹi ji bonda lema?"

Kẹ tẹi ji ndenga yẹ "Nya mua nya nyaha mue yie ngẹẹ ngi ma nẹnẹ. Ngi kọ bẹ kẹ nya mia nya lẹẹngọ ngi ma, ina naa i ngi bonda gbi liama, gbọ le nga pie nga li lọ a ngaka ma wie ngi ngi hiya gbi. A yẹ ngi yama na, ba tọlọ a lewe a pimẹ."

Ji lengọ-o, kẹ kenẹi ji i hiyea i gbundẹ nyapoi ji ma. I ngi ba hu gbolẹ yila; kia i ye gbọma yamamana, kẹ nungẹi nasia ti ye na ti ngi hounga. Kẹ nyapoi ji tọni kenẹi ji a wa ngi mahu kẹ i lenga a pimẹ. Kia i lini hu lẹmbi haa kẹ i yama i nde ngi bonda ma yẹ ti kenẹi ma nẹnẹ.

Tẹi na mia wọ i pieni kenẹi na ii haani.

Famia, tẹnga foloi ji bẹ ti ya ti nyahanga lema ti li ti gama a yakama wielọ.

---

1. Recorded by young man from Bunumbu in Freetown on April 10, 1960. A Mende text and English summary of a version of this tale occurs in Stott's manuscript.
2. Dogs also figure in Tales 17, 58, 70, 74, 78, and 86; cows (nika) in Tales 19, 23, 39, 50, 52, and cats (gọnẹ) in Tales 14, 46, 53, 75, 87, and 91.
3. Marriage payments are gathered by grooms from senior relatives given to the brides' parents and maternal uncles. They may include paying brides' Sande initiation expenses. If a wife leaves her husband without justification, her marriage payment must be returned by her family (Little /Household 1948/; Little /1967 ed./:153-162; Hollins /Marriage 1928/:29; Crosby:250). Bridewealth is also a concern in Tale 39.
4. Bushyams (ngawu) are a rainy season food; see Tales 42, 44, and 69. In Tale 25, a spirit assumes the form of a bush-yam before taking the form of a human being.
5. Snakes (kali) often are the form that spirits of the dead may assume, as in Tale 31.

Co-Wives

TALE 15: A WITCH AND HER CO-WIFE[1]

At one time there was a man in a town who had two wives.
At first these women were very friendly. Later one of them
began to hate her companion; she had a witch in her stomach.[2]
They had both entered the Sande society the same year.[3]

Then the man laid a farm for them both. When the farm
had been made and just as the rice started to grow, the witch
woman bewitched the rice. The rice did not grow even a
little; the rice did not grow at all.

Then the man said, "Let me divide the farm in half.
I will farm part for one woman and I will farm part for the
other." So the man divided the farm in half.

Just when one wife's rice started to grow well, at night
the woman who was a witch went into her companion's farm. She
went into the farm, she came out of her skin; she turned into
an animal; she ate a great deal of the rice. Then she took
her human skin, she got into it, and she returned to the town.
The next morning the woman who owned the farm went to the
farm and found that her rice had been eaten.

When they put a fence around the farm as a trap, they
failed to catch anything. Then the woman who owned the farm
went to a diviner in order to find out how it happened that
some animals were destroying her rice that had been growing
well.[4]

Then the Muslim said to her, "Someone is going into this
farm to eat the rice. But before you can know who it is, beat
a lot of pepper; beat the pepper, wash it; beat it, wash it."
He said, "Go and put this pepper water at the entrance to the
farm; put it just where one enters the rice field."

Then the woman did exactly as the diviner had instructed
her to do.

When night came, the other woman told all her witch companions that they should go to the rice farm and they went
there. Just where the woman put her skin was where the woman
had put the pepper pan--just as if the great God had arranged
it. As soon as the woman said, "Let it come off; let it come
off; let it come off," her skin came off, and she put it in
the pepper water. She went and ate a great deal of rice.
Then the woman and all her companions decided to get back into
their human skins. When the woman came and put her skin on,
the pepper burned her naked flesh. Then she said, "Let it

come off; let it come off; let it come off." She went and
dove in the river; she returned and said, "Let me put the skin
on my flesh." As soon as she put on her skin, she said, "Let
it come off; let it come off; let it come off." She kept putting on her skin and taking it off until morning came. All
her companions had left her and returned to the town.

That morning the woman who owned the rice farm was lying
down. When the sun rose, the woman realized that her co-wife
was unfriendly toward her. When she went to the farm house,
she found her co-wife standing there in her nakedness, and
she knew that her co-wife was the person who had bewitched
her rice.

Too much jealousy, therefore, is bad.

They killed that woman at that time.

The story is ended.

Kenẹi ji gbe wọ i yẹ tẹi ji hu hoe. Nyahangẹi jisia ti
yẹ ngi yeya fele. Nyahangẹi jisia ti yẹni ti longọma vuli yo
halei kẹ gbọma ye nalọ na ngi li hu nọhọngọ ngi mba ji va.
Tawao huani yẹilọ wa ngi go hu. Kẹ kenẹi ji a kpalẹi la wọ
ti venjọ lọ wọ wẹ. Ti venjọ kpẹlẹ ti wani hale hu a fo yilakpe
lọ.

Kẹ ji wọ ta kpalẹi ji la ji kini mbẹi ji a tato a
gbekpela kẹ huana nyahẹi ji i ya hu ta mia a mbẹi ji a huana.
Mbẹi ji ẹẹ gbekpe kulo bẹ va haani.

Kẹ kenẹi ji ndea yẹ "Gbẹ lẹ ngi kpalẹi ji luahu gọlẹ" yẹ
"nga ya nda numui ji wẹ nga nda ji wẹ." Kẹ i kpalẹi ji luahu
gọlẹnga.

Kẹ nyapoi ye ji huanamọi ji ji kini ngi mba ji ti kpaa
ji laa ti kpẹlẹ wẹ-o ngi mba ji bẹi ji gbekpeni kini bi wuanga
hu kia ngi wọpọ piema, kpindi wẹlẹnga wọ kẹ i ya i ya a ngi
gọlẹi ji gbua ngi ma kẹ i ya i wote a huẹi ji a mbẹi ji lọ
mẹ kakakakakakaka. Kẹ i wanga kẹ i ngi nu gọlẹi na wumbua kẹ
i wuanga hu kẹ i yama tẹi hu. Nyapoi ji ngele wonga na i ya
a male ngi bẹi ji mẹngọ.

Ti koko gbi gọni na kpa ji ma, tii gbaha. Kẹ nyapoi ji
bẹ kẹ i ya tọtọgbẹmọ kọ i kọ gbọ na vuli wienga huẹi jisia ti
ngi bẹi ji nyanima hi jifa bẹi ji gbekpengọ yẹla kpa hu.

Kẹ mọi-mọi ji bẹ kẹ i ndea ngi ma yẹ "Na nyandengọ" yẹ
"numu mia i lima kpa ji hu a li a mbẹi ji mẹ," yẹ "kẹ a yẹma
bi ngi gọ" yẹ "pujẹi mia ba hiya ba ngua" yẹ "bi li bi ye njẹi
ji lọ kpalẹi la ngi kini ba yẹ wama mbẹi hu" yẹ "bi to na."

Kę ta bę kę i hindęi ji wienga kia leke kenęi ji ndei la
ngi ma.

Kpindi węlęnga wǫ kę nyapoi ji kę i ya na. Kia leke tia
ngi mbangęi jisia gbi a ndelǫ ti ma yę "ti li." Kę ti ya. Kę
ta mia le kini a ngi gǫlęi ji wu na na mia nyapoi ji puję hakęi
ji loi na-kia leke ngewǫ wa a hinda hugbatę. I lini wǫ i ngi
gǫlęi ji gbuanima. Kia leke i ndeni yę "Kǫkǫkpuama kǫkpuama
kǫkǫkpuama," kę ngi gǫlęi ji gbęlę kę i gbuanga ngi ma kę i
punga puję yęi ji hu. I li i mbęi ji mę kakakakakaka. I wa
na ngi mbanga gbi kę ti ndenga na tę ti yama na numu vulu
gǫlǫ hu. Kia i wani yę i ngi gǫlǫi ji wumbu i pę ngi ma ingę
kę pujęi ji vonga ngi luwu ngęyęi ji ya. Kę i ndea yę
"Kǫkǫkpuama kǫkpuama kǫkǫkpuama kǫkpuama." Kę i ngamanga
gbǫma hu ii lęmbi haani i li i lǫmbu njęi hu i wa ingę pujęi
na voma kę "Gbę lę gbǫma ngi kǫlęi gbǫma nya luwuma." Kia
leke i kǫlǫni ngi ma kę i ndenga yę "Kǫkǫkpuama kǫkpuama
kǫkǫkpuama kǫkpuama." I loni wǫ na lǫ wiema haani i lǫhu
ngele i wo ngi mbanga gbi kę ti ya na ti ngi longa.

Nyapoi ji ngele wona na wǫ ngi ma lalǫ i heini haani kę
foloi ji lawǫnga kę ta nyapoi ji a yę "tii ndomahu-o" ta bę i
kǫnga na. Kę nyapoi ji loni a ngie. Kia wǫ na i lini kpuęla
i lini i ngi maleni loni na ngi ma ngęyęi ji kę i kǫnga kę ta
mia wǫ a li a ngi bęi hua na.

Famia tolo kele kele gbuala ii nyandeni.

Nyapoi na ti ngi walǫ wǫ.

Dǫmęi yę kęlęmęi mia.

---

1. Recorded by young woman from Bo in Freetown on July 11,
1960. I published an English translation of this tale in
"Supernatural Beings in Męnde Dǫmęisia," (1961); Innes (1965)
presents a summary version of the tale.
2. Mende beliefs about witches (hǫna) are discussed in Chapter 1.
3. Co-initiates in Sande are expected to have extremely close
relations; the fact that the co-wives in this tale were co-
initiates (ti wani hale hu) emphasizes the immorality of the
bewitching wife. Aspects of Sande initiations are mentioned
in Tales 39, 62, and 87.
4. Diviners (tǫtǫgbęmǫ) are protagonists in Tales 95 and 97
where the association between Islam and divination in Mende
minds is noted again.

TALE 16: A JEALOUS WOMAN AND HER CO-WIFE[1]

At one time there was a chief who married two women. The senior wife gave the junior wife to her husband. The man loved the junior wife more than his senior wife. The senior wife was jealous of the junior wife, because her husband loved his junior wife more than he loved her.

One morning the women went to the river. The senior wife had said that they should go fishing and they had gone to fish in a very deep river. As soon as they arrived at the river, the senior wife said, "Come, bend over; let us throw out this water /to make a dry hole in which to trap fish/."

The girl said, "Mother, my head aches; I cannot throw out water."

"Oh," replied the woman, "you must throw out the water yourself. Since you came into this house, my husband loves you more than me; you have become too proud."

The girl said, "Then, Mother, let us throw out this water."

Then the women threw out the water until they had made a dry place. Then the senior wife said that the junior wife should go into the hole which she did. The senior wife was jealous and wanted to kill the junior wife by letting water into the hole. So the senior wife broke the dam, the water reached the girl who was unable to get out of the hole. The girl tried to climb onto the bank of the river; her head was on the bank so she could not sink, her body remained in the water. The fishes ate the girl; she encountered all sorts of things.

When the senior wife returned to the town, her husband asked, "Where is my wife with whom you went out today?"

"Oh," she said, "I don't know where your very high status wife is." She said, "By the way, she did not go fishing with me. I don't know where she went."

Then the man sent a messenger to the girl's family to ask if their child had visited them that day. Her family replied, "We did not see her."

Then the chief trembled a lot; his heart was greatly troubled. The chief's companions did not see the child whom he had lost. Meanwhile, for almost a week they searched for the girl; they did not find her.

A man who wove baskets went to cut some rope from a palm tree that stood over the river.[2] As soon as he cut the tree "kpǫkpǫ," the girl in the water said:

"Who is hitting the palm tree?
"Who is hitting the palm tree?
"Go tell some men to come after me in the water;
"Ta mba ya njei njei ya kumande.
"They should come after me in the water;
"Ta mba ya njei ya njei ya kumande."

At once the man ran back to the town. He said to the chief, "Chief, something is singing in the river; I am very afraid."

The chief was lying on his face; his heart was troubled about his wife. He said, "My heart is troubled. I do not want anyone in this country to bring foolish talk to me; I can't listen to him."

Then the chief sent his servant to the river; he cut the palm tree; the thing in the water sang the same song; the servant returned to the chief. The servant said, "Father, come, let us go; something is singing a song in the water. If you go there, you will be able to decide wisely about the thing in the water."

Then the chief himself took a knife; he cut the palm tree, and the thing sang:

"Who is hitting the palm tree?
"Who is hitting the palm tree?
"Go tell someone to come after me in the water;
"Ta mba ya njei ya njei ya kumande.
"They should come after me in the water;
"Ta mba ya njei ya njei ya kumande.
"They should come after me in the water;
"Ta mba ya njei ya njei ya kumande."

Then the chief said, "I want to put a Poro prohibition on this river bank that no woman may come here. The prohibition concerns a secret matter: no one may tell that I am taking my wife out of the river."

Then they established this Poro prohibition that no woman could come there. When the prohibition was established, the men threw out the water, they threw it out and took the chief's wife out of the water. Of course, the fishes had eaten her so that only her head remained.

The chief asked her, "How did you happen to come here?"

The girl said, "My big mother came here with me to fish. I entered the hole to look for fish and she broke the water on me. She was going to kill me but God did not agree to my death."

He said, "Is that true?"

She said, "It is. You passed searching for me."

Then they returned to the town. The junior wife's entire family came; her senior wife's relatives all came. When they had come, the junior wife again explained everything.

Then the chief himself was able to kill the woman at that time, because she had wanted to kill her co-wife, the chief's junior wife. In those days whatever chiefs wanted happened. If anyone passed and the chiefs decided to kill him, he was killed without discussion.

That is how long ago the killing of people came into this world.

Maha yila na wọ kẹ i nyahẹi jisia jọnga. Ti fele kẹ nyahẹi jẹmbẹi ji kẹ i nyahẹi gọinga ngi hini ji wẹ. Nyaha woi ji kẹ i longa na a nyaha woi ji i lewe nyaha jẹmbẹi ji ma kẹ nyaha wai ji bẹ kẹ i lolinga a nyaha woi ji jifa ngi hini longa wa a ngie wonga ta i lewenga ngi ma.

Kẹ ngele wonga kẹ ti ya njẹi hu yẹ "Ti li nyẹ gbẹmẹi" kẹ ti ya nyẹ gbẹmẹi njẹi ji yo hu bọngọ wa kpali hu mia. Kia leke ti lini "Kuo" yẹ "wa bi wẹ mu njẹi ji wili."

Ndopoi bẹ yẹ "Ye" yẹ "nya wui lọ gbalẹma" yẹ "ngii guma a nja wili la."

"Kuo" yẹ "ba gulọ vuli bi pili jifa bi wanga wọ pẹlẹi ji bu. Nya hini ji i longa na a bie i lewenga nya ma famia bi yama lengọ."

Ndopoi ji bẹ yẹ "Kẹ ye mu njẹi ji wili."

Kẹ ti njẹi ji wilinga njẹi ji wilingọi ji i bẹlilọ kinẹi yẹ i jọkọ kpukpui hu kẹ i jọkọnga kpukpui hu. Ngi longọ i ngi wa kẹ i njẹi ji wonga ngi ma tolei hu mia na-o ngi lolongọ a ngie ngi longọ i ngi wa. Kẹ i njẹi ji wonga ngi ma kẹ njẹi ji wunga ndopoi ji ma ẹẹ yaa gu a gbia la njẹi bu. I pie lọ na kẹ i lenga ngiyei ma ngi wui ji i lo ngiyei ma i yaa guni a lọmbu ngi gbekpe ta i lo njẹi hu. Nyẹnga ta ngi mẹ gbẹ-o-gbẹ lole a ngi male na.

Kẹ nyapoi ji kẹ i ya tẹi hu kẹ ngi hini ngi mọlinga yẹ "Ọ nya nyahẹi ji ha wa ta wu ya."

"Kuo" yẹ "bi jama nyaha wai na ngii ngi loma gọ" yẹ "ha lẹ pẹing ii lima nyẹ gbẹma mia i ya na ngii na gọ."

Kenẹi ji bẹ kẹ i nu longa ndopoi ji ngi bonda gama yẹ "Ina woi ndopoi i ya ha ngi bonda gama lọ?" Ngi bonda bẹ tẹ "Mu yaa tọni."

Kẹ ndọlọi na gọ gbẹlinga wa ngi li mọnẹngọ wa ta ngi mahẹi mbanga ti loi na longa na hu ngi yeya ii yaa tọni a yẹ kẹ tia lọ lewema i bẹ wuki yilama ta ndopoi ji lọlọ tẹ tọ.

Kena yila a sambẹi ji vẹ kẹ i ya ngeya lewemẹi tambẹi ji i loni ye njẹi na mahu lọ. Kia leke i kẹni "kpọ kpọ," kẹ ndopoi ji longa ji hu kẹ i ndenga

yẹ "Ye mia a tambẹi yẹ kpọkiti kpọ
  "Ye mia a tambẹi yẹ kpọkiti kpọ"

yẹ "Li bi nde hiwa lenga ma ti wa nya woma njẹi hu
  "Ta mba ya njẹi ya njẹi ya kumande
  "Ti wa nya woma njẹi hu
  "Ta mba ya njẹi ya njẹi ya kumande
  "Ti wa nya woma njẹi hu
  "Ta mba ya njẹi ya njẹi ya kumande."

Kẹ kenẹi ji i yamanga yakpe a pimẹ kẹ i ndenga mahẹi ma yẹ "Mahẹi" yẹ "hani lọngolei yama njẹi bu" yẹ "ngi luwanga wa kẹlẹ ma gbii ma."

I maleni mahẹi ji lani ngi ya pẹngọ ngi li mọnẹngọ ngi nyahẹi va. Mahẹi bẹ yẹ "Nya li ji mọnẹngọ; ndọlọi ji hu ngii loni numu gbi i wa a baba yẹpẹ nya gama" yẹ "ngẹẹ gu ngi woloma."

Kẹ i gbenga ngi bọilopoi ma i wani gbọma lọọ kẹ hani ji ngolei ji yanga njẹi ji bu kẹ ngi bọilopo bẹ ya i nde ngi ma yẹ "Kẹkẹ" yẹ "wa mu li" yẹ "hani lọ ngolei yaa ma njẹi bu" yẹ "bi fongalọ na" yẹ "ba kili ya ọ nẹmahu le jọlọ hani na hinda ma."

Kẹ mahẹi ji wanga ta vuli lọ mbọwẹi wumbuni i tambẹi lewe kẹ hani ngole yanga yẹ

"Ye mia a tambẹi yẹ kpọkiti kpọ
"Ye mia a tambẹi yẹ kpọkiti kpọ
"Li bi nde hiwa lenga ma ti wa nya woma njẹi hu
"Ta mba ya njẹi ya njẹi ya kumande
"Ti wa nya woma njẹi hu
"Ta mba ya njẹi ya njẹi ya kumande
"Ti wa nya woma njẹi hu
"Ta mba ya njẹi ya njẹi ya kumande."

Kẹ mahẹi bẹ pienga na yẹ "Nya longọ na ngi hale wa njẹi la hinda kpẹlẹ" yẹ "nyaha gbi ẹẹ yaa fo bei" yẹ "halei i wote a ndọwu ma hinda" yẹ numui gbi ẹẹ hugọ" yẹ "ngi nya nyahẹi ji gbia."

Kę ti halei wuanga nyaha gbi ęę yaa fo na kę halei ji wuangǫi ji kę ti njęi ji yilinga ti pili ti ngi nyahęi na gbia njęi na bu ingę nyęnga ti ngi męngǫ na kę leke ngi wumęi ji longǫ.

Kę i ngi mǫlinga yę "Bi ye pieni na bi wani mbei?"

Yę "Nya nje wai mia" yę "wani a ngie nyę gbęmę" yę "ta mia ngi wuani leke kpukpui ji hu ngi wanga ngi nyęnga jęsianga kę i njęi wonga ngi ma" yę "i nya wamalǫ" yę "ngewǫ ii lumani nya walęi ma."

Yę "Ta mia hi?"

Yę "Ta lǫ, wu lewema a nya gǫkǫli."

Kę ti ya tęi hu na kę nyahęi ji ngi bonda kpęlę ti wanga ngi nje wai ji ngi njeini kpęlę kę ti wanga ti wani na kę i jiangama gbǫma i hugę.

Kenęi bę i gui lǫ na wǫ i nyapoi wa yę "Ngi longǫ i mba ti maha loi wa." Kę wǫ woma mahanga na leke wǫ ta nde ta lǫ a loma. Numu a ye lǫ lewema tę ma palǫ loma jia gbima.

Fale na mia wǫ wani a numu walęi i ndolęi ji hu.

---

1. Recorded by young co-wife in Bo on April 16, 1960. A summary of a version of this tale appears in Innes (1965):59-60.
2. Among the palm trees important to Mende are tamba, the large rattan palm; nduvu, the raffia palm, and tǫkpǫ, the oil palm.

TALE 17: THE PALM OIL WIFE[1]

At one time there was a chief. One day he got up and decided to go hunting. When he entered the forest, he found a big pot in the middle of the forest. Oil was in the pot-- very clear palm oil.[2]

Then the chief said, "Ah, how fine this oil is. I wish that this oil would turn into a wife for me."

Then the oil said, "Sir, I would like to turn into your wife, but first you must answer a question. You have a senior wife in the town who shares your responsibilities. When we marry, will you explain my transformation to her?"

"Oh," said the chief, "I will not do that. Just turn into a wife for me; I will do everything for you."

Then the palm oil said to the chief, "Turn your back."

When the chief turned away, the oil changed into a very beautiful woman. She said, "Sir, let us go now."

When they returned to the town, the chief brought his new wife and presented her to his senior wife. He said, I have brought you a present: a little wife for me." The woman thanked him a lot.

At night when they were lying down, the senior wife said to the chief, "Sir, where did you find this woman?"

He replied, "She was given to me."

She said, "Who gave this woman to you?"

He said, "Oh, now that I have brought her, she will do all the work for you; your only task will be to give her work. But there is one kind of work that you must not give her to do: she must not cook. Be sure that she never cooks."

She said, "All right."

He said, "Be sure that she does not go near the fire."

She said, "All right."

They lived there.

The chief had a dog named Kebele. This dog could do anything: he could speak as people speak.

Now the woman was very jealous of the girl and she nagged the man continuously about her origin.

Finally, the man said, "I said that this girl should not go near the fire, because she is palm oil."

One morning the man got up and went hunting in the forest. Then the woman said to the girl, "Go to wash the clothes."

The girl said, "Senior wife, the sun is hot. Let me wait until the sun has cooled a little then I will go to wash the clothes."

Then the woman turned to her, "Hi," she said, "I do not see you! You are nothing but oil!"

The girl said, "Senior wife, what did you say?"

She said, "Bah, I will not speak to you!"

The girl got up.

When the sun's edge had cooled, the girl went, washed the clothes, and returned.

After that the woman would tell the girl to do things even if the sun were hot. If the girl refused, the woman would turn to her and say, "I do not see you! You are nothing but oil!" Then the girl would remain where she was.

One day the man went hunting again.

The woman said to the girl, "If you do not cook today, we will not eat any food here!" She kept nagging at the girl.

Finally, the girl got up and went into the cooking house. She laid the fire; she prepared the food for cooking; she sat near the fire cooking. Then her foot began to melt; she melted as far as her waist.

Then the woman said to her, "Aren't you melted yet? If you had melted completely, that would be lovely."

The girl sat there until she melted completely and turned into oil.

When the woman saw that the girl had finished melting, she called their dog, Kebele, to lick up the oil.

But Kebele said to her, "Recently when father killed an animal and brought it, did you ask Kebele to eat the animal? Now that father's wife has turned to oil, you tell Kebele that he should lick it up. Kebele will not do that; I, Kebele, will not do that." Kebele kept saying this until the man came.

When the man returned, he first called the girl; he kept calling the girl, but she did not come.

Then Kebele came out and said, "Recently when father brought an animal, you did not ask Kebele to eat the animal. When you cooked sweet food, you did not tell Kebele to eat the food. Now that father's wife has melted and turned into oil, you tell Kebele that he should lick it up. Kebele will not do that."

When the man heard this, he called his senior wife. He said, "Where is the girl?"

"Oh," she said, "I do not know where she went."

He said, "I asked you where is the girl? You and she were in the house. Where is she now?"

She said, "I do not know where she is."

Then the man said, "All right, let me search for her."
He looked about inside the house; he did not see her. He went
outside looking carefully for her; he did not see the girl.
Then he went into the cooking house. When we went there, he
found this big puddle of oil. He asked the woman, "Who is
this oil melted here?"

The woman said, "Is it not your wife who has turned to
oil?"

Then the man shot the woman with his gun.

That is why jealousy is bad.

Lọ yila ma maheị gbe wọ heini hoe. Kẹ i hijea yẹ ta lima
kpandẹwilimẹi ji i yẹ lima kẹ i fonga ngoleị ji hu. Kẹ i
kọvẹ wai ji malenga heini ngoleị ji lia kọvẹi ji ngulọ yẹlọ
hu. Semale loke loke yẹ la.

Kẹ i ndea yẹ "Ah," yẹ "ngulẹi ji nyandeni kpa" yẹ "ngulẹi
ji i wote leke na a nya nyaha."

Kẹ i ndea yẹ "Kẹkẹ" yẹ "nga wotelọ a bi nyaheị yẹ "kẹ kia
hu na" yẹ "bi nyaha wai na teị hu" yẹ "ji le mu heima" yẹ "kẹ
bi hungẹnga a ngie" yẹ "ngi gunngọi bi bu" yẹ "ba hungẹlọ a
ngie?"

"Kuo" yẹ "ngeẹ na wie" yẹ "wote le a nya nyaha" yẹ "na le
gbi" yẹ "nga pielọ bi wẹ."

Kẹ ngulẹi ji ndea ngi ma yẹ "Bi woi ve."

Kẹ i wovenga kẹ ngulẹi ji wotea a nyaha nyande nyande
nyande wa. Kẹ i ndea yẹ "Kẹkẹ," yẹ "mu li na."

Jima ti yamani teị hu kẹ i waa a nyaha nineị ji kẹ i ngi
magọnaa ngi nyaha wai ji gama yẹ "Bi yoyo wo lọ ngi wa la" yẹ
"nya nyaha wo mia." Kẹ nyapoi ji ngi jẹ gbua ka. Jina ti yẹ
lani a kpindi kẹ ngi mọlia yẹ "Kẹkẹ" yẹ "bi ye hijeni a nyaheị
ji?"

Yẹ "Ti fei lọ mbẹ."

Yẹ "Yelọ nyaheị ji veni bi wẹ?"

Yẹ "Kuo," yẹ "jina ngi waa a ngie ta na ngengei bi wiema
bi va" yẹ "bia bi nda mia le a ngenge vela ngi wẹ" yẹ "kẹ
ngenge yakpe mia le bẹẹ fe ngi wẹ, na wọi hi aa pie" yẹ "ta
mia a ngundei wa lẹi" yẹ "aa ngunde wa-o."

Yẹ "Ọ."

Yẹ "Aa li ngọmbui gbla-o."

Yẹ "Ọ."

Fale tia na.

Kẹ mahẹi ji ngila ngi yeya ngilẹi ji laa a Kebele. Hinda gbi le ngilẹi ji a pie lọ ngilẹi ji a yẹpẹ lọ saha. Kia mua mu yẹpẹ ma.

Kia hu na nyapoi ji kẹ i lolonga wa a ndopoi ji kẹ i longa kenẹi ji ma haani kẹ kenẹi ji ndenga ngi ma yẹ "Hani fa ngẹ ndopoi ji aa li ngọmbui gbla" yẹ "ngulọ mia."

All right kẹ kenẹi ji hijea gbọma ngelei ye pekẹi i wo kẹ i ya gbọng ngolẹi ji hu kpandẹwilimẹi kẹ nyapoi ndea ndopoi ma yẹ "Li bi kulẹi wa."

Kẹ ndopoi ndea yẹ "Ye" yẹ "folei gbaningọ" yẹ "gbẹ ngi mawulo folei ya i lẹli kulo" yẹ "nga lilọ ngi kulẹi jisia wa."

Kẹ i wotea ngi gama yẹ "Hii" yẹ "mbọ ngi bi lọni mangulọ."

Kẹ ndopoi ngi mọlia yẹ "Ye, bi yẹ gbẹ?"

Yẹ "Ẹngẹng" yẹ "ngii yẹpẹi bi ye."

Kẹ ndopoi ji hijea.

Ji folei ya ndẹlini kẹ i ya kẹ i kulẹi jisia waa kẹ i waa.

Na na le gbi i ndea ndopoi ji ma i ndea yẹ i ji wie ina folei gbandingọi yo ọ ina liva ngundẹi wamẹi-yo yẹ "Ngii bi lọni ma ngulọ."

Kẹ ndopoi ji kẹ i heinga.

Lọ yila ma kẹ kenẹi ji ya kpandẹwilimẹi ji gbọma kẹ nyapoi ndea ndopoi ma yẹ "Ha ta" yẹ "bii liilọ ngundẹi hu" yẹ "kọ le kẹ mu gbi muẹ mẹhẹ mẹ mbei." I nọ ndopoi ji ma haani.

Kẹ ndopoi ji hijea kẹ i ya ngundẹi ji hu. Kẹ i ngọmbui ji la so mẹhẹi ji lọ na i yẹ heini ngọmbui ji gbla a ngili. Kẹ ngi gọẹ tọtoa a wu la. I wu haani i fo ngi lia.

Kẹ nyapoi ji ndea ngi ma yẹ "Bii yaa wuni!" Yẹ "Kẹ bẹ bi wunga panda" yẹ "na lọ a nyande."

Ndopoi ji i hei na ngi gbi i wu i wote a ngulọi.

Jina nyapoi ji tọni kẹ ndopoi ji wunga i kpọyọa kẹ i ti
yilẹi ji lolia yẹ Kebelema i wa i ngulẹi ji gọmi.

Kẹ Kebele bẹ i ngolei ji gbua (kẹ ngole ta ngẹẹ gu ngii
nga jifa nya wo nyamungọi) kẹ Kebele ndea ngi ma yẹ "Ji gẹ kẹkẹ
a huẹi wa a wa la" yẹ "bia yẹma Kebele ma bẹ wa bi yẹ i mẹ?"
Yẹ "Jina kẹkẹ nyahẹi wotea a ngulọ bẹ Kebele ma i wa i kọmi!"
Yẹ "Kebele ii le," yẹ "nya nda Kebele i yaa na!" Yẹ "Ngẹẹ
pie." Naa i loima haani kẹ kenẹi ji wa.

Tao ji kenẹi ji a wa a ndopoi ji lọ yese loi i ndopoi ji
loi haani ii wani.

Kẹ Kebele gbia kẹ i longa yẹ "Ji gẹ kẹkẹ a wa a huẹng"
yẹ "bẹẹ yẹma Kebele ma Kebele wa bi huẹng mẹ," yẹ "bi bi mẹhẹ
nẹnẹ yili bẹ bẹẹ yẹma Kebele ma wa bi mẹhẹ mẹ" yẹ "jina kẹkẹ
nyahẹi wunga i wotea a ngulọ bẹ Kebele ma i wa i kọmi" yẹ
"Kebele ẹẹ pie."

Kẹ kenẹi ji na humẹninga kẹ i ngi nyaha wai ji lolinga
yẹ "A ndopoi?"

"Kuo" yẹ "ngii ngi lima gọ."

Yẹ "Ngẹ bi ma a ndopoi wua ta walo pẹlẹ bu?"

Yẹ "Taami" yẹ "ngii ngi yẹma gọ."

Kẹ kenẹi ndea yẹ "All right" yẹ "gbẹ ngi ngi gọkọi." Jina
i lewea kulo haani pẹlẹi ji gohu ii tọni kẹ i hitẹa ngitiiya
ina gbi gbekpe ii ndopoi ji lọni kẹ i ya na ngundewẹlẹi ji bu.
Jina i lini ngundewẹlẹi ji bu kẹ i ngulẹi ji ye popa wai ji
malea kẹ i nyapoi ji mọlia yẹ "Yọ gulẹi ji wui mbei?"

Yẹ "Bi nyahẹi ii le a wote a ngulọi?"

Kẹ kenẹi ngi bonga a kpandẹi.

Famia tolo ii nyandeni.

---

1. Recorded by woman from Rotifunk in Freetown on September 2,
1960.
2. Palm oil (ngulọ) in its clearest form is semale that is
used with rice as noted in Tale 30.

Parents and Children

TALE 18: GBELO AND THE ELEPHANTS[1]

Once there was a man and his wife living in their house. The man was a hunter. He took a little wife.

The girl and the senior wife were there together; the senior wife had the junior wife in her charge; the junior wife had not borne a child. The senior wife was so mean to the girl that she ran away.

One day the girl went very far away until she came to a big grass field. When she entered the field, she walked continuously until she saw some broad rocks stretching out far away. She turned and saw a big tree.

When the girl climbed the tree, she looked at the rocks and saw a big elephant lying on top of the rock. The elephant saw the girl also; it got up and went to the girl.[2]

The elephant said, "Oh, my child, what have you come to look for here?"

She said, "Sir, my senior co-wife troubles me, and my relatives are not nearby. My husband paid bridewealth for me and brought me here, but this senior co-wife taunts me all the time, so I ran away."

"Very well," he said. "But this place where you have come is bad. Since you saw me, I shall tell you that my family is here. There are a great number of us, but I will hide you. When they come to the place where I have hidden you, they will say that they smell a new person's scent, but do not come out."

Then the girl said, "All right."

Then the old man took this girl into the town. He gave her water, she bathed; he gave her food, she ate; then he hid her.[3]

Before long some elephants came. When they had just reached the door of the house, they all said, "Grandfather, there is a new person's scent."

He said, "What do you mean? Why do you say 'there is a new person's scent?' All the time I turn myself into a person; all the time you turn yourselves into living people. How is it that you say 'there is a new person's scent?'" He said, "No one is here at all."

He continued to hide the girl. Behold he turned the girl into his wife. The girl remained there until she conceived. When the girl conceived, he said, "Child, I will explain your situation to my senior wife, because her heart is good and she will not reveal you to others. But those children, those young men, should they hear that you are here, they would kill you."

Then the girl said, "All right."

When twilight came, the elephants returned to the town.

Then the man called his senior wife and explained everything to her. "That is what I was doing while I remained behind," he said. "Because you are in the right, do not tell my secret."

And the old woman agreed.

Then the man said to his wife, "The girl should return to her people. If she is going to give birth, she ought to bear it yonder among her family."

Then the girl left.

When the girl left, she bore a child. Then the elephant turned into a living person and went into the town.

When he came to the town, they said to him, "A girl was here recently; she hid herself and went far away; she conceived; she returned and has given birth to the child. The child is a boy."

Then the man went and thanked the midwives; he thanked the man and his wife. He said, "I want to give the child's name."4 They agreed; in fact, they were very happy with the things that he had brought them. He said, "This child is named Gbelo."

Then the girl said, "All right." The girl's husband also agreed to the name. Then the man returned to his home.

After the man had gone, Gbelo grew up very quickly; he matured. One day he said that he was going for a walk. When he went, he surprisingly went to the tree that his mother had once climbed. He climbed the tree.

Then the elephant saw him; the elephant got up and came to him. The elephant said, "Child."

He said, "Yes, sir?"

The elephant said, "What have you come to pluck here?"

Gbelo said, "Father, I only came for a walk. Night over-
came me here, so I climbed into this tree."

The elephant said, "What is your name?"

The child said, "My name is Gbelo."

Then the elephant seized the child; it embraced him. The
elephant said, "Eeh, you are my child! I gave you that name.
So come, let us go into the house."

The elephant went and concealed the child carefully. As
soon as the young men and his senior wife returned, he called
the old woman. He said, "Do you remember the child that the
girl once bore? As a matter of fact, the very child came
today." He said, "But what should we do now?" He said, "Look
your grandchild has come!"

Then the old woman took the child and hid him in another
place.

Then the young men said, "There is a new person's smell."

Then the old woman scolded them; she said, "You, your
father is a person; even I myself am a person. How can you
say 'there is a new person's smell?'" She said, "I do not
want to hear that sort of thing!"

Then the young men were quiet.

Early in the morning the old woman took the child out of
his hiding place. She, the child, and the old man went out
of the town.

Then the man said to the child, "Gbelo," he said, "I have
only two things to give you: this bag and this gun." He said,
"Any animal that you shoot at with this gun will be killed
with only one shot. But if you meet an elephant and you shoot
at it, it will only be wounded; it will not die. Therefore,
as long as you live, do not shoot an elephant; do you understand?"

The child said, "Yes."

The man said, "Do not shoot an elephant; do you understand?"

He said, "Yes."

Then the old man and woman escorted the child as far as
the town.

When the child returned to the town, he said, "Mother, something happened to me today." He explained his experiences to his mother.

But his mother did not explain that those people yonder had borne him. She said, "All right, but be sure to keep it only in your mind."

When the child's kinsmen had sown cassava, they put rice in the swamp. The elephants went and trampled the rice; they kept trampling the rice; they broke the rice. Then the child's senior mother /that is, his mother's co-wife_/ saw them.

She said, "Gbelo, some animals are always in the rice field. Please go and shoot them."

The child arose; he took his gun and went to the rice field; he found the elephants there. "Oh, Mother," he said, "I cannot shoot these elephants."

She said, "If you do not shoot them, I will kill you right here."

Since he was a small child, he shot at the elephants; he injured the foot of one. At once all the elephants came running; they were looking for the person who had shot at them. Then the child turned into a leaf and fell into his father's bag; he lay there trembling. Then the elephant looked in the bag, he saw that it was Gbelo.

The elephant said, "Let us go; let us take the wounded elephant and cure him."

Then the elephant went. He said to the child, "Gbelo, did not I tell you never to shoot elephants?"

He said, "Yes. But my mother's senior co-wife said that I should shoot and that if I did not shoot, she would kill me; I was afraid."

Then the elephant said, "All right." The elephant escorted him to his town and said, "Do not shoot at elephants, do you understand?"

The child said, "Yes."

(Do you know the reason why we women always tie our lappas leaving an extended piece, a mouth? I am about to explain the reason.)

Another time Gbelo got up and went walking. When he returned from his walk, his senior mother called him.

She said, "Gbelo, there are some animals in the rice field. It appears as though hogs are in the rice field. Come, you go and shoot them."

When Gbelo went he saw that hogs were in the rice field. But really the animals were not hogs but little elephants. Gbelo went and shot at the animals; he wounded one; they all came running looking for the person who had shot at them. Then Gbelo again turned into a leaf; he lay down in the ear of his grandmother's cloth; he was trembling with fear. The woman dropped her head down; she looked at the ear of her cloth and saw Gbelo.

Then she said to her husband, "Sir, let us go; we will take him to be cured; really the person who wanted to kill us today; we have not seen him; let us go."

When the woman said that, the man immediately knew that it was Gbelo who had shot at them. Then they took the wounded elephant to be cured.

Then he said, "Gbelo, this is what we are going to do to you. Forever after if you see an elephant, if you load your gun, if you fire your gun, it will not shoot. Any other animal that you shoot at, you will kill, but if you fire at an elephant, the gun will not shoot. Now go."

They packed up many things for Gbelo to take home.

When Gbelo got home, his senior mother said again, "Gbelo, some animals are in the rice."

Then he said, "Mother, you keep calling me to go to kill the animals. When I shoot at them, they almost kill me." He said, "Now you go first. When you go first, if you see any animals, call me. When you call me, I will shoot this gun."

Then the woman went to the rice field; she found the elephants there. She called, "Oh, Gbelo."

Then Gbelo came running. When Gbelo came running, he did not observe what kind of animals were there. He fired his gun; the gun sounded. When the gun sounded, the old woman cried out. Gbelo had shot her with the gun. She was taken into the house; shortly afterward she died.

That is why jealousy is bad. If you are always jealous, you will lose your life. Because of jealousy, this happened.

Lo yila gbǫma kenęi ji mia ta ngi nyahęi. Ti heini ti
węlęi ji bu. Kenęi ji ta kpandęwilimǫ mia a ngie kę i nyahęi
ye kulowoi ji gǫinga gbǫma.

Kę ta nyaha wai ji lǫ heini. So nyaha wai ji ta ndoi
yęlǫ ngi yeya nyaha wuloi ji ta ii yaa ndo leni kę nyapoi ji
ngi wie nyamungǫ yęla a ndopoi ji nyaha woi ji ta kę ndopoi
ji welanga.

Lǫ yila ma kę i ya i li i li i li kę i fonga foni wai ji
hu. Ji i foni foni ji hu kę i heia haani kę falai jisia i ti
maleni ti lani so falai ji ii yaa lukpeni gblanga kę i wotea
kę i ngulu wai ji lǫnga. Kpindi lǫ na węlęma ngi ma kę i
lęnga ngului ji hu.

Jina i lęnga ngului ji hu a falai ji gama gbe kę i hele
wai ji lęnga i lani falai ji ya. Hele ji wa i ndopoi ji lǫnga
gbǫma kę i hijea kę i ya ndopoi ji gama.

Yę "E nya lo," yę "bi wa gbǫ gǫima mbeindo?"

Yę "Kękę" yę "nya nje wai mia a nya mǫnę" yę "tao" yę
"nya bondani tii mbei gblanga kenęi ji ya i nya gǫinga i wa a
nge" yę "kę mamęi ji lǫ le nya vawǫle ma" yę "famia ngi
welanga."

Kę i ndea yę "All right" yę "kę hindęi ji bi wa na yę "na
nyamungǫ" yę "bi nya lǫma hi ngi yępęi ma bi gama" yę "nya
bondanisia mbei" yę "mu vahangǫ wa le" yę "ke" yę "nga bi
lǫwulǫ" yę "mia ngi bi lǫwuma na" yę "ji wǫi ti gǫmęma ti nde
bę tę numu nina magui" yę "baa gbua-o."

Kę ndopoi ji ndea yę "Ei."

Ke kena wovęi ji i ndopoi ji wumbua kę i ya la tęi hu. I
ngi gǫ a nja i mua i ngi gǫ a męhę i mę kę i ngi lǫwua.

Hu ii lę mbini kę helengęi jisia kę ti wa. Jina ti wai
ti foilǫ le kinęi pęlę la kę ti gbi ti ndenga a lenga "Maada,
numu nina magu."

Ye "Ange wa ye nde wuę 'numu nina magu'? I lęmbia haani
nya ngi wote a numu wua wu wote a numu vu" yę "ta mia wa nde
wę 'numu nina magu'?" Yę "Numu gbii mbei-o."

I ndopoi ji lǫwua i lǫnga na ma haani męma i ndopoi ji
wotea na a ngi nyaha ndopoi ji loa haa kę i gonga. Jina
ndopoi ji koi ji wumbua kę i ndea yę "Ndopoi" yę "ha ta" yę
"ngęę gu ngaa bi ma lǫwu wa" yę "nga bi hinda hungę lǫ a nya
nyaha wai" yę "jifa" yę "ngi lii gama nyandengǫ" yę "Ęę gu aa
bi gbua ngitiiya" yę "kę ndopoi ye jisia kǫngęi ye jisia" yę
"ti bi malǫ męninga le wǫi mbei" yę "ta bi waa."

Kẹ ndopoi ji ndea yẹ "E."

Ji kpọkọ volei ji hitini kẹ helengẹi jisia ti yamanga ta hu kẹ i ngi nyaha wai ji lolinga kẹ i na kpẹlẹ hugẹnga a ngie yẹ "Hi lọ ngi loa a pie bi woma" yẹ "fale bi lemọ le" yẹ "nya mawẹ."

Kẹ mamẹi ji lumaa.

Kẹ kenẹi ji ndea ngi nyahẹi ma yẹ "Ndopoi ta" yẹ "i yama" yẹ "ina a ndoi le lọ" yẹ "i li i nde mia ngi bonda gama."

Kẹ ndopoi ji ya.

Jina ndopoi ji lini kẹ i ndoi ji lenga. Kẹ kenẹi ji helei ji kẹ i wotea a numu vu kẹ i ya tẹi ji hu.

Ji i wai folei na ma kẹ ti ndea ngi ma tẹ "Ndopoi yila gẹ mbei i lọwua gẹ i ya i ya i gonga i waa i ndoi lenga ye ndoi ji hindolo le."

Kẹ i ya ti gama ke i sẹ gbua koimawaisia ma i sẹ gbua kenẹi ji ma kẹ ngi nyahẹi yẹ "Nya longọ ngi ndopoi ji la hei." Kẹ tia bẹ ti luma; ingẹ ti gohunẹingọ wa hakẹi nasia i wai a tie na. Yẹ "Ndopoi ji" yẹ "ngi la a Gbẹlo."

Kẹ ndopoi ji ndea yẹ "E." Kẹ ndopoi ji ngi hini bẹ lumaa kẹ kenẹi ji yamaa.

Jina kenẹi ji lini hu i lẹmbi haani kẹ Gbẹloi ji kẹ i lola kẹ i lakpaa. Lọ yila ma kẹ i hiyea yẹ "Nya lima jẹsia ma." Kẹ i ya i li lọọ ngului ji wọ ngi nje lẹi hu kẹ ta bẹ lẹnga hu.

Kẹ helei ji kẹ i ngi lọnga kẹ helei ji hijea kẹ i waa ngi gama yẹ "Ndopoi."

Yẹ "Na."

Yẹ "Bi waa gbọ gọima mbei?"

Yẹ "Kẹkẹ, ngi wa lọ le jẹjiama," ye "ta mia kpindi nya malea mbei" yẹ "fa ngi lẹa ngului ji hu."

Ye "Bi lẹi?"

Kẹ ndopoi ndea yẹ "Nya laa a Gbẹlo."

Kẹ helei ji gbundẹa ndopoi ji ma i ngi gulu yẹ "E!" Yẹ "Nya loi lọ a bie" yẹ "nya mia ngi mbiyẹi na veni bi wẹ" yẹ "famia wa mu li pẹlẹ bu."

I li i ndopoi ji lọ wu sọ. Kia le kọngẹi jisia ti yamani
ta ngi nyaha wai ji kẹ i mamẹi ji lolinga yẹ "Ba ndopoi ndoi
lea wọ le" yẹ "ye ndoi gbe i wa" yẹ "kẹ ma ye na pie" yẹ "bi
laloi gbe wa."

Kẹ mamẹi ji bẹ kẹ i ndopoi ji gbua mia kenẹi ji ngi lọwui
na kẹ i ngi lọwua hinda weka.

Kẹ kọngẹi jisia tia na ndema tẹ "Numu nina magui."

Kẹ mamẹi ji jọlẹa ti ma yẹ "Wua wu kẹkẹ numu, nya-o numu
wua wa ye nde wẹ 'numu nina magu'?" Yẹ "Ngii loni nga ye na
humẹni."

Kẹ tia heini.

Ngele wo hu kẹ mamẹi ji ndopoi ji gbua ta kenẹini gbi kẹ
ti ya.

Kẹ kenẹi ndea ngi ma yẹ "Gbẹlo" yẹ "hani felekpe mia nya
nga fe bi wẹ" yẹ "ta mia a kpavẹi ji kẹ kpandẹi ji." Yẹ
"Kpandẹi ji" yẹ "hua-o-hua bi mboi la" yẹ "a mbo yilakpe" yẹ
"a palọ"; yẹ "kẹ bi hele malenga" yẹ "bi mboa" yẹ "a ngi nẹmulọ
le kẹ ẹẹ ha." Yẹ "Fale kunafọ i lo hu bi ngelei ji bu" yẹ
"baa hele bo hoe."

Yẹ "Mn."

Yẹ "Baa hele bo hoe."

Yẹ "Mn."

Kẹ ti ngi laloa haani kẹ ndopoi ji yama.

Jina i yamani tẹi hu yẹ "Ye," yẹ "hinda nya maleni." I
jiama kinẹi i hungẹ a ngi njẹ.

Ke ngi njẹ bẹ ii hungẹni aa yẹma nungẹi nasia mia ti ngi
leni ọ helengeẹi nasia mia ti ngi leni kẹ i ndea yẹ "Eye" yẹ
"kẹ na i" yẹ "bi nẹmahu-yo."

Lọ yila ma tangẹi ji ngi kẹkẹni ta hi kẹ mbẹi ji ta pu
kpetei ji hu. Helengẹi jisia ta lilọ ti mbei ji yọlọ ta
njọmbọ njọmbọ haani ta ngale ngale. Kẹ ngi njẹ wai ji malea.

Yẹ "Gbẹlo" yẹ "huanga lọ le mbẹi ji hu" yẹ "kọnẹ wa bi
li bi ti bo."

Ndopoi ji i hiyea kẹ i kpandẹi ji wumbua kẹ i ya kẹ i
helengẹi jisia malea "O" yẹ "Ye," yẹ "nya ngẹẹ gu nga helengẹi
jisia bo."

Yẹ "Bii ti boilọ," yẹ "nya ngi bi wa ma hindẹi ji."

Tao ndopo wulo mia ke i kpandẹi wilia helengẹi jisia ma
ye ngila kẹ i ngi gọẹ yalẹa hu gbandi na kẹ ti gbi ti wa a
pimẹ ti waa numui ji gọkọlema i helengẹi jisia boni. Kẹ
ndopoi ji kẹ i wotea a ndawẹi ke i ya kẹ i gulaa ngi kẹkẹ
gbafẹi ji hu a hẹlẹ ngi ma i lai na a gbẹli ni ni ni. Kẹ
kenẹi ji kẹ i gbafẹi ji hugbenga kẹ i tọnga kẹ Gbẹlo mia.

Kẹ i ndea yẹ "Mu li" yẹ "a mu ngi wumbu mu li mu li mu
ngi hale."

Kẹ i ya. Kẹ i ndea ngi ma yẹ "Gbẹlo" yẹ "ngii ndeni bi
ma ngaa" yẹ "ma baa helenga bo?"

Yẹ "Mn," yẹ "Kẹ ngi nje wai mia ndeni yẹ ngi mbo yẹ ngii
mboilọ yẹ a nya wa lọ" yẹ "naa ngi luaima."

Kẹ i ndea yẹ "Ọ." Kẹ i yamaa gbọma kẹ i ngi laloa tẹ
"Baa yaa kpandẹwili hoe."

Yẹ "Mn."

(Ang hanifasïe nyahanga mu kulẹi ji yilima ma ye nda ma
gbua ye sabui lọ ngi wama hungẹ mahi.)

Tẹmi ye pekẹi ma kẹ i hiya gbọma kẹ i ya. Jina i ya
jẹjiamẹi ji i wa kẹ ngi nje wai ji ngi lolinga gbọma.

Yẹ "Gbẹlo" yẹ "huanga lọ hindẹi ji" yẹ "bi tọa bẹ
ndondanga mia ti mbẹi ji hu" yẹ "wa bi li ti bo."

So ji i lini i tọi lọ vuli kẹ ndondanga mia kẹ mama
ndondanga yaa na hele numui jisia mia. Kẹ i ya kẹ i kpandẹi
ji wilia 'so' ti ma kẹ i yena bonga kẹ i ngi nẹmua kẹ ti gbi
ti wa gbọma a pimẹ ti waa numui ji gọkọi ma. Kẹ i wotea gbọma
a ndawẹi ngi mama ji kẹ i laa ngi gulẹi ji ye ngoli ji hu ta
wa gbẹlima na a nduwa. Kẹ mamẹi ji ngi wui hitẹa kẹ i kulẹi
ji ye ngoli ya gbea kẹ i Gbẹlo lọnga.

Kẹ i ndea ngi hini ma yẹ "Kẹkẹ" yẹ "mu li" yẹ "mu ngi
wumbu mu li mu ngi hale; ingẹ" yẹ "numui ji" yẹ "haai mu wa
mui ngi lọma" yẹ "mu li kenẹi ji."

Kia nyapoi ji na leni kẹ i kọnga yakpe kẹ ngi loi mia
kpandẹi ji wilini kẹ ti hele na wumbua ti li la ti li ti ngi
hale.

Kẹ ti ndea ngi ma tẹ "Gbẹlo" tẹ "na na mu piema a bie,
kunafọ bi hele lọbẹ bi bi gbandẹi jọsọ bẹ bi pili ẹẹ yaa yia"
yẹ "kẹ hua gbi na le bi kpandẹwilini ngi ma" yẹ "ba ngi waa
kẹ bi pilia helema kpandẹi ji ẹẹ yaa yia" yẹ "kẹ li na."

Ti haka gbotonga hugbatẹ ngi wẹ.

Kę Gbęlo ya kę mamęi ji ngi mǫlia gbǫma yę "Gbęlo" yę "huanga mbęi ji hu."

Kę i ndea yę "Ye" ye "huangęi jisia wǫgba ba nya loi bę ngi li ngi ti wa" ye "ngi kpandęi ji wilia ti ma" yę "a lo te ti nya wa" yę "kia hu na" yę "biaa ba li biaa ba lo kulǫ" yę "bi longa kulo" yę "bi yaa" ye "bi ti lǫngaa" yę "ke bi nya loinga" yę "bi nya lolinga lǫ" yę "nga kpandęi ji wili lǫ."

Kę i ya kę i helengęi jisia malenga. Kę i ndea ngi ma yę "Oo Gbęlo."

Kę Gbęlo humęninga kę i wa a pimę ngi wangǫi na pimę ii yaa mabęni ina huangęi ye jisia gbe huanga le ii ti mabęni kę i kpandęi ji wilia kę kpandęi ji yiaa kpandęi ji yiangǫi na kę mamęi ji yele gulaa; Gbęlo ngi bonga a kpandęi ji ti ngi wumbu na ti li a ngie pęlęi bu. Ji ti lini a ngie pęlęi bu i yaa lęmbini kę i haa.

Famia tolo ii nyandeni baa lo tolo gbuama haani bi l vui juku tolo woma so kę ji le.

---

1. Recorded by woman from Rotifunk in Freetown on September 2, 1960.
2. In this tale and in Tale 56, elephants (hele) are able to assume the form of human beings; Męnde generally believe that ancestral spirits frequently assume the form of elephants. Several Męnde in both Bumpe and Bunumbu mentioned that in the far eastern part of Męndeland, it was customary for very old people to turn into elephants. In the mid-nineteenth century, Thompson observed that "Elephants are numerous here, and are often killed by the natives, and eaten... From the bottom of the foot the natives make wristlets, which are much valued as ornaments" (Thompson:247-248).
3. The old elephant welcomes his guest according to Męnde etiquette, with water in which to bathe and food to eat.
4. Męnde children receive their first names three days after birth for girls and four days after birth for boys (Sawyerr and Todd:30). When initiated into Poro and Sande, Męnde youths assume new names (F.W.H. Migeod, "Some Observations on the Physical Characters of the Mende Nation," Journal of the Royal Anthropological Institute 49 /1919/:266). Teknonymous names are also used after people become parents. Moreover, certain individuals, such as twins and their succeeding siblings are given special names (see Tale 96).

TALE 19: MUSA WO AND HIS FAMILY[1]

At one time Musa Wo was with his father, his mother, and his uncle.

One day Musa Wo got up. He said to his father, "Father, give me a cow. I will take it to my uncle so that he can train it."

His father gave him a cow. When Musa Wo took the cow, he left it with his uncle. The cow remained with his uncle for a long time.

Musa Wo got up one day. "Father," he said, "I want to go to my uncle. Today he is giving me my cows; they say that my cow has borne three calves."

Then his father said, "Go."

As Musa Wo was going to his uncle's place, he met a man on the road.

The man said, "Musa Wo."

Musa Wo said, "Yes, Sir."

He said, "Good morning."

Musa Wo said, "Father, thank you."

The man said, "What are you setting a trap for in the middle of this road?"

He said, "Oh, Father, the road has crossed the road before I am setting a trap for it."

The man said, "What does that mean?"

Then Musa Wo said, "I will explain later."

Then the man asked, "Musa Wo, where is your father?"

He replied, "My father is between the sky and the earth."

He said, "What does that mean?"

Then Musa Wo again said, "I will explain later."

Again the man asked, "Musa Wo?"

He said, "Yes, Sir."

He said, "Where is your mother?"

"Oh," he said, "my mother is between a razor and a needle."

He said, "What does that mean?"

He said, "Oh, Father, I will explain later."

Then the man passed and Musa Wo went on until he reached his uncle's place.

Musa Wo said, "Uncle, good morning."

His uncle said, "Yes."

He said, "Uncle, I have come to take my cows."

"Oh," he said, "you do not have any cows here; the only cow you own is here. My bull is the one who bore the calves."

Musa Wo said, "Oh, Uncle, does a man bear a child?"

Then his uncle said, "Yes, a man bears a child."

Then Musa Wo said, "All right." He started for home.

When Musa Wo had almost reached his father's place, he ran with a big shout to his father. He said, "Father, Father, Father," he said, "please come; take me across the river; the river has risen a lot and I cannot cross it; I want to go to my uncle."

Then his father got up and followed him. His father put him on his shoulder. Just as they reached the middle of the river--the river did not cover a person's foot--Musa Wo said to his father, "Father, put me down; I stepped on a fish in the water."

"Oh," said his father, "Musa Wo, you are on my shoulder. How could you step on a fish in the water?"

"Oh," he said, "just let me down."

As soon as his father let him down, he ran quickly to his uncle. "Uncle, uncle, uncle," he said, "what, are you sitting?" He said, "Father, look at the child bearing my responsibility at the side of the river."

Then his uncle turned. He said, "Oh, Musa Wo! Child, you are a great liar! Does a man bear a child?"

Musa Wo said, "Hurrah, Uncle, you have justified my argument. Give me my cows."

When his uncle gave him the cows and he was returning home, Musa Wo met the man again who had asked him the questions.

The man said, "Musa Wo."

He said, "Yes, Sir."

He said, "When I asked you 'what are you setting a trap for in the middle of the road?' You said, "the road has crossed the road before you are setting a trap for it."

He said, "Yes, Father, a rat crossed this road; I am setting the trap before him."

The man said, "Yes, all right. When I asked you 'where is your father?' You said, 'your father is between the sky and the earth.' What does that mean?

Musa Wo said, "Yes." He said, "When I left my father today, he has gone to settle a quarrel between paramount chiefs. Therefore, he will be in difficulty: if he decides in favor of one, the other will kill him or do something bad to him; if he decides in favor of the other, that one will also think he has done wrong."

Then the man said, "When I asked you 'where is your mother? You said 'your mother is between a razor and a needle.' What does that mean?"

Musa Wo said, "When I left my mother was suffering the pain of childbirth; therefore, I said, 'Mother is between a razor and a needle.'"

The story is finished.

Lọ yila ma Musa Wo mia wọ heini ngi kẹkẹ-o ngi nje-o ngi kenya-o.

Kẹ ta ngi Musa Wo kẹ i hijenga lọ yila ma. Kẹ i ndenga ngi kẹkẹ ma yẹ "Kẹkẹ nya gọ a nika nga li la kenya gama i li i makẹ."

Kẹ i ngi gọnga a nikahẹi ji. Ji Musa Wo lini a nikẹi ji kẹ i ndonga ngi kenya gama. Nikẹi ji lẹmbinga haani ngi kenya gama.

Jina i hijeni lọ yila ma. "Kẹkẹ" yẹ "nya longọ ngi li kenya gama ha i li i nya nikangẹisia ve tẹ i ndenga lenga ti sawa."

Kẹ ngi kẹkẹ ndea yẹ "Li."

Jina i yẹ lima kẹ ta kena yila ti kọmẹnga pelei ma.

Kẹ i Musa Wo mọlia yẹ "Musa Wo."

Kẹ i ndea yẹ "Na."

Yẹ "Bua."

Kẹ i ndea yẹ "Mn, kẹkẹ bi sie."

Yẹ "Gbọ bi ma yatẹma hi pelei ji lia?"

Yẹ "Kpuo," yẹ "kẹkẹ," yẹ "pelei mia pelei ma lewea" yẹ "ta mia ngi ma gulọ yatẹma."

Yẹ "Na hu lọ a gbẹ?"

Kẹ i ndenga ngi ma yẹ "Nga hugẹlọ kẹ kulọ ma le."

Kẹ kenẹi ngi mọlia yẹ "Musa Wo," yẹ "ọ bi kẹkẹ?"

Yẹ "Nya kẹkẹ lọ ngelei luahu a ndọe."

"Na hu lọ a gbẹ?"

Yẹ "Nga hungẹlọ kẹ kulọma le."

Kẹ i ngi mọlia gbọng yẹ "Musa Wo."

Yẹ "Na."

Yẹ "Ọ bi nje?"

"Kuo," yẹ "nya nje lọ kpeka lua hu a miji."

Yẹ "Na hu lọ a gbẹ?"

Yẹ "Kuo, kẹkẹ," yẹ "Nga hungẹ lọ" yẹ "kulọ ma le."

Kẹ kenẹi lewenga ngi ma kẹ ta bẹ i ya. Ji i lini kẹ i fonga ngi kenya gama.

Yẹ "Kenya bua."

Yẹ "Mn."

Yẹ "Kenya" yẹ "ngi wanga nya nikanga woma."

"Kuo" yẹ "bi nikanga gbii mbeindo" yẹ "nikẹi yakpe mia bi yeya mbei." Yẹ "Nya nikẹi ye hinẹi mia ndengẹi jisia lenga."

Yẹ "Kuo" yẹ "kenya" yẹ "hindo a ndo le lọ?"

Kẹ i ndea yẹ "Eh," yẹ "hindo mia ndo le."

Kẹ i ndea ye "Ọ." Kẹ i yamanga.

Ji i lini ii foni panda ngi kẹkẹ gama ke i lewenga a pimẹi a yele wa kẹ i ya ngi kẹkẹ gama. Yẹ "Kẹkẹ kẹkẹ kẹkẹ" yẹ "kọnẹ" yẹ "wa bi njẹi lewe a nge" yẹ "njẹi vengọ wa" yẹ "ngẹẹ gu nga njẹi lewe nya longọ ngi li kenya gama."

Kẹ ngi kẹkẹ bẹ hijea kẹ i tonga ngi woma kẹ i ngi wumbunga kẹ i ndanga gbaki ma. Ji na i yẹ lima ti foi lọ leke kinẹi njẹi lia njẹi wa ẹẹ numu gọ ma windẹ kẹ i ndenga ngi kẹkẹ ma yẹ "Kẹkẹ," yẹ "nya hitẹ" yẹ "ngi nyiminga nyẹi ma njẹi bui."

"Kuo," ngi kẹkẹ yẹ "Musa," yẹ "bi nya gbaki ma ba ye pie bi nyimi nyẹ ma njẹi hu."

"Kuo" yẹ "nya hitẹ le."

Kia le ngi kẹkẹ ngi hitẹni kẹ i lewea vaung a pimẹi kẹ i ya ngi kenya gama yẹ "Kenya, kenya, kenya," yẹ "biaa heini" yẹ "kẹkẹ gbe ndoi lema nya yeya njẹi la."

Kẹ ngi kenya wotea yẹ "Kuo, Musa Wo," yẹ "ndopoi" yẹ "bi lẹni kpa" yẹ "hindo mia a ndo le."

Yẹ "Hoiyo!" Yẹ "Kenya" yẹ "bi nya lemunga" yẹ "nya nikanga ve."

Jina ngi kenya nikẹi jisia veni i yẹ yamama kẹ ta kenẹi ji ti gomẹnga gbọma kenẹi ji ha ngi mọlini a njẹpẹi jisia.

Yẹ "Musa Wo."

Yẹ "Na."

Yẹ "ngi bi mọli lọ ngẹ gbọ bi ma yatẹma pelei lia" yẹ "bi ndeilọ nya ma bẹ 'pelei mia pelei malenga ta mia bi kulọ yatẹma.'"

Ye "Eh kẹkẹ" yẹ "nyina mia le pelei ji malenga" yẹ "ta ngi ngi gulọ yatẹma."

Yẹ "E," ye "ji wọi ngi bi mọlini nge 'ọbi kẹkẹ' bẹ bi kẹkẹ lọ ngele lua hu a ndọẹ" yẹ "na hu lọ a gbe?"

Yẹ "Eh." Yẹ "Nya kẹkẹ" yẹ "ngi ndoni ha ndọmahanga ti fele ti yianga i ya ye njiẹi ji lọ le ma. Fale a yẹ kiti luahu lọ na i temu vea ye ngila wẹ ina tii ngi wai lọ ta hinda nyamu wielọ a ngie." I ndenga ye na ma yẹ "Bia" yẹ "bi lẹle" yẹ "ye na bẹ a ngili lọ a ngie," yẹ "ii kpekpe wieni."

Kẹ ti ya kẹ i ndea yẹ "Ji wọi ngi bi mọlini ngẹ 'ọ bi nje?'
bẹ 'nya ma bi nje lọ kpeka lua hu a miji'" yẹ "na hu lọ a gbẹ?"

Yẹ "Ngi ndoni ha ye goi gbalẹma ndole gohu gbalẹi" yẹ "ngi
ma" yẹ "fale 'ngi ye na leni ngẹ ye lọ kpekẹi lua hu a miji.'"

Kẹ ji lọ wieni hoe.

---

1. Recorded by woman from Rotifunk in Freetown on September 2,
1960. This tale mentions three most important senior kinsmen,
parents and maternal uncle (kenya). See Chapters 1 and 4.

TALE 20: MUSA WO AND HIS PARENTS[1]

At one time there was a story about Musa Wo.[2]

Once there was a chief who was a very wealthy man. He
had a big town; he had many wives; he had many young men. The
women were there, and some of them conceived.

One of the women was pregnant for some time, but she did
not bear the child. She remained pregnant. All her co-wives
bore their children; the children began to walk. The woman
had not borne her child. For ten years the woman was pregnant
which disturbed the chief. He was afraid of the unusual
length of her pregnancy.

One day the chief said, "This young woman has been pregnant for ten years; she has not borne her child. I have decided that I will drive her away." Then the chief drove the
young woman away.

The woman went far away into the bush. She found a hut
where she stayed alone. Whenever morning came, she would go
to chop her firewood; she would bring it; she would stack it.

One day she went to chop firewood in a recently vacated
farm. When she went, she took an ax.

Just as she started to cut firewood, she heard a human
voice saying, "Strike the ax gently on the front of your calf."

She stopped. Where was this human voice coming from?
She asked, "Who is speaking?"

As soon as she struck the ax on the front of her calf,
Musa Wo jumped out--kọkọlọ. He was completely grown up, his

beard had grown. Then he cut up the firewood very quickly; he tied it in bundles: six bundles for his mother and eight bundles for his father. Then very quickly he took his mother's share first and threw it down in the village. Then he took his father's share to the village. As soon as he had dropped the firewood, he went to greet his father, the chief.

The chief asked him, "Who are you? Where did you come from?"

Then Musa Wo said, "I am your son. The woman whom you once drove away and who was pregnant for ten years has borne her child."

Then the man asked, "When were you born that you have grown up so?"

"Oh," he said, "today."

"Oh, what is your mother's name?"

"Oh," he said, "as for that, I will explain but not now."

When the chief heard that, he became very afraid. When Musa Wo left, the chief spoke to the town elders. He repeated everything; he explained everything to them; he said, "That is what happened to me."

"Oh," said the elders, "Chief, if such a thing happened, you should kill that person, because never have we experienced such a thing before."

Then the chief said, "I think that you should help me; we must do that; you show me how we shall walk on the road."

Then the elders said, "What would be good: let us go and dig a very big hole on your large farm. When we have dug the hole, we will put sharp sticks and thorns in it. Afterward we shall call him; we will put a chair over the middle of the hole. When he comes, let him sit on the chair then he will fall into the hole. Then Musa Wo will be killed."

Then they went.

But Musa Wo is a person who can understand the bush-cows' language. All of the animals in the world can speak to him; he can speak to them.

As soon as they started to dig the hole, the ants went to Musa Wo. They said, "Musa Wo, this is truly what your father has started to make for you: they are digging a big hole; they are going to set a chair over it so that if you go there, you will drop into the hole and you will die."

"Oh," he said, "let them be; let them do it."

Then the ants left.

Musa Wo's father went, he had them dig a hole; then they put pieces of bottles, thorns, and all kinds of bad things in the hole; then they put a mat over the hole and set a chair on it; then they sent a person to call Musa Wo.

The messenger said, "Your father wants to see you."

Musa Wo came. When he came, they offered the chair to him. They said, "Please sit on that chair."

Musa Wo said, "No, customarily if you come into a house, your father shows you a chair; if your little brother is there, you should tell him to go to take that seat." Then Musa Wo said to his little brother, "Go, take the chair and bring it."

Just as his little brother was about to go there, they said, "Don't go there; there is a hole there!"

"O ho," said Musa Wo, "I am the one for whom you dug a hole so that I would fall into it; isn't that so?"

Then Musa Wo left.

They were unable to catch him that way so they tried another way.

Then the chief's heart was troubled again. He said, "What shall I do now so that this child will die?"

Then the elders said, "Since you have failed to get him with the hole, the second thing that you should do is this: tell him to come to carry your palm thatch tomorrow."

Musa Wo went to the place where the palm thatch was kept. Before he came, people were lined up under the thatch in order to shoot him with their guns.

When Musa Wo arrived, he said, "Customarily if you go to carry thatch, you should beat under the thatch so that if a snake is there, he will not bite you."

Just as Musa Wo was about to beat the people, the people under the thatch began to shout. They said, "Don't kill us! We are here!"

"Oh," said Musa Wo, "today you wanted to kill me too; isn't that so."

Musa Wo left without transporting any thatch. Therefore, his father was not able to kill him by that means at that time.

That is why they were unable to kill Musa Wo at one time.

Dọmẹi na wọ kọloni Musa Wo ma.

Maha yila gbe wọ i hijeni. Mahẹi ji navo wamọ yẹ la ta lakpa wa ngi yeya ngi nyahanga ti vahangọ wa. Ndakpaloisia ti ngi ma ti gbotongọ wa yẹla; nyahangẹisia ti loni lọ na na kẹ ti lẹnga kẹ ti gonga.

Ye ngila yẹ lọ na ta bẹ i yẹ koi ji hu lọ i koi ji wumbu haa. Ẹẹ ndoi ji le i loni koi ji hu lọ. Ngi mbaanga gbi ti ti nda lenga le ti jia tia na haa ii yaa ndoi ji leni. Fo pu i lenga na taa koi ji hu kẹ ji i gbalẹnga mahẹi ma. Kẹ mahẹi bẹ i luanga hindẹi ji ma.

Folo yila kẹ i ndea yẹ "Nyapoi ji numu i ko wumbu fo pu ẹẹ ndo le. Ngi piema ngi gbẹ." Kẹ i nyapoi ji gbẹnga."

Kẹ nyapoi ji i ya i lini ndọgbọi hu lọ polong. I li i bafa wẹlẹ na na mia i yẹ na ta yakpe. Ngele wongalọ wọ i li i ngi gọwui yale i wa i pu. I yẹ nalọ.

Folo yila i li lọ na kọwui ji yalemẹi ji njọpọi ji hu kẹ i ya koni ji lọ ngi yeya. I li i koni ji.

Ji i tọtoni leke a tewe tewe la kẹ i numui ji yia woi mẹninga yẹ "Koni na họlẹ kulo bi haka yamẹi."

Kuo kẹ i longa kulo. Mi lọ njẹpẹ woi ji gbuama na? Kẹ i mọlia "Ye mia njẹpẹi lema?"

Yẹ "Ngẹ bi koni họlẹ kulo bi haka yamẹi."

Kia leke i koni na họni ngi haka yamẹi na kẹ Musa Wo i gbujanga kọkọlọ. Ngi lakpangọ vaung ngi gbẹlẹ gbi gbiangọ. Kẹ i koni ji hounga ngi nje yeya. Kẹ i kọwui na lewetewenga fulo fulo fulo. Kẹ i ngilinga i ngi nje ndẹi yili ngili wọita i ngi kẹkẹ ndẹi yili ngili wayakpa. Kẹ i ya fulo fulo fulo fulo a ngi nje ndẹi na yese kẹ i pilinga fulẹi hu kẹ i ngi kẹkẹ ndẹi na wumbunga kẹ i ya. Kia leke i kọwui gulani bing kẹ i ya famẹi ji wiema ngi kẹkẹ ma mahẹi ji. Kẹ i ya i famẹi ji wiema ngi ma.

Kẹ mahẹi ngi mọlinga yẹ "Yelọ a bie? Bi ye hijenga milọ bi gbianga na?"

Kẹ i ndenga yẹ "Bi loi mia a nge;" yẹ "nyahẹi ji mia wọ" yẹ "bi ngi gbẹni i yẹ koi hu fo pui na va wọ" yẹ "i ndoi leni."

Kę kenęi ngi mǫlia yę "Migbe lǫ ti bi lenga na bii lakpanga bi fonga hęing?"

"Kuo" yę "ha."

"Kuo, bi nje lęi?"

"Kuo" yę "na ta" yę "nga hungę lǫ kę kia hu na ya na na."

Kenęi bę ji lengǫ-o kę i luanga wa. Kia Musa Wo gbuani, ke kenęi i ndea ta gbakoi nasia ma i jia hindęi ji ma i hungę a tie yę "Hi mia hindęi ji nya malenga."

"Kuo" tę "Mahęi, na bonda i wienga lǫ pie bi numu bondęi na waa jifa wǫgba mua mu yaa na hulǫni wǫ."

Kę ta bę ndea yę "Ba wua wa gbǫ nyama mu na wie-o wua wa pelei gę a nge. Kia ma ye lewe la?"

Kę ti ndea tę "Na mia nyandengǫ bi gba wai na ma a mu li mu ndowa lakpa wa bǫ na ndowęi na mu bonga lǫ na ngulu-ya-fǫ-na-o ngali-o ta mia ma pu na kpęlę mu pienga lǫ mu ngi loli i wa mu heiwui ya gbatę na panda. Mu to ye ndięi na. I wa i hei ma i wanga leke i heinga heiwui na ma a gula lǫ ndowęi na hu kę ta ngi Musa Woi na kę mu ngi wanga."

Kę ti ya.

Kę Musa Woi ji numu mia wǫ a ngie a tewuisia ti la yięi mę lǫ fuhani na gbi leke ndunya ta yępę lǫ ngi ma ta teini ta yępęlǫ.

Kia leke ti tǫtoni a ndowęi ji bǫ la kę pupuni kę ti ya ti li ti hungę a ngie tę "Musa Wo hi mia bi kękę i tǫtoa a pie la bi va-o" tę "tia lǫ ndowa wa bǫma" tę "ti heiwui hei na kǫwoi bi ya lǫ bi gula ye ndowęi na hu kę bi hanga."

"Kuo" yę "wua a gbe na leke ti ma ti pie."

Kę ti ya.

Ngi kękę i li i pie ti ndowęi na bǫ sani gękęlę ngali hani na leke gbi jani nyamunyamu le kę ti ya ti li ti pu ndowęi na hu. Kę ti ndowęi na hu bonga wa kę ti ngalęi ji langa mahu falafela kę ti heiwui ji heinga mahu kę ti numu longa Musa Wo loli ma.

Tę "Bi kękę longǫ i bi lǫ."

Kę Musa Wo wanga. Kia i wani kę ti heiwui ji ya ngenga a ngie tę "Heiwui mia-e ba heilǫ bę miando."

Kɛ Musa Wo bɛ ndea yɛ "Hmm," yɛ "ba wa wɔ pɛlɛ bu bi kɛkɛ a heiwu gama gɛ a bie ina bi nde wo lɔ na ba ndelɔ ngi gama bɛ i li i heiwui na wumbu." Kɛ i ndea ngi nde wuloi ma yɛ "Li bi heiwui na wumbu bi wa la."

Kia leke yɛ i li na kɛ ti ndenga tɛ "Baa li na ndowɛi lɔ na!"

"Oho," yɛ "nya mia ha wu longɔ wuɛ wu ndowɛi bɔnga nya gulɔ kɔ ngi gula la hi ye?"

Kɛ i yamanga.

Tii guni ngi ma mia kɛ pekɛi kɛ ti pienga.

Kɛ kenɛi ji li hu mɔnɛnga gbɔma yɛ "Nga ye na vuli pie ndopoi ji i ha-e?"

Kɛ ti ndea tɛ "Na na bi gbahanga ngi ma ndowa hindɛi na hu. Hindɛi ye fele ge na na ba pie ta lɔ a ji. Ba ndelɔ ngi ma bɛ i wa sina i bi yasɛi belɛ."

Kɛ Musa Wo ya njasa belɛmɛi na. Kia i lini kɛ ti nunga lɔkpɔnga njasɛi ji bu kɔ ti kpandɛi ji wili ngi ma ti ngi wa.

Kia wɔ Musa Wo lini kɛ i ndea yɛ "Bi ya wɔ njasa bele ma ba mbu lendelɔ" yɛ "kɔwɛi na kali lɔ na aa bi ɲyi."

Kia leke wɔ Musa Wo yɛ i nungɛi nasia lewe ti njasɛi na bu kɛ ti yele gulanga tɛ "Baa mu waa mua mia."

"Kuo wu longɔi ha wɛ wua bɛ wu nya wa hi ye?"

Kia wɔ ti na leni Musa Wo ii yaa njasɛi na bele fɔ. Fale ngi kɛkɛ ii guni wɔ ngi ma a pelei na.

Na mia wɔ i wieni tii guni Musa Wo ma.

----

1. Recorded by young man from Pujehun on February 16, 1960. A summary version of this tale appears in Innes (1964):13.
2. In this tale Musa Wo's unusual birth is associated with unusual powers enabling him to understand the speech of animals.

TALE 21: THE FLEDGLINGS[1]

A bird laid five eggs; then she left them and went away.
When she went away, the eggs became smooth by themselves. And
the Kanji River swelled until it almost touched the eggs. The
eggs hatched. But the little birds stayed in the nest where
she had put the eggs in a high tree; the river did not touch
them. The birds stayed in the nest until they were able to
eat the earth; they pecked at the earth. God continued to feed
the little birds; their feathers began to come out and they
were able to shout. They remained in the nest until they were
bigger and able to trap insects, but their feathers had not
come out completely. Then they began to go from place to place.

A crow saw the little birds; she said that they were her
children.[2]

"Oh," they said, "you can say that we are your children,
because we are small. But our mother used to make a special
cry; if you make it, we are your children."

She said, "Make your cry."

They said, "First you make your cry."

"Gor-gor-gor."

They said, "Then we are not your children."

"Children, you make your own cry."

Of course, their heads were small, and they shook; their
feathers were small, but their voices were beautiful:

"Our mother bore us long ago;
"Our mother bore us long ago;
"Our mother bore us on the Kanji.
"The Kanji River sat on the eggs;
"The eggs became smooth;
"And the eggs have hatched.
"Kanji jo gbẹti jo;
"Kanji jo gbẹti jo;
"Kanji jo gbẹti jo."

The crow said, "Friends, you are not my children, but you
are beautiful."

Then the little birds got up and went away.

A bushfowl saw them.[3] She said, "Hush, my children; hush
my children; hush my children."

They replied, "Don't say 'hush my children; hush my children.' We are looking for our mother; she used to make a special cry. If you make that cry, we are your children."

Then the bushfowl said, "kọkọyẹ, kọkọyẹ, kọkọyẹ, kọkọyẹ, kọkọyẹ."

"Oh," said the little birds, "we are not your children."

The bushfowl said, "Friends, make your cry now."

"Our mother bore us long ago;
"Our mother bore us long ago;
"Our mother bore us on the Kanji.
"The Kanji River sat on the eggs;
"The eggs became smooth;
"And the eggs have hatched.
"Kanji jo gbẹti jo;
"Kanji jo gbẹti jo;
"Kanji jo gbẹti jo."

Now the bushfowl was dancing to their song. "No," she said, "I have changed my mind; it is clear that we are different." Then the bushfowl gave the little birds many presents and told them that they were very beautiful.

Then the little birds went on their way until they met a woodcock.[4]

The woodcock said, "My children have come; my children have come." She prepared food for them and a nest for them. They slept until the morning when the woodcock gave them water in which to bathe.

The little birds said, "Yesterday when we came, you said that we were your children. We don't mean to offend you; you have treated us well. But we are looking for our mother; she used to make a special cry. If you make that cry, we are your children."

The woodcock said, "Kpọu, kpọu, kpọu, kpọu, kpọu, kpọu."

The little birds said, "Woman, we thank you for your kindness, but that is not how our mother used to cry."

"Then, friends," said the woodcock, "make your own cry now."

"Our mother bore us long ago;
"Our mother bore us long ago;
"Our mother bore us on the Kanji.
"The Kanji River sat on the eggs;

"The eggs became smooth;
"And the eggs have hatched.
"Kanji jo gbẹti jo;
"Kanji jo gbẹti jo;
"Kanji jo gbẹti jo."

"Oh," said the woodcock, "children, your voices are sweet."

Then the little birds went on their way; the woodcock accompanied them for some time before she returned.

Now we are going to find their mother; they will see each other.

But first the little birds met a hummingbird. She said that they were her children; she would not let them leave; she made a house for them; she prepared food for them; she gave them many presents; she gave them some money. The little birds, however, said that they were going to travel on.

The little birds said, "Don't say that we are your children. It is true that we are looking for our mother. She used to make a special cry. If you make that cry, we shall agree that you are our mother."

Then the hummingbird said, "Kawung, kawung, kawung, kawung, kawung, kawung."[5]

"Well," said the little birds, "we are not your children."

She said, "Friends, make your own cry now."

Now, of course, they had grown bigger and their voices were more beautiful like their mother's voice.

"Our mother bore us long ago;
"Our mother bore us long ago;
"Our mother bore us on the Kanji.
"The Kanji River sat on the eggs;
"The eggs became smooth;
"And the eggs have hatched.
"Kanji jo gbẹti jo;
"Kanji jo gbẹti jo;
"Kanji jo gbẹti jo."

"Well," said the little birds, "goodbye; we are going now. We thank you for your hospitality, but we are not your children. We are looking for our mother; you are not she."

Then the little birds went and met their real mother. Of course, as soon as they reached their mother, they could not mistake her. They said, "Mother, we have come!"

She said, "My children have come looking for me."

The little birds knew that she was their mother. They were very happy. They looked at her; they looked at her. Of course, they all looked alike.

The little birds said, "Truly, you bore us. We are looking for our mother. There was a special cry that our mother used to make before she left us; if you make it, we are your children."

But their mother said, "Of course, children, don't worry. Sit down now; don't worry about anything. I shall decide when to make that cry."

Their mother made food for the little birds; they ate it; she prepared a nest for them; they slept in it.

The next morning their mother came and put her head over the edge of the little birds' nest--they did not sleep in the same place that she did. She threw back her head and sang:

"I bore my children;
"I bore my children;
"When I bore my children on the Kanji,
"The Kanji River swelled and sat on the eggs;
"The eggs became smooth;
"The eggs hatched in the Kanji River."

Of course, the little birds in the nest responded!

"Hu-hu gbẹti jo kanji jo."

That day there was a big dance in that nest; liquor flowed freely.

Of course, these little creatures brought riches into the world.[6]

What I have explained is what happened at one time.

I ngawui ji la i ndai lọlu kẹ i ndonga na kẹ i ya. Jina i ngawui ji longa na i ya ngawui ji lọ na gbongbonga a ngi gbongbo haa i longa na hu. Kẹ Kanji venga na i lẹnga ngawui ji ma na tẹtẹngọ. Kẹ ngawui ji ndengei jisia ti loi na tẹi ji hu lọ kẹ i ti wumbunga na kẹ i ti lẹnga ngului na hu ii yaa foi ti ma ti loi na na haa haa kẹ ti gunga na a pọlẹi jisia mẹ la ta pọlẹi jongba jongba na ti loi ma na haa. Ngewọ loi na ti gọma kẹ ti gbaki jisia ti gbua kẹ ti gunga na kẹ tia vui tia na gbawoma ti loi na na haa kẹ ti jẹmbẹnga kulo na hi ta gu na ta fuhaninga manẹ kẹ ti gbaki tii yaa li wa kuhama, tao ti loi na telei ji wiema.

Kę gǫma ji ti lǫnga yę ngi lenga mia a tie.

"Kuo" eh tia bę ti ndenga tę "Hu ba ndelǫ bę bi lenga mia a mue jifa mu gulongǫ" tę "kę kpawo lǫ na wǫ mu nje a pie. Bi pienga kę bi lenga mia a mue."

Yę "A wu ndęi wie lę."

Tę "Bia yese bi ndęi wie lę bia bi gǫma."

"Gor-gor-gor."

Tę "Kę bi lenga yaa a mue-o."

"Ndopoisia wua bę a wu ndęi wie lę."

Ingę ti wui na kulongǫ woi na a gbęli ti gbaki yaa i woni wa panda kę ti woi manęngǫ:

"Mu nje mu lea wǫ;
"Mu nje mu lea wǫ;
"Mu nje mu leilǫ Kanji ma-o.
"Kanji pienga i lęnga ngawu ma;
"Ngawui na kpongbonga kę ngawui na tętęa,
"Kanji jo gbęti jo;
"Kanji jo gbęti jo;
"Kanji jo gbęti jo."

"Kpo" yę "ndakpęisia" yę "nya lenga ya a wue kę wu nyandengǫ."

Kę ti hijia kę jisia kę ti gbua.

Kǫkǫyę yama yę "A gbe a nya lenga-o a gbe a nya lenga-o a gbe a nya lenga-o."

Tę "Baa yęma 'a gbe a nya lenga a gbe a nya lenga.' Kpawoi lǫ na wǫ mu nje a pie mu nje mia mu ndǫlǫma. Kpawoi wǫ ye a pie bi pienga kę bi lenga mia a mue."

Kuo kǫkǫyę mia nde yę "Kǫkǫyę-kǫkǫyę-kǫkǫyę-kǫkǫyę-kǫkǫyę-kǫkǫyę."

"Kuo" tę "kęma wieni mu pele yila."

Yę "Hu ndakpęisia wua bę a wu ndęi wie lę."

"Mu nje mu lea wǫ;
"Mu nje mu lea wǫ;
"Mu nje mu leilǫ Kanji ma-o.
"Kanji pienga i lęnga ngawu ma;
"Ngawui na tętęa.

"Kanji jo gbẹti jo;
"Kanji jo gbẹti jo;
"Kanji jo gbẹti jo."

Ingẹ ta bẹ ta ngi kọkọyẹ kẹ ta na magama "As" yẹ "ngi wotea" yẹ "mia mia na ma wieni mu kpulaninga." Kẹ i ti bẹ hua hinda wie kẹlẹma gbi ma i gbẹ-o-gbẹ wie. Yẹ ti nyandengọ wa.

Kẹ tia bẹ kẹ ti ya kẹ ti ya ti ku le wọ kpula mahu.

Kẹ kpula ndea yẹ "A nya lenga ti wa ko nya lenga-o a ndopoisia ti wa-o nya lenga-o." Kẹ ti gbi i pienga gbe-o-gbẹ i mẹhẹnga yili kẹ i ndama gbatẹ gbi ti yi gbuu. Nge i wo i nja ve ti mua panda.

A tẹ "Kẹ jina bi ndea na mu wa na" tẹ "kaye gbi bi ma vui ta bi ndea bẹ bi lenga mia a mue bi gahu gbia na mu ma gaye gbi ma" tẹ "kẹ kpawoi lo na wọ mu nje a pie mu nje mia mu ndọlọma; kpawoi na wọ ye a pie bi bi pienga kẹ bi lenga mia a mue."

"Kpọu-kpọu-kpọu-kpọu-kpọu-kpọu."

A tẹ "Nyapoi, bi lenga mia seẹ a mue" tẹ "kaye gbi bi ma." Tẹ "Kẹ hi yaa na wọ ye a yẹ kpawoi wiema."

"Kẹ bọisia a wu ndẹi wie lẹ."

"Mu nje mu lea wọ;
"Mu nje mu lea wọ;
"Mu nje mu leilọ Kanji-ma-o.
"Kanji pienga i lẹnga ngawu ma;
"Ngawui na tẹtẹa.
"Kanji jo gbẹti jo;
"Kanji jo gbẹti jo;
"Kanji jo gbẹti jo."

"Kpo" yẹ "ndopoisia wu wo nẹngọi."

Kẹ ti lewea i li polong ti lawoma kẹ i yama.

Kẹ kẹ ti ya kẹ ti fua ti gbia kpula gama mu lima na ti nje gama-o ta tieni ti lọ na.

Kẹ kọti bẹlẹi gbuanga ma kẹlẹma gbi ma yẹ ngi lenga mia a tie ti li ẹe luma bẹ ti le ngi ma-e kẹ i pẹlẹi ji gbatẹa ti wẹ i kpọyọ gbẹlẹng i mẹhẹ hinda wie i hoe hani ma kpoto kọpọma i fe ti wẹ ti pele ma.

Tẹ "Baa yẹma bi lenga mia a mue jina bi ndema bẹ bi lenga mia a mue mua-o mu nje mia mu ndọlọma fale kpawoi ji na wọ ye a pie bi pienga kẹ na woeni kẹ mu nje mia a bie."

Kɛ ngawui lɔ a jia ngulu wa ya "Kawung-kawung-kawung-kawung-kawung-kawung-kawung-kawu."

"Kɔ" tɛ "bi lenga yaa a mue."

Yɛ "Bɔisia a wu ndɛi wie lɛ."

Kɛ ti lewea na ingɛ tia na jɛmbɛma ti wo nɛngɔwa na ta ti njemi.

"Mu nje mu lea wɔ;
"Mu nje mu lea wɔ;
"Mu nje mu leilɔ Kanji ma-o.
"Kanji pienga i lɛnga ngawu ma;
"Ngawui na tɛtɛa.
"Kanji jo gbɛti jo;
"Kanji jo gbɛti jo;
"Kanji jo gbɛti jo."

"Kɔ" tɛ "kɛ mu kpɔyɔ-o mu ya-o; bi lenga yaa a mue; kaye gbi bi ma kɛ mu nje mia mu ndɔɔma; bia yaa na."

Kɛ ti ya na kɛ ti foa vui ti nje ma na. Ingɛ kia le ti foi ti nje ma ngi wui ii yakama tia ngamɛi ngi wu ndia ta ɛɛ yaka. Kia leke ti foi ti nje ma kia leke ti ndei tɛ "A ye na ti wa-o."

Yɛ "Nya lenga ti wa gɔima a nge."

Kɛ ti kɔnga na tɛ "Kɛ ti nje mia." Manɛngɔ wa na kpɔo. Ti kpe ti kpe. Ingɛ yakpe ta bɛ.

Tɛ "Kulungɔi ji ɛh i na vui" ti ndei tɛ "bia mia vuli bi mu leini kɛ kpawoi na wɔ mu nje piema wɔ i ya wɔ mu yeya mu ndɔɔma. Bi ye kpawoi na wienga kɛ bi lenga mia a mue."

Kɛ ta bɛ ndea "Inge" yɛ "bɔisia" yɛ "wa wu mɔnɛ" yɛ "a hei na le" yɛ "wa yaa gili gbɛ-o-gbɛ va" yɛ "kpawoi na ngi nɛmahu gɔima ma." I mɛhɛ hinda wie ti wɛ, ti mɛ. I pɛlɛ bu gbatɛ gbɛ-o-gbɛ kpɛlɛ kakɛi kpɛlɛ i ko na ti ma pɛlɛi bu i kpɔyɔ gbɛlɛng.

Kɛ nge wonga na kɛ i le mia kɛ i ngi wui gbia kanyamɛi la ha na ti nda wɛlɛ bu mia tii yii bɛ hinda yila ta tieni kɛ i ngi wui gbua yɛ

"Ngi nya lenga lea wɔ;
"Ngi nya lenga lea wɔ;
"Ngi nya lenga lea wɔ Kanji gohu.
"Kanji venga lɛnga ngawu ma;
"Ngawui na kpongbonga;
"Ngawu na tɛtɛa Kanji jo."

Inge̱ ke̱ tia be̱ ti nda hoa mia pe̱le̱ bu.

"Hu-hu gbe̱ti jo Kanji jo."

Kome̱ wa mia folei na pe̱le̱ bu. Ndo̱ gbuengo̱ see̱ ke̱le̱ma
gbi ma. Inge̱ boi nasia tia wo̱ ti wai wo̱ a kpate̱ ndo̱hu. A
na mia wo̱ ngi hunge̱i wo̱ nunge̱isia ti pie wo̱.

---

1. Recorded by a man from Bumpe in Bo on April 16, 1960.
2. The pied crow (corvus albus: Mende, go̱ma; gokole) also
appears in Tale 33. In the mid-nineteenth century, Thompson
wrote that "Crows are numerous wherever I have been. In size,
voice, and disposition, they are exactly like the American
crow. The body is all jet black, except the breast and neck,
which are a beautiful snow white. Crows and hawks are very
troublesome in the farms, and among the fowls" (Thompson:308).
3. The bushfowl (ko̱ko̱ye̱; Francolinus bicalcaratus) also is a
protagonist in Tales 33 and 73. In the latter tale the life-
ways of domestic fowl (te̱) and bushfowl are sharply contrasted.
Bushfowl are ground birds that "spend most of their time
moving in small parties through grass, farms and the like in
search of food... No real nest is made, the five or six eggs
being laid in a natural hollow on the ground" (John H. Elgood,
Birds of the West African Town and Garden /London:1964 ed./:6).
4. The woodcock (kpula; Lophoceros semifasciatus), which is
also a gregarious bird, "feeds on fruits and insects in tree
tops morning and evening, but comes lower down in the heat of
the day" (Elgood:17).
5. Humming bird (Ngawui).
6. Dances (kome̱; ndoli) also figure in Tales 33, 39, 64, 65,
85, and 93.

TALE 22: JOSE, HIS MOTHER, AND THE WATER SPIRIT[1]

At one time there was a very handsome boy named Jose.
The only work that he did was to canoe on the water. His
mother and father kept advising him to look for some other
occupation, but Jose only wanted to paddle on the water. All
day long he would ferry people across the river.

Jose and his parents lived near a big river. The water
was very rough and many bad spirits lived in the river.

Jose's mother constantly advised him to give up his pad-
dling on the river. One day when she lay down, she dreamt
that a river spirit came out of the river and changed into a
person and came to Jose to be ferried across the river.[2]

In the morning Jose's mother did not want to tell him about her dream. She said, "I am going out, but if anyone comes today, do not take him across the river." She said, "Do not cross the river with anyone today."

Jose said, "All right."

Then Jose's mother went out.

Not long after Jose's mother left, a very beautiful woman approached--her skin was very white, she shone.[3] Then the woman came to ask for Jose.

The woman said, "Is Jose here?"

"Oh," some people said, "he is here today."

She said, "Let me meet him."

Someone went to call Jose and he came.

The woman said, "My friend, I am traveling, and I want you to take me across the river."

Jose still remembered what his mother had said; he replied, "No, I am sick today."

The woman pleaded and pleaded with Jose. She said, "Friend, take me across the river; consider your responsibility to your work."

The woman kept begging until the sun reached its zenith.

Finally, Jose said, "Then I agree; jump into the boat."

The woman jumped into the boat.

Just as the boat was approaching the middle of the river, Jose's mother returned. "Oh, Jose," she cried, "you have ruined yourself. Today I said to you, 'If anyone comes, do not take him across the river.' Now this woman has come and you have decided to put her in the boat to take her across the river. Hurry back here."

But what happened?

The boat began to turn around; it kept turning around and turning around. Just as the boat reached the middle of the river, it sank with Jose--mọng. When the boat sank, Jose was killed; that is how he died, no trace of him was ever seen.

At that time Jose disobeyed his mother's advice. He died in the river; the spirits took him away at that time.

That is why you must obey whatever advice your mother
gives to you. Do not disobey her advice, because she has seen
what you have not seen.

At one time Jose died in that river.

I have explained what I heard.

Ndopoi yila i hiyelọ wọ. Ndopoi ji nyandengọ wa. Ngi
lei mia a Josẹi. Ndopoi ji ngi yenge yeka gbi wo na ke nja
wili la. Ngi njei i lewe ngi woma, ngi kẹkẹ i lewe ngi woma
tẹ i ngenge gọkọi i pie ii loni a ngenge gbi kẹ nja wili la.
Ngele wonga wọ a luva njẹi na wiema kpẹing a nunga.

Tawao mbeindo ti ye na nja wa gbla mia ti ye na yẹ njẹi
na nyamungọ wa jina nyamuisia gbi ti ye njẹi na hu-o.

Wati gbi va ngi nje a ngi lahi yẹ i gbe nja wili lei na
ma. Folo yila kẹ ngi nje i lailọ kẹ i kibaunga a ngie jinei na
i njẹi na hu kẹ i gbua i mawovẹnga a numui i wa yẹ i njẹi lewe
a ngie.

Kẹ ngele wonga kẹ ngi nje ii loni i kibau yẹpẹi ji hugẹ
a ngie. Kẹ ngele wua kẹ ngi nje ndenga yẹ "Nya lima kẹ foloi
ji kpẹing" yẹ "numui i wa" yẹ "baa lima bi nja lewe a ngie,"
yẹ "baa nja lewe a numu gbi a folei ji."

Yẹ "Kulungọi."

Kẹ ngi nje i gbua na.

Kia leke ngi nje lini hu ii guhani kẹ i nyaha nyande
nyande yila lọnga kolengẹ fofo ngi lui na hu ngi wanwangọ
wa kẹ i gbuanga kẹ i wa kẹ i ngi hinda hu mọlinga.

Yẹ "Jọsẹi lọ mbei?"

"Kuo" tẹ "Ta ha mbei."

"Yẹ "A pie le ma ta mu lọ."

Kẹ ti ya ti ngi loli kẹ i wa.

Yẹ "Nyande," yẹ "ngi wa" yẹ "ngi lewema" yẹ "kẹ nya longọ
bi njẹi lewe a nge."

Ta bẹ njẹpẹi ji ngi njei ndeni kulo le ngi wo hu kẹ i
ndenga yẹ "Mm" yẹ "nya gahu ii gboi ha."

Nyapoi ji i ngi manẹnẹ i ngi manẹnẹ yẹ "Nyande njei lewe
a nge," yẹ "gili le bẹ kulo ngenge ye va."

I ngi manẹnẹ i loni haa ngi manẹnẹma kẹ foli fonga kinẹ ngundenga.

Kẹ ta bẹ i ndenga yẹ "Kẹ ngi kulunga kẹ wa bi wili ndẹndẹ hu."

Nyapoi ji wilinga ndẹndẹi ji hu.

Kia leke ti gbuale ngakui bu ti gifẹi le ti ye lima njẹi lia kẹ ngi njei i gbuanga "Eh, Jọsẹi," yẹ "bi bia yekpe jukunga! Ngi ndenga ha bi ma ngẹ 'Numu gbi i wa baa nja lewe a ngie.' Taa nyapoi ji a wa ba li lọ baa ngi wili ndẹndẹ hu baa nja lewe a ngie!" Yẹ "Mavula, bi wa!"

Kẹ gbọ wie?

Ndẹndẹi na loni lọ wọ bembema i lọ bembema i lọ bembema. Kia leke wọ ti foni njẹi na lia lia ndilina kẹ ndẹndẹi na i lọmbunga a Jọsẹi mọng. Kia wọ ndẹndẹi na lọmbui a Jọsẹi i wa i gẹlẹ hi i ha nguwusa bẹ ti yaa tọi.

Ngi nje layẹi na wọ ii kpuai hu i ha wọ fo njẹi na hu jinẹi nasia ti li wọ a ngie.

Na va mia numui na i bẹ leni njẹpẹi gbi le i ndenga bi ma bi humẹni baa ngi layẹi gbua hu jifa na i tọnga bii ya tọi.

Jọsẹi ha wọ njẹi na la.

Ngi na wẹ mẹni ngi hugẹ.

---

1. Recorded by a young man from Pujehun on May 30, 1960 in Freetown. I published an English translation of this tale in "Mende Folktales," West African Review 1960/61.
2. Dreams (kiabu; kibalo) are often the means whereby living and dead kinsmen communicate; moreover, dreams frequently presage future events (e.g., Hofstra /1941/:190-191; Tales 23, 24, 39, and 91). Certain dreams have stock interpretations in Mende culture: if a person dreams of dried fish, it means conspiracy; if a person is breaking wood in a dream, it means hardship (see Migeod /1926/:271-273). When a child is able to relate dreams, the child is considered to have achieved a new level of intellectual maturity.

TALE 23: A SORROWFUL MOTHER'S REWARD[1]

At one time there was a woman who had only one child. She bore only that child; she never bore another. Her child did everything for her.

One day it happened that her child became ill and before long he died.

The woman wept continually for her child, because he was her only child. The child drew water for her; he pounded her rice for her; he did all the work for her. The woman kept weeping for her child; everyone felt sorry for the woman.

Now one evening, the woman lay down and she dreamt that her child was with her in the village. Her son said to her, "Stop weeping. Tomorrow morning go to my grave; sweep it clean; then sit down and sing there." He said, "Just when the sun reaches its zenith, you will see me; I will arise."

When morning came, without telling anyone the woman went to sweep her child's grave. She swept the grave clean; she sat down near the grave to sing; she kept singing.

While the woman was singing, the sun reached its zenith; the woman saw the grave shake. When the grave shook, it divided in half: part of it fell one way; part of it fell the other way. Then these boxes began to come out of the grave, then sheep began to come out of it, then goats came out of it, then cows came out of it, and people carrying bags of money in their hands came out of it. All these creatures and all these things came out of the grave. Finally, the child began to come out of the grave; his head emerged little by little; he came out of the grave completely. When his mother saw him, she was very happy.

Then they began to carry all those things to their house in the town. When they had carried everything to their house, all his relatives came to the house. They all were very happy about the riches which the child had brought. He brought wealth at that time.

When the other people in the town saw all those riches, they began to kill their children in order to gain wealth. But none of their children ever returned; they never gained any riches at that time.

Nyapo yila ye lo wọ na ngi loi i yẹ yakpe. Ye ndoi na yakpe mia i ndeni. I loilọ na haa kẹ i ya ndo yeka leni. Ndoi na mia i yẹ hindei kpẹlẹ wie ngi wẹ.

I wie lo na folo yila ke ndoi na i higbenga. Hu ii guhani ke i hanga.

Nyapoi ji woelo haa ngi loi na jifa yakpe mia leke ndo le i ngi yeya a nja wuli ngi we, a mba hiya ngi we ngengei gbi leke ta yakpe mia i ye pie ngi we. Nyapoi ji i woelo na haa i lo na haa woma numui gbi ngi ma mamao hu.

I hiti lo na gboko yila i lailo i kibao heinga a ngi loi ji ti vulei na hu ti ye na. Ke ngi loi ji ndenga ngi ma ye "Gbe a wola." Ye "Nge wonga lo sina bi li nya gambei na ma" ye "bi li bi mayela fo" ye "bi hei na ba ya ngolei ya" ye "wati na kinei folei i folonga lo leke ngundia" ye "ba nya lolo ngi hije."

Kia ngele woni ta be ii hungeni a numu gbi ke i gbuanga i li ngi loi gambei na gama i lilo a mayela i mayela fo. Ke i heinga kplanga a ngulei na ya. I ngulei na ya haa.

I loni ngulei na ya ma lo ke folei i fonga ngundia ke i tonga ke kambei na ke i gbelinga. Kia i gbelini ke i golenga ndia na fele ji i li a mbewe ji i li a mbewe ke i tonga hakei jisia ta gbua kakakaka kangei jisia ti gbua haa ke mbalangei jisia ti totonga a gbuala ke njengei jisia nasia ti gbua haa ke nikangei jisia totonga a gbuala haa nasia ti hu i lewe. Ke numu vuisia be ti gbuanga ti lenga navo begi jisia ti ti yeya. Ti kpele ti gbua hakei nasia gbi ti gbua. Kia na hakei kpele gboyoni a gbuala ke ta vuli ke i totonga a gbuala i gbua haa ngi wui na a gbua kulo kulo ngi wui a gbua kulo kulo haa ke i fonga ngi lia i loni haa gbua ma lo ke i gbua i gboyo kambei na hu. Kia ngi nje ngi loni ngi gohunengo wa.

Ti toto na a hakei nasia bele la tei hu ti ye pele bu. Ti hakei nasia gbi bele ti ye pele bu. Ta vui i gbua na tia ngi njeni kpele ke ti ya na ti ye pele bu. Ti li na na ti gbi ti gohunengo wa yela. Kpate gboto mia ndopoi na wanila. Tia mia wo ti kpate la gbuani.

Kia nunga wekeisia be tei na hu lo ni ti yelo na a ti lenga wa ko ti li tia be ti li ti wa a kpatei ji. Ke tia ti ndei ta kia le wo na ti hani ii wa i gele hi be numu yilakpe be ii yaa wo yamani wo.

---

1. Recorded by a young man from Pujehun in Freetown on May 13, 1960. I published an English translation of this tale in "Supernatural Beings in Mende Domeisia," <u>Sierra Leone Bulletin of Religion</u> (1961).

TALE 24: A DEAD WOMAN'S SON[1]

When you stand on a hill, you should not speak slander-ously.[2] This termite hill was there.

At one time a boy's mother died; she went to the land of the dead. At night the boy used to dream of his mother. She was buried on top of a hill and a tree with many fruits was planted on her grave. If someone went to the tree and spoke to it, the tree would bend down so that the person could pluck its fruits. If someone said something slanderous about the boy's mother, the tree would not bend down.

Whenever people went to the tree, they spoke slanderously of the boy's mother. They did not know that the tree had been planted on her grave. They wondered why it was that when they came to the tree, it stood straight and tall and that when the boy came to the tree, it would bend to the ground.

There was a song that the boy sang:

"Answer so that I may hear soon;
"Answer, my mother;
"It is Jomo pleading.
"Answer so that I may hear soon;
"Answer, my mother;
"It is Jomo pleading."

The boy would say, "My mother who bore me, I have come to this tree and sung this song. I have not said anything bad. Make the tree bend down so that I may pick some fruit to eat, because my mother is not here to give me food. When I come from work, I do not have any food to eat; when I eat the fruits of this tree, my heart is refreshed. My mother's co-wife does not love me; when I come from work with her children, she does not give me any food to eat. So I come to this tree to pluck fruit to eat. But when others come here, they say slanderous things about my mother."

If a person came and said something abusive to the boy on this hill, the woman's spirit would hear. When the person climbed to the top of the hill, the tree would stand tall.

Then if the boy sang,

"Answer so that I may hear soon;
"Answer, my mother;
"It is Jomo pleading.
"Answer so that I may hear soon;
"Answer, my mother;
"It is Jomo pleading."

If he said, "As I sing this song, make the tree lift this
abusive person into the sky.

"Answer so that I may hear soon;
"Answer, my mother;
"It is Jomo pleading."

As soon as the boy sang the song, the tree would pick up
the abusive person and lift him far into the sky. The person
would scream and scream and scream.

Then the boy would sing again:

"Answer so that I may hear soon;
"Answer, my mother;
"It is Jomo pleading.
"Answer so that I may hear soon;
"Answer, my mother;
"It is Jomo pleading.
"Answer so that I may hear soon;
"Answer, my mother;
"It is Jomo pleading."

So you should not speak slanderously, while you stand on
a hill. That is how this proverb originated at one time.

Baa yẹ loni hiwi mahu baa yẹpẹ a pọlẹ. Hiwi ji lọ loni.

Ndakpei ji ta ngi nje hanga wọ. I ya ndọwu na. Kpindi
wẹngalọ kẹ i kibaonga a ngie. Ngului na nguangọ wa. Numu bi
yaa bi fonga ngului ji ma, ngului ji loni hiwi ji ma, bi yaa
na, bi longaa na ba njẹpẹi ba nde kẹ ngului lọ yeima. Kẹ bẹẹ
ngẹli wili ti waa kẹ ti ndakpẹi ngi nje kẹ ti ngi yẹlinga.

Tẹ "Ngi nda njei hanga wọ ngului ji wọ mu hini wọ hindẹi
ji ta mia wotenga na a hiwi wa i loni hindẹi ji." Kẹ tẹẹ luma
numu i ngului ji i wa i kọle ang tia ii le ti wo a yẹ a ngului
ji ti hini wọ kamba ma lọ ta gulọ na ta ngi nje yẹ li. "Gbẹ
va lọ mua mu wanga ngului gama kẹ ngului ji lẹnga polong kẹ
tia ti wanga lọ na kẹ ngului ji yeinga ndọma gbẹe ti na wiema
na?" Njẹpẹi na mia ta nde.

Kẹ ngole lọ na a kpia ta mia a nde:

"Ndumabe ngi mẹni wọi;
"Ndumabe nya nje;
"Jọmọ-e.
"Ndumabe ngi mẹni wọi;
"Ndumabe nya nje;
"Jọmọ-e.

"Ndumabe ngi mẹni wọi;
"Ndumabe nya nje;
"Jọmọ-e."

Yẹ "Nya nje" yẹ "bia lọ bi nya leni. Kia ngului ji ngi
wanga ngi ngolei ji yanga. Nya ngii njia gbi leni ngi ngolei
ji yanga" yẹ "ngului ji yei ngi nguluwẹi ji gọi ngi mẹ kpe nya
nje ii na a nya gọ a mẹhẹ ngi gbiaa ngengemẹi ngi waa ngẹẹ
mẹhẹi jọ mẹi va nga nguluwẹi ji lọ mẹ nya lii i lẹli nya njei
ji wo ta ngi mba-nyahẹi ti sọẹ ji hu wọ ta ii loni a nge mua
ngi lenga mu hijenga ngengemẹi mu wa ngẹẹ mẹhẹ wa jọ ngaa mẹ
ẹẹ nya gọ a mẹhẹ ngaa mẹ nya go a ve ngului ji lọ nga wa ngi
mẹ ngului ji lọ ngi waa nga taa ngọe ngi mẹ kẹ tia ti waa ta
nya nje yẹlilọ kakakaka."

Numu bi waa bi njẹpẹ lenga lọ njẹpẹ lọ na bi ndenga lọ
hiwi ji ma mamẹi a humẹni lọ ngi yafẹi a humẹni lọ gbi i kpọyọ
ẹẹ lalima. Kia leke ba lẹ hiwi ma leke kẹ i lẹnga a bie polong
a lẹ lo a bie na. Kia tia ti yaa kẹ ti lẹnga hiwi mahu ti
lẹnga lọ hiwi mahu.

Kẹ i ngole gbianga na:

"Ndumabe ngi mẹni wọi;
"Ndumabe nya nje;
"Jọmọ-e.
"Ndumabe ngi mẹni wọi;
"Ndumabe nya nje;
"Jọmọ-e.
"Ndumabe ngi mẹni wọi;
"Ndumabe nya nje;
"Jọmọ-e."

Yẹ "Ngului ji kia ngi ngolei gbia ma" yẹ "li a ngie polong
ngeleya" yẹ "li a ngie."

"Ndumabe ngi mẹni wọi;
"Ndumabe nya nje;
"Jọmọ-e."

Kia ti ngolei na gbianga lọ kẹ ta leke lẹma a tie polong
a lẹlọ a bie polong ngeleya bẹ gu ba hitẹ gbi yelei na mia i
yẹ kula na a kula a kula a kula a kula a kula a kula a yelei
na gula.

Kẹ i ngolei gbianga gbọma,

"Ndumabe ngi mẹni wọi;
"Ndumabe nya nje;
"Jọmọ-ẹ.
"Ndumabe ngi mẹni wọi;
"Ndumabe nya nje;

"Jǫmǫ-e.
"Ndumabe ngi mɛni wǫi;
"Ndumabe nya nje;
"Jǫmǫ-e."

Bɛɛ yɛ loni hiwi mahu baa njɛpɛ a pǫlɛ. Salei na i hijeni wǫ na lǫma.

---

1. This proverb tale was recorded by a man from Mattru Jong in Freetown on September 6, 1960.
2. "To speak slanderously" (yɛpɛ a pǫlɛ) means literally "to speak with mud."

TALE 25: BUSHYAM'S TRANSFORMATION[1]

At one time there was a woman who was very wealthy but barren.[2] She wanted a child very much; but she did not have one.

Whenever she went walking on a road, she would weep, "I am barren; I do not have a child."

One time she was weeping as she was walking on a road. She was weeping because she did not have a child; if she died without a child, who would look after her money?

Then the woman heard a voice. The voice asked, "Who is weeping?"

The woman turned; she looked, but she did not see anyone. She asked, "Who said that?"

Then the bushyam standing in the bush said to her, "It is I; I am the bushyam." It said, "It is I who spoke. You earth people do not protect others; if you would protect someone, I would turn into your child. I, the bushyam, am speaking."

"Oh," said the woman, "I will protect you."

The bushyam said, "If you really could sleep somewhere and then in the morning not tell the secret to anyone! But whatever enters your mouth, you tell! Otherwise, I would turn into your child."

"Oh," said the woman to the bushyam, "I would not tell your secrets in the town."

Then the bushyam said, "Turn away."

When the woman turned her back, the bushyam turned into a very handsome boy. The bushyam turned into a very handsome boy and stepped onto the road.

The boy repeated the rule to the woman; he said, "This is my rule: if you and I go into town, you must not tell my secret to anyone. If anyone asks how you got me, you say, 'This is the only son whom I have ever borne. At one time I sent this child to my family in my own town, because people would not put their eyes on him there. Today I went for him; now he and I have come together.'"

When they went into the town, the woman's friends said, "Friend, where did you find your very handsome child?"

The woman did as the bushyam had instructed; she did not reveal anything about him. As soon as her friends asked, she said, "My child whom I brought was in our town; today I went there for him, he and I have come together."

But when she said this to one of her friends, he kept asking questions; he pressed her to explain.

He kept pressing her for an explanation until she said, "Recently a bushyam turned into a living person; it is this child. He said that I should not explain his origin in the town. If anyone asked me about him, I should just say, 'It is my child!' I should say that I bore him, that he was in our town, that I went for him today and brought him here. But the rule that the bushyam made is if I explain about him in the town, he will return and I will continue to be barren."

When the woman told the man this, he began to say to his friends, "Of course, what the woman was saying recently was completely untrue. Really a bushyam has changed into the child."

Then the woman's story began to scatter.

When the woman's child was with his companions, little children whose mouths cannot stay shut, his companions said to him, "Didn't you say that you are a living person? But really you are a bushyam that was recently brought to the town."

As soon as the boy heard that, he knew that his mother had explained his origin. Immediately he went away from them looking for a place to hide. After he had hidden from them, he returned to the bush and stayed there.

The woman returned to her barren state; she did not have any children.

Lọwọ lẹnga lengọ woma wọ nyapo yila yẹ lọ na. Ye nyapoi ji ngi gbatẹngọ wa kẹ ngi gohu bengọ yela. Ngi longọ wa a ndo hinda kẹ ndo gbi ii yẹ ngi yeya.

I pele gbi wo i hounga i ya lima a ya a ngọlẹi ji wie pelei ji ma yẹ "Ngi gbemangọi ndo gbii ngi yeya."

Kpema yila i yẹlọ a ngọi ji wie pelei ji ma a ngọi ji wie jifa ta yakpe ndo ii ngi yeya i jiama. Tao in na bẹ kuna na le yọ ngi navoi jisia taa lo ngi yeya.

Kẹ i njẹpẹ woi ji mẹninga kẹ i njẹpẹi woi ji ngi mọlia yẹ "Yema i ngọi na wiema?"

Ta bẹ i wote i na gbe ii numu lọi kẹ i mọlia yẹ "Yọ njiẹi na leni?"

Kẹ ngawui ji i loi ndọgbọi hu kẹ i ndea ngi ma yẹ "Nya mia, nya nya ngawu"; yẹ "nya mia ngi njẹpẹi na leni" yẹ "ji wu lakala wẹ numu bawo a yẹ wa" yẹ "bẹ numu bawoma. Kia bi ngọlẹi na wiema" yẹ "nga wotelọ a bi lo. Ngawu mia njẹpẹi ji lema-o"

"Oh," yẹ "nga bi bawolọ."

Yẹ "Ina vuli wa gulọ wu yii hinda nge gbi i wo wẹ njẹpẹ gbi njẹpẹ gbi ii lele a yẹ gbuama wu la wa nde" yẹ "nga wotelọ a bi lo."

"Kpo-o" yẹ "ngẹẹ bi hinda hungẹ tẹi hu."

Nyapoi mia ji lema ngawu ma. Kẹ i ndea yẹ "Wote."

Kẹ nyapoi wotea, ngawui na i wote a hindolo nyande nyande kẹ i gbua.

I yama i sawẹi gẹ a ngie yẹ "Nya jawẹi yẹni a ji hi ji mua bie mu lima tẹi hu, baa li ba nya hinda hungẹ a numu gbi. Numu gbi bi mọlia bi ye hijeni a ngie bi bi nde ngi ma bẹ 'Nya loi ji yakpe mia wọ gba ngi hijia ngi majọa. Ye ndopoi ji ngi njoyonga wọ nya bonda gama nya yetahu jifa nunga ta li yama lo wẹi ngi ma taa haa ngi ya na ta mu wa.'"

Kia ti li tẹi hu kẹ ngi mbanga ngi ndiamọisia ti tọtonga ngi mọlila "Nyande, bi lo nyande nyande wa ji bi ye gbua la?"

Ta bẹ kia lọ ngawui ma ndei la ngi ma i ta wie ii ngi yẹpẹ gbi hungẹi. Kia le ti ngi mọlia a ndelọ yẹ "Nya loi ji

ngi gbuala i mu yetahu lo gẹ taa haa ngi ya ngi wama ma taa
mu wa."

Kẹ kia i ji leni ngi ndiamọ yila ma kẹ i tọtoa na a ngi
mọli la i tọtoa ngi mọlila i humbu a hindẹi ji hugẹ.

Kia na i kpọndẹi ngi ma haa kẹ ta bẹ i ndea yẹ "Ngawu
mia gẹ i wotea a numu vu ta lọ a ji," yẹ "numu ẹẹ ngi hinda
hugẹ ta hu ti nya mọlia le ngi nde le ngẹ 'nya loi mia' ngẹ
'ngi ndea lọ wọ i mu yetahu lọ famia haa ngi ya na ta mu wa,'
kẹ sawẹi wọ ngawui feingọi i ngi hinda hugẹna wọ le ta hu i
yamama kẹ i loa a ngi gbemẹi."

Kenẹi ji bẹ kẹ njẹpẹi ji i hugẹni a ngie kẹ i tọtonga
hugẹ la a ngi ndiamọisia, "Ingẹ nyapoi na njẹpẹi na gẹ i
ndema wu ma tọnya yẹpẹ yaa na. Ngawu mia gẹ i wotea a numu."

Kẹ ngi lọwẹ tọtoa a vaya la.

Kia le wọ ndopoi ji loi lema ta ngi mbaangẹi jisia. Ndopo
mumuisia tia ti la ẹẹ hei kẹ ngi mbaangẹisia ti ndea ngi ma tẹ
"Bia bi yẹ ma gẹ bẹ numu vu lọ a bie mẹma ngawu lọ gẹ a bie ti
wa gẹ a bie bi tẹi ji hu?"

Kia le ta bẹ i na humẹi wọ i kọlọ kẹ ngi nje mia ngi hinda
hugẹa. I yẹ na le a le ta tia li ta le a le a pele gọli lọwu
va ti ma. Kia wọ i lọwui ti ma i yamai lọ wọ fọ i li i hei
ngi lọgbọi na hu kẹ i hei wienga na.

Nyapoi na i lo wọ fọ hi ngi lẹi na i pie wọ i yama kpe
ma yẹ i na hu ndo gbi ii yaa yẹ ngi yeya.

---

1. Recorded by young man from Pujehun in Freetown on February
16, 1960. Versions of this tale have appeared at least thrice
already: Migeod (1908) published a Mẹnde text and English
translation; Innes (1965) presented a summary of the tale; I
published an English translation ("Supernatural," /1961/).
2. Barren, lit., stomach was dry (ngi gohu bengọ yẹ la).

TALE 26: A YOUNG WIFE'S DISGRACE[1]

At one time there was a girl who was growing up. Every
day her mother said to her, "Child, you are a woman; stay in
the house and learn the work that I do. I will teach you how
to do a woman's work."

The woman always said this to the girl. But as soon as
morning came, the girl would leave the house and spend the day

wandering about; she never came into the house. In the evening she would return just as her mother was putting her spoon into the rice to serve it.

Her mother would say to her, "Child, you are a woman. Why are you behaving like this? In the morning when I am doing a woman's work and I tell you to come to watch me, you refuse to stay; you wander about; people say that you lead a useless life. One day you will reach that riverside."

The girl continued to behave in the same way. She did not listen to her mother's advice. Then the girl became mature and a man fell in love with her. When she came out of Sande, she was given to her husband.

When she went with her husband, he called many people, including his good friends, to come. He called them to come to meet his wife. He brought a lot of food; he killed an animal. He told his wife that she should cook so that the people could eat.

Of course, when the girl's mother used to tell her to come to watch her cook, the girl never came. When the girl came to her husband, she did not know how to sweep a house; she did not know how to do any work.

As soon as the girl's husband gave her the animal, she cut it up; she put it in the pot without salt; she did not sprinkle pepper on it; she did not even put tomatoes into the pot; she just put the pot on the fire. Throughout the day the tasteless animal was cooking. In the afternoon she set the pot of rice on the fire; she cooked the rice; she took it off the fire; she took it to her husband.

The girl said, "Father, I have brought the food."

Then the man called all his good friends to eat the food. As soon as one person brought a spoonful of rice to his mouth, he said, "Friend, I have eaten enough." Then another took the spoon, he put just one spoonful of rice into his mouth. Then everyone left.

When the girl's husband tasted the rice, he could not eat it. He called the girl; he said, "How did you learn to cook food? What have you learned to cook? This food is tasteless!"

Then the man took her to the cooking place. He said, "When you are cooking food, slant the cover on the pot; put in enough salt and oil to make the food sweet."

Because the girl had never stayed in the house, she was ignorant about a woman's work.

Then the man said, "I am going to tell your family what you have done to me."

The man took the food and sent it to her family.

He said, "Go home. Let them teach you how to cook food, how to make a bed, and how to do all the housework that a woman does."

When the girl went to her mother, all her relatives were ashamed.

Her mother said to her, "You see; I used to tell you to watch me work, you would not listen; you said that I was scolding you. But now you have reached the riverside." Her mother wept before she began to show the girl how to do household chores. After the girl had learned those tasks, she returned to her husband's house.

That is why it is appropriate that when a girl is at home, she should learn how to do household chores from her family.

Nyahalo yila gbe wọ i hiye. Nyahaloi ji fo gbi va ngi nje ye wọ a nde ngi ma yẹ "Ndopoi ye nyaha lọ a bie ba hei pẹlẹ la bi ga a ngenge nasia nga pie nyaa nga bi ga."

Kpema gbi va nyapoi ji i yẹ hi a nde ngi ma kẹ ndopoi ji ji le wọ ngele woma i gbua pẹlẹi na bu i ya a luva lema kpeing ii wa pẹlẹi na bu kẹ kpọkọi i wa a male. Kine ngi nje i mitẹi la mbẹi ma i kọikọi va.

Kẹ ngi nje lọ ndema ngi ma "Ndopoi, bia nyaha a bie. Bia bi ji wiema? Nge wua ngenge jisia hi nyaha yenge le nga ye piema ngẹ bi wa bi na lọ bẹ luma ba ye na ba le tẹ lenga ba lewe a batiya" yẹ "folo yila ba folọ njẹi na la bia bẹ."

Ndopoi ji i loi ji wiema haa...ii nyapoi ji layẹi mẹni kẹ i longa hu kẹ i gbela kẹ hindo longa a ngie. Jina ti ngi gbuani kẹ ti ngi venga ngi hini wẹ ji hu na.

Kia ti li ngi hini ji nunga gboto wa ngi ma loma yakpenga-o nasia ta tie ti hinda yekpe hu i ti lolinga yẹ "Ti wa ta ngi nyahẹi na ti lọ." I mẹhẹi gboto lema i hua wa yẹ "Ngi nyahẹi na i ngili tia nungẹi nasia ti me" yẹ "kumẹi na hu."

Ingẹ nyapoi ji ta ngi nje ya wọ ndema ngi ma yẹ "I wa i mẹhẹi yilimalọ" ii pie. I wani ii bẹ a ka yela la pẹlẹ bu ngenge gbi le ii bẹla.

I li le kenẹi ji huẹi ji i fe ngi wẹ i tewelọ le i pu fẹi ji hu ii kpalo wiema ii pujẹ vaifaima ii tamatisi bẹ ii pui ma kẹ i heinga. Huẹi na yẹ tawẹi na i luva yilima kpeing kpọkọvuli kine kẹ i mba vẹ heinga i mbẹi ji yili kẹ i kpuanga i hugbatẹ kẹ i ya la.

Yẹ "Kẹkẹ, ngi wa a mẹhẹi."

Kenẹi na ngi malomẹi yekpe nasia gbi i ti lolinga na mẹhẹi na go bu. Numui na a mitẹi wumbulọ le i mbẹi na wa le la yẹ "Nyande, i gua na"; i mitẹi na wumbu i mbẹi na ma la kẹ ti kpẹlẹ ti vayama.

Kia ngi hini vuli i wani i mbẹi na gọmi ii guni a mẹ. I ngi loli i ngi mọli "Mẹhẹi ye kani?" Yẹ "Gbọ bi ngilini?" Yẹ "Mẹhẹi ji tawẹi ye ji."

Kẹ na ta ndopoi ta i wẹi lo le wọ la yẹ "Bi ya mẹhẹi ji yilima bẹ kọbẹi lekpenga le, kpolẹi i hou, ngulẹi i hou, mẹhẹi na gbi le a mẹhẹi nẹ" yẹ "Kẹ i wunga."

Jifa ii hei wọ pẹlẹ bu i houngọ.

Kẹ kenẹi bẹ ndenga yẹ "Ji bi pieni a nge ngi hugẹ ma a bi bonda, ti houngọ."

Ta bẹ mẹhẹi na i mbumbu i njoyo ngi bondanga ma.

Yẹ "Li, ti li ti bi ga a mẹhẹ yila, kpọku hou la, kẹ pẹlẹ bu yengei na gbi le na nyaha a pie."

Ndopoi na kia wọ i li ngi nje gama ngi njeni gbi ti wufenga wọ yela ta vuli.

Kẹ ngi nje ndenga ngi ma yẹ "Bi tọnga ngi ya wọ ndema bi ma bẹ humẹni bẹ nya yiama bi ma kẹ bia vuli bi fonga na" yẹ "njẹi lai." Ngi nje i wọ i ya tọto a gẹnga la ngenge nasia haa pẹlẹ bu yenge nasia pẹing i yama wọ hini wẹlẹi na hu.

Na va mia mahoungọ numu bi ya kuhun kaka yẹ nyalo bi lapi bi ga pẹlẹ bu yenge nasia bi bonda ma.

---

1. Recorded by young man from Pujehun on May 30, 1960 in Freetown.

TALE 27: A DISOBEDIENT CHILD[1]

If someone follows you everywhere, it is not good.

At one time there was a woman whose child followed her a lot. Everywhere the woman went, her child would follow after her. She used to beat him for always following her until she got tired.

Once the woman went to wash clothes at a place where a spirit used to drink water. At this place there was a large and very beautiful rock. But if a person sat on the rock, his buttocks would stick to it; he would not be able to get up until the spirit came and pulled him off.

Once the woman gathered all the dirty clothes together; she went to wash them. When she went, she left her child in the town. She distracted his attention so that he would not follow her. As soon as the woman left, the child followed after her; she did not know that he was following her. The child continued to follow her until she reached the edge of the river. Then she turned and saw him standing behind her.

"Oh, child, today I left you in the town! I told you not to come and now you have come. All right, stand here; we will wash the clothes and then we will go; do not sit down."

The child stood there for some time. He got tired of standing; he sat down on the rock. As soon as he sat down on the rock, his buttocks stuck to the rock; he was unable to get up. When the woman had washed the clothes, she returned to the town. She told the child's father what had happened.

What did they do?

The child's parents came and built a house over him. In the morning his mother cooked food and brought it; she knocked on the door, the child opened it; he ate the food. They did this for the child until the time for the spirit to drink arrived; the spirit came.

When the spirit came, he saw the house on the rock; the spirit was confused; he did not know what to do. The spirit had not built the house there; that was his drinking place; he had not left the house there, but when he came, he found the house there. Then the spirit hid near the house in order to discover what was in the house or why the house was there.

The spirit sat there for a day. Then he saw a woman coming with some food; she knocked on the door; her son opened it; she brought the food; he ate the food. As soon as the woman came out of the house, the spirit chased her. He ran after the woman; he was unable to catch her. When the woman got to the town, she fell on the ground; people had to fan her face before she could get her breath.

As soon as the spirit opened the child's house, he grabbed the child. He ripped the child in half: he swallowed one part; he swallowed the other part.

The woman never returned to that place. When she went to the town, she said, "The spirit has eaten our child."

No one went to that place. Everyone was afraid of the spirit. The spirit sat there for a long time; he did not see any other person; he went away.

That is why it is bad to follow someone everywhere. That child used to follow his mother everywhere until the spirit ate him.

Hani ngakpẹ lọ hinda ma ii nẹnẹ.

Nyapo yila gbe wọ i hiyeni ngi loi ji a ngakpẹi ji wie wa. Hinda gbi le wọ i ya lima na ngi loi ji a hitẹlọngi woma a ngakpẹi ji lọ wie. Ti ngi lewe kulo hindẹi na va ti gbaha.

Kẹ wati yila ma hindẹi lọ wọ na ta kulẹi wua na ye hindẹi ji hani wai ya gboime mia. Hani wai ji a njẹi ji gboi wọ hindẹi ji foma ye fala wa ji hu a li polong na nyandengọ wa kẹ numu ẹẹ hei na bi heinga le na bi wotoi na ndọlẹi hou lọ ẹẹ ya kunafọ gbua na kẹ leke hani wai na i wa kuna ta i bi gbua na.

Wati yila nyapoi ji i kula nọhuẹisia lelọma kpẹlẹ i li i ti wa. I ye lima kẹ ngi loi ji longa tẹi ji hu. I ngi ya mbamba yẹ a hitẹ wẹ ngi woma. Kia le i li i ye lima ndopoi ji a to ngi woma ii hungọ i ye lima a to ngi ma a li a to ngi ma a li a to ngi ma a li a to ngi ma ti lonima kẹ i fonga njẹi ji la. Kia le i woteni kẹ i ngi lọnga loni ngi woma.

"Kuo, ndopoi ji, bia ha ngi bi longa tẹi ji hu ngẹ 'baa wa' bia bi wa" yẹ "kẹ" i ndenga yẹ "kulungọi ya na a lo mu kulẹi wua mu li kẹ baa hei yọ."

Kẹ ndopoi ji longa. Kia le i loi seẹ toi ji gboi le ngi la a mẹ nyẹvu kẹ i heinga fawẹi ji ma. Ngi heingọ fawẹi ji ma-o a mẹ naati kẹ ngi wotoi na i fawẹi na hounga ẹẹ ya gu a gbua na kẹ nyapoi ji kulẹi ji wuanga i kpọyọ i yama tẹi ji hu kẹ i yama i hugẹ a ngi kẹkẹ.

Gbọ ti pie?

Ti wani lọ ti pẹlẹ wa lo ngi mahu i pẹlẹi ji bu. Ngele wonga wọ ngi nje mẹhẹi ji yilinga i wa la i pẹlẹi ji la lewe kẹ i ndawoa i mẹhẹi ji mẹ. Ti loi ji lọ wiema haa kẹ hani wai ya gboue gbe ji hitinga kẹ i wa.

Kia i wani i pẹlẹi ji lọni loi fawẹi ji ma ngi wuhu baa lọwa ii ya kọ gbọ a pie ji ii pẹlẹ loni wọ na tao ngi ya gboimei mia ii pẹlẹi loni wọ na i wa na i pẹlẹ malenga na. Kẹ i lọwunga pẹlẹi ji gbla kọ i kọ gbọ pẹlẹi ji bu ọ gbọ pẹlẹi ji loni hindẹi ji piema.

I loni hei lọ a folo yila kẹ i nyapoi ji lọnga i wa a
mẹhẹi ji kẹ i pẹlẹi ji la lewengá kẹ ngi loi ji hijenga kẹ
i pẹlẹi ji la wua i wa mẹhẹi ji i mẹ. Kia le i mẹhẹi ji me
le hani wai ji nyapoi ji gbuani le kẹ hani wai ji hitẹnga
ngi woma i nyapoi ji gbẹ haa ii guni ngi ma. Kẹ nyapoi ta
ya tẹi hu i li i gula ya gba ti ngi ya fẹ haa ndẹvu i ya wa
ngi hu.

Kia le wọ i pẹlẹi na lawoi ndopoi na ma i hou i ti ndia
i ji gbọi i ji gbọi.

Nyapoi ta i ya wọ yame hindẹi ji i lilọ na le i nde tẹ
hu yẹ "Hani wai i mu loi mẹa."

Numu gbi ii ya wani na. Tia bẹ ti luwama hani wai na.
Hani wai i hei na kẹ ii ya numu yeka lọni kẹ i gbua i li.

Na va mia ngakpẹ lọ hinda ma ii nẹnẹ ndopoi na ngakpẹi
na wie wọ haa hani wai lọ ngi mbe mẹni.

---

1. Recorded by young man from Pujehun in Freetown on May 13,
1960.

TALE 28: A COWARD AND HIS SON[1]

At one time there was a man. When a very fierce war came
to his country, the man and his son went to hide in the bush.
They walked for a long time in the bush until they unexpectedly
came to some recently farmed land.

As soon as they stepped into the farm, they were caught.
"Man," said their captors.

He said, "Yes."

They said, "If you speak the truth, we shall let you go."

He said, "How shall I speak the truth?"

They said, "Which of you two shall we seize and let his
companion go free?"

The man said, "Oh, my child that I begat; he is quite
old."

"Oh," they said, "you have not spoken the truth. Now
see this sluggish pond."

He said, "Yes."

They said, "You have a big beard; soak up all the water with it."

When the man was bending over, he said, "When something becomes difficult, it is difficult; when something becomes difficult, it is difficult." The man kept soaking up the water with his beard.

When he had soaked up the water completely, he and his son were set free. They went away.

Kena yila mia wọ kẹ kọi ji gula ngi lọlọi ji hu kẹlẹma ii ma. Kẹ ta ngi loi ji kẹ ti lọwua ti loni lima ndọgbọ wa ti loni lima haa ndọgbọ hu mẹma njọpọi ji ti kakpa ma na mia kine ti ya na. Ti li lọ wọ leke a mẹi kungau kẹ ti nyimia kpalamẹi.

A mẹi kpa kẹ ti ti houa tẹ "Kenẹi."

Yẹ "A."

Tẹ "Tọnya yia yẹpẹ le mu gbei bi ma."

Yẹ "Nga ya tọnya yẹpẹ le?"

Te "Wuvenguẹi ji numui na le mu gbama ngi mba ma mu ta wama?"

Yẹ "Kuo" yẹ "ndopoi ji bẹ" yẹ "nya ngi ndeni" yẹ "kẹ ngovangọ-o"

"Kua" tẹ "bi ya tọnya yia leni. A na" tẹ "bonga wa gbe heini njẹi ji."

Yẹ "Hn."

"Bi gbẹlẹi ji kpontongọi ji ba hube a kpẹlẹ lọ njẹi na."

Na wọ a mahu wẹlẹ a nde yẹ "Hinda gbọwunga i gbọwua hinda gbọwua i gbọwua." I loi wọ njẹi na bema a ngi gbẹlẹi na.

I kpọyọ seng ti ya gbe wọ ngi ma ta ngi loi; ti li.

---

1. Recorded by man from Bo in Freetown on January 20, 1960.

TALE 29: A HUNTER AND HIS SON[1]

My father, at one time there was a hunter who had a son. The man used to get up early all the time.

One day the hunter and his son got up early to go hunting. As they were preparing to leave, the moon came up; the hunter thought that morning was coming. He took his gun and loaded it in the house. The hunter and his son started on their way. When they went, the boy forgot to take fire with him.

When they came to an old farm, the hunter saw a bushcow and a deer.[2] He killed them. When the hunter killed the deer, he put it on his shoulder and carried it away. Just as they reached the edge of the forest, the moon went down; it was dark.

"Oh," said the hunter, "that was the moon; morning has not come yet." He said, "Child, we will sit here until it begins to get light then we will go into the thicket."

While they were sitting there, the man wanted to smoke his pipe. He asked his son for fire.

The boy said, "Oh, I did not bring any fire today."

The man exclaimed, "That's good! There isn't any fire!"

The man did not know that a spirit was sleeping nearby at the base of a hill.[3] The spirit's head was bald and it shone. If you saw his head, you would see it shining brightly.

The hunter turned and saw the spirit's head shining, he thought it was fire. The man thought that the little marks around the spirit's head were shining coals.

"Oh," said the hunter, "child, look there's a fire yonder. The women must have left it where they were making palm wine. Go and bring some fire to put in my pipe."

Then the boy took his loading rod and loaded his gun. When the boy went, he hit the spirit's head right in the center of his bald spot with his iron rod.

The spirit said, "What?"

"Oh," said the boy, "Father said that you should come."

The boy and the spirit walked to the hunter.

The spirit said, "Did you ask for me?"

The hunter said, "What? Oh," he said, "I killed a bush-goat and this deer today. I told the child to ask you to come so that I could give you the deer."

They gave the deer to the spirit.

Then the man and his son returned to their town. The man beat the child; he said that the child had behaved stupidly.

So that is what the hunter said at that time, but I say that the child's wisdom was greater than the man's.

Nya kekę, kpandęwilimǫ yila mia wǫ ta ngi loi ji. Ndakpaloi ji a humbu kpele gbi, a humbu kpele gbi.

Kpandęwilimęi ji a humbu lǫ yila ma kę ta ngi loi ji. I ndenga ye "Ti li kpandęwilimęi ji." Ti loilǫ leke seę, kę ngawui ji wanga ta ngilima yę tǫ a yę ngele mia wonga kę i kpandęi ji wumbunga kę i sǫsǫnga pęlęi bu i kpǫyǫ chęng kę ta ngi loi ji ti pelei hounga. Ngi loi yę limalǫ ii lini a ngǫmbui kę i loni kenęi ii hugǫ.

Kia wǫ ti lini ti gbiailǫ leke njǫpǫ wovęi ji hu kę i tęwęi ji lǫnga ndǫpęi ji kę i panga. Kia i ndǫpęi ji wani kę i ndanga gbaki ma kę i ya la. Kia wǫ ti ngolęi ya houni leke kę ngawui ji gulanga hu gbindinga.

"Kua" yę "ngawui ji yę ngele ii yaa lę haaa woni-e" yę "na nyandengǫ" yę "ndopoi" yę "mu hei mbei yę hu yalǫwǫi woma" yę "mu li kului hu."

Ti lǫnga heinilǫ kę tavę gbǫe mani kenęi ji lǫnga. Yę ngi loi i ngǫmbu ve ngi wę.

"Kuo" ngi loi yę "ngii wani ha a ngǫmbu."

Kę ta be ndenga na yę "Na nyandengǫ" yę "kpele ngǫmbu gbi na."

A yę ma i wotenga ngafęi ji lani miando męma ngafęi a yi hindęi na lǫ ngiyei na bu. Ngafęi ji yęlęi ngi wu hu, hu a volo bi tǫngalǫ hu a vo kana kana kana.

Yęlęi ji hu vo ngi lǫ i tǫnga ta a tǫ a ngǫmbu yatęngǫ mia. Ngi wui ye tewǫi jisia ti hei hu ta yę tǫa a teka mia kia a vola.

"Kuo" yę "ndopoi, ngǫmbui gbe mia. Nyahanga ti ndonga ha wahi hu. Li bi wa la ngi pu tavęi hu."

Kẹ ndopoi kọlu valẹi ji wumbunga ta kpandẹi jọsọla. Kia wọ i lini hani waẹ wui ye yẹlẹi na hu vulii ndia ndiẹi na nga mẹni na i kọlu valẹi ji jọsọnga na.

Hani waẹ yẹ "E."

"Kuo" yẹ "kẹkẹ yẹ bi wa."

Ta ta ti jianga ti wanga ti fonga kenẹi ma.

Yẹ "Bia lọ bi nya mọlini?"

Yẹ "A," yẹ "gbee? Kuo," yẹ "tẹwẹ kẹ ndọpẹi ji mia ha ngi panga" yẹ "ta mia ngi bi mọlinga ngẹ ndopoi i bi mọli ngi fe bi wẹ."

Kẹ ti ndọpẹi ji venga hani waẹ wẹ.

Kẹ ta ngi loi ji ti yamanaga ti yamanga ti ye tẹi hu. Kẹ ta lọ ndopoi lewe ma yẹ "Ndopoi lọ kpowa wieni."

Hi na lọ wọ ngi ndeni ngẹ: Ndopoi nẹmahu leweni kenẹi ma.

---

1. Recorded by man from Bo in Freetown on January 12, 1960.
2. See note to Tale 3. The deer (ndopa) also figures in Tale 82.
3. In this tale, the spirit is called ngafa and hani wa interchangeably.

TALE 30: SPIDER AND HIS CHILDREN[1]

How Spider's waist became very slender at one time.

We all know that Spider is a very greedy creature. Once four feasts were being held in four nearby towns. Spider wanted to go to all four feasts to eat the different food. He did not know that all four feasts would take place at the same time.

Spider made an arrangement with his children. He brought a big rope that was very long. He told his children that each of them should go to a different town with a piece of the rope; /the other end of the rope would be tied around his waist/.

He said to the children, "When the people start to make their sacrifice and to divide the rice there, you pull on the rope. Then I will know that the time for the feast has come in that town; I will go there and eat their rice. When I have finished eating, perhaps the time for feasting will have come in another town and the child there will pull on the rope."

Spider's children agreed to his plan.

Now what happened was that the time for food sharing in all the towns occurred at the same time. Spider's children began to pull on the rope; they pulled very hard; they did not slacken the rope. Spider went to his children; he told them to slacken the rope, but they refused to do so. The children continued to pull on the rope. Not one grain of any of the four feasts reached Spider's mouth; Spider did not eat any of the food.

That was how the rope burned Spider's waist and his waist became very slender at one time.

Kasilo gbọ wọ pieni Kasilo lia yẹ lengi lengi.

Mu kpẹlẹ mu kọlọ kẹ Kasilo ta fuhani mia a ngie ngi mẹhẹ hindango wa. Wati yila lengọ woma wọ mẹhẹ gomẹ nani i yẹ lo gbla gbla tanga hu. Komẹi ji naningọ kpẹlẹ Kasilo longọ i li na kọ i li i ye mẹhẹi jisia mẹ.

Kẹ i hugbatẹa ta ngi lenga yẹ "Komẹi ji sina," kẹ ii yẹ hungọ kẹ komẹi ji kpẹlẹ i wiema a lenga kẹ i hugbatẹa kẹ i ndea ngi lenga ma i li i wa a ngeya wa ngeyẹi na ngọlọngọ wa. Kẹ i ndea ngi lenga ma i ti longa nani ya ti kpẹlẹ ti li ti lo na.

Yẹ "Wati wẹle nasia ti tọtonga ti nda jaa na gbua va mbẹi na golẹkọlẹ va," yẹ "numui ji" yẹ "bia bi nya lala kẹ ngi kọnga kẹ tia ti nda wati hitea. Nga li lọ na ngi li ngi ye mbẹi na mẹ. Wati na hu na mu ya kpọyọma kẹ nga nasia bẹ ti nda wati hitea" yẹ "bia bẹ bi nya lala."

I ji lọ lei kẹ ndopoisia kpẹlẹ ti luma.

Hindei ji i ngi wielọ na kẹ mẹhẹi jisia kpẹlẹ kọlẹ gbe ji i hitea a lenga kẹ ti tọtonga na a ngi lala ti kpẹlẹ ta ngi lala hugbọwungọ. Numu gbi i ya na a ngeyẹi kulọ bẹ yọkọ ngi ma. I ya na i nda jisia ma kọ ti ngeyẹi ji yọkọ i li mbeindo tẹ luma jia bẹ tẹ luma ta ngeyẹi ji yọkọ. Kia lọ i ndei la yẹ ti ngi lala ti toi haa ngi lalama. Mẹhẹi na ye ngi la bẹ ti kpẹlẹ hugbatẹ ye ngila bẹ i hitẹi hu. A mẹhẹi na kpẹlẹ i baalọ hu.

Na mia wọ i wieni. Kia bẹ hu na ngi lia na ngeyẹi na na i yẹ ngi mọ ngi lia ta wọ pieni Kasilo ngi lia i yẹ lengi lengi.

1. Recorded by young man from Pujehun in Freetown on February 12, 1960. A summary of a version of this tale appears in Innes (1965).

TALE 31: MASE AND HER MOTHER'S CO-WIFE[1]

At one time there was a man who married two women. The man loved one of these women very much. Each of the women bore a child. While one of the children was still creeping, her mother died.

When the woman died, her family said, "Look, this child is too small to remain with her mother /i.e., her mother's co-wife/. We want to take her to bring her up."

Then the man said, "If you do this to me, you will make me weep. Leave the child with me, because I cannot see her dead mother."

So they left the child.

The time for scarifying the child came.

When the scarification time came, the child went to her father's other wife. She said, "Mother, put this mark on me too."

The woman had put the scarification mark on all her children, but she said, "I will not put this mark on you. Your conduct is such that I cannot put it on you."

The child wept all day.

The next morning they went to the farmhouse. The child took a pail and went for water. As she walked, she wept. Then she saw her mother's spirit in a cave; her mother's spirit had changed into a snake.

Her mother's spirit said, "Mase."

The child said, "Yes."

She said, "Why are you weeping?"

The child said, "Mother, the time for scarification came recently. I asked mother to scarify me, but she refused. That is why I am crying."

The woman's spirit said, "Then come here. Stop weeping."

The child approached.

She said, "Close your eyes."

The child closed her eyes and the woman's spirit put the marks on the child's belly.

She said, "Turn around."

The child turned around and put the mark on her back.[2]

She said, "Until the fourth day, please do not untie your cloth."

The child said, "Yes, Mother."

The child returned.

On the third day her mother's co-wife said, "What is wrong with you, child, that no one sees your nakedness?"

The child said, "Mother, nothing is wrong; I have a cold."

The woman said, "Mase, I shall see your body today."

The woman took the cloth off the child. "Oh," said the woman, "my children, come see this creature's scarification.[3] Who put this mark on you?"

The child said, "I myself put it on."

The woman said, "Someone put this mark on you. Today I will find out who it was."

Then the woman beat some rice; she beat the rice and cooked it; it finished cooking.

Then the woman said to the child, "Go, fetch some water; go, fetch some water."

When the child had gone for water, the woman put the child's rice in an iron pot under a board. She made a trap with the board and put the rice below it.

As soon as the child returned, the woman said, "There is your rice; take it and eat it. Then let us go into the town."

As soon as the child stooped down to take the rice, the board caught her hand.

Then the woman sang,

"Plank ma wasa a wasa,
"Who made your marks?
"Plank ma wasa a wasa,
"Who made your marks?
"Plank ma wasa a wasa,
"Who made your marks?
"Plank ma wasa a wasa,
"Who made your marks?"

Already the plank was pressing the child's hand, her hand began to swell.

Finally the child said, "A snake made my marks." Then she died.

"Aha," said the woman, "that is what I wanted to know from you! You have died!" She said, "My children, take the bundles; let us go now into the town."

As soon as they arrived in the town, the man asked the woman, "Where is Mase?"

"Of course, man, you are in civilization! As soon as we arrived at the farmhouse, the child became cold. She returned much earlier to the town. Why, hasn't she arrived yet?"

"Oh," said the man, "no; no, we have not seen her here today."

Then the man gathered twenty messengers. He said, "Look for the child."

The messengers looked for the child all over the town; they did not find her.

The man said, "Go to the farm hamlets."

The messengers went to the farmhouse; they found the dead child lying there. Then they took her body; brought it to the town; laid it in the barre. Then the woman was called.

The people said, "How is it that you went with the children to the farmhouse today; now the child has been brought and she is dead?"

"Oh, my people," cried the woman, "I do not know anything about the child. She ran into the bush today. After we left the farmhouse, she returned there. Oh, my family, I could not have done such a thing!"

Then the man sent a messenger to the woman's relatives. When the woman said, 'Oh, her family, she could not have done such a thing,' of course, they did not ask her, 'Did you kill the child?' As soon as the people said, 'How is it that you went with the children to the farmhouse today; now the child has been brought and she is dead,' the woman cried, 'Oh, I could not have done such a thing.' Now the woman's own children were old enough to be held as witnesses to that conversation.

Then the /dead/ child's grandparents were called and they came. When they came, they heard about the entire conversation; they questioned all the people.

Then the child's mother's spirit approached; she had changed herself into a caterpillar. The caterpillar bowed jigi jege:

"With jege jigi her body is scarred;
"Her best witness is the chief.
"With jege jigi her body is scarred;
"Her best witness is the chief.
"With jege jigi her body is scarred;
"Her best witness is the chief.
"With jege jigi her body is scarred;
"Her best witness is the chief."

Then the people said, "Be quiet, some mourners are coming on the road. Their voice is very sweet; listen to their lament."

Everyone was quiet; they remained sitting. The caterpillar came.

People said, "Make way for her!"

Then an entry way was made for the caterpillar. The caterpillar entered the barre; she approached the shrouded corpse. She blew on the child's hand and she blew onto the middle of her head; the child moved in the shroud.

People cried, "The corpse is moving! The corpse is moving!"

Then the child jumped up. When the child arose, the caterpillar had disappeared without a trace; the child was alive.

People asked the child, "What happened to you?"

The child said, "My mother /i.e. father's wife/ caused everything that happened. We went to the farmhouse; my mother made a trap out of a board and caught my hand. She has denied knowledge of what happened, but her children are witnesses to it."

Then the woman's children were called and questioned.
They said, "That is what she did to our sister."

Then some men took that woman and threw her so far into
the sky that we cannot see her at all.

Do not tell lies!

If I am telling a lie, tadpoles tell lies.

How do tadpoles lie?

When the sun goes down, stand over by the gbonjei trees.
They sing a song:

"Gbembele ma wasa a wasa;
"Who put on your marks?
"Gbembele ma wasa a wasa;
"Who put on your marks?
"Gbembele ma wasa a wasa;
"Who put on your marks?

If they are telling a lie, I am telling a lie.

Kenęi ji mia wǫ i hijeni i nyahanga jǫ ti fele. Ye
nyahangęi jisia i loilǫ a ye ngila hulengǫ gbong ta ta kę ti
ndo yila lenga. Ye ndoi ji i loni a kǫyięi hu lǫ kę ngi nje
hanga.

Ngi nje hangǫi ji kę nyapoi ngi bonda ti ndenga tę "Kpe
ndoi ji gulongǫ lova ngi nje gbla" tę "mu longǫi mu li la mu
ma laa."

Kę kenęi ndenga yę "Wu ji wiengalǫ a nge" yę "kę ngaya
mia wu tukpenga nya wu hu" yę "fale" yę "a ndoi ji lo" yę
"ngę ya ngi nje haa."

Kę ti ndoi ji longa.

Kę so welęi ji wanga mark wulęi ji.

Jina ye marki wulęi ji wanga kę nyapoi ji ti ndoi ji loni
a ngie ngi hini nyahęi ye ji. Kę i ndenga yę "Ye" yę "nya bę"
yę "soi ji wu nya ma."

Kę i punga ngi lenga gbi ma kę i ndenga "Ngęę pu bi ma"
yę "bi nyikǫi ji" yę "ngęę gu ngi na wu bi ma."

Haa na tia lo na ndopoi ji a wuva wǫmalǫ.

Kę ngele yila wonga kę ti ya kpuęla kę i faji ji wumbunga
a ngendęi kę i ya njęi hu. Ngi lingǫi ji ta lǫ ngǫę wiema

kẹ i ngi nje yafẹi ji lọnga miando pui hu i mawuvenga a kali.

Kẹ i ndenga yẹ "Mase."

Yẹ "Na."

Yẹ "Gbẹ wọ lọ bi piema?"

Yẹ "Ye" yẹ "so wulẹi ji mia gẹ wanga" yẹ "ngẹẹ ye i pu nyama" yẹ "ẹẹ pu" yẹ "ye ngọ mia ngi piema."

Yẹ "Kẹ wa mbei" yẹ "gbe na ye ngọẹi ma!"

Kẹ i wanga.

Yẹ "Bi yamẹi liwi." Kẹ i ngi yamẹi ji liwinga kẹ i punga ngi gọi ji hu.

Yẹ "Wote."

Kẹ i punga ngi womẹi ji.

"Ha ye nji sawa ye nani volema bi ya kulẹi vulo bi ma hoe."

Yẹ "E ye."

Jina i wanga haa nji fele ye sawa volei ma kẹ ngi nje mbaa nyahẹi ji ngi mọlinga yẹ "Gbọ bi ma, nyahẹi numu ẹẹ bi luma hakẹi lọ?"

Ta bẹ yẹ "Ye" yẹ "hinda ii le" yẹ "kọlẹi mia nya ma."

Yẹ "Mase," yẹ "nga tọlọ ha."

Kẹ i kulẹi ji gbianga ngi ma. "Kuo" yẹ "nya lenga" yẹ "a wa wu fuhani so lọ. Gbẹe soi ji wu bi ma hi?"

Yẹ "Nya yekpe mia ngi puni."

Yẹ "Numui na soi ji wu bi ma" yẹ "nga lọlọ ha na ngi ngi gọọ."

Kẹ i mbẹi ji hijanga i mbẹi ji hija i ngili i kpọyọ.

Kẹ i ndenga ngi ma yẹ "Li bi wa a njẹi, li bi wa a njẹi."

Kẹ i ndopoi ji nda bẹi wunga kọ vẹi hu kẹ i nguanga gbembelei bu. I gbembelei ji mbei lo hani i ngatẹ kẹ i nguanga mbu.

Kia wọ leke ndopoi na wani yẹ "Mbẹi wumbu na bi mẹ mu li tẹi hu."

Kia leke ndopoi mawęni yę i wa i mbęi wumbu kę gbembelei
hounga ngi lokoi ma.

Ta mia wọ i ye ngolei gbiani

"Gbembele ma wasa a wasa,
"Yọwọ bi joi wieni-e?
"Gbembele ma wasa a wasa,
"Yọwọ bi joi wieni-e?
"Gbembele ma wasa a wasa,
"Yọwọ bi joi wieni-e?
"Gbembele ma wasa a wasa,
"Yọwọ bi joi wieni-e?"

Ta ngulęi ya ha na gbembelei na i lọha ngi lokoi na ya
kę ngi lokoi loni vema.

Ta bę kę i ndenga yę "Kali mia nya joi wieni." Kę ndopoi
hanga.

"Ęhęng," yę "na mia ha ngi ndọlọma bi ma" yę "bi ha" yę
"nya lenga" yę "a hakęi wumbu mu li na tęi hu."

Kia leke ti foni kę kenęi ngi mọlinga yę "Ọ Mase?"

"Ingę, kenęi, bia bę pu loi ji kia ha leke mu wani kpuęi
la ndopoi na kọlę wunga ngi ma i yamanga ha kpo tęi ji hu.
Gbę ii ya le a foni?"

"Kuo" yę "mn mn mn mn" yę "mu ya le ha a ngi lọni mbei."

Kę i masenji jisia gbi yianga numu nu gbọyọngọ yę "A ndopoi
gọkọli."

Ti ndopoi na gọkọli haa tęi hu tii ngi lọni.

Yę "A li kpalatęisia hu."

Kę ti ya kpuęla. Ti lini ti ndopoi maleni lai na lọ ngi
hangọ kę ti mbumbunga ti wa la kę ti mbumbunga ti wa la ke ti
ndenga sęmęi bu kę ti nyapoi lolinga.

Ti ngi mọli "Gbęe wa ndopoi jisia wu ya kpuęla ta ti wa
la ngi hangọ?"

"Kuo nya bonda ndopoi ngii kọ i wilinga ha ndọgbo hu lọ,
mu gbianga kpuęla i yamanga na. Kę nya bonda nya vuli ngęę gu
nga ji wie."

Kę kenęi bę kę i numu longa mambla gama. A gbę hani wie
na? Ji i ndenga yę 'Kuo ngi bonda ęę gu a ji wie' mn tii ngi
mọlini a yęma 'bia ya lọ bi ndopoi wani?'" Kia leke ti ndeni

tẹ 'Gbẹe na ha wa ndopoisia wu ya ha kpuẹla ta i longa na' ti
ya ti malenga na ngi hangọ." 'Kuo' yẹ 'ngẹẹ gu nga na wie.'
Ngi lenga ye nyaha lenga ti jẹmbẹ jẹmbẹngọ-o tia mia ti ti
houma a seli yẹ njẹpẹi na ma.

Kẹ ti ya kẹ ti ndopoi ngi mamani lolinga kẹ ti wanga.
Jina ti wa kẹ ti hei ji ma yẹpẹ lenga ti kpọyọ seng; ti nunga
gbi mọli.

Ndopoi ji ngi nje yafẹi ji kẹ i gbianga i ngi mawuve a
kpekpeli ye kpekpeli ji hi kine na wẹ jigi jẹgẹ:

"A jẹgẹ jigi ngi ma lọ gbọma-o;
"Ngi lima na jeli lọ a mahẹi.
"A jẹgẹ jigi ngi ma lọ gbọma-o;
"Ngi lima na jeli lọ a mahẹi
"A jẹgẹ jigi ngi ma lọ gbọma-o;
"Ngi lima na jeli lọ a mahẹi.
"A jẹgẹ jigi ngi ma lọ gbọma-o;
"Ngi lima na jeli lọ a mahẹi."

Kẹ nunga ti ndenga tẹ "A lando lẹ" tẹ "ngomabla lọwa ma
pelei ji hu" tẹ "ti wo nẹngọ wa" tẹ "a londo lẹ ngọẹma."

Kẹ nunga ti londonga ti loni wọ heinilọ kpekpeli na i wa.

Kẹ nunga ti ndenga tẹ "A hije le ngi gulọ."

Kẹ ti hijenga pẹlẹi la i jọkọ sẹmẹi na bu kẹ i wanga pomẹi
na mahu kasangei na hu nọ i fẹfẹi wu ndopoi na yeya i pu i
leke ngi wulia i pu na mia leke gbi ndẹvu na hi i pu na kẹ
ndopoi jẹsianga kasangei na hu.

Kẹ ti ndenga tẹ "Pomẹi jẹsianga! Pomẹi jẹsianga!"

Kẹ i hijenga sa. Ngi hijengọi ji kpekpeli na ta ngi
logbo bẹ tii tọni kẹ i longa hu kẹ ndopoi vulunga ngi vulungọi
ji.

Kẹ ti ngi mọlinga "Bi ye na pieni?"

Yẹ "Nya nje kẹ nja hounga na kine" yẹ "ye mia ha" yẹ "mu
ya kpuẹla" yẹ "i gbembelei yatẹnga" yẹ "i punga nya lokoi ma"
yẹ "i mawolinga lọma" yẹ "ngi lenga mia seli a tie."

Kẹ ti ngi lenga lolinga ti ti mọli tẹ "Hi na i pieni a mu
nde na."

Kia wọ hingaa ti nyapoi na wumbuni wọ ti teni wọ ngele ma
ti kpajini na kpoe i gẹlẹ hi mu ngi vofo lọni.

Baa ndẹ gula-o.

I ya lọ a ndẹ nga kula kẹ ndẹ mia kputisia ta kula.

Ta ye kula ji?

Folei a ye lima li fọ bi lo gbonjei mahu. Ngole mia ta
nga:

"Gbembele ma wasa a wasa;
"Yọwọ bi joi wieni-e?
"Gbembele ma wasa a wasa;
"Yọwọ bi joi wieni-e?
"Gbembele ma wasa a wasa;
"Yọwọ bi joi wieni-e?
"Gbembele ma wasa a wasa;
"Yọwọ bi joi wieni-e?"

Ina ndẹ mia ta kula kẹ ndẹ mia nya bẹ nya kula.

---

1. Recorded by young woman in Bo on April 16, 1960.
2. Both men and women are scarified (so) on their backs;
boys during their Poro initiation, girls at any time. These
marks represent both maturity and fortitude. "The more the
marks and the more complicated they are, the greater is your
strength of endurance. That is why Mase's mother's spirit
put the marks not only on the back which is the normal place
but also on the belly which is done only in the case of those
with maximum strength of endurance" (Personal communication,
Reverend Isaac M. Ndanema, December 13, 1961).
3. The wicked co-wife shows her hatred for the child by re-
ferring to her as a creature of a lower order of being (fuhani)
than a human being.

Siblings

TALE 32: THREE BROTHERS[1]

At one time there was a man who begat only three children.
These three children were boys. They were there for a long
time.

Whenever the boys passed by, the man would warn them. He
would say, "You three are the only children I begat. I did
not beget a girl; I only begot you. I want you to adhere to
my wish: like one another; let none of you deceive the others
even after my death; do not scatter. If you adhere to my
wish, you will be able to make your way in the world."

At one time these three children chose their occupations.
Ones only work was sexual adventures; another's only work was
feats of strength; the other's mind was very clever. They always remained together. Whenever they went walking, they went
together.

One time they walked until they reached a country. One
of the strongest laws of this country, which was explained to
all visitors, was that if anyone flirted with the chief's wife,
he and all his people would be killed. A second rule in this
country was that if a person killed the bushcow which was
killing the people of the country, the country would be divided
into four parts and three would be given to the slayer of the
bushcow. The three brothers remained in this country.

One night the brother who was sexually promiscuous went
to the chief's senior wife. The night that he went there,
the chief was there. As soon as the man knocked on the door,
the chief caught him arm and cut it at the wrist. The man
ran back to his brothers; his arm was bleeding badly. When
his brothers saw his bleeding arm, they asked what had happened, and he explained.

The man said, "So it is: when I went to the chief's house
yonder, they cut my hand."

"Oh, child," cried his brothers, "you have killed us.
When we came, the law was explained to us; you have trans-
gressed the law. Let us go away tonight."

Then the brothers arose and went out in order to leave
the country. As they went, they came to a big grassfield
where the man-killing bushcow was. The bushcow rushed toward
them.

Then the strong man said, "Stand back; let me go ahead."

When his brothers stood aside, the strong man stepped
ahead and killed the bushcow.

After he had killed the bushcow, the strong man said, "Let us go on now in the night. We have nothing to fear in the farm, for there is nothing more to harm us."

Then the wise man said, "We are not going!" He said, "Let us return to the town."

"Oh," said his brothers, "Elder Brother, let us not return. If we return, the people will kill us."

He said, "Let us return."

The three brothers returned to the town and went to sleep.

In the morning the court was in session. The three brothers came into court.

The wise man said, "I want to ask the chief something."

The chief said, "Well, ask me."

"When we came to this town, what did you explain to us?"

"Oh," he said, "I told you that a spirit is on the road; he kills people. If anyone kills the creature, we shall divide the country into four parts and give three parts to the slayer."

The wise man said, "Why is it that last night when we saved you, you are killing us?"

The chief said, "What do you mean by that?"

The wise man said, "Last night we killed this spirit. I told my brother to go to your own house; he went, he did not find you there. When he came and told me that, I said, 'Then go back and look for his senior wife.' As soon as he went to knock at her house, you cut his hand; until now he is wounded in the house!"

When the wise man had spoken, the chief acknowledged his error. Everyone in the country knew that the chief had done wrong.

Then the country was divided in four parts. Three parts were given to the three brothers.

The three brothers were sitting talking.

One said, "I will become chief, because I am the strongest. I killed the spirit. After the spirit was killed, we got all this property. Therefore, I shall be chief."

Then another said, "Before you killed this spirit, I was responsible for what happened. If my hand had not been cut, we would not have killed the spirit."

Then the wise man said, "You have said that your hand was cut; you have said that you killed the spirit. But I say that my wisdom is responsible for our achieving what we have."

Then the three brothers fought. They quarrelled over the chieftaincy. None of them got the chieftaincy, it was given to another person.

If you had been asked to give the chieftaincy, to which of the brothers would you have given it?

Kena yila gbe wo i hiyeni. Kenęi ji i hi hei i ndenga leni sawakpe ye ndenġęi jisia kpęlę ti kpęlę hinga lenga yęla a tie kę i longa hu ta ti ti yę na haa.

Kę kpelema gbi wǫ ta ti ti ya lewema a ti lahilǫ yę "Wua ngi wu lenga" yę "wu sawakpelǫ ngi wu lei. Ii nyahalo hei na wua lele mia, fale na nya longǫ la wu pie nya lima hindęi le ta lǫ a ji a lo a wunyǫnyǫ numu gbi a gbua ngi mba woma i yę a nya hangǫ bę woma wua gbua wu nyǫnyǫ woma a le kuma wu loahu a vaya na lǫ a wie wu gu wu wu jiawi jǫ ndunyęi hu."

Kę ndenga sawa jisia ti kpęlę kę ti yengeisia lǫ wǫ na ti bumbui: ye ngila lǫ wǫ na ta yę ngi nda yenge gbina kę pue gbuala, yę pekęi lǫ na wǫ ngi nda yenge gbi na kę kpaya, ye ngila lǫ wǫ na ngi nęmahu lewengǫ wa. Ti yę na na kę jia bę wǫ ti ya limahu ta le wǫ woma ta le kuma.

Wati yila ti loi lǫ ye tewei ji wiema haa kę ti wa ti foa ndǫlǫ yila hu. Ye ndǫlǫi ji hu ti jawęi ye kpaukpau kpaukpau yeni wǫ a ye ji lǫ. Numu gbi bi ya na ta ji hungę a bie tę 'Mahęi nyahęi mbeindo numu gbi bi sai gula la ta bi wa ti kpe bi bonda kpęlęma" tę "fale ndǫlęi ji hu jawęi yeni a na ye fele ye tewu yila mu yeya ndǫlęi ji hu a nunga wa ye tewui na numu gbi bi gua bi pa mua ndǫlęi ji gǫlę na nai mu kaka sawa lukpe bi ma." Ti loi lǫ na.

Na kpǫkǫ yila ndakpęi ji pue gbuamǫ wa ji kę i ya mahęi nyaha wa ji gama. Kia i lini na le kpǫkǫi na mahęi i yę na. Kia le i li i pelei ji la leweni le ngi longǫ i pęlęi ji lawo kę mahęi i ngi lokoi houa i tewe kpe ye heimęi ngi loko laa. Kę i yama ngi ndewenga mahu a pime ngamęi ji a wa bǫ ngi lokoi na. Kia na i wai kę ngi ndenga ti ngamęi ji lǫ a kę tia bę ti ngi mǫlia kę i jia hindęi ji ma i hungę.

Yę "Hi mia na" yę "mahęi ye pęlę bu mia nya ya na ti nya lokoi ji lenga."

"Kuo ndopoi bi ma wa mu wa gẹ ti njẹpẹi ji hugẹnga a mue ta bi gbua lọ poma bi hitia poma bi pienga. A mu li a kpindi ji."

Kẹ ti hiyia ti gbua kọ ti li kẹ kia ti li kẹ ti fonga foni wa ji hu mbeindo hi tewui ji na a nunga wa kẹ tewui ji i foa hu kẹ i wa ti mahu.

Kẹ kpayamọi ji i ndenga yẹ "Ti kpeya" yẹ "i lewe kulọ."

Ti kpeya i lewea kẹ i tewui na wa.

Tewui ji wangọi ji hu kẹ i ndenga yẹ "A mui na kpindi ji hu" yẹ "mui ya luwa kpamẹi" yẹ "hani yeka gbi ii ya mu gulọ na a mu gbalẹ."

Kẹ mẹmahu le mọi ji ndenga yẹ "Mui lima" yẹ "a mu yama tẹi na hu."

"Kuo" tẹ "ngọ mua yama. Hindẹi ji maluwangọ wa le mu yama nungẹi jisia ta mu wa."

Yẹ "A mu yama le." Ti yama ti li ti gbu.

Ngele i wo kẹ koti gomẹa kẹ ti kpẹlẹ ti wa koti hu.

Kẹ i ndenga yẹ "Ngi longọ i mahẹi mọli."

Kẹ mah i ndea yẹ "Kẹ nya mọli-e."

"Ye ji wọ mu wai tẹi ji hu gbọ wọ bia bi hungẹni a mue?"

"Kuo" yẹ "ngi ngi lọwọ wuma ngẹ hani wa lọ pelei ji ma a nunga wa ye hani na numu gbi le bi pa mua ndọlẹi ji gọlẹ na nani mu kaka sawa lukpe ngi ma."

Yẹ "Eke gbe gbuẹi mua mu bi bawoni bia bi mu va!"

Yẹ "Na hu lọ a gbẹ?"

Mu hani wai ji lọ gbuẹi wa kẹ ngi ndenga nya ndewei ma ngẹ i li bi ye pẹlẹ bu," yẹ "i ya ii bi maleni na." Yẹ "Kẹ i wa i nde nya ma ngẹ 'kẹ yama bi ngi nyaha wa gama gbe jifa mahẹi ii yẹilọ ngi ye pẹlẹ bu a yẹ ngi nyaha wa gama.'" Yẹ "Kia na i li kọ i pẹlẹi ji lawoi le" yẹ "bi ngi lokoi ji lewea gbuẹi. Kia bẹ na" yẹ "kpe mia ngi minisangọ ta pẹlẹ bu!"

Kia le i ji leni kẹ mahẹi i temu lewenga. Kẹ ndọlọbla kpẹlẹ ti kọnga kẹ mahẹi i hinda yọmu wua.

Kẹ ti ndọlẹi ji gọlẹnga kaka nani kẹ ti kaka sawa lukpea ti ma.

Kę nunga sawęi jisia kpęlę ti heia.

Ji yę "Nya nga mahayęi mę jifa nya lǫ mia nya kpayangǫ
ngi hani wa ji wa hani wa ji woma mu hani ji kpęlę majǫa fale
nya nga mahayęi ji mę."

Kę ye pekęi ji bę ndenga yę "Pęing bę bi ye hani wa ji
wa." Pui gbuamǫi ji yę "I hiyeni nyama na gę ngii nya lokoi
ji lewe a wa a lo mu wala ma" yę "falǫ mu hani wai ji wa."

Kę nęmahu lemǫi ji bę ndea yę "Ji bia bi ndema kia bę ngę
ti bi lokoi na leni, kia bę bia bi ndema bi hani wa na wani,
ina ngę ngi nęmahu lewe gbatęi mua yama tęi hu nga njępęi ji
hungę a mahęini. Kia i jiani la a nya nęmahu le" yę "mua
wangę mu hani ji majǫ."

Ti kpęlę kę ti lapia. Ti yi wǫ ndapi na gǫma ti kpęlę na
le. Kia tia tia ti ndapi na gǫi ti yiani mahayęi na va, numu
gbi ii mahayęi na majǫni. Ti mahayęi na veni numu yeka lǫ wę.

Ina wǫ bia mia ti bi mǫlia tę "Bi mahayęi ji ve." Ba fe
wǫ ye lǫ wę?

---

1. Recorded by young man from Pujehun in Freetown on February
12, 1960. Innes (1964) presents a summary of a version of
this tale.

TALE 33: THE BROTHERS' PACT[1]

This story is about two brothers, Fasila and Gbuande.
They had the same mother. They planted a tree so that it
would bear sweet fruit.

They said, "When the fruit comes, let us distribute it
among the people in our town."

The tree stood there; the fruit had not yet come. Then
Fasila went into the country, he became a top player.[2]

As soon as the tree bore fruit, the townspeople came to
Gbuande. They said, "We have come, because the tree has borne
fruit. Give us our fruit so that we may divide it."

Gbuande refused; he said, "My brother Fasila is not
here; therefore, I will not do that."

The people said, "Let us send a person to call Fasila
so that he will come and we may divide the fruit."

They sent bushfowl to call Fasila. When the bushfowl went, he came to a cassava farm; he ate cassava until his belly was filled; he returned.

He said, "I did not see Fasila."

Then they sent a crow to call Fasila. When the crow went, he found a lot of palm nuts; he ate many palm nuts; he returned.[3]

He said, "I did not see Fasila."

Then they sent a sparrow to call Fasila.[4] He went; he found Fasila playing tops in a big town among a large crowd. He delivered the message to Fasila in a song; he sang about the fruiting of the tree, about the people coming to divide the fruit, and about what Gbuande said. The sparrow told Fasila all about the fruit in a song.

Then Fasila left the top game. He gathered all the people for a big farewell dance. They all said goodbye to Fasila who had arranged for the dance. Fasila returned to his own village.

When Fasila returned home, he and Gbuande had a big fight. They fought until Fasila killed his brother.

That is the end of the story.

Dọmẹi ji ndalongọ ndenga felenga lọ ma, Fasila ta Gbuandẹ. Nje kuhunga mia a tie. Kẹ ti ngulu hinga na hi a wa panda ye nguẹi ji-o nẹngọ.

Kẹ ti ndenga yẹ "Nguẹi ji i wanga lọ mua nungeisia kinẹng mu tẹi ji hu ma kọlẹ lọ a ngo yila."

Ngului ji loni ji ngọi lọi ya lẹ a wani. Kẹ Fasila ta i ya ndọ hu i wotenga si gọ gu gbawa.

Kia na ngului wani kẹ tablẹisia ti wa Gbuandẹ gama tẹ "Mu wanga na kpe nguẹi wanga a mu nguẹi gọle na mu kọkọlẹ."

Gbuandẹ ii luamni yẹ "Nya nde Fasila ii mbei famia ngee na wie."

Kẹ ti ndenga tẹ "A mu numu lo họ mu Fasila loli i wa kọ mu ngulu wọi ji gọlẹkọlẹ."

Kọkọyẹi kẹ ti ngi longa kẹ i li i Fasila loli. Kia i lini kẹ i wanga tanga gbalẹi hu kẹ i tangẹi ji mẹnga haani ngi go i ve kẹ i yamanga.

Yẹ "Ngii Fasila lọ ni."

Gokole kẹ ta bẹ kẹ ti ngi longa tẹ "Li bi Fasila loli."
Kia i lini kẹ i malenga towui ye nguẹi ji gbotongọ na kẹ
towui ji i mẹnga ka ka ka ka, kẹ i yamanga.

Yẹ "Ngii Fasila lọni."

Sukẹi kẹ ti ngi longa ta bẹ tẹ "Li bi Fasila loli." Ta
lini i liilọ vuli i Fasila lọ i maleni ta si ji gọ ta yila
hu kẹlẹma gbi ma faha wa kẹ i gọnga Fasila ma ngole hu ngolei
ji kinẹi i ngani nda longọ ngului ji ngi walẹi ji ma nda
longọ nungẹisia ti wa ngi gama, gbọ le kenẹi wienga. Fasila
woma ndalongọ ngulu wọi ji ma kẹ i hungẹnga kpẹlẹ ngole hu.

Kẹ Fasila gbenga si gọlẹi ji ma. Kẹ i nunga kpẹlẹ
yandọnga kẹ ti komẹ wa gulanga fẹlimangọ wa mia ti kpẹlẹ ti
vẹlinga ngi ma. Ta mia i hindẹi kpẹlẹ hugbatẹni i navo gbua
i haninga kpẹlẹ yeya ti vẹ lima kẹ i yamanga ngi ye fula hu.

Kia i yamani kẹ i ndapi wa hitẹnga ngi nde gọ ba ti lapi
haa i ngi nde wa.

Njẹpẹi ngi gẹlẹmẹi mia.

---

1. Recorded by man from Tikonko in Bo on April 18, 1960.
2. Tops (si) is a popular game which Vivian described at
the close of the nineteenth century:
"Gambling is a favorite pastime; the popular game is
called 'Sigo,' and is played on a skin, with ivory
tops. Four players are a set, and arrange themselves as if for whist, only seated on the ground.
A goat's skin or square piece of cowhide is placed
in the center of the group, the space beneath the
hide being carefully packed with banana leaves and
stalks, so that the edges of the skin are raised
and a hollow produced in the center. Play begins
by naming the stakes: the ivory tops are spun
with the finger and thumb into the hollow of the
hide, and the victor is the one whose top knocks
those of his opponents off the skin." (Vivian:28)
3. Oil palm nuts (towu) are also mentioned in Tales 58 and
76.
4. Sukẹi, "sparrow."

Affines

TALE 34: SPIDER AND HIS MOTHER-IN-LAW'S PLUMS[1]

At one time Spider went to visit his mother-in-law.
Spider and his wife went to visit his mother-in-law. Of
course, Spider's mother-in-law liked him very much and she
knew that he would eat a lot. She cooked a bushel of rice
and some good meat just for him. Spider ate all the meat
and all the rice.

The room that they brought Spider into was beside his
mother-in-law's room. When bedtime came, his relatives-in-
law came into the house and lay down; Spider's wife lay down
too. Spider lay there not knowing that a big plum tree stood
outside the room.[2]

A big wind came and Spider heard a plum fall--popopo.
Spider sat up; he turned to look at his wife to find out if
she were asleep; he wanted to go to collect the plum and eat
it. When Spider looked at his wife, she was sleeping. Very
quickly Spider ran outside; he collected eight plums and
brought them inside.

Now Spider was grumbling to his wife, "Your relatives
don't give a person enough to eat! Today they cooked a bushel
of rice for me; is that sprinkling of rice enough for me? Look
I am still hungry; I am going to eat some plums."

Spider ate the eight plums. When he finished them, he
ran outside again--kuku kuku; he went and gathered ten plums.

When he returned, he missed his way. He went into his
mother-in-law's room; he sat near his mother-in-law on the
bed; he thought that she was his wife.

Spider said, "Move over for me. Your relatives! If a
person comes here, they give him just one bushel of rice.
How can that satisfy me? She cooked one bushel of rice for
me to eat; she said that she would give me some food. That
is all a person gets here! When we were at home, you said,
'Let us go to our relatives; let us go to my people; they
will give you food.'" Spider kept talking like this.

When his mother-in-law took her cloth off her head, she
said, "Why, son-in-law!"

As soon as Spider saw his mother-in-law's face, he ran
out of the house; he ran to his own town; he said that his
relatives-in-law had taken his wife away from him.

Kasilo mia wo i lini ngi yemo welei hu. Kasilo ji ya
ngi yemo welei ji hu ta ngi nyahei ti ya ti fonga. Kpokoi
na kia leke ti foninga inge mamei longo wa a ngie. Tao ngi
yenoi ta kolo ke a mehe me ngongo ke i mbei yilinga buse
yila. Mba buse yila mia ti ngilini ti ndahani yekpe yilima
ta yilakpe va ke i kpele menga i tewe kpe. Kia wo i mbei ji
meni i teweni kpe.

Lumui ji ti ngi wani hu. Ngi yemoi lumui gbe ta be ngi
ndei gbe tia na na ke nda gbei ji hitinga ke ngi yemoini ti
wa pelei bu ke ti langa ke ngi nyahei be longa la. Ta lo
heini mema gboji wulu wai lo loni ngitiiya.

Ke fefe wai ji gulanga a meni leke gboji ji a wu leke
po po po. Kuo i hei ke i wotenga i ngi nyahei ji gama gbe
a ngi nyahei gama gbe kenga woi ngi nyahei yinga ngi longo
i li i gboji i woyo ngitiiya i me. I ngi nyahei ji gama gbe
ngi nyahei nji hu. Kaka kaka i lewe a pime ngitiiya ke i
gboji woyonga wayakpa ke i wanga la.

Ta lo na yiama ngi nyahei ma "Bi njeni te numu go! Mba
bondei ji ta wa ha ta mba buse yila kpe yili mbe. Na vaili
a ye pie a nge? Ndole bondei ji gbe le nya ma i lukpe mbe
nga gboji me."

Ke i gboji wayakpei ji menga ke i kpoyonga. I kpoyo ke
i gbianga gboma ngitiiya a pimei kuku kuku ke i ya ke i
ngoyonga pu.

I wanga na ke i yakanga ngi welei ma. A me kpole i
wilinga ngi yemoi gama ke i ya ke i heinga ngi yemoi gblanga
kpukei ji ma. Ta a to a ngi nyahei mia.

"Lukpe mbe wu njeni numu wangalo mbeindo mehei mia a na
lo mba buse yila vulii. A ye pie a nge? Mba buse yakpe mia
ta ngili ngi menga ta wa a lewema a nde ti mehe venga mbe! Ji
mia numu wangalo mbei, mu yalo heini miando be, 'E ma e mu li
mu njeni gama, mu li nya njeni gama; mehe lo ti feni mbe.'"
I loni wo na lema lo.

Kia ngi yemoi kulei wumbuni ngi wumba ye "Gbee lemia!"

I ngi yemoi yama loni a mei vaung i gbianga i ya a pime
i ya i fonga ngi ye ta hu ye "Ti nyahei gbianga ngi yeya."

---

1. Recorded by man from Bo in Freetown on January 7, 1960.
Njemo, mother-in-law.
2. Hog plum (gboji).

TALE 35: SPIDER AND HIS MOTHER-IN-LAW'S CLOTH[1]

At one time there was an old woman who had a very beautiful daughter. She was to be married to Spider. One evening Spider went to visit his mother-in-law; it was during the rainy season and the house to which they brought Spider leaked a lot.

The people said, "It is very late, let us lie down now. In the morning, you will see the woman's daughter."

When Spider was lying down, the rain was coming down. His mother-in-law had put a big white cloth in a basin in Spider's room. When Spider saw something white in the room, he thought it was rice. Spider went and touched it; he came with a spoon of palm oil and turned it on the rice, which was with his mother-in-law's cloth. Just as Spider was preparing to eat the "rice," a drop of water fell on the basin "taa"; Spider thought that someone was calling him (he went to see; he saw no one; he returned). Every time he prepared to eat the rice, "taa kolon" (he went to see who it was; he returned). He kept doing that all night.

As soon as the morning came, Spider saw the cloth and that he had put palm oil on it. Spider ran away; he went to his siblings; he said that his wife had been taken away.

That is what happened at one time because of Spider's greed. He never returned for that woman, because he had spoiled his mother-in-law's cloth.

Mama wova yila mia wǫ. Nyahaloi ji i yę ngi yeya. Ndopoi ji nyandengǫ wa. (Kę mamęi ji ndea yę "Numu gbi le ęę ngi loi ji ve bi wę kę bia.") Kasilo ji i li ngi yemǫ welei ji hu a kpindi ji lǫ kę i ya. Kę hamęi ji yęla. Pęlęi ji ti ngi wa mbu a bǫ wa kę i ya kę ti ngi wa pęlęi ji bu a ye wati na.

Kę ti ndea na tę "Kpindi ji ngǫlǫngǫ wa" tę "fale gbę mu la na. Ngele i wo i wa mamęi ji loi ji gama." 'Tao Kasilo lǫwǫ ti fei ngi wę.)

Ji na Kasilo i la haa njęi ji lǫ wama kę ti kulęi ji kula wai ji kę ti pua hakęi ji hu. Wati na hu kpindi welia kini kę ti kulęi ji wunga pani ji hu fęnggbei ji. Njęi ji yę na wama Kasilo ji ti kulęi ji wanga pęlęi ji bu a boi ji lǫ kowengoi ji kę i tǫa yę mbęi mia i ya i bǫ wienga kę i waa a mitęi ji ngulǫgbǫli ji i ya i mbumbunga i pote mba ti gulęi na ma, a mitęi wa lǫ le hu fǫǫ. A tǫ yę mbęi mia, a tǫ yę mbęi mia. Njęi ji gbuja pani ji ma i ndea yę 'Taa.' Kuo kę Kasilo lǫma a ye mia nya lolima. 'Taa kolon' i loi wǫ na wiema haa.

Kę ngele kia le wǫ hu yę "Puun!" I kulęi na lǫi le i
tǫi kę mba ti gulęi mia i ngulǫgbǫli na wuama kę i lewea a
pimę. I li i li ngi ndenga gama i li yę "Ti nyahęi gbua nya
yeya."

Wati na lǫ wǫ wieni Kasilo męhęi hindęi ye ngila mia wǫ
i hitii hu i lilǫ ii ya yamani wǫfǫ nyahęi na woma jifa i mba
ti gulęi nasia kpęlę nyaningǫ miando.

---

1. Recorded by young man from Pujehun in Freetown on February
12, 1960. Reverend Stott (MS) presents a Mende text and
English summary of a version of this tale.

TALE 36: SPIDER AND HIS MOTHER-IN-LAW'S PEANUT[1]

At one time Spider and his mother-in-law were. Spider
got a wife from an old woman.

Spider said, "Let us go to your parents; I will work for
your mother this year."

Spider and his wife went /to his mother-in-law's house/.
In the morning Spider was going to cut trees to make a farm;
his mother-in-law roasted a bushel of peanuts for him to eat
on his way. As Spider was walking, he was eating peanuts.

One peanut fell out of Spider's hand. Spider bent down
to look for the peanut. He searched and he searched; he did
not see the peanut. Spider put his bag down; he took his
matchet to cut the brush. He cut and he cut around that
place. Spider spent the entire day cutting brush while
looking for the peanut.

Spider's mother-in-law cooked some food to take to him.
When she went, she met him cutting grass on the bush path.
She said, "Oh, what is the matter, son-in-law?"

"Oh," he said, "Mother-in-law, I am searching for my only
diamond ring."

The old woman began to look on the ground. As she was
looking on the ground, she saw the peanut. She knew that her
son-in-law was greedy. She took the peanut. She said, "Son-
in-law, I have only seen this peanut."

At once Spider took the peanut from the old woman's hand;

he threw it into his mouth. He ran away; he went home; he
said that they had taken away his wife.

This is the end of this story.

ma.   Kasilo ta ngi njemǫ mia wǫ.   I nyahẹi ji jǫnga mamẹi ji
Tia na.

foi ji."   Ye "Mu li mu fo bi njeni gama, nga yengelǫ bi nje wẹ a

Kẹ ti ya. Kia wǫ ti lini nge wonga i ya lima ndoimẹi
ji kẹ ngi yemǫi ji kẹ i nikili ji yelenga ngi wẹ busẹ yila
yẹ "Ya mẹ pelei hu bi li." I loni wǫ nikili ji mẹma a li
pelei hu ngi wui hitẹngǫ.

Kẹ nikili gbuanga ngi yeya yila kẹ i gulanga. Aya Spida
i wẹnga ndoima hindẹi na hoe. I nikili ji gbǫkǫi i kǫkǫi i
kǫkǫi i kǫkǫi ẹẹ tǫ kẹ basaki langa kẹ i mbogbẹi vuli wumbua
ndoi va i ndoi wie i ndoi wie i ndoi wie hindẹi na i luvani
ndoi wiema kpẹing a nikili ji gǫkǫi.

Ngi yemǫi ji mẹhẹ yilinga na ta lima la ngi woma. I lini
i ngi maleni a pelei galẹi ji ma hawa. "Kuo!" Yẹ "Gbẹe,
demia?"

"Kuo," yẹ "nya yemǫi," yẹ diamǫn ring yakpei nya yeya"
yẹ "ta mia ha i gulanga hindẹi ji" yẹ "ta mia ngi kǫkǫlima."

Mamẹi ji loi na ndǫmẹi gbema ta bẹ a lewe a ndǫmẹi gbe.
Kẹ mamẹi i nikili ji lǫnga kia i ngi mbelẹi ji gǫlǫ mẹhẹ lingǫ
kẹ i mbumbunga. Yẹ "Demia," yẹ "kẹ leke nikili ji ngi tǫnga."

A mẹ kpa i nikili hounga mamẹi yeya kẹ i pilinga la. A
mẹ vaung i lewenga a pimẹ kẹ i ya i nde yẹ "Ti nyahẹi gbianga
ngi yeya."

Dǫmẹi ji ye kẹlẹmẹi lǫ.

---

1. Recorded by man from Bo in Freetown on January 12, 1960.
Nikili, peanut. Reverend Stott's manuscript includes a Mẹnde
text and English summary of a version of this tale.

TALE 37: SPIDER AND HIS MOTHER-IN-LAW'S STEW[1]

At one time Spider went to his mother-in-law's house.
Spider was a very skillful house builder.[2] At his mother-
in-law's place, Spider was doing house building.

His mother-in-law said, "Let me cook him some food."

Then Spider's mother-in-law cooked some food for him;
she finished cooking. The rice was drying and the sauce was
near the fireplace. The sauce was very hot. Spider's mother-
in-law took the sauce and set it aside. Then she went to
fetch water.

Immediately the house builder looked to see where his
mother-in-law had gone; then he ran into the house--kuku. He
went inside; he took the cover off the pot; he took out one
piece of meat.

As Spider came out, he saw his mother-in-law approaching.
He threw the meat into his cap. The meat was hot, it burned
his head; he moved his head this way, the meat burned his head;
he moved his head that way, the meat burned his head; he kept
tilting his head this way and that. When his mother-in-law
reached him, Spider took his hat off his head; a big piece of
meat fell out of his cap; Spider took the meat; he ran away.
When he got home, he said that his wife had been taken from
him.

This is the end of this story.

Kasilo ji mia wọ i li ngi yemọi gama ngi yemọ wẹlẹi ji
ta Kasilo ji pẹlẹ mahọwọmọ yengei mia wọ a pie. A pẹlẹi ji
mahọ mbẹlingọ wa i loa pẹlẹ mahọmẹi ji lọ.

Kẹ ngi yemọi ji i ndenga yẹ "Gbẹ ngi kọnda yili."

Ke ngi yemọi ji mẹhẹi ji ngi wẹ i gbọyọ seng. Ngi yemọi
ji yi i mẹhẹi ji yilinga ngi wẹ-o i gbọyọa. Kẹ mbẹi ji
hubenga hakpẹi ji lọ hei koloi gbla; hakpẹi ji-o kpandingọ
wa i kpua i heinga i toa. Kẹ i ya njẹi hu i ya njẹi hu va.

Gbue pẹlẹ mahọmọi ji i pelei hugbe ngi yemọi ya kẹ ta
be i wa pẹlẹ bu kuku a pimẹi. Kẹ i ya kẹ i fẹi ji la wumbunga
kẹ i huẹi ji wumbunga kate yila.

Kia ye i gbua kẹ i ngi yemọi lọa mia. A mẹ kpole i
pilinga ngi wumbua bọlọi hu. Huẹi ji-o kpandingọ a ngi
wumbu mọ ngi wui ji a hitẹ na, i ngi wumba mọa kẹ i ngi
wui yama mbei i ngi wumba mọa kẹ i ngi wui lẹkpẹnga mbei
yaka i loi wọ ndẹkpẹma. Ngi yemọi foloni lọ wọ le ngi gọbu

ke i bǫlǫi gbua ngi wumbua. A mę gbu ke hua gate wa gbua i gula. Ke i ye hua gatei wumbunga. A mę vaung i lewenga a pimę i kpęlę ngi wumbua bǫlǫi ma. Ke i ya i nde yę "Ti nyahęi gbua ngi veya."

Dǫmęi ji ye ke lęma ye mia.

----

1. Recorded by man from Bo in Freetown on January 12, 1960.
2. Mahǫmǫ, house builder. Housebuilding occurs in Tales 40 and 80; in Tale 40, the man also builds for his mother-in-law.

TALE 38: ROYAL ANTELOPE AND THE CHIEF[1]

At one time there was a very wealthy chief who had only one very beautiful daughter. Anyone who saw the girl wanted to marry her.

At one time the chief gathered together all the people in the country, he said, "My daughter is mature now. If you want to marry her, you must drink a pail of boiling water."

This situation was very difficult for the people.

Whenever a person came saying, "I want to marry this child," the chief said, "Look there is a pail of water; drink it; then you can marry this woman."

Whenever a man drank the water, his heart would dry, he would fall, and he would die.

The chief kept doing this; people kept dying; many people died.

When many people had died, Royal Antelope came. He said, "Father."

The chief said, "Yes."

Royal Antelope said, "I have come to have you give me this child. I will marry her."

"Oh," he said, "if you want to marry this child, it is only necessary for you to drink one pail of boiling water; then you can take the girl and marry her."

"Oh," he said, "is that all?"

He said, "Yes."

He said, "I agree, but before I drink this water..."

The chief said, "Yes?"

Royal Antelope said, "Let me go; I will tell my whole family to be there."

The chief said, "Yes."

The chief did not know the clever plan that Royal Antelope had made.

Then Royal Antelope went and got all his family. They were many. They came and gathered. Royal Antelope came to the chief, he said, "My family has come now."

Then the chief himself put some very hot water into the pail; he gave the pail to Royal Antelope; Royal Antelope held the pail.

Royal Antelope said, "But, Father."

The chief said, "Yes?"

He said, "Before I drink the water, I must say goodbye to my family."

The chief said, "I agree."

Then Royal Antelope went to his father, he said, "Father."

He said, "Yes?"

Royal Antelope said, "I have said that I want this woman, but the chief said that I have to drink this pail of boiling water."

He said, "Oh, is it agreed?"

Royal Antelope said, "I have agreed."

His father said, "Drink it truly."

So Royal Antelope kept walking among those people until he had completed the circle. When he had finished walking among all those people, he drank the water. When Royal Antelope drank the water, he did not die and he got the woman.

That was how Royal Antelope got his wife from that wealthy person at one time.

Maha yila mia wọ kpatẹngọ kẹlẹma gbi ma. Kẹ i ndoi ji lenga. Ndo nyahaloi yakpe nyandengọ wa. Numu gbi le bi tọngalọ ba lolọ la. Ndoi ji mia wọ.

Kẹ i ndọbla kpẹlẹ yandọnga ye "Ndoi ji gbela na; bi longọ bi mani hei kole" yẹ "ba njā gbandii lọ gbọle faji yila nja nẹngọi, faji yila ta lọ ba kpọle."

Ah hindẹi ji mini lọ ndọbla ma.

Numui na gbiangalọ yẹ "Nya longọ a ndoi ji."

"Kuo" yẹ "njẹi gbe mia faji yila," yẹ "kpọle bi nyahẹi ji jọ."

Kena ta njẹi na mẹ. Ti fengalọ na wẹ, kẹ i gbọlenga wu kpọlengọ-o, kẹ ngi li benga, kẹ i gulanga kẹ i hanga.

I loni wọ piemalọ kẹ nunga ti loi lọ hama, nu gboto ti hailọ.

Jina wọ nungẹi jisia ti hei ji wieni, kẹ Hagbe ji wanga yẹ "Kẹkẹ."

Yẹ "E."

Yẹ "Ngi wanga bi ndoi ji ve mbẹ. Ma ta mu hei."

"Ko," yẹ "bi ya bẹ wa ndoi ji wu hei," yẹ "njia weka ii ma" yẹ "nja nẹngọi ji faji yila," yẹ "bi kpọlenga lọ leke," yẹ "ndoi ji wumbu" yẹ "wa ta wu hei."

"Kuo!" Yẹ "Na lele?"

Yẹ "I."

Yẹ "Nya lokolọ ma," yẹ "kẹ pẹing wọi ngi njẹi ji kpọle."

Yẹ "I."

Yẹ "Gbẹ ngi li ngi nde nya bonda kpẹlẹma ti wa ti yẹ na."

Ta bẹ yẹ "Eye."

Ii kọ a yẹkẹ nẹmahu le mia Hagbe kpianga a ngie.

Kẹ Hagbe ya kẹ i ngi bonda kpẹlẹ lẹnga ti gbotongọ wa, kẹ i ti lẹnga kẹ ti wanga ti yandọ. Kẹ i wa kenẹi gama yẹ "Nya bonda ti wanga na."

Kẹ kenẹi bẹ i nja nẹngọ wai ji wumbunga faji ji hu, kẹ i fenga ngi wẹ kẹ i hounga.

Yẹ "Kẹ kẹkẹ."

Yẹ "E?"

Ye "Pẹing ngi njẹi ji gbọle," yẹ "kẹ nga vẹli pẹing nya
bonda ma."

Ta bẹ yẹ "Nya lokolọ ma."

Kẹ i ya ngi kẹ gama, yẹ "Kẹkẹ."

Yẹ "E."

Yẹ "Nyahẹi ji mia ngẹ nya longọ la, kẹ kenẹi yẹgẹ nja
nẹngọi faji yila," yẹ "ta lọ nga kpọle."

"Ko" ta bẹ yẹ "kulungọ?"

Yẹ "Nya lokolọ ma."

Yẹ Kpọe yo."

Kẹ i lewenga i loni haa jiama nungẹi nasia mahu lọ ha i
lewe i kala i komẹ. Kpẹing i jia nungẹi jia kpẹlẹ mahu i
kpọyọ seng kẹ i njẹi ji gbọlenga. Kia wọ i njẹi gbọeni, ii
ya hani; kẹ i nyahẹi ji jọnga.

Na mia wọ Hagbe nyahẹi ji jọi la wọ kpatẹmọi ji ma.

---

1. Recorded by man from Bo in Freetown on January 7, 1960.

TALE 39: KPANA AND HIS WIFE[1]

At one time there was a very poor man named Kpana.
Kpana was so poor that he was unable to buy cloth for shorts;
he was so poor that he was unable to get any food except
what people gave him. He continued to be poor.

Once they had a Sande ceremony in this town. Before
they held the Sande ceremony, they called all their daughters
and asked them to name their lovers. They called the children
and asked them to name the lovers whom they would marry. One
child named Kpana; she said that he was her lover.

Her family said, "Child, you have named this poor man
Kpana. What does he have? He can't even buy cloth to wear!"
They beat the girl.

The girl said, "No matter how much you beat me; I will say that I love Kpana; he is the one I love."

Everyone in the girl's family beat her; they were unhappy; they said, "Let her be."

They stopped beating her and called Kpana. They said, "Our daughter says that she loves you."

(The girl who said that she loves Kpana was very beautiful; she was more beautiful than any of her companions.)

Kpana sat; he considered this information; he could not find any way out. He said, "Then I agree."

When Kpana went to gather money for the marriage payment, he did not have one shilling. Kpana went searching /for money/. He spent three weeks in the bush gathering palm kernels to sell so that he could get one shilling; he was unsuccessful.

What did he do?

Kpana arose; he said that he was going on a journey; he went to the river. As he continued to travel, he reached a road; he lay down, he slept, and he dreamt.

Kpana dreamt: he reached where some thieves who had gathered many good things had put the things. What did he do? When he saw these things and he saw that no one was there (they had gone to steal more things to add to what they had), he began to transport the things to his own house: boxes, money, cloth, cows, sheep, table utensils, chairs, beds--all the things that are considered as wealth in this world. Kpana transported all those things that he had been unable to get in the past. And God arranged that the thieves did not catch him. He kept transporting all those things that he could carry until he had carried everything. He filled his entire house--his room and his parlor with that load of wealth. All this time he was in a dream; his family did not know about it; the girl's family did not know about it. As soon as the last things had been transported, he arrived at his own house. And Kpana trembled; he awoke.

As soon as Kpana awoke, all the things that he had dreamt about were in his own house. All those riches were in Kpana's house.

In the morning Kpana went to his mother-in-law. In the meantime before he went to his mother-in-law, he sent a person to call his wife; she came.

Kpana said, "Jise, I have come now for the feast about which you spoke to me recently. When I said that I loved you and you said that you loved me. We shall marry; let us feast, let us have a dance, let us call people."

Then Kpana sent a person to call all his family and his wife's family. They all came; they were very happy now. The people, who had beat the girl and had said that they did not want her to marry Kpana who was so poor, were all very happy now. All those people for whom the matter had not been sweet at first were happy now, because Kpana brought riches.

That is why if a person says that he is thinking about doing something and you do not know how it will end, you tell him to forget the idea. At that time those people said that the plan was bad at the beginning, but they were happy at the end. Kpana and his wife became happy people.

Nyanimọ wai wọ. Kenẹi ji ta ngi nyaningọ wai yẹla, ngi lẹi mia wọ a Kpana. Kpana ji i ye na ngi mambẹi vuli wọ a ngi guma gula gbii ngi ma. Ina leke ngi nyaningọ ngila mẹhẹi ji vuli ẹẹ guma kẹ nunga ti mẹhẹi majọ wọ ti ngi gọ. I loi lọ na ma.

Wati yila kẹ ti Sande wama tẹi ji hu kẹ ti ya wọ Sande wama pẹing tia Sande wa ta ti lenga kpẹ loli lọ ti ti mọli na hi ti ti mọli ti ti malomẹisia gẹ kẹ i loa hu na kẹ ti ndopoisia lolinga kẹ ti ti mọlia tẹ "Ti malomẹisia gẹ nasia ta ti ti heima." Kẹ ndopo yila kẹ i Kpana ji gẹnga yẹ "Ta mia ngi nda malomẹi le."

Kuo kẹ ngi bonda ti ndea "Ndopoi, bia ba Kpana ji gẹ. Nyanimọ bondẹi ji gbọ ngi yeya? Kulẹi vuli numu la ngii guma ma." Ti ngi le haa.

Yẹ "Wu nya lewe bẹ haa" yẹ "wu nya le bẹ haa na le wie nya na" yẹ "nya longọ a Kpana na. Ta lọ nya nda malomẹi le."

Ti ngi le haa numu gbi ti ngi bonda le ti li nyaningọ. Kẹ ti ndenga tẹ "Ti gbe ngi ma."

Kẹ ti gbia ngi ma kẹ ti Kpana lolinga ti ye hindẹi ji wu ngi gulọ tẹ "Hi lọ mu nyapoi i njẹpẹi lea yẹ ngi longọlọ a bie."

(Ndopoi ji wọ i nde yẹ 'ngi longọi a Kpana,' i nyandeni wọ ngi mbangẹi nasia gbi ma ngi nyandenọ wa.)

Kuo Kpana i hei i njẹpẹi ji gbekpe. Kẹ ta bẹ i piegi ii na i lumalọ yẹ "Kẹ ngi lumanga."

Kia Kpana i li hindei ye tọto kọpọi vuli wọ na ii yẹni
a si yila Kpana li kọkọima i loi lọ na haa hoki sawa i ndọgbọ
hu a lewe a tọlu wọyọ kọ i wa i li i majia i sili yilẹi na
majọ ii gui ma.

I gbọ wie?

Kẹ i hiyenga yẹ i li majia hu lọ kẹ i ya njẹi ji hu. Kia
i li haa i foi pelei ji hu kẹ i laa i yi kẹ i kiabunga.

Kia i kibauni kẹ i ya i fo humabla ti haka yandọngọ wa ji
mia humabla ta haka yekpeisia gbi wumbu ta ta pu na kẹ i fonga
na. Ta bẹ i gbọ wie? Hakẹi jisia kia i tọni le kẹ nungẹisia
tii na na hu ti ya humamẹi ye pekẹi kọ ti wa ti pu hakẹi jisia
ma. Ta bẹ i na gbe kpẹ ii numu lọi kẹ i tọtonga a hakẹi jisia
belẹ la ngi ye pẹlẹ bu kanga, navo, kula, nika, mbala, hani
na gbi leke gbatẹ haka le nikanga-o, table magbatẹ hakanga-o,
sianga-o, kpukọ-o hani na gbi le ndunya gbatẹ haka le i male
lọ na. Kẹ ta bẹ i tọtonga a mabelẹ la, i mabelẹ haa. Ye na
le gbi le ngi loko ẹẹ guma ta mia i yẹ a lila. Tao Ngewọ
pielọ tii ngi hou. Na haa i hakẹi na belẹ hakẹi na le gbi i
guni mbu i kpẹlẹ mbelẹ hindẹi na kpọyọ. I pẹlẹi na lave
kpang ngi lumui na hu kẹ paua ma kpẹlẹ kẹ na lavea a gbatẹ
hakẹi na. Na hu gbi ii hungọ kẹ kibau hu mia; ngi bonda-o
tii hungọ; nyapoi ji ngi bonda-o tii hungọ. Ta bẹ kia le
hakẹi jisia kpẹlẹ belẹi hakẹi ye kẹlẹma kẹ i lila le. I fo
le ngi ye pẹlẹ bu. Kẹ i gbẹinga i wu.

Kia le i gbẹi i wui hakẹi nasia kpẹlẹ ti ngi ye pẹlẹ bu.
Kia lọ ha i kibaui na wie la. Kpatẹi haka hakẹi na gbi le.

Kẹ ta bẹ kẹ nge wonga kẹ i ya ngi yemọi ji gama kẹ ayẹ
pẹing i li ngi yemọi gama kẹ i halẹi kẹ i numu longa ngi
nyahẹi ji gama kẹ ti ya ti ngi loli ti wa.

Yẹ "Jise, njẹpẹi ji gẹ bi ndeni nya ma ngi wa na" yẹ
"komẹi va" yẹ "mua komẹinga na kẹ nya kia lọgẹ ngi ndeni nge
nya longọi a bie bẹ bia bẹ bi longọi a nge pẹing ma bi mu ya
hei kẹ mua komẹnga mua ndoli gbatẹ mu nunga lolima."

Kẹ ta bẹ i nu laa ngi bonda kpẹlẹ gama ta ngi nyahẹi
kẹ ti kpẹ ti gohunẹngọ wai yela na. Tia gẹ ti yẹ nyapoi ji
lewe-o tẹ tii loi a hindoi ji Kpana ji jọ jifa ngi nyaningọ
wa le. Ti gbi ti gohunẹngọ wa yela na. Kẹ ti loli ti
kohunẹi ji wie kẹ ti ti jọei ji wiea na numui nasia kpẹlẹ
wọ hindei na ii yẹ nẹ ti wẹ ye tọtomẹi na ti gbi i
nẹlọ na ti wẹ jifa Kpana wa kpatẹ.

Na va mia numu a nde leke a yẹma hinda wiema bii ye
gbui gọ bii ye kẹlẹma gọ kẹ bi ndea bẹ i gbe ye hindei na ma.
Tia ti ndei wọ nyamungọ yela tọtomẹi kẹ nga gbuamẹi manẹlọ
ti wẹ. Kpana woteni fo a kohunẹmọ ta ngi nyahẹi.

1. Recorded by young man from Pujehun in Freetown on May 13, 1960.

TALE 40:   AN URCHIN AND HIS MOTHER-IN-LAW[1]

At one time there was a woman who had one very beautiful daughter. The woman said that she would give her daughter in marriage only to a person who could build a house on a big rock. (She said that) because she did not want her daughter to marry; she loved her a lot.

The child was very beautiful. Men came from every land for this girl. The woman said that she would not give her to any man unless he built a house for her on stone and she lay in that house before she gave her child to him. When all these people came for the girl, they were unable to get her.

One day a young man came; he was unwashed and very filthy. He said that he had come because of the girl. He appeared very little.

Then the woman said to him, "Child, all those grownups came for the girl; they did not get her. Have you, this little person of the family of the little, come for this girl!"

One day the young man went fishing; he caught a crab; he brought the crab to his mother-in-law.

He said, "Cook this crab for me until it is very soft, for my teeth are not as strong as grownups' teeth. I want you to cook this crab until it is as soft as an ordinary animal. Cook it. Tomorrow after I have eaten it, I will go to work."

Then the youth gave the crab to the woman. She put the crab in a pot; she set it on the fire; it cooked all day long.

Then the youth said, "Mother, isn't the crab cooked yet?"

The woman said, "No, it is not done yet; it's really very raw."

Then she called the youth, she said, "Child, do you still mean to tell me to cook the crab until it is soft?"

Then the youth said, "Woman, can you say to me that on a rock, on which a person cannot dig a hole, I must build a house before I can marry this girl?"

The woman gave the girl to the youth. She said, "You have shown that you are clever; you are the one who must have this girl. Take her."

At one time that little youth got that girl. His wisdom enabled him and no one else to get that girl.

Mama wovei ji gbe wo i hijeni. Nyahalo nyande nyande yila i yelo ngi yeya. Nyahaloi ji ye ee fe numui gbi we ke numui ji wo ba pelei lo. Koti ma fawai ji ma. Fale jifa ii yee loni i ngi ve numu gbi we; ngi longo wa la.

Ndopoi yo nyandengo wa. Nunga ti yelo a gbua ndolei hu gbi leke. Ta wa nyahei ji va. Ye ee fe ti we ye ke leke numui na ba pele lo ngi we koti ma a ye lani ye pelei na hu lo peing i ya nyahei ji ve bi we. Jina nunga gbi ti wanga nyahei ji va ke ti gbahanga ma.

Folo yila ke ndopo wulo yila i wanga. Ndopoi ji ngi muango be ii yela. Ngi lui na nohongo wa ke i wanga ye i wanga nyahei ji lo va. I ya kulo hing.

Ke ti ndea ti ma te "Ndopoi, kpakonga gbi ti wanga wo nyahei ji va mui feni ti we; bia mia bi wulongo bondei ji ba wa nyahei ji va."

Lo yila ke i ya ndoli wilimei ji ke i ngaku vila hounga. Ke i wanga la ye ngi yemoi ma.

"A ngakui ji yili mbe, i ye bewe kpe nya yongoli ii gba kpauni kia kpakoisia ti ndei na." Ye "Nya longo ngakui ji bi ngili i ye bewe bewe. Kia lo hua gbama na" ye "bi ngili; sina" ye "ngi mengalo na ke ngi ya ngengemei" ye "na lo a wie ngi gu ngi gbaya ngi ngenge wie."

Ke ndopoi na ngakui na venga mamei na we. Ke mamei ngakui na wunga fei na hu. I heinga i wuva yilima kpeing.

Ke ndopoi ndenga ye "Ye, ngakui ii yaa yilini le?"

Mamei ye "Mn, mn gbe-o-gbe ii yaa wieni le" ye "ngundungo wa le."

Ke i ndopoi ji lolinga ye "Ndopoi, bia vuli bi longoi bi nde nya ma be ngakui ji i yililo i ye bewe bewe kia hua na?"

Ke ndopoi be ndenga ye "Ba gulo ye bi nde nya ma be fala hu ta hani mia numu ee gu a mbo ba li lolo bi nde nya ma be nga pelei lo na peing ngaa ya nyahei ji majo?"

Ke i nyahei venga ndopoi we. Ye "Bia mia wo ngewo wa bi genga" ye "bia mia ba nyahei ji majo. Fale nyahei ji wumbu."

Ndopo wuloi na lọ wọ i nyahẹi na majọni fọ ngi nẹmahu le
va na mia wọ i wieni ndopoi na ta i nyahẹi na majọni.

---

1. Recorded by young man from Pujehun in Freetown on February
16, 1960. Migeod (1908) has published a Mẹnde text and English
translation of a version of this tale.

TALE 41: ROYAL ANTELOPE AND A FIGHTER[1]

At one time there was Ndapigbou and he had only one sibling, a sister.[2]

Ndapigbou said that if he and another man fought and the
man knocked Ndapigbou down, the man could marry his sister.
Ndapigbou fought many people; he beat them; he knocked them
down; they cooked him an ewe. He continued to do this.

Then Royal Antelope came and said, "Comrade."

He said, "Yes, you have come."

Royal Antelope said, "Yes, thank you." He said, "I want
your sister."

"Oh," he said, "Comrade, there is nothing to discuss except that we must fight. If you knock me down, you may take
the woman."

Oh, my father, what a fight it was! They joined hands;
they began to fight; they fought for two days; they continued
to fight. Then Royal Antelope took Ndapigbou; he lifted him
up and dropped him on the ground. Royal Antelope and
Ndapigbou's sister got married.

Now, did you hear the little story that I told?

Ndapigbou mia wọ i hiyeni ta ngi ndewe ti felekpe ti ti
leni.

Ngi ndewei ye nyahaloyiẹi ji yẹ "Kẹ numu gbi wa ta wa
lapi pẹing" yẹ "wu lapia bi ngi gulanga" yẹ "wu ngi nde wu
hei." I loni wọ ndapi na gọma haa i numu gboto leweilọ i
ti gulanga kẹ ti mbala ha yila yii. I ji loni wọ hu lọ.

Kẹ Hagbe ji gbuanga. Yẹ "Ndakpẹi."

Yẹ "E, bi wa."

Yẹ "E, bi sie." Yẹ "Nya longọ a bi ndewei ji bi ndewe wuloi ji" yẹ "nya longọ la."

"Kuo" yẹ "ndakpẹi" yẹ "jia yeka ii ma-e" yẹ "mu lapia le" yẹ "bi nya gulanga," yẹ "bi nyahẹi wumba."

A nya kẹ, ndapi mia ti loko wulinga na ndapi ji hu hei. Ti ndapi ji lọ wọ gọni ti ndapi ji gọ hu i yili fele ta ndapi gọ. Ti loni wọ ndapi gọma. Kia Hagbe i Ndapigbou wumbuni i tẹ a mẹ gbuọ kẹ i kula Hagbe ta Ndapigbou ndei na ti hei lọ wọ fọ.

Bi na wuloi na mẹni nga hungẹ?

———————————

1. Recorded by man from Bo in Freetown on January 20, 1960. Innes (1965:56-57) has presented a summary of a version of this tale.
2. Ndapigbou, Tireless Fighter.

Uncles and Nephews

TALE 42: SPIDER, ROYAL ANTELOPE, AND THE BANANAS[1]

At one time Spider went walking with Royal Antelope. When they went looking for bushyams, the rainy season was very heavy. They were searching for bushyams; they kept walking until they saw this yam foliage; they looked for the root.

A tree with bananas was near the water; the ripe bananas were reflected in the water, as the tree bent over the water.

When Spider was searching for the yam root, he looked into the water and saw the sweet banana hanging, he did not look upwards.

"Oh," he said, "Uncle, come and see the ripe banana in the water!"

Spider took off his clothes; he jumped into the water; he remained moving about in the water.

And Royal Antelope looked upwards; he saw the ripe bananas; he climbed into the tree; he tore off a bunch of bananas; he jumped over Spider into the water. Spider and Royal Antelope came out of the water together.

Royal Antelope said, "Did you see it?"

"Oh," said Spider, "Uncle, my hand touched it."

"Oh," Royal Antelope said, "I ripped off one bunch; look at it."

Royal Antelope handed the bananas to Spider. Spider said, "I will not eat any." He thought that Royal Antelope had cut all the bananas without giving him any.

Royal Antelope said, "Father, let us not dive again."

But Spider dove into the water again.

As soon as Spider dove, Royal Antelope climbed the tree; he cut two bunches; he jumped over Spider /into the water/. Spider and Royal Antelope came out together.

Royal Antelope said, "Did you see any?"

Spider said, "I did not see any."

Royal Antelope said, "I cut two bunches."

Spider said, "Oh, Uncle, you are foolish! If I had reached them, I would have cut them all. Eat your part; if you gave me any, I would not eat it."

Then they undressed again and came into the water. Royal Antelope took some bananas again. Finally Royal Antelope finished all the bananas. If he gave Spider any bananas, Spider would not eat them.

When the fruit of the banana tree was completely plucked, Royal Antelope tapped Spider. He said, "Turn, look up."

Spider looked up at the banana tree; he saw the fruitless banana stump hanging there. Spider became angry; he said that Royal Antelope was foolish in his head.

Spider and Royal Antelope quarrelled there; they had a big fight.

What I heard someone say long ago, I have repeated.

Kasilo mia wọ. Ti lini wọ jiasiamẹi ta Hagbe. Kia wọ ti lini ngawu lọlọmẹi ji hamẹi wọlọngọ wa. Ti lilọ ti ngawui ji lọlọmẹi ji ti loni jiamalọ kẹ ti ngawu vọvọi ji lọnga. Ti loni ye tukpulọi gama gọkọlema lọ.

Sẹlẹi ji loni njẹi gblanga mẹmai i hẹlẹnga kẹ i ligbinga ngului ma njẹi mahu i loni hẹlẹni na lọ kẹ i gbowunga. Kpọwungọi ji na.

Kia Kasilo lini i loni ngawu lukpulọi ji gọkọli ma lọ a yẹma i njẹi ji bu gbenga kẹ i sẹlẹi nẹnẹi ji lọnga hẹlẹni njẹi bu. I nẹnẹi ji lọnga hẹlẹni, ii yaa ngelei ya gboni.

"Kuo," yẹ "kenya wa lẹ ngi sẹlẹ gbọlu lọnga njẹi bu!"

I ngi ma gbianga hindẹi na i kpọyọnga i wilinga njẹi hu i loni wilimalọ njẹi hu.

Ke Hagbe ngelei ya gbenga kẹ i sẹlẹ gbọlui ji lọnga kẹ ta bẹ lẹnga ngului ji hu gaya gaya kẹ i mbelanga ma tisa yila kẹ i wilinga ngi mahu njẹi hu kẹ ta ta ti gbia a lenga.

Yẹ "Bi tọi lọ?"

"Kuo," yẹ "kenya nya lokoi yẹlọ vuli a jala!"

"Kuo," yẹ "nya ngi mbelanga ma tisia yila," yẹ "ta gbe."

I ngi gọ yẹ "Ngii mẹma," gbẹva ta kaanga na lii hu ngi longọi ta i kpẹlẹ lewenga lọ na i wa lọ la ẹẹ ngi gọ.

Ta bẹ yẹ "Kẹ, maa lọmbu gbọma."

Kẹ i lọmbunga.

Ngi lọmbungọ leke, Kasilo lọmbunga hu kpọ, kẹ ta lẹnga ngului na hu kẹ i mbelanga ma tisa fele kẹ i wilinga Kasilo mahu kẹ ta ta ti gbianga a lenga.

Yẹ "Bi tọi lọ?

Yẹ "Ngii tọni."

Yẹ "Nya ngi mbelani ma tisa fele."

Yẹ "O, kenya," yẹ "bia bi malamangọ-e," yẹ "nya kpemẹi ngi fonga lọ ma" yẹ "nga kpẹlẹ lọ lewe na. Kuo" yẹ "bi ndẹi na mẹ bi fe bẹ mbẹ ngii mẹma."

Kẹ ti ti ma gbianga gbọma kẹ ti yeinga na kẹ Hagbe sẹlẹi ji gbianga na ta yila kpe i kpọyọ seng i fe bẹ ngi wẹ ẹẹ mẹ.

Kia wọ sẹlẹi ji gbọyọni na na seng kẹ i Kasilo mawọndẹnga yẹ "Wote lẹ bi ngelei ya gbe!"

Kẹ Kasilo ngelei ya gbenga sẹlẹi ji dagba gbamẹi hẹlẹni na na kẹ Kasilo lii lewenga yẹ "Hagbe ngi wu hu banga!"

Ti yianga hindẹi na, ndapi wa mia ti yẹ kọma.

Na ngi na woi na mẹni wọ ngi hugẹ.

---

1. Recorded by man from Bo in Freetown on January 12, 1960.

TALE 43: SPIDER, ROYAL ANTELOPE, AND THE FISH[1]

At one time Spider and Royal Antelope made an agreement. They said that they were going to fish; when they had caught the fish, Spider would divide the fish that they caught. If there were many fish, Spider would put the large fishes in his basket and the small fishes in Royal Antelope's basket. /After they had fished,/ Royal Antelope went to dry his fish; Spider cooked all his fish and ate them all at one time. Spider finished all his fish; he did not know that Royal Antelope was drying his fish. As soon as the rainy season came, hunger became severe; Royal Antelope crushed all his dried fish and made this fish flour very sweet by putting a lot of honey in it.

Ah, Royal Antelope and Spider made farms side by side. When Spider and his son went to the farmhouse at one time, they did not bring fire with them.

Spider said to his son, "Go yonder to Royal Antelope's farm to fetch fire."

Then the child went for the fire. When the child reached Royal Antelope's farmhouse, he met Royal Antelope's children eating sweet roasted flour. /Royal Antelope had made the powdered fish into flour.7 Then Royal Antelope cut off some flour and gave it to Spider's child. As Spider's child carried the fire, he was eating the flour; he licked it; he did not finish it quickly; it was sweet.

Spider sat until he saw his son. Then he went to meet his son on the road. When he met the boy, he did not look at the fire.

He said to the child, "What are you eating?"

Then Spider tore off a piece of the child's food; it was very sweet. Spider took all the food out of the child's hand and ate it. Then he took the firebrand out of the child's hand and threw it into the water. Then he walked off grumbling; as he went, he was trembling a lot.

"This very stupid child! Today I sent him after fire. Look, the boy went and dropped it into the water; the fire was completely extinguished. Uncle, good afternoon."

Spider had reached Royal Antelope's farmhouse, and his uncle answered him.

"Oh," Spider said, "what kind of sweet food did you give to this child?"

Now before Spider reached the farmhouse, as soon as Royal Antelope saw him coming, he hid all his children.

"Oh," said Royal Antelope, "my friend, while you were at your house, when this famine became severe, I killed my children. I made my children into the roasted flour that you saw; I beat them; I ground them up well; I made them into this sweet roasted flour."

"Oh," said Spider, "Uncle, I must decide what to do."

Then Spider took some fire and returned home. When he returned, he put out the fire. He caught one of his children; he threw the child into a mortar; he put all his many children into the mortar; he pounded them. Oh, blood filled the mortar; Spider killed all his children at that time out of greed.

Ah, that was how Spider and Royal Antelope behaved at one time.

Kasilo ta Hagbe mia wọ. Ti hinda hu gbatẹni tẹ ti ya nyẹ gbẹ. Ti nyẹi ji gbẹnga wọ, Kasilo mia a kọlẹ ti nyẹi hounga wọ. Kpotongọ nyẹ kpogboi le mia a pu ngi nda yivẹi nu, nyẹi ye mumuisia na ta mia a pu Hagbe nda hakẹi hu. Hagbe bẹ yalọ kẹ talọ mbema a mbe ta ngi Kasilo ta ya lọ ngi nyẹi kpẹlẹ mia a ngili i kpẹlẹ mẹ hindẹi lọ. Na i pieni haa kẹ ti kpọyọnga na mẹma nyẹi ji wọ mbema. Kia leke hamẹi gulani ndọlẹi gbọwoni kẹ i fukanga kpẹlẹ kẹ i gbatẹnga a kpọhu ji nẹingọ wa i kọmi ji wu hu vuli.

Ang kpaẹ ji ti ndani Hagbe nda gbaẹ lọ mbei Kasilo ndẹi lọ mbei. Kasilo ti yẹ wọ lima kpuẹla tii lini a ngọmbu.

Kẹ i ndenga ngi loi ye hindogẹi ji ma yẹ "Li miando Hagbe ye kpama" yẹ "bi li wa a ngọmbui."

Kẹ ndopoi ji ya ngọmbui woma. Kia wọ ndopoi ji lini i foni leke kpuẹla i maleni Hagbe lengẹi jisia ta kpọhui mọngọi ji mẹ nẹingọ wa. Nyẹ vukẹi ji i kpatẹni a kpọhui ji. Kẹ Hagbe mbelanga ma kẹ i fenga ndopoi ji wẹ. Ndopoi ji loni mẹmalọ i ngọmbui ji wumbunga i loni mẹmalọ haa a wa a lewe a ma gọmi i loni ii humbu a kpọyọ nẹingọ.

Kasilo ji i heinga haa i ngi loi lọni kẹ i ya ngi loi gulọ pelei ji hu i ya ta ndopoi ji ti gomẹnga. Ii ngọmbui gama gbeni.

Yẹ ndopoi ma "Gbọ lọ bi mẹma?"

Kẹ i kulo belangama kẹ i mẹnga ndopoi ji yeya nẹingọ kẹ i kpẹlẹ gbianga ndopoi ji yeya kẹ i mẹnga. Kẹ i ngọmbu gọtii gbianga ndopoi yeya kẹ i pilinga njẹi hu. Kẹ ta lọ na lewema a lumbe a li a gbẹli kpakpa.

"Kpowa kpowa lo bondẹi ji ngi ndenga wọ ngi tonga ha ngọmbu woma. Kpe ndopoi ya i gulanga i gulanga njẹi hu ngọmbui ji kpẹlẹ lufenga. Kenya, bia na."

I fonga kpuẹ ji la kẹ kenya lumanga.

"Kpua," yẹ mẹhẹ bondẹi ji bi feni ndopoi ji wẹ nẹingọ
bondẹi ji?"

"Kuo," yẹ "ingẹ nya nde" yẹ "ji bia bi ndẹi" yẹ "ji
ndọlẹi ji gbọwongọ."

Kẹ pẹngi fo kpuẹi ji la. Kia leke Hagbe tọni miando a
wa kẹ i ngi lengẹisia kpẹlẹ lọwunga.

Yẹ "Ji bi hindẹi" yẹ "kia hu na ndọlẹi ji gbọwongọ" yẹ
"nya lenga nya lenga mia" yẹ "ngi ti kpẹlẹ wanga" yẹ "tia mia
ngi ti kpẹlẹ gbatẹnga a kpọhu mọngọi ji bi tọma" yẹ "ngi
humanga ngi kpọgbonga a panda" yẹ "ta mia ngi kpatẹnga a kpọhu
mọngọi ji nẹingọ bondẹi ji."

"Kuo," yẹ "kenya ii ya bi ma."

Kẹ i ngọmbui wumbunga kẹ i yamanga ngọmbui ji. Kia wọ
i lini i ngọmbui lani i kpọyọni seng ngi loi na a hou lọ leke
a pili kondẹi hu kẹ ta na hu vakama i ti kpẹlẹ wu kondẹi hu a
yẹma i hinjanga ti kpẹlẹ o kẹ ngamẹi ji kondẹi vendanga fae
i ngi lenga kpẹlẹ wa wọ mẹhẹ hinda woma.

Ang hi wọ Kasilo ta Hagbe ta jiani.

---

1. Recorded by man from Bo in Freetown on January 7, 1960.
Reverend Stott's manuscript includes a Mende text and English
summary of a version of this tale; Innes' 1964 article presents a summary of a version of this tale. Innes (1964):9-10.

TALE 44: SPIDER, ROYAL ANTELOPE, AND THE BASKETS OF RICE[1]

Spider and his uncle Royal Antelope.

One time long ago Royal Antelope went searching for food;
he was looking for bushyams. Royal Antelope spent the whole
day looking for bushyams; he did not see any.

When the evening sun arose, Royal Antelope came to a large
and beautiful clearing. He saw some baskets with whips hanging
/from a tree/. There were baskets of many sizes: big ones
and small ones. Then Royal Antelope turned and saw a little
paper with writing on a basket; the paper said, "Rice is in
the basket. If anyone says that he wants to eat some rice,
the basket will come down and he will be whipped. If the
person does not cry out, he can eat the rice; if the person
cries out, the basket will rise again."

Then Royal Antelope did not worry about digging up bush-yams. He went to a very small basket of rice.

He said, "Let the very small basket of rice whip me once; let it stay on the ground so that I can eat it."

Then the basket of rice came down-vuu. The whip beat Royal Antelope once; Royal Antelope did not cry out; the basket settled on the ground; Royal Antelope ate some rice. Royal Antelope ate some but not all of the rice. He put the remainder in a basket and took it with him.

Royal Antelope carried the basket; he called Spider, and gave it to him.

"Oh!" Spider said, "Uncle, how did you get this food?"

"Oh," said Royal Antelope, "I got the food at a certain place. I will show you where but not today."

He said, "When will you show me the place?"

Royal Antelope said, "When the old women begin to cough, you come to me; we will go there."

What did Spider do?

As soon as he went, he put some pepper into the fire. People began to cough, "o-gbǫhu-gbǫhu."

Then Royal Antelope said, "Don't kill people!"

And Spider came; he said, "Uncle, they have begun to cough."

"Oh," said Royal Antelope, "no. Go back; go and lie down. Just at the time that the chief's wives are going for water, come to me."

Then Spider went again; he took a bucket and dropped it. Then he came to Royal Antelope again, he said, "Uncle, they have gone."

Royal Antelope said, "Go; lie down. Lie down until early in the morning. Go; be patient."

Spider went but he kept counting the hours. Morning came; Spider came to Royal Antelope, and they went.

As soon as they reached /the clearing/, Spider with his great greed went and stood in front of the big basket of rice which he wanted. As soon as the rice came down and he was slapped, he cried out; immediately the rice basket rose and hung in the tree; he did not eat anything.

Oh, this situation was difficult for Spider. He went to Crab, he said, "Uncle, help me so that I will not disgrace myself. Go, dig a hole for me. When the rice comes down, it will beat the hole, it will remain on the ground. Then you and I will eat the rice. Let me show you."

Crab agreed /to the plan/. The rice came down--vuu. Just as the whip was about to beat Spider, he went inside the hole; the whip beat the hole thinking that it was beating Spider; it did not hear a cry; it stayed on the ground. Then Spider ate some rice; he gave a little rice to Crab; he put a lot of rice in a basket. Then Spider called another basket down; it came down; he put the rice into his basket. The basket was very heavy. Then Spider and Royal Antelope started to walk to the town.

As Spider and Royal Antelope were walking, they reached a place where many vampire bats were hanging.[2] Royal Antelope caught a bat; he broke its neck; he dropped it in his basket. Spider joined in killing bats, but he did not catch as many bats as Royal Antelope. Spider decided to catch living bats; he caught the bats and put them into his basket on top of the rice. Spider and Royal Antelope continued on their way with the bats that they had caught.

They were going with their baskets. The living bats that Spider had put in his basket ate all the rice. Then the bats got out of Spider's basket and flew away. Only one bat remained in the basket. The bat went into a corner of the basket and lay down. Spider was very happy; he thought he was carrying rice and bats to eat that night.

Spider and Royal Antelope went on until they arrived in the town. Spider dropped his basket /on the ground/; he began to open his basket to look at the rice and bats he had brought. As soon as Spider opened the basket, he found only bat defecation inside it. As soon as Spider took out a leaf, the bat came out--kpui and flew up to the ceiling.

Spider called his children. They brought firewood; they set a big fire in the house.

Spider said to his children, "I am going to climb up to the ceiling. When I go up, if anything should fall, do not look at it; just beat it."

When Spider climbed up in order to catch this bat, he climbed a little way; he slipped and fell into the fire; he roasted there. Spider did not eat any rice; he did not eat any bats; he died. So that was how Spider reached the end of his greediness at one time.

That is why if your companion invites you to a feast, do not say that you alone should eat. Spider said that. At one time that is why Spider did not eat any food and he died.

Do you understand the little story that I told? Spider's own life was spoilt.

Kasilo ta ngi kenya Hagbe.

Wati lenga lenga woma wọ Hagbe ji i li lọ jẹsiamẹi ji mẹhẹi gọi mẹhẹi ji kẹ mẹhẹi na wọ ti yẹ kọkọi a wati na hu ta mia wọ a ngawui ji ndọgbọi yawui ji. Hagbe lilọ na ngawui ji gọkọima i luva lima kpẹing ii humbuni a ngawui ji lọ.

Kpọkọ voloi i yẹ hitima kine kẹ i ya i fo hinda wali wa hu yẹla ye wali ji hu na gbatẹngọ wa yẹla kẹ i kahẹi jisia lọnga felengọ fomẹisia ti lani ma ti hẹlẹ kpẹ. Kahẹi na ye mbawai ye kulowuloi ye saisingọi gboto hẹlẹ na. Kẹ i yama kẹ i kọlọ wulo lọnga nyẹngọ kahẹi na ma yẹ "Mba mia kahẹi na hu. Kẹ numu bi loa bẹ bi mbẹi na mẹ kẹ mbẹi na a wa i bi vogba bii wọẹ lọ kẹ bi mẹ kẹ bi wọa a yama lọ mẹhẹi na."

Hm kẹ Hagbe bẹ ta bẹ i ya bẹ ngii mọnẹi ngawu gbua va. Kẹ i ya mbẹiyẹi kulo wuloi na mia.

Kẹ i ndea yẹ "Mbẹi ye kulo wuloi na mia i wa i nya vogba voli i hei ngi mẹ."

Kẹ mbẹi na wavu. A ngi yeya vomẹi na kẹ i Hagbe vogba voli Hagbe ii wọẹ kẹ mbẹi na heinga kẹ Hagbe i mẹa, i tẹnga mẹ ii gbọyọni. Kẹ i na wua kahẹi hu kẹ i ya la.

Kia i li la kẹ i Kasilo lolinga kẹ i ngi gọnga.

"Kuo," Kasilo yẹ "kenya bi ye hiyeni a mẹhẹi bondẹi ji?"

"Kuo" yẹ "mẹhẹi ji mia ngi gbua la na" yẹ "nga na gẹ kẹ ha yama ẹẹ."

Yẹ "Migbe lọ ba na gẹ?"

"O" yẹ "mẹhẹi ji" yẹ "nga na gẹ" yẹ "kẹ kpe leweni kine mama wovẹisia ti wunga tọhẹi hu" yẹ "bi wa" yẹ "mua bie mua lilọ na."

Kpọ Kasilo ji pie?

I lilọ lee kẹ i pujẹ vokẹi ji wua koloiya. Nunga ti wua tọhẹi hu. O gbọhu gbọhu ti wua tọhẹi hu.

Kẹ Hagbe ndea yẹ "Baa nunga wa le."

Kẹ i wa yẹ "Kenya ti wua tọhẹi hu."

"Kuo" yẹ "mm" yẹ "yama" yẹ "yama vuli bi li bi la gbe wẹi kine mahẹi nyahanga ti ya lima njẹi hu" yẹ "ye wati na hu bi wa."

Kẹ i ya i li gbọma kẹ faji ji wumbua i tọtonga a ye ji gulala kẹ i wa gbọma yẹ "Kenya ti ya."

Ta bẹ yẹ "Li bi la bi la nge wo na vuli" yẹ "bi li i lẹi."

Kẹ i ya kẹ i loi na haa lowọi gbawama. Kẹ ngele wonga kẹ i wanga kẹ ti ya.

Kia le ti foi Kasilo ta ngi mẹhẹi hinda wai ji gama foisi i li i loni mbẹi ye mbawailọ gulọ ta ngi lọngọ. Kia le wọ mbẹi ji yẹi ngi vogbẹi kẹ i wọlọnga a mẹ lenjẹ kẹ mbẹi yama i hẹ na ii mẹni.

Kuo! Hindẹi ji gba kulo ngi ma. Kẹ i ya ngaku gama yẹ "Kenya" yẹ "ba lo nya woma" yẹ "nga jambo" yẹ "li bi bi ndowẹi bọ nya wẹ. Mbẹi ji wa nguama ndowẹi ji hu i ndowẹi ji la vogba" yẹ "a heilọ. Kẹ mua bie mu ngi mẹa." Yẹ "Fale" yẹ "nya kẹ."

Ngaku bẹ luma kẹ mbẹi ji i wa vuu. Kia le yẹ i Kasilo vogba a mẹ kpui kẹ i wanga ndowẹi hu. Ii ngọ wo mẹnini kẹ i heinga. Kasilo ji kẹ i mbẹi ji mẹa i Ngaku gọi kulohi mbẹi ji kẹ a pu le kahẹi ji hu a pu le kahẹi ji hu a pu le kahẹi ji hu a pu le kahẹi ji hu kẹ i peka ma loli wenga. Kẹ i wa gbọma kẹ i pua kahẹi ji hu miningọ wa kẹ ti tọtoa tẹi hu kẹ ti jẹi humbua na li va tẹi hu.

Tia Hagbe ji ti lilọ le kẹ ti ya ti fo ndẹvẹi jisia ma tẹ hẹngọ wa tia taja jisia kẹ Hagbe ta i ndẹvẹi ji hounga i mbo gbini i kula kahẹi ji hu. Kasilo ta yẹ i wulio wọ ndẹvẹi ji wa lẹi ji hu ii ndẹvẹi ji houa gboto. Na wienga Hagbe a le lọ ngi ma yẹ "Fuli hi le" a hou a sọsọ mbẹi ji mahu a sọsọ mbẹi ji mahu a soso mbẹi ji mahu kahẹi ji hu kẹ ti longa hu. Kẹ ti ndẹvẹi jisia houa kpẹ kẹ ndẹvẹi jisia ti hounga ti kahẹi ji wumbua na.

Tia lima Kasilo nda lẹvẹ vulisia ha ti wama kahẹi ji hu ti mbẹi na gbi mbẹi na mẹilọ heefi ti gbi ti gbua ti li. I lo na yakpe kẹ i wa kahẹi na yẹ skọku skọku yila hu i wẹ na. Kasilo gohunẹngọ wa yẹ ta lima a mbẹi kẹ ndẹvẹisia ti mẹma a kpọkọi na.

Kẹ i ya kẹ ti ya ti fo a kahẹi ji gula kẹ ta i tọtonga a mavulo la i kọ kia i yeya a mbẹi na kẹ hani nasia i ya la. Kia le wọ i mavuloni ndẹvẹi gboi na le mia i yẹ wui na. Kia le yẹ i ndawẹi na gbua le kẹ ndẹvẹi gbua yẹ kpuli kẹ i lẹnga ngelei ya.

Kasilo hiyea i ngi lenga kpę loli ti wa a kǫwui ti
ngǫmbu wa yatę pęlęi na bu.

Kę i ndenga ti ma yę "Nya lęma ngelei ya" yę "ngi lęa
hani gbi leke gula" yę "waa mabę" yę "wu nde."

Kia Kasilo le kǫoi lę i ndęvęi ji hou i le lǫ le kulo
kę i namunga kę i gula Kolei na ya i mǫ wǫ kpaye ii mbęi na
męni ii ndęvęi na męni i yama i ha. So na mia wǫ i wie
Kasilo. Kę i hitenga męhęi hinda gęlęma.

Na va mia nu wa bi mba bę wa li męhęi hinda gomę hu bę
bia yakpe bi mę, Kasilo ngi nde na wie wǫ ii męhęi na męni
ęę yama i ha.

Ba na woi mę ngi hungę? Kasilo lę vui nyani wo mia.

---

1. Recorded by young man from Pujehun in Freetown on May 13,
1960. Thrice versions of this tale have been presented:
Migeod (1908) published a Mende text with English translation;
Stott (MS, n.d.) presented a Mende text and English summary;
Innes (1964) published an English summary.
2. Bat (ndęvę) figures as a protagonist in Tales 64 and 65.

TALE 45: LEOPARD, TIGER, AND ROYAL ANTELOPE[1]

My father, something that happened at one time in the
country.

Many years ago Leopard used to catch animals all the
time, Leopard kept catching animals; for some time he oppressed
them. Then the animals went and hid. When the animals hid,
Leopard went about; he did not see any animal; he got up
quickly.

At that time the animals did not have any food unless
they crossed a big river; across the river was food. Leopard
went and carved a big boat; he put it at the river crossing;
he became a ferryman.

The animals were very hungry.

When an animal came and called across the river; Leopard
came and said, "Jump in the boat. You can go to eat food."
As soon as they crossed the river, Leopard would catch the
animal that had jumped into the boat and eat it. Leopard
killed the animals there; he oppressed them.

One day Royal Antelope went to Tiger; he said, "Tiger."

Tiger said, "Yes?"

Royal Antelope said, "I beg you. I hid all my children some time ago. But when they go to the eating place, Uncle Leopard who went and sat at the river crossing, just eats them. What would be good.

Tiger said, "Yes."

Royal Antelope said, "Uncle, lie down in a basket; we will cover you with cloth. When we have covered you, I will take you; I will say that I am going to sell country cloth." He said, "If water is in the boat, I will go into the bow of the boat; I will sit there. As soon as Leopard has crossed the river, you catch him and kill him so that he will not chase us."

Tiger agreed to this plan.

Royal Antelope put Tiger in a basket; he covered him with a cloth; he wrapped a little cloth around his face; he carried him /to the river/.

Royal Antelope said, "Uncle, come for me."

Leopard paddled to the river crossing. As soon as Leopard arrived, Royal Antelope took the basket and put it in the boat; Royal Antelope got in the boat; he went and sat in the bow of the boat and Leopard stayed in the stern.

When the boat reached the middle of the river, Leopard said, "When we have crossed the river, I will eat you."

Royal Antelope kept sitting in the bow; he said, "Of course, when we have crossed the river--if you eat me, Tiger will eat you."

Leopard said, "What did you say?"

Royal Antelope said, "Uncle, I said when we have crossed the river, I will go to sell this cloth."

When they had just crossed the river and Leopard said, "Get out there," Tiger got out of the basket; he swung Leopard and turned him upside down.

At one time Royal Antelope was saved.

Nya kẹkẹ, hinda yila mia wieni wọ ndọlẹi hu.

Folo gboto lewengọ na kọli mia wọ yẹ huanga hou kẹlẹma gbii ma. I huangẹi jisia hou lọ haa i gbou to la tia bẹ kẹ ti ya ti lọwu. Kia ti ndọwui ji wieni kọli i lewe i lewe ẹẹ huang lọ ta bẹ kẹ i hijenga kpa.

Kẹ kakẹi na ma wọ huangẹi nasia ti na mẹhẹi gbi na kẹ leke ti njẹi lewe nja wa na woma mia na mia mẹhẹi na. Kọli bẹ li lọ i li i ndẹndẹ wa hawa kẹ i wa kẹ i nda njẹi ji la kẹ i wotenga bẹ na a kutuwoba.

Huangẹi jisia ndọlẹi ji mininga ti ma.

Kia na a wa kẹ i toli wienga njẹi woma kia a wa yẹ "Wili ndẹndẹi hu bi mẹhẹ mẹ." Na wilima ndẹndẹi hu le ti njẹi lewenga kẹ i na houa kẹ i mẹa. I ti wa lọ na i gbou.

Folo yila ma kẹ Hagbe bẹ kẹ i ya sugbu gama yẹ "Sugbu."

Yẹ "A."

Yẹ "Konẹle" yẹ "nya lenga kpẹlẹ ngi ti lọwunga wọ" yẹ "kẹ ti ya lima mẹhẹi mẹmẹi" yẹ "kenya kọli gbe i ya i heinga njẹi la" yẹ "ta le ti mẹma na." Yẹ "Na nyandengọ."

Yẹ "Hn?"

Yẹ "Kenya la kahẹi ma mu bi mayili" yẹ "mu bi mayilinga," yẹ "ngi ya a bie" yẹ "nga ndelọ" yẹ "ngẹ kọndi gula mia ngi lima majia ma." Yẹ "Ina nja ndẹndẹi hu" yẹ "nya ngi lima mia ndẹndẹi yẹ hokpamẹi." Yẹ "Nga" yẹ "hei na." Yẹ "Kẹ ji le i njẹi lewenga" yẹ "kẹ bi hounga kẹ bi paa kọ ii hiye mu woma."

Kẹ i luma bẹ.

Kẹ i nda kahẹi ma i mayili i kpọkọ i kula wo mbembe ngama kẹ i ya la.

Yẹ "A kenya wa nya woma-o."

Kẹ i njẹi wilia kẹ i wa njẹi ji la. Ngi fongọ leke-o kẹ i kahẹi ji wumbua kẹ i nda ndẹndẹi ji hu kẹ ta ya mia ndẹndẹ yẹ hokpalẹ i li i hei kẹ kọli ta longa mbeindo poma.

Kia wọ ti li ti foni njẹi lia lọ kẹ kọli lọ na ndema yẹ "Mu njẹi lewe njẹi woma ngi bi mẹ."

Hagbe i loni hei mia lọ bawoemẹi yẹ "Ingẹ mu njẹi lewe njẹi woma bi nya mẹa lọ sugbu lọ a bi mẹ."

Yẹ "Bẹ gbẹ?"

Yẹ "Kenya ngẹ mu lewe njẹi le njẹi woma ngi li ngi kulẹi
ji majia."

Kia wọ ti njẹi lewe le njẹi woma leke kọli yẹ "I hije mia"
kẹ sugbu hijenga kahẹi ma a mẹi vaung kẹ i vẹmbẹ a la kẹ i
kpu ma.

Hiagbe mia i bawo wọfọ.

---

1. Recorded by man from Bo in Freetown on January 27, 1960.

TALE 46: CAT AND LEOPARD[1]

A long time ago Leopard and Cat were very close friends.

Once Leopard met Cat in the bush. Cat knew that Leopard
would eat all living creatures. When Cat saw Leopard, he was
afraid. Rain was coming and Cat was very afraid. He thought
that Leopard wanted to eat him.

Cat said, "I did not know that it would rain today. I
just put a lot of skins in the sun; I put them out in the sun
today in order to dry them. This rain will get everything
wet."

As soon as Cat spoke, Leopard asked, "What kind of skin
could this little creature get?"

"Oh," Cat said, "leopard skin, bushcow skin, chimpanzee
skin--I have gotten lots of skins."

"Oh, yes," Leopard said, "you little creature, you got
such things! How were you able to get those skins?"

Cat said, "What happened to them; I know that I am small;
I can crouch down. As soon as I crouch down, I grow bigger;
I catch an animal; I kill it; I take his skin off. That is
what I do to get those skins."

When Cat said this, Leopard said, "Then by all means
crouch; go on; I want to see that."

When Leopard said that Cat should crouch, Cat started to
get bigger; he stretched his eyes and cheeks--fff. As soon as
Leopard saw this, he was very afraid; what did he do? As soon
as Cat just began to crouch and to grow bigger, Leopard ran
away into the rain; the rain beat on him; he ran away. As soon

as Cat saw that Leopard had gone so far away that he would not
be able to return to catch him, Cat also came out and went
away.

That was how Cat saved himself at one time. That is what
happened so that up to this time, if Leopard calls Cat, he
calls him "Uncle."

Lọ hu guhangọ lengọ woma wọ kọli ta gọnẹ ti yẹlọ wọ
ndiamọ ya yekpe wa hu.

Kẹ wati yila kọli ji i liilọ i gọnẹ male ndọgbọi hu. Kia
i ngi maleni tao gọnẹ kọlọ kẹ kọli a huanga mẹlọ kẹ fuhanisia
kpẹlẹ. Kia i ngi lọni kẹ i luwanga. Njẹi ji i wama kẹ i
luwanga wa ta bẹ kẹ i ndenga kọli longọ gọnẹ mẹ.

Kẹ ta bẹ i ndenga yẹ "Ngii na ha njẹi ji i wanga nya woma"
yẹ "kọlẹi jisia kpẹlẹ gẹ nga puma folei ji ya, ngi kpua ha
folei ji ya gẹ kọ ti be." Yẹ "Njẹi ji i wanga i gbi lẹli ma
lọ lọọ."

Kia le i ndeni kẹ kọli ngi mọlinga-e yẹ "Gbẹ gọlọ mia bi
wulo ji ha gu ma?"

"Kuo," yẹ "kọli kọlọ-o, tewu kọlọ-o, ngolo kọlọ-o" yẹ
"kọlọ gboto wa" yẹ "nga gulọma."

"Kuo, e" yẹ "bi bi wulo ji ẹ bi gulo hingọ bondẹi ji ba ye
hi pie ba gu kọlẹi nasia?"

Yẹ "Pelei na gula ti ma" yẹ "nya ngi kọlọ mumui mia a nge"
yẹ "nga luvẹlọ hu." Yẹ "Ngi luvẹngalọ le hu" yẹ "kẹ ngi
wọlọnga wa" yẹ "kẹ ngi huẹi ye na hounga ngi pa ngi ngi gọlẹi
gbua." Yẹ "Hi mia nga pie nga gu kọlẹi nasia ma."

Ji lengọ kọli bẹ kẹ i ndenga yẹ "Kẹ luvẹlẹ hu họ yo ngi
na lọ."

Kia kọli i ndeni yẹ "Gọnẹ i luvẹ" kẹ gọnẹ i tọtonga a vela
vọwu a ngi yamẹi ji lalahu kẹ ta na ngi gomẹi ji yẹma fff. Kia
kọli i ji hu lọ ni le kẹ i luwanga wa, ta gbọ i pieni? Kia
leke gọnẹ i tọtoni leke a luvẹla hu i tọtoni a vela hi kẹ i
lewenga a pimẹ i gbua njẹi na bu i gbua njẹi na i loilọ haa...
ngi lewe ma a lewe a pimẹ. Gọnẹ bẹ kia leke i tọni kẹ kọli
i ya ha gutangọ na hi ẹẹ ya gu a wote a yama a ngi hou kẹ
ta bẹ i gbua na i li.

Na lọ wọ fọ i pieni kẹ ngi na baonga na mia wieni kọli
kia bẹ hu na a gọnẹ loli na yẹ ngi kenya.

1. Recorded by young man from Pujehun in Freetown on February 12, 1960.

TALE 47: THE MONKEYS AND LEOPARD[1]

What happened at one time so that Leopard does not jump like Monkeys.

At one time Leopard went to Monkey. Leopard said that Monkey should enable him to jump into a tree as Monkeys do. The Monkeys sat in one place and they agreed; they came to Leopard.

Monkeys said, "Oh, how are we going to arrange that?"

"What would be good."

They said, "Yes."

Leopard said, "Come, give me your medicine."

Monkeys said, "We agree."

Then the Monkeys returned.

One Monkey said to his companions, "Before we give our medicine to this man, let us call Kejei Monkey. We will take Kejei Monkey to Leopard and tell him to put him under his head in order to be able to jump. Let Leopard sleep with Kejei Monkey under his head until morning; then we will give Leopard the jumping medicine."

When Monkeys took this bundle and gave it to Leopard, he laid it under his head.

When night came, Leopard boasted, "When tomorrow morning comes, Monkeys will give their medicine to me, with God's help. I will destroy them all. Danger will fall on them. Let me meet them, God will make the medicine that they will give me. I will kill two monkeys each day; I will not kill them /all at once/."

In the morning Monkeys came and took the bundle; they carried it away. At once Kejei Monkey got out of the bundle.

Kejei Monkey said, "You want danger to fall on us! If you give the jumping medicine to Uncle Leopard, he will cut all our heads off. Last night that is what he was saying yonder."

At that time what did Monkeys give to Leopard? /The kind of medicine that they decided to give him was:/ If you are on the ground, you will jump far only on the ground. Monkeys came with the medicine.

Monkeys said, "Uncle, we have come to bring you the medicine."

As soon as they rubbed the medicine on Leopard's face, he jumped.

"Ah," Monkeys said, "that is the only kind of jump in the world that you will make."

That is what happened at one time so that Leopard does not jump upwards, he /only/ jumps on the ground.

Do you hear the little story that I have related?

This is the end of the story.

Na wọ i wieni kọli ẹẹ windẹ kia kuanga ti na.

I li lọ wọ kua gama ta ngi kọli yẹ i pie ta bẹ i windẹ ngului hu, kia ta windẹ la. Kuanga bẹ kẹ ti heinga hinda yila kẹ ti gulunga kẹ ti wa ngi gama.

"Kuo," tẹ "mu ye na hugbatẹi wiema?"

"Gbọ nyandengọ."

Tẹ "Mn."

Yẹ "Wu wa wu halei ve mbẹ."

Ta bẹ tẹ "Mu lokolọ ma."

Kẹ ti yama.

Kẹ ti mba yila ndenga ti ma a yẹ "Pẹing mu mu halei ji ve kenẹi ji wẹ," yẹ "a mu kua kejei loli, jifa pẹing hi" yẹ "mu li mu nde muẹ i nda wu kọ kia a wili la. A nji la. I yi ngi wu lọ ngele wua kẹ mu pindẹ halei venga."

Kia wọ ti ye hakẹi ji wumbuni ti veni ngi wẹ i ndani wu.

Kia kpindi wue lọ kẹ ta na yonga lewema. "Kpẹlẹ sina ngele i wo Ngewọ ja hu jia ti halei ji ve mbẹ nga ti gbọyọlọ seng. Kpundẹ vuli mia gula ti ma. Kẹ gbẹ mua ti mu bẹ hu Ngewọ le i pie ti hale ta ve. Ngi ti wa fele folo na kẹ ngii ti wa."

Ngele woi lọ wọ kẹ ti wa kẹ ti mbumbua ti ya la kẹ ti
kua kejei ji lọa i gbuanga te gbe.

"A" yẹ "kpundẹi mia wu longọ wẹ wu kula mu ma." Yẹ "Wu
pindẹi halei fea Kenya Kọli wẹ" yẹ "a mu wu le lọkpẹ a yẹ hi
mia kini i ndea kpindi ji."

Tia bẹ na na wọ ti vei ngi wẹ? Ji ba lo loi ndọlọmẹi
bi lo loi bi windẹ huguhangọ kẹ na mia wọ. Kẹ ti wa na a hale.

Tẹ "Kenya, mu wa halei vema bi wẹ."

Kia wọ ti siani ngi lama a mẹ kuja i windẹnga.

"A" tẹ "bi windẹ wie kpẹlẹ mia ndunya."

A na mia wọ wieni kọli ii windẹni ngeleya a windẹ
ndọlọmẹi lọ.

Bi na wuloi na mẹi ngi hugẹ?

Dọmẹi ji gẹlẹngẹi mia.

---

1. Recorded by man from Bo in Freetown on January 27, 1960.

TALE 48: GOAT, LEOPARD, AND LION[1]

Why Leopard and Lion do not like each other is what I am
going to tell you now.

At one time Goat was in a town and he said that he was
going to Mecca. When he was going to Mecca, he had a jar of
honey in his hand. And he started on his way.

He remained walking for two years until he reached a
farm. The rain was falling heavily. Goat entered the farmhouse so that the rain would not hit him. He remained there;
the rain came; it beat down.

While Goat was sitting inside, before long Leopard /came/;
he too was going to Mecca and he too had been walking for two
years. Leopard reached this farm; he saw the dark rain.

Leopard said, "Let me go into this farmhouse so that the
rain will not beat me."

When Leopard came into the farmhouse, Goat saw him and he
came out.

Goat said, "Uncle, good afternoon."

Leopard said, "Yes, good afternoon."

Goat said, "Uncle, where are you going?"

"Oh," Leopard said, "I am going to Mecca."

Goat said, "All right; Uncle, I am going to Mecca too."

"Oh," Leopard said, "you have reached." So Leopard said to him, "you have reached," which means that Leopard is going to eat Goat at that place; Goat is not going to pass on.

Ah, and Goat was very afraid. Goat sat there trembling inside.

Before long Lion also /came/ going to Mecca; Lion came out in this farm, the rain was dark.

Lion said, "Oh, let me enter this farmhouse where the rain will not beat me."

As soon as Lion entered the farmhouse, Leopard saw him.

Leopard said, "Uncle, good afternoon."

Lion said, "Yes, Leopard, good afternoon."

Leopard said, "Yes, Uncle, where are you going?

"Ah," Lion said, "I am going to Mecca."

"Oh," Leopard said, "Uncle, I also am going to Mecca."

Lion said, "Where, Goat, is it that you /are going/?"

Goat said also, "I am going to Mecca."

And Lion turned and saw the bottle in Goat's hand; he said to Goat, "What is in your hand?"

"Oh," Goat said, "Uncle, I have food in my hand; it is very sweet. But a person does not eat this food with any kind of meat except leopard meat."

Leopard turned and looked at Goat sideways. Goat knew that he was not saved, /because/ big Lion would not be able to eat Goat; he would only eat Leopard. Then Leopard was worried. When Lion heard Goat say that a person ate his food with leopard meat, Lion turned and killed Leopard. Goat knew that he was saved; he went.

This is what happened at one time so that Leopard and Lion do not like each other.

Na Kọli ta Njala tii loni ma na mia na ngi na gẹma a wue.

Wọ Nje ji ta tẹi ji hu kẹ i ndenga yẹ "I lima Mẹka lọ." I ya lima Mẹka lọ kọmi jani lọ yila ngi yeya. Kẹ i pelei ji hounga.

I loni wọ limalọ fo fele a jia kẹ i fonga kpaẹ ji hu kẹ njẹi ji gbilinga ngọngọ kẹ nje wanga kpuẹi ji la nje ji aa ngi lewe wọ.

I loni njẹi ji i wa i lewe i longa heinilọ hu ii guhani kọli bẹ mẹma ta lọ lima Mẹka ta bẹ jianga fo fele. I fonga kpaẹ ji hu i nja gbili lọnga.

Yẹ "Gbẹ ngi wa kpuẹ ji la ji fa wọi njẹi ji a nya lewe."

Ngi wangọ kpuẹi ji hu yo. Kẹ nje ngi lọnga i kpua.

Yẹ "Kenya bua."

Yẹ "I," yẹ "buwae."

Yẹ "Kenya bi lima mi lọ?"

"Kuo," yẹ "ngi lima Mẹka lọ."

Yẹ "kungọi" yẹ "Kenya," yẹ "nya bẹ ngi lima Mẹka lọ."

"Kuo," yẹ "bi fonga." Ji i ndenga ngi ma yẹ "Bi fonga" na kẹngọ i ngi mẹma hindẹi na la ii yaa lewe ma.

Aah kẹ nje luwanga wa i heini na ngi ma a gbẹli hu.

Ii guhani mẹmai sugbu ji bẹ lima Mẹka lọ kẹ i gbianga kpaẹ ji hu njẹi ji gbilingọ.

Ta bẹ "Kuo" yẹ "gbẹ ngi wa kpuẹ ji la njẹi ji hu i lewe a nge."

Kia lewe wọ i wani le kpuẹ bu kia leke kọli ngi lọni.

Kẹ i ndenga yẹ "Kenya bua."

Yẹ "I," yẹ "kọli," yẹ "bua."

Yẹ "I," yẹ "kenya," yẹ "bi lima mi lọ?"

"Ang," yẹ "ngi lima Mẹka lọ."

"Kuo," yẹ "kenya," yẹ "nya bẹ ngi lima Mẹka lọ."

Yẹ "Ọ nje bia bẹ?"

Nje bẹ yẹ "Ngi lima Mẹka lọ."

Kẹ sugbu wotenga kẹ i sani ji lọnga nje yeya yẹ nje ma ye "Gbọ mia bi yeya?"

"Kpo," yẹ "kenya," yẹ "mẹhẹ mia nya yeya"; yẹ "nẹngọ wa," yẹ "kẹ mẹhẹi ji numu ẹẹ mẹ a hua-o-hua weka," yẹ "kẹ leke kọli hua."

Kẹ koli wotenga i ngi gbe a jẹngbẹ hu wele nje ta kọnga na kẹ ngi ma bawonga ji va. Sugbu wa kẹ ẹẹ gu i ngi mẹ kẹ leke kọli a mẹ fale koli bẹ kẹ ngi li hẹlẹnga. Kia wọ na sugbu humeni nje ndeni na wọ yẹ mẹhẹi ji ngi yeya numui a mẹ a kọli huа lọ i woteni lọ wọ i kọli wa. Kẹ nje la ngi ma bawong i li.

Na va mia wọ kọli ta sugbu tii loni ma.

---

1. Recorded by man from Bo in Freetown on January 7, 1960.

Leaders and Followers

TALE 49: THE CHIEF AND THE TURTLE[1]

My father, at one time there was a young man who was made chief in a town. No one could tell a lie. If you told a lie, they would kill you immediately. At one time this situation oppressed all the country. If you told a lie, you would be killed; the situation continued; it was serious.

A jovial man came into this town; he said, "Father."

The chief said, "Yes."

The man said, "A chief in a nearby town is coming to visit you soon."

The chief made a lot of preparations. They spent the whole day sitting; they did not see the /visiting/ chief.

"Oh," the chief said, "Comrade, you are a stranger who came today. There is a law in this country that a person cannot tell a lie. Why, today, you said 'the chief is coming'; he did not come; therefore, we will kill you."

Then they killed the man. When they killed the man at one time, they did not know that he could transform himself. When they killed the man, he transformed himself.

When this chief was going to the river to bathe, this young man (to whom they had said that he told a lie and they killed him not knowing that he was a magician) had changed into a turtle. The chief saw him on the road.

The chief said to his servent, "Take the turtle yonder; we will carry it into the house; we will train it."

And they took the turtle; they carried it into the big house; it stayed there; they trained it.

When everyone in the town had gone out, the turtle got up at once and came to the chief's mother who was the only person in the house.

"Oh," the turtle said, "Mother."

She said, "Yes."

He said, "Let me tell you something."

She said, "Yes."

He said, "They are going to make this whole country one;
your son is going to become a big chief over all this country.
I am telling you; it is true."

Oh, she ran outside; her son asked, "What is the matter?"

She said, "The turtle said that you are going to be chief
of the entire country."

He said, "Who said that?"

She said, "It was the very turtle that you recently brought
into this house."

"Oh," the people said, "then let us go there."

And the people went into the town. They questioned the
turtle. Of course, the turtle was drawn up /in his shell7;
he lay there on the ground. They questioned him--he was quiet.

"Oh," the people said, "Chief, your mother told a lie."

"Oh," said the chief, "there is no way out of it."

Then they took the old woman and they killed her.

The night passed; morning came. The chief's beloved wife
went to bathe. At one time she stood bathing in the yard.
Immediately the turtle went to her.

The turtle said, "Mother."

She said, "Yes."

He said, "Let me tell you /something7."

She said, "Yes."

He said, "About the chieftaincy--if the chief died, they
would make you the chief. If you want to have it happen now,
all you do is go, say to the chief, 'Make it so that I become
chief.' If he asks you who said it, you say, 'the turtle.'"

Then the noble woman ran out of the yard; she went and
said, "Father, your chieftaincy--I am the one who will become
chief."

"Oh," he said, "who told you?"

She said, "The turtle."

Then the chief went; the people went; they questioned the

turtle who kept silent, and they killed the chief's senior
wife.

When morning came, the chief was lying in his hammock,
and the turtle came and bowed down right under his hammock.
Immediately the turtle blew a horn; he blew a horn; he blew
a horn. The chief turned away from the noise of the horn
which was blowing in his ear.

The chief said, "Oh, what is the matter? My people,
who is making that sort of horn blowing noise?"

"Oh," the people said, "where chief?"

The people sat; they did not see any hornblower; the
turtle had returned into the house long ago; they listened
there for a while; they listened.

They said, "Oh, Chief, you yourself have told a lie."

And they killed this chief.

When they killed this chief at one time, the young man
returned. The turtle changed back into a living person.

He said, "Ah, this man, who laid this law on the country
at one time, was bad. Therefore, I wanted to remove the law;
I changed into the turtle. I am the one who came and told the
chief that his companion chief was coming to visit him."

"Oh," the people said, "what would be good."

He said, "Yes?"

They said, "To have the kind of person who came in this
country /as our chief/. Although he is a stranger in this
country, let us make him our chief."

At one time they made the turtle their chief; he became
the chief in that country.

This is the end of this story.

Nya kɛ, ndakpao yila mia wɔ ti ngi heini a mahɛi te hu.
Numu gbi ɛɛ ndɛ gulama. Bi ndɛ gulanga le ti bi wama. Hindɛi
ji lɔ wɔ i gbɔluni ndɔlɔi kpɛ la i gbɔu na ndɔlɔi kpɛla. Bi
ndɛ gula ta bi wa lɔ na hu ɛɛ nyani hindɛi i mini.

Ndakpao yila ta ngeyangemɔ mia a ngie, kɛ i gbuanga tɛi
ji hu yɛ "Kɛkɛ."

Yẹ "Eẹ."

Yẹ "Tẹi ji hu hindẹi ji" yẹ "ye maha yila" yẹ "ta wama vama bi makulọ."

Gbatẹ gboto mia i pieni. Ti luva heini kpẹing tii mahẹi ji lọni.

"Kuo," yẹ "ndakpẹi," yẹ "hota mia a bie bi wa ha ta sawa ndọlọi ji hu numui ẹẹ ndẹ gula. Gbe ha bi ndenga bẹ 'Mahẹi lọ wama," yẹ "ii wani," yẹ "fale" yẹ "mua bi walọ-o."

Kẹ ti ngi wanga. Ti ngi walọ wọ fọ ta bẹ ngi hangọi ji mia mẹma maluve mia. Ti ngi panga, i maluvelọ.

Mahẹi ji i ya lima njẹi hulọ muamẹi kẹ ndakpaoi ji na (ti ndenga tẹ "I ndẹ gulanga ti ngi panga" mẹma kọvomọ mia a ngie.) Kẹ i wotea a hakui. Kẹ mahẹi ji tọnga pelei ma.

Kẹ i ndenga ngi boilopoi ma yẹ "Kẹ hakui na wumbu mia mu li la pẹlẹ bu mu makẹ."

Kẹ ti hakui ji wumbua kẹ ti ya la pẹlẹ wa bu ta na ta makẹ.

Kia wọ nunga gbi ti vaya tẹi hu, a mẹng kpui hakui ji gbua ta ngi mahẹi ngi nje yilakpe ji mia i lọni pẹlẹi bu kẹ hakui ji gbia.

"Kuo," yẹ "Ye."

Yẹ "Mn."

Yẹ "Ngi nde ngi ma."

Yẹ "Mn."

Yẹ "Ye ndọlọi ji hu kpẹlẹ ti wama ndagbọma;" yẹ "bi loi mia wama wotema a maha wa ndọlọi ji kpẹlẹ hu," yẹ "fale, ngi nde wu ma," yẹ "sala bẹ ii ma."

Kuo kẹ i gbua a pimẹ ngi loi mọlinga yẹ "Gbẹe?"

Kẹ ngi loi mọlinga kẹ i ndenga yẹ "Hakui" yẹ "ngi nde wu ma" yẹ "bia mia bi wama lọma ndọlọi ji kpẹlẹ gulọ."

Yẹ "Ye mia ndeni?"

Yẹ "Hakui ji vuli pẹlẹi ji bu gẹ bi wa la."

"Kuo," tẹ "kẹ a mu li na."

Kẹ ti ya ti ya tẹ hu ti hakui ji mọli. Ingẹ i gbokpau miando ndọlọmẹi i wie na ti ngi mọli lọ.

"Kuo," tẹ "mahẹi, bi nje ndẹ gulanga."

"Kuo," yẹ "pie ngi ii ma."

Kẹ ti ya la kẹ ti paa.

Hu i yoi gbuu ngele i wo ngi nyahẹi ji vuli ngi longa la i ya mua ma. I loni wọ kului hu lọ muamẹi a mẹn kpole kẹ hakui wilinga ngi mahu.

Yẹ "ye."

Yẹ "Mn."

Yẹ "Ngi nde bi ma."

Yẹ "Mn."

Yẹ "Mahayẹi na" yẹ "mahẹi na hanga" yẹ "bia mia ti bi heima a mahẹi." Yẹ "Bi longa bẹ kẹ na i lọ na" yẹ "kpẹlẹ mia ngi ndema bi ma," yẹ "li bi nde mahẹi ma bẹ 'bia ba pẹ nya nga mahayẹi mẹ.' I ya yelọ ndeni bẹ 'Haku.'"

Kẹ mua i gbua kului hu a pimẹ i ya kẹ i ndenga yẹ "Kẹkẹ," yẹ "Mahẹi ji bi yeya" yẹ "nya mia ta nya hei a mahayẹi."

"Kuo," yẹ "yelọ ndeni bi ma?"

Yẹ "Haku."

Kẹ i ya ti li ti haku mọli mayalong. Kẹ ti ngi nyaha wa waa.

Ngele woa ta ngi kenẹi i loni wọ la mbomẹi hu i loni laa lọ kẹ haku wilinga mbomẹi ji bu vu i welẹnga. I hului ji vele, i bului ji vẹ, i bului ji vẹ. Mahẹi ji yẹ i wote bulu vẹ woi ji i ngi woli hu vẹngọ ngi ma.

"Kuo," yẹ "gbee," yẹ "nya bonda," yẹ "bului vẹ woi bonda ye na hi wama?"

"Kuo," tẹ "mahẹi miando?"

Nunga na ti heinga tii bulu vẹmọi ji loni hakui yama ha kpọlọ pẹlẹ bu. Ti woloi lọ na haa tii wolo.

Tẹ "Kuo, mahẹi, bia bẹ bi ndẹ gulanga."

Kẹ ti mahẹi ji wanga.

Ti mahẹi ji walọ wọ kẹ ndakpoi ji yamanga hakui ji i yama maluve kpa a numu vulu kẹ i loa na.

Ye "Aa kenei ji ta sawei ji wọ i nda ndọlọi ji hu nyamungọ
falọ wọ nya longọ ngi kpua hu falọ wọ ngi woteni hakui ngi wani
ngi ndeni wọ ngẹ ngi mba maha" yẹ "ta wama ngi gama."

A nunga bẹ tẹ "Na nyandengọ."

Yẹ "Eh."

"Numui bondẹi ji i wanga mu yeya ndọlọi ji hu. Kia bẹ
hota mia ndọlọi ji hu mu ngi hei a mahayẹi."

Ti haku lọ wọ heini a mahayẹi fọ i wote a maha ndọlọi na
ma.

Dọmẹi ji ye kẹlẹma ye mia.

------

1. Recorded by man from Bo in Freetown on January 12, 1960.

TALE 50: THE THIEF AND HIS APPRENTICE[1]

A long time ago there was a very rich man who did not get
his wealth by any other means than by stealing. He continued
to steal and he had more wealth than anyone in the country.
Cows, sheep, everything that wealthy people have the man used
to steal from his companions; he brought them /to his house/;
he kept them. He continued to do that; he became very rich;
his name was well known in the country. At one time everyone
was afraid of him because of his wealth.

One day a man who had only one son said, "I am bringing
my son to this man to have him teach my son to steal, because
this man has greater happiness than any chief in this country;
because this man is rich, he is very happy; he is a wealthy
man."

Then the man took his son and gave him to the rich man.
The small child went /to live with the wealthy man/.

When the child went to the stranger, he remained with
him. Some people came; they brought a (two) cow that they
were taking to sacrifice. They came and rested for some time
in this town; then they went on with the cow.

Then the child who had just been brought to the wealthy
man said to his teacher, "Teacher, I want to steal the cow
that those people have."

"Oh," the rich man said, "I have never done such a thing. They are two people walking with one cow. If you steal it from them, I am not skillful at that kind of stealing."

"Oh," the child said, "I myself will do it."

The man said, "Child, you will not be able to do that."

The child said, "I will be able to do it."

"Oh," the man said, "I will not advise you to go. But you have said that you can do it; you may follow and steal the cow; so go."

Then the boy said, "Just give me your shoes; I will take them."

And the rich man gave the boy his shoes; the boy took them--the shoes were very fine.

When the boy went and was approaching these people, he entered the bush; he was walking quickly--vu vu--in the bush; he went ahead of the people and dropped one shoe. The boy left it and went on.

Then the people came and reached the shoe. They wanted to take the shoe, because it was very fine, but they saw that there was only one shoe and no one puts on one shoe. When the people passed, the boy went on; he went a fair distance and he dropped the other shoe. Then the people came and reached the second shoe. As before one shoe was there so the other was here.

Then one man said, "The shoe that we saw today yonder, this is its companion. Let us go back /for the other shoe/."

And the other man said, "It is agreed."

Then the men tied the cow at that place; the boy had hidden near the second shoe. When he had dropped the second shoe, he had not gone away. Then the men tied the cow; they both returned for the first shoe.

As soon as the men had gone beyond a bend in the road and the boy knew that they could not see him, the boy untied the cow quietly. The boy brought the cow into the bush; he brought it and passed the people when they were returning to take their cow. The boy returned with the cow into the town.

When the boy's teacher saw the cow, he said, "Oh, child, you know this skill better than I. So tomorrow we will go to your father; I will go to him for my payment."

Then the people went reached /where they had left/ the
cow; they did not see the cow; they decided to return to the
town. At that time they had brought the cow into the big
yard with its companions. The people arranged to give the
rich man /something for the cow/.

"Oh," the rich man said, "of course, you left me lying
here in this hammock. I have not gone anywhere. I have been
lying here."

So the people never saw their cow at all.

The rich man took the boy to his father; he said, "Your
son whom you recently left with me knows this skill better
than I. So I have brought him /to you/."

At that time the child remained there /with his father/.
So he did not get the wealth that the rich man did, because he
showed too much cleverness.

Gbema lenga ma wọ kena yila wọ yema kpatengọ wa kẹ ngi
nda gbatẹi ji ii majọ wọ a pele yeka gbi kẹ huma. I loni humẹi
ji wiema i gbatẹi na ndọlẹi na hu ngi yatenga gbi yẹ na.
Nikanga, mḅalenga, hani na gbi le kpatẹbla a yẹ ti yeya a lilọ
a huma mba yeya a wa a ngandọ. I loni na wiema i gbatẹ hulengọ
wa ngi lọ wẹi i gbua na wa ndọlẹi na hu. Nunga gbi le ta luwa
wọ ngi ma ngi gbatẹi na va.

Folo yila i hitilọ na kena yila na ngi loi ta bẹ i yilakpe
hindolo a ngie kẹ i ndenga yẹ "Ngi wa a nya vuli loi kenẹi ji
gama i ngi ga a humẹi gbamaile kenẹi ji ta ngi gohunẹi ji
bondẹi ji gbẹlẹ maha bẹ ii ndọlẹi ji nahi a hiti ngi hu
gbamaile ngi gbatenga ngi gohunẹngọ wa le ta kpatẹ ma mia a
ngie."

Kẹ i ya a ngi loi ji kẹ i ngi venga ngi wẹ. Ndopo wuloi
ji i ya.

Kia wọ ta li a numu hota i yẹ heilọ i loi heilọ, kẹ nunga
ti wa ti fele nikaha wa i ti yeya ti mala. Ti mala sa gbuamẹi
kẹ ti wa kẹ ti lẹvu haa tẹi ji hu kẹ ti lewea a nikẹi ji.

Kẹ ndopoi ji ha ti wa a ngie a nikẹi ji kẹ i ndenga ngi
kenẹi ji ma, ngi kamọi ji ha ti wa a ngie ngi gama, yẹ "Kamọ,"
yẹ "nya longọ ngi ngi nikẹi na huma nungẹi nasia yeya."

"Kuo," yẹ "ndakpẹi" yẹ "nya ngii ya wọ a na nyọkọ wie-o.
Nunga ti fele ti jiama a nika yila bi bi huma ti yeya" yẹ
"nya ngi bẹni a humẹi ye na bonda."

"Kuo," yẹ "nya nga pielọ."

Yẹ "Ndopoi," yẹ "bẹ gu na ma."

Yẹ "Nga gulọ ma."

"Kuo," yẹ "nya nge yẹ ma bi li-o," yẹ "kẹ na wei bẹ ba gulọ ba lolọ bẹ bi bi huma." Yẹ "Kẹ li-o."

Kẹ ta bẹ ndenga yẹ "Kẹ nya gọ lẹ bi gọwẹi na hu" yẹ "ngi li la."

Kẹ kenẹi ngi gọwẹi ji venga ngi wẹ kẹ i ya la, kọwẹi ji nyandengọ wa.

Kia i li i yẹ foma nungẹi jisia ma kẹ i wa ndọgbọi hu i jia ndọgbọi na hu vuvu kẹ ta ta hitia lewenga ti gulọ kẹ i kọwẹi ji gulanga kaka yila ti ngi lo kẹ i hiyenga na kẹ i ya gbọma.

Nungẹi jisia kẹ ti wa kẹ ti fonga kọwẹi ji ma mbumbumẹi ta ma jifa nyandengọ wa kẹ ti tọ kọwọ yilakpe mia tao numu ẹe kọwọ yila wa. Kẹ ti lewenga ma. Kẹ i ya gbọma. Kia i li polong hu ii guhani wa kẹ i pekẹi na gula. Kẹ nungẹi jisia kẹ ti wa gbọma kẹ ti wa ti foa kọwẹi ji ma. Kia lọ ha ji na hi lọ ji bẹ na.

Kẹ i ye na ndenga yẹ "Kọwẹi na ha mu tọni mia" yẹ "ngi mbalọ," yẹ "mu li poma."

Kẹ na ndenga yẹ "Kulungọi."

Kẹ ti nikẹi na yilinga hindẹi na kẹ ndopoi i lọwui lọ kọwẹi ye na gblanga-o. Kia i na kulai ii ya li. Kẹ ti nikẹi ji yilinga ti venja kẹ ti yamanga kọwọi ji ye pekẹi na woma.

Kia le wọ ti gbuani le ti li huguhangọ pele wu yila wangọ ti luahu i kọ kẹ tii yaa ngi lọma kẹ i nikẹi na vulonga yelẹng. I wa la a ndọgbọi na hu wie. I wa ingẹ ta nungẹi nasia ti velanga ma. Wati ji na tia ti ma ti ti nikẹi ji wumbu ta i lewenga a nikẹi ji. I yama la tẹi ji hu kẹ i yama la.

Kia wọ ngi kamẹ nikẹi ji lọni lee yẹ "Kuo," yẹ "ndopoi," yẹ "bi ka ji gọni nya nyama so sina mua lilọ bi kẹkẹ gama i li nya nga pawẹi va."

Kẹ nungẹi jisia ti ya ti fo nikẹi ji gama tii nikẹi ji lọni kẹ ti ngahounga ti yama tẹi ji hu. Na hu ma ti nikẹi ji wanga wa lẹi hu ti mbanga ma. Ti hindẹi ji gbatẹi ti kenẹi ji gọ.

"Kuo," yẹ "ingẹ wua vuli we nya longa mbei lani mbomẹi ji hulọ. Ngii yaa lini hinda gbi. Nya lọ ngi lani mbeindo."

So tii nikẹi na lọni wọ fọ.

Kenẹi bẹ i ndopoi na wumbu i li la ngi kẹkẹ gama yẹ "Bi loi gẹ bi la mbẹ ngi ngi nga ta ka jingọ nya ma. Fale ngi wa la."

I lo wọ fọ na. So ii yaa kpatẹi na majọni wọ kia kenẹi na piengọ jifa i ngi nẹmahu lewei lọ wa gbuani.

---

1. Recorded by young man from Pujehun in Freetown on February 16, 1960.

TALE 51: SPIDER AND THE CHIEF[1]

At one time there was a very wealthy chief. If any stranger went to him and remained there until he died, he would bury the person with a lot of money; he would bury the person with a lot of gold; he would bury the person with a lot of diamonds. Anyone who went to the chief, who stayed there and became sick and died, would be buried by him that way.

As soon as Spider heard about that, he said that he must go to the man and pretend to die; when he was buried, he would bring the things into his own town. And Spider went to the chief; he arrived at the chief's town. Spider was there only four days; on the fifth day Spider got a fever and he pretended to die. Then the chief went and laid Spider down and prepared him /for burial/; bags of money were put down, bags of diamonds were dropped, gold was put down also; Spider was lying down.

And the chief said, "When this stranger came, he did not stay here long before he died. I am going to ask someone to sing for him."

The chief went /to find a singer/. There was a woman of high status who used to sing very sweetly. The chief went and asked her /to sing/; she came. Now these women of high status began to sing; they sang a song over the corpse in the house; they sang not knowing that the sound of the song was sweet to Spider's ear; Spider lay there.

When the people came outside the house, Spider got up a little to watch; when they came into the house, Spider lay down quietly. Spider kept doing this, he became tired; he kept doing this, he became tired. When the people came out /of the house/ and went far off, Spider really jumped down

from the bed. Throughout the night Spider kept watching the
dance; he wanted to go to it. When the people came /into the
house/, Spider returned and lay down quietly. So Spider kept
doing this corpse business; he continued at that time to do
this.

When Spider got up once, he did not know that people
were coming to look at the corpse in the house.

The people said, "Come, the corpse has come out; look,
it is the stranger!"

When Spider was about to return to lie down, the people
saw him. When the people saw Spider, he came out /of the
house/--tsen; he did not return. At one time Spider came
suddenly out of the house into the midst of the crowd; he ran
away. At one time Spider did not get the wealth that he wanted
to get.

Maha mia wọ kpatengọ kẹlẹma gbii ma. Hota gbi bi li ngi
gama bi longa lọ na bi hanga lọ a bi gbọwo lọ a kọpọ gboto, a
bi gbọwo lọ a kani gbọli gboto, a bi gbọwo a diamọ gboto. Numu
gbi lini ngi gama leke bi longa lọ na bi higbẹ ya lọ bi hanga
lọ a bi gbọwo a na lọ.

Kasilo ji i na humẹni lọ leke yẹ i lima lọ kenẹi gama, i
ha a kaso; ti ngi gbọwonga lọ i wa a hakẹisia ngi ye ta hu.
Kẹ i ya i lini kenẹi gama i fonga na. I yẹ na lọ nani leke i
lọlui ma kẹ kọlẹi wunga ma kẹ i hanga a kaso. Kẹ kenẹi ya i
nda kẹ ti ngi magbtenga kọpọ bẹgi mia ti pupuni ma diamọ bẹgii
jisia ta kulama gbọli jisia ta puma, ta lọ lani.

Kẹ kenẹi ji bẹ ndenga yẹ "Hotẹi ji wanga ii lẹmbini
mbeindo i hẹi ji wienga." Yẹ "Ngi lima lọ ngi ngolemọ mọli
ngi va."

Kẹ i ya. Mua yila a ngolei ji ya ngo nẹngọ kẹlẹma gbii
ma. Kẹ i ya kẹ i ngi mọlinga kẹ i wanga kẹ muai jisia ti
tọtonga na a ngolei ji yala kẹ ngolei ji ti ngolei ji ya ti
ngolei ji ya pomẹi ji mahu pẹlẹi ji bu ti nga memai ngolei ji
wo nẹnga ngi woli hu i lani.

Nunga ti yalọ gbuama ngitiiya kẹ i hijenga kulo i na gbe;
ti ya lọ wama pẹlẹi bu kẹ i langaa kpẹ. I ji lọ wieni i gbọwo,
i ji wie a gbọwo nunga ti gbiangalọ ti ya lọ kuhama kẹ i
gbujanga vuli kpukẹi ma. I lo pi gohu a ndolimẹi ji gbe ngi
longọ i li na. Ang nunga ti ya lọ ti wa kẹ i yamanga i la kpẹ
kpẹ kia poma hindẹi ji lọ i pieni haa. I loni wọ ji lọ wiema.

Kia wọ na i hijeni mẹmai tia lọ wama pomẹi ji gama gbema
pẹlẹ bu.

Tẹ "Wa pomẹi gbianga kpe hota mia."

Kia wọ na yẹ i yama i la kẹ ti ngi lọnga kia wọ ti ngi
lọni wọ i gbiani wọ tseng ii yaa yamani i gbiani wọ kpuleng
i li a pimẹ. I ba wọ fọ a kpatẹi na hakẹi ji i lini fa ii
yaa majọni.

---

1. Recorded by man from Bo in Freetown on January 7, 1960.

TALE 52: THE RICH MAN AND HIS WATCHMAN[1]

The old watchman whom at one time a rich man hired.

Once there was a very rich man who hired a watchman. The
watchman's mouth was in the exact middle of his head where no
one could see it. The rich man hired this man; he sent him to
watch over sheep, goats, and cows.

As soon as everyone in the town had gone away, the watchman went and caught a big ewe or a big female goat; he killed
it; he cooked it very quickly; he ate it; he threw away the
leftovers; he sat there. (In fact, if you yourself came and
saw him, you would not see his mouth.) All the time the
watchman used to do that, and the sheep like the goats began
to decrease.

One day the rich man called the watchman; he asked him,
"What is the matter? No other people are coming into this
town; they are not going to the sheep, but the sheep are de-
creasing. Who is it that is eating the sheep?"

"Of course," the watchman said, "Master, you yourself
know that I do not have a mouth. How could I eat the sheep?
I myself know nothing; I do not know about the sheep."

Oh, the rich man believed this answer; he said, "As you
say that you do not know about the matter, I am going to have
you taken to prison."

The rich man called some people; he told them to shave
the watchman's head and to take him and put him in prison.

When at the time the people were shaving the watchman's
head, they saw his big mouth in the very middle of his head;
he had many teeth; his mouth was very big; in fact, he wanted
to bite them.

Then the people went and explained the situation to the rich man; they said, "You recently hired this man whom you said did not have any mouth; his mouth is in the middle of his head."

"Oh," the rich man said, "so that it how it is! So it is he who has been eating the sheep as he denied! Therefore, take him to prison; let him sleep there for the night."

When the morning came, the rich man had the watchman killed. As soon as they killed the watchman, the rich man hired another watchman who would watch over his sheep.

At one time they killed that bad watchman. They left him in the middle of the road, because his mouth was in the very middle of his head and also he did all that evil to the headman. The rich man had the watchman killed; he hired another person to take his place; his sheep were saved.

Pẹlẹmahugbemọ wovẹi na wọ kpatẹmọi i ngi wumbuni.

Wati yila i yẹ wọ na kena yila ye na ngi gbatẹngọ wa kẹ kenẹi ji i pẹlẹmahugbemọ yila wumbunga. Ye kenẹi ji ta ngi lẹi i ngi wui liandia liandia lọ wọ kẹ numui ee tọ. Kenẹi ji kpatẹmọi ji i ye kenẹi ji wumbuni na. Kẹ i ngi loa yẹ "I ya mbalanga, njenga, kẹ nikanga" yẹ "i ya ti mahugbe."

Kenẹi ji ji le wọ nunga kpẹlẹ ti vayama tẹi ji hu i li i mbalẹi ye ha wai na hou ọ i njei ha wa hou i paa i ngili fulo fulo fulo kẹ i mẹa. Ye mọni na loa i pili i hei na. (Sao ingẹ bi wa bẹ bi ngi lọ bii ngi la lọma.) Wati gbi va i yẹ ji wọ wie, wati gbi va i yẹ ji wọ wie, kẹ mbalangẹi jisia ti mahu i tọtonga a yeila kia njengẹisia.

Folo yila kẹ kenẹi ji i ngi lolinga kẹ i ngi mọlinga "Gbẹe? Nunga yeka tii wama tẹi ji hu, tii lima mbalangẹisia gama kẹ mbalangẹisia ti ma yeima le. Yọ mbalangẹisia mẹma?"

"Ingẹ" yẹ "bia, Masta, bia vuli bi kọlọ nya nya la ii na ngii ye piema a mbalanga? Nya bẹ ngii hungọ hinda gbi ngi hungọ kọloni mbalangẹi nasia ma."

Kuo, kenẹi bẹ kpẹmboi ji gua i ye le la kẹ i ndenga yẹ "Ina họ bẹ bii hindẹi na hungọ kẹ ngi piema ti li a bie kpindiwẹlẹ bu."

Kẹ ta bẹ i nunga lolinga yẹ "Ti ngi wui wole ti li a ngie ti ti gu kpindiwẹlẹ bu."

Kia na le wọ nungẹisia ti ye ngi wui ji wiema male kẹ ti ngi la wa ji lọnga i heini ngi wui ji liandiẹi ji, ngi yọngọi

na i wui na kakakaka ngi lęi gǫlǫngǫ wa ngi longǫ pęing i
ti nyi.

Tia bę kę ti ya ti ti hindęi na hungę a kenęi tę "Ba
kenęi ji gę bi ngi wumbunga bę ngi la gbi na ngi lęi lǫ ngi
wui lia-e."

O, ta bę yę "Hi wǫ na hi ye!" Yę "Fale ta mia gę i lema
a nya mbalangęisia mę a ma wǫima!" Yę "Fale a li la a li la
kpindiwęlę bu ti hu i nyi gbu."

Nge i wo, kenęi na i pie ti pa. Tia bę kia le ti ngi wa
kę i numui yekanga wumbunga pęlęmahugbebla yekanga wumbunga a
ya na a ngi mbalęnga mahugbe.

Pęlęmahugbemǫi nyamui na ti ngi wa wǫ fǫ. Pelei lia ti
gbe ngi ma jifa ngi wui ta ngi lęli ngi wui liandia liandi i
lǫ wǫ tao i pie nyamui na kpę i yę pie i ya ngui kenęi nahu;
ta bę na wǫ i pie. I pielǫ ti ngi wa i numui yeka wumbu i ngi
wu ngi womęi ngi mbalangęi nasia ti bawo fǫ.

---

1. Recorded by young man from Pujehun in Freetown on May 13,
1960.

Insiders and Outsiders

TALE 53: CAT, RATS, AND A BELL[1]

How Rats came into a hole at one time--that is what I have come to relate to you today.

Cat annoyed Rats; he caught them. When he caught them, he always killed them. The situation became intolerable.

Rats said, "Let us go to the chief."

And they went to the chief /of the rats/.

Rats said, "Chief, Cat catches us a lot. So what are we going to arrange to do?"

The chief said, "What would be good: let us buy a bell. When we have bought the bell, we will put it on Cat's neck. When Cat is coming, we will know. That would be good."

"Oh," Rats said, "we have agreed."

Although Rats had not arranged how they were going to put the bell on Cat's neck, they agreed. They contributed money; they went and bought a bell; they brought the bell.

Rats said, "Look we have brought the bell. How are we going to do it?

"Oh," the young male rats said, "what would be good: the chief's linguist should put the bell on Cat's neck."

The linguist said, "Oh, where will I stand to put the bell on Cat's neck? What would be good: the chief should take the bell and put it on Cat's neck."

"Oh," said the chief, "I cannot do that. Where would I stand to put the bell on Cat's neck? I cannot do that."

"What would be good:" they said, "let us arrange something else. How will we do it?"

The chief said, "Yes, we will put the bell on Cat's neck."

Not knowing that Cat was spying on them, Rats remained standing at that time. Suddenly Cat jumped among them; he killed four rats. Some ran away; some jumped into the hole.

That is what happened at one time that Rats came into a hole. Until this day Rats have not put any bell on Cat's neck; up to this time, Cat catches Rats.

Gbǫ wǫ wieni Nyinanga ti wani ndowa hu ta mia na ngi wa ha hugǫma a wue.

Nyinanga gǫnǫi gbandingǫ ti ma a ti hou. I ti hou lǫ na a ti wa kpua kǫ i gbǫwoa na.

Ti la tia bǫ tǫ "A mu li mahǫi gama."

Kǫ ti ya mahǫi gama.

Tǫ "Mahǫi" tǫ "gǫnǫ mu hounga na wa fale mu ye hugbatǫ wiema?"

Ta bǫ yǫ "Na nyandengǫ le" yǫ "a mu bamandei yeya." Yǫ "Mu bamandei yeyanga" yǫ "mu kula gǫnǫ boloma." Yǫ "I ya wama ma kǫlǫ" yǫ "na lǫ le a nyande."

"Kuo," tǫ "mu kulua."

Tii yaa na hugbatǫni pǫing ta ye pie ti bamandei ji gula gǫnǫ boloma. Kǫ ti lumanga, kǫ ti kǫpǫi gukula kǫ ti ya, ti bamandei ji yeya kǫ ti wanga a bamandei ji.

Tǫ "Bamandei gbe mu wanga la. Mu ye na piema?"

Kuo, kǫngǫi nasia tǫ "Na nyandengǫ" tǫ "mahǫi lavale wai i li i bamandei ji gula gǫnǫ boloma."

Yǫ "Kuo," yǫ "nga lǫ mi lǫ nga bamandei ji gula gǫnǫ boloma? Na nyandengǫ, mahǫi vuli i li a bamandei ji i kula gǫnǫ boloma."

"Kuo," mahǫi bǫ yǫ "Ngǫ gu ngi na wie." Yǫ "Nga" yǫ "loni mindolǫ nga bamandei ji gula gǫnǫ boloma? Ngǫ nga yǫ ngǫǫ gu."

"A na nyandengǫ," tǫ "a mu hinda weka hugabtǫ, ma ye pie?"

Yǫ "Bamandei ji mu kula gǫnǫ boloma."

Mǫma gǫnǫ lǫ ha ti manǫma. Ti loi wǫ loni lǫ. A mǫ gulugulu kǫ gǫnǫ wunga ti hu. Kǫ i panga na nani kǫ ti lǫnga ti lenga a pimǫ kǫ nasia lǫnga ti wilinga ndowǫi hu.

A na lǫ wǫ wieni nyinanga ti wani wǫ ndowa hu. Foloi ji bǫ tii yaa wǫ bamandei gulai fǫ gǫnǫ boloma. Kia bǫ hu na ta lǫ ti houma.

---

1. Recorded by man from Bo in Freetown on January 7, 1960.

TALE 54: ROYAL ANTELOPE, CHIMPANZEE, AND MONKEY[1]

At one time the animals were all in one place.

They said, "Let us go walking."

And they went. When they went walking, they walked until they came to Hitembaum. When they arrived, they did not have any water; they were thirsty and they wanted to cook food.

"Oh," Royal Antelope said, "the ugly person is the one who will go for water."

Chimpanzee said, "My head aches."

"Oh," Monkey said, "My head aches."

"Ah," Royal Antelope said, "really what I said was not directed at anyone. You yourselves said that you are ugly; you are the ones to go for water."

Chimpanzee and Monkey went for water; they returned; they cooked the food.

Huanga mia wọ. Ti kpẹlẹ ti le lọ heima yila.

Tẹ "A mu li jẹsiama."

Ke ti ya. Kia wọ ti li jẹsiamẹi ji ti loi jei mia kẹ ti nde a Hitẹmbaum. Ti foa nja gbi tii yeya nja gbọle mani ji ti ma ti-o ti longọ ti mẹhẹ yili.

"Kuo" kẹ Hagbe ndenga yẹ "Numu na nyamungọ" yẹ "ta i li njẹi hu."

Ngolo yẹ "Nya wui lọ gbalẹma."

"Kuo" kualẹi yẹ "ngi wui lọ gbalẹma."

"A," tẹ "ji vuli mu ndea wẹ wua mu toni gbi wu ma. Wua wua kpẹ wu ndenga wẹ kẹ wua wu nyamungọ. Wua wa li njẹi hu."

Ngolo ta kuala ti li njẹi hu, ti wa ti ya mẹhẹi na yili.

---

1. Recorded by man from Bo in Freetown on January 20, 1960.

TALE 55: SPIDER AND THE PROVIDENT CHIEF[1]

At one time a chief said, "Let me buy food in the country; the time of hunger is coming."

Then the chief gathered a lot of food; there was a lot of food. When the big rainy season came, great hunger was in other lands. Of course, in the chief's own country there was plenty of food; they spent the days dancing.

When Spider heard about the chief's country, he decided to go there. He went there; he said that he was a dancer. He held a big bag around his neck; the bag could hold eight bushels of rice.

When Spider went to the chief's country, he fell at the chief's feet--bum. He put seven bushels /of rice/ in his big bag and carried the rice away. When Spider carried the rice away, he ate all of it; he did not leave any rice. When morning came, Spider returned again. At that time Spider continued to put rice inside the bag.

On another day Spider went /to the chief's country/, he put twelve bushels of rice in this very big bag. When Spider said that he was leaving, the bag split; immediately the rice scattered.

At one time Spider was caught. Spider's face was shamed yonder at one time.

Maha yila mia wọ yẹ "Gbẹ ngi mẹhẹ yeya ndọlọ hu" yẹ "kpe ndọlẹi lọ wama."

Kẹ i mẹhẹi ji yandọnga kaka mẹhẹi gboto mia. Kia wọ na hama wa ji wai ndọlẹi wọngọ ndọlọ yekẹisia hu. Ingẹ ta ngi gama mẹhẹi gbotongọ na ndoli le ta luvama.

Kuo Kasilo ji kia i na humẹini yẹ ngi lima na yẹ ngi lima i ya yẹ ndolimọ mia a ngie-o, i wotea a ndolimọ. Beki wa mia i houni i kula booma. Beki na a mba bushẹ wayakpa bẹ i wumbu lọ.

Kia wọ i li wọ ndoli ji ti ya kama ji gulama mia mahẹi gọwọ bu na bmm, mba bushẹ wọfla a lo lọhu beki wa na hu ngi yeya kẹ i yala. I ya la a kpẹlẹ lọ mẹ ẹẹ ndo. Ngendẹi wa kẹ i wa gbọng Kasilo loi wọ i gula mbẹi ji hu.

Lọwọ yẹkẹi ma i li i gulae mbẹi ji mbẹi ji bushẹ pu mahu fele i punga na beki wa ji hu yẹ i li na kẹ beki blaa a mẹi wai mbẹi ji vaya.

Ti Kasilo hou lọ wọ tọ. Ngi ya i wuve wọ mia.

---

1. Recorded by man from Bo in Freetown on January 20, 1960.

TALE 56:   KPANA AND THE ELEPHANTS[1]

At one time there were many elephants in the bush. One young man, who hunted, was more skillful than anyone with a gun. This man killed some elephants; all the other elephants hid and returned to their town. When the elephants returned to their town, they turned into old people. The young man continued to search for the elephants. The professional hunter's name was Kpana; he continued to search for the elephants.

Suddenly one elephant changed into a very beautiful girl. She met the young man.

He said, "Young lady, good afternoon."

She said, "Yes."

He said, "Thank you."

She said, "Yes."

He said, "How are you?"

She said, "I am well. Sir, why are you walking here?"

"Oh," he said, "young woman, I am looking for elephants. They used to go on this road. I am searching for them."

"Oh," she said, "please be my friend."

He said, "All right."

The elephant who had changed /into a young woman/ was named Sombo.

Now she said, "You are my friend. You get up and go with me."

She loved this hunter a lot--endlessly; she loved him endlessly.

Then the hunter and the woman went on a road. He did not know that she was an elephant. They went and came into a town. The hunter met living people there; he did not know that they were elephants. When they arrived, the elephants sat in council; the hunter stated the purpose of his visit; he said that he was hunting elephants.

The elephants sitting in council said, "Let us go and kill him in that round house yonder. When night comes, let us go and break that house down; we will fall on him; we will kill him."

Now Sombo heard this and she loved Kpana very much. Just as night fell, Sombo went quietly and took Kpana out of the house; he went and she left him.

Sombo said to Kpana, "Go."

When night came, the elephants went; they broke the house down completely; they did not see Kpana; they turned to Sombo.

The elephants said, "Sombo!"

She said, "Yes."

They said, "What did Kpana say yesterday?"

She said, "Kpana only said, 'Goodbye.'" She said, "I do not know how he went."

Helei ji mia wo kẹ ndọgbọi hu ti gbotongọ kaka ti na. Ndakpao yila a kpandẹi wili ngi jọngọ gbi na kpandẹi ji lọ. Kenẹi ji i helengẹi jisia wa i helengẹi jisia wa kẹ ti gbi ti lọwua kẹ ti yama ti ye ta hu. A ti foa ti ye ta hu ti kpẹlẹ ta wotea a nunga wova lọ. I loi wọ helengẹi ji lọlọma i loi ti lọlọma. Kamasọi ngi la a Kpana i loi ti lọma i loi ti lọma.

A mẹi gbaung kẹ ta helei i wotenga a mbọgbe lopo nyande nyande kẹ ta ta ti gomẹa.

Yẹ "Mbọgbe bi wa."

Yẹ "Hn."

Yẹ "Bi sie."

Yẹ "Hn."

Yẹ "Ọ bi gahu?"

Yẹ "Kaye ii Ngewọ ma. A" yẹ "gbẹi kenẹi" yẹ "bi lima hi kena wọvẹi?"

"Oh," yẹ "nyapoi" yẹ "helenga mia ngi ti lọlọma" yẹ "ti ya wọ a pelei ji lọ." Yẹ "Tia lọ ngi lọlọma."

"Kuo," yẹ "nya ndiamọ mia a bie, hoe."

Yẹ "Eye."

Helei ji mawoveni ngi la a Sombo.

Kẹ i ndenga na yẹ "Nya ndiamọ mia a bie. Bi hiti bi li nya gama."

I longa wa a kamasọi ji kẹlẹma ii ma i loa la kẹlẹma ii ma.

Kẹ ta ta ti ya pelei ji hu. Ii kọ kamasọi ii kọ a yema helei mia. Kẹ ti ya kẹ ti gbuanga tẹi ji hu. I nunga vulunga le male na mẹma helenga mia. Kia wọ ti li wọ kẹ helengẹi jisia ti heinga woma yila i konẹi ji wia i kpọyọa seng yẹ "I helenga lọ gbẹma."

Kẹ tia bẹ ti heia woma yila tẹ "A mu li mu ngi wa mia pẹlẹi na bu mia kilikili na bu. Kpindi wẹlẹa mu li mu pẹlẹi na wo mu wẹlẹma mu paa."

Kia wọ Sombo ji ji humẹninga tao i longa wa na a Kpana kẹlẹma gbi na. Kia wọ le kpindi wẹlẹni kẹ i ya yẹlẹng kẹ i Kpana gbia pẹlẹi na bu kẹ i ya kẹ i ngi longa.

Yẹ ngi ma "Li."

Kia wọ kpindi wẹlẹi kẹ ti ya ti pẹlẹi na wonga ti kpọyọ seng tii ngi lọi kẹ ti wotea na ngi mahu.

Tẹ "Sombo."

Yẹ "A."

Te "Kpana yẹ gbengi gbẹ?"

Yẹ "Kpana ndeilọ le yẹ 'Mu kpọkọ.'" Yẹ "Kẹ ngii kọ i ye lini."

---

1. Recorded by man from Bo in Freetown on January 27, 1960.

TALE 57: ROYAL ANTELOPE AND LEOPARD[1]

Leopard and Royal Antelope.

A long time ago Royal Antelope and Leopard were all in one place. You know that Royal Antelope is very clever.

One morning came; Leopard was eating the other animals; the situation was serious for them all.

Royal Antelope got up; he said, "I am going to tie up Uncle Leopard. When I go, I will go cleverly."

Royal Antelope sat and thought about what to do first, then he came /to Leopard/.

One morning Leopard was sitting and Royal Antelope came running fast.

He said, "Uncle, Uncle Leopard, I am coming to you."

Leopard said, "What is the matter?"

"Oh," Royal Antelope said, "I heard that a big wind is coming! Can it be that you have not heard that a wind is coming. If a person is not tied, the wind will come and take him away."

"Oh," Leopard said, "is that true?"

"Oh," Royal Antelope said, "Uncle, I came here for you to tie me. Tie me quickly!"

Then Royal Antelope ran into the house; he came back with a rope; he put his hands behind him; he wanted Leopard to tie him.

But Leopard in his great stupidity believed Royal Antelope; he thought that Royal Antelope was speaking the truth.

Leopard said, "Child, you are a little child; I am very big. You tie me; you tie me to this tree."

Then Leopard went behind the tree. Little Royal Antelope tied Leopard's hands very intricately; he tied Leopard's feet; he left Leopard lying down.

Royal Antelope said, "Uncle, I am going to find someone who will tie me so that when this wind comes, it will not carry me away. Someone will tie me to a big tree."

But what happened?

As soon as Royal Antelope went, he called all the animals together.

Royal Antelope said, "Come; I tied Uncle Leopard with deceit; he does not understand it; I have tied him!"

Then all the animals came; they encircled Leopard; they surrounded him; they laughed at him; they said foolish things in his face.

Leopard remained tied there. Little by little the rope was rotting; the rope rotted completely so that he was able to leave the rope quickly. Now Leopard had become thin; he had become thin; he had become thin; he had become thin. Leopard had not eaten any animal there; he had not eaten any food there.

At that time all the animals ran away from Leopard; they went into the bush. Royal Antelope said to all the animals, "Everyone should go and hide now. What we have done to Uncle Leopard will have made him angry; he will take revenge on us."

Since the time that happened until this day, if Leopard meets any animal, he will catch it; he will eat it; he will say, "At one time you tied me up." That is why Leopard and all the other animals are not friendly. He goes about alone. If Leopard and other animals meet, he will eat them, because at one time they tied him up.

Kọli ta Hagbe.

Wati hu guhango yẹ la wọ Hagbe ta Kọli ti yẹ kpẹlẹ hinda yila kẹ wu kọ Hagbe ta kasongọ wa le.

Ngenda yila i wani lọ kẹ ji Kọli i yẹ ti mẹ ye hindẹi ji i mini ti kpẹlẹma.

Kẹ i hijenga i hinda hugbatẹ yẹ "Kenya Kọli ji ngi lima ngi ngi yili kẹ ngi ya lima nga li a nẹmahu le womawẹi lọ."

Kẹ i heinga i gili la pẹing, kẹ i wa.

Ngenda yila Kọli yẹ hei lọ i wa a pimẹ wa.

Yẹ "Kenya, Kenya Kọli, Kenya Kọli, ngi wa bi gama lọ."

Yẹ "Gbẹe?"

"Kpo-o," yẹ "ngi mẹninga fẹfẹ wa wama," yẹ "ii na bia bi ya humẹnini" yẹ "fẹfẹi na wama" yẹ "numu bi yilingọ i yelọ le" yẹ "fẹfẹi na wa a lilọ a bie."

"Kuo" kẹ Kọli ndenga yẹ "Tọnya?"

"Kuo," yẹ "Kenya, ngi wa mbei bi nya yili." Yẹ "Nya yili ka ka."

Kẹ ta ngi Hagbe i lewenga pẹlẹi bu i wa a ngeyẹi kẹ i ngi lokoi lewenga poma. Ngi longa na Kọli i ngi yili.

Kẹ Kọli ta ii hungọ ngi gbowa wai ngi ma kẹ i la bẹ la yẹ "Tọnya yia mia Hagbe ndema."

Kẹ i ndenga "A ndopoi bia bia ndopo wo lọ a bie nya nya jẹmbẹngọ wa bi nya nya yili. Bia nya yili ngului ji ma."

Kẹ Kọli i lewenga ngului na woma. Hagbe wulo i ngi lokoi na i hu yili nẹvẹ nẹvẹ nẹvẹ i ngi gọwẹi na hu yili i ndoni lani lọ.

Yẹ "Kenya, nya bẹ ngi lima numu lọ gọkọi ma i nya yili, jifa fẹfẹi ji a wa ii li a nge i nya yili ngulu wama."

Kẹ gbọọ wie?

Kia leke i li i huanga gbi lo leima.

Yẹ "A wa" yẹ "ngi kenya Kọli yilinga kẹwẹ kẹwẹi ẹẹ yaa gu a humẹ la" yẹ "ngi yilinga."

Kẹ ti kpẹlẹ ti wa ti ngi gala ti ngi gome tia na ta ngi yele ta ndeni baba nasia jea ngi yama.

Kọli i loni haa ngili na hu-o kẹ ngeyẹi na i lo lulama kulo kulo kulo kulo kulo i lula i gbọyọ gbẹlẹng ngi ma na hi i ya gu i ta yekpe fulo ngeyẹi na ya. Na hu na i benga i benga i benga i benga huang gbi na a mẹ mẹhẹ gbi na a mẹ.

Na hu huanga kpẹlẹ tia bẹ ti kpẹlẹ ti vayalọ ngi ma ti ti li ndọgbọi hu. Hagbe i nde ti kpẹlẹ ma yẹ "Numu gbi a li na wu li wu lọwu-o. Kenya Kọli ji ji mu pienga a ngie ngi li na wama hijema i piema mu woma."

Ta bẹ kia na wọ le na wie foloi ji bẹ ta hua gbi ti gomẹa na le hua mia a bie i hounga le i bi mẹma yẹ "Wua wọ wu nya yilini." Na va mia Kọli ta huanga kpẹlẹ tii loni ma. Ta yakpe mia a lewe ta tieni ti gomẹa le a ti mẹ jifa wọ ti ngi yililọ.

---

1. Recorded by young man from Pujehun in Freetown on May 13, 1960.

TALE 58: GIANT RAT AND DOG[1]

At one time Giant Rat and Dog competed.[2]

One time Giant Rat and Dog made a bet about fear.

One day Giant Rat went to Dog; he said, "Dog, I will make you, all your relatives, and your friends very afraid.

I will make you afraid so that you will do some very evil
things."

Then Dog said to Giant Rat, "Me?"

Giant Rat said, "Yes."

Dog said, "Comrade, it is a lie!"

Giant Rat said, "Or if I do?"

"Oh," said Dog, "what happens if you do make us afraid,
if all my relatives and all my friends become afraid, we will
be your slaves.[3] But what happens if you come and you cannot
make us afraid?"

"Oh," Giant Rat said, "if I am unable to make you afraid,
then what you have said will happen to me too."

Then Dog agreed. They made this bet. At that time their
uncle Royal Antelope was there, when they both said that they
would make each other afraid and they agreed on a day.

The day before the day that they were going to scare each
other came, Giant Rat and all his family went and collected
palm kernels. Giant Rat begged them to help him chew the palm
kernels; they spent the whole day chewing /palm kernels/.

Now the morning came when Giant Rat was going to make Dog
afraid. As soon as morning came, Giant Rat went into the bush
and fetched palm husks and filled both his cheeks with them.
As soon as Giant Rat saw Dog coming yonder; he started to suck
the palm husk--he cleaned it; he cleaned it; he cleaned it.
Giant Rat kept cleaning the palm husk until Dog came.

Dog came and reached Giant Rat; he said, "The little fear
that you made does not scare me. Now prepare yourself for my
own time."

Then Dog's own time for scaring Giant Rat was approaching.
When the time was coming, Dog went to his family and said that
they should go and make all kinds of instruments. When all the
instruments were made, Dog went to Giant Rat and said that in
the morning he would come to frighten him at his house.

Very early in the morning Dogs ate enough food; they all
dressed themselves; they started to bring the instruments. As
soon as they arrived near Giant Rat's house, Giant Rat heard
the noise of these instruments; he took a pot out of the house
and ran. Whenever he met any creature on the way, he explained
to him and that creature also ran away with him; they all
joined together.

Little Royal Antelope was sitting cooking this rice; he saw the creatures; they came running kpoli kpoli kpoli.

Then the creatures said to Royal Antelope, "Uncle, something strange is happening to us; we hear something's voice!"

Royal Antelope said, "Which things?"

"Ah," they said, "the voice spoke very loudly! Never have we heard such a thing! Therefore, we are all afraid."

As soon as they said that, Royal Antelope knew about the scaring agreement between Dog and Giant Rat and he knew that the time for Dog's turn had come. Then Royal Antelope took the rice that he was cooking; he cut a banana leaf; he put a little rice on the leaf.

When Royal Antelope had put the rice on the road, he remained waiting; he saw Dog and his family coming kpoi kpoi kpoi. Dog and his family were dressed in iron instruments; they passed beating their instruments; the noise was very loud and the whole bush trembled. As soon as Dog came out where Royal Antelope had thrown the rice on the road, Dog went and put his mouth in the rice and ate it.

At one time Giant Rat lost that bet. Dog made slaves of Giant Rat and his relatives, the bush creatures, because of the competition they had. That is why if Dog sees any bush creature he runs after it saying, "You are my slaves." If Dog can, he will catch the creature and eat it. That was how at one time the bush creatures became Dog's slaves.

Mawai wọ kuwulọ ta ngila ti hou.

Wati yila i yẹ wọ na, kuwulọ ta ngila mawai hou i yẹlọ ti luwa hu kọlọni houluama.

Folo yila kuwulọ i lilọ ngila gama yẹ "Ngila nga peilọ bi luwa wa bi bondẹisia gbi leke wu lei hu i gbẹ bi ndiamọisia kpẹlẹma" yẹ "nga pielọ wu luwa vuli wu hinda nyamu nyamu wie."

Kẹ ngila ndenga kuwulọ ma yẹ "Nya?"

Yẹ "Mm."

Yẹ "Ndakpẹi, ndẹ mia."

Yẹ "Ọ ji nga pie?"

"Kuo," yẹ "na wie bi pienga mu luwa mu lei hu kpẹlẹ kẹ nya ndiamọisia kpẹlẹ mu luwa mu hẹi nya-o nya bonda-o kpẹlẹ

mu wote a bi luwǫ kę ǫ-na wie bia bę wa bii ya gui ba mu
huluwa?"

"Kuo," yę "nya bę ngi guilǫ nga bi huluwa kę na lǫ bi
ndenga ta bę i wie nya bę gama."

Kę ngila bę kę i luma kę ti mawai ji hounga. Wati na hu
Hagbe ta ti kenya i yę na lǫ ti venja kpęlę tę ta ti nyǫnyǫu
huluwalǫ kę ti kulanga lǫ ma.

Yę lǫwęi ji ta huluwęi ji wiema kę lǫwęi ji pęing lǫwęi
ji i ya hiti kuwulǫi ji i li ta ngi bondęisia kpęlę ti lilǫ
tǫlui ji ti ngǫyǫ. I ti gbi manęnę yę "Ti li ti gbǫ ngi ma
ti nyuma tǫlui na." Ti li ti luvani nyumama pęing.

Ngelei ji a wo na i wa i ngila huluwa. Kia leke ngele
woni kę ti ya ndǫgbǫi ji hu kę ti ya tǫlu gbęlęi ji ti kpęlę
ti goma la vengǫ la. Kia leke ti ngila lǫi mia wama kę ti
tǫtonga a tǫlu gbęlęi ji gbǫlela ta kole fu ta kole ta kole
ti loni haa kolema ngila i wani.

I wa i fofa ngi ma yę "Kulǫ huluwęi lǫ gę haa nya
huluwala" kę i ndenga yę "ba bi ma gbatęlǫ na nya nda wati
va."

Kę ngila bę kę ngi nda wati i lukpenga gbla. Kia i ye
hitima ma kę i ya i li i nde ngi bonda ma yę "Hani na gbi leke
ta nde ngaihaninga le i li i pie." Ti kpatę ti kpęlę ti tę
ti ma. "Ngele na woi na ta wa huluwamęi na."

Ngele wo wa ti gbi ti męlę mę na a gu a tie ti ti mayi
kpęlę a ngaihani nasia kę ti tǫtonga a wala ingę kia leke ti
yę foloma kuwulǫ ngi gbla i sǫlewoi ji ngaihani jisia ti
jǫlewoi ji męi kę i fę gbua bu i lewenga a pimę. I ya i fonga
le fuhani na ye na ma i hugęnga leke a ngie kę na bę lewenga
a pimę. Ti kpęlę ti la tǫngǫ wai ji.

Hagbe wuloi ji i loni heilǫ a mbęi ji yili kę i ti lǫnga
le ta gbuanga kpǫli kpǫli kpǫli ta li a pimę ji.

Kę ti ndenga tę "Kenya kama hinda i mu wiema" tę "mua
haka wo męma."

Yę "Hakei nasia?"

"Ah," tę "ngoi wolongǫ wa le wǫgba mu ya na mę." Yę
"Hindęi na hu kia mu luwa hu mu kpęlę."

Ta bę kia le ti na leni kę i kǫnga huluwęi ji ngila ta
kulo ti ti lema kę ye wati mia ngila ndęi hitinga kę ta bę i
ya mbęi ji i yę ngi ma kę i manalai ji kę i tewenga i mbęi ji
kulo wunga hu.

Pelei ji hounga kę ngilani ti ya ti loni heilǫ kę ti
ngilani lǫnga, ta ngi bonda ti gbuanga kpoi kpoi kpoi ti gbi
ti mayilinga a kolidia-o na le gbi ngaihani le ta lewe a
ngaihani ji yale yę "Ngoi na komęngǫ wa." Kę ndǫgbǫi na gbi
a gbęli. Kia le ti gbuenga mbęi na i ye wili pelei na hounga
ngila i li le i lawęi la hu kę i męnga.

Mawai na i gula wǫ fǫ kuwulǫma. Ngila i kuwulǫ ngi bondęi
nasia kine tia le kine ndǫgbǫ vuhaninga a tie ngila luwǫnga
mia wǫ a tie. Mawai na va ti houni. Na va mia foloi ji bę
ngilęi i yama wienga le ndǫgbǫ vuhani ma i hitema poma yę "Nya
luwǫlǫ a wue." I gungama houma i mę. Wati na mia wǫ ti wani
ngila luwǫyęi hu.

---

1. Recorded by young man from Pujehun in Freetown on May 30,
1960.
2. Giant rat or Pouched rat (kuwulǫ; Cricetomys gambianus)
"grows up to fifteen inches long, with an eighteen inch tail...
The 'pouches,' which give it one of its English names, are
pockets of skin inside the cheeks...used to collect food which
...the animal carries away to its hole" /A. H. Booth, Small
Mammals of West Africa (London:1960):55/.
3. In traditional Męnde society, slavery (slave, nduwǫ) was
the fate of war captives often enabling the victors to enlarge
their farms (see Little, 1967 ed., 37-39).

TALE 59: ROYAL ANTELOPE, ELEPHANT, AND HIPPOPOTAMUS[1]

How little Royal Antelope tested Water Elephant and Bush
Elephant in order to discover which one was stronger.[2]

At one time the sun came out; little Royal Antelope arose
and went to Water Elephant.

Royal Antelope said, "Ah, this elephant is huge; but when
I fought with him, I beat him. In that fight I beat him; I
dropped him /on the ground/. So I am going to do with Water
Elephant too."

Then Water Elephant said, "What nonsense this child is
talking!" He said, "You tiny creature, can you fight with an
elephant?"

"Oh," said Royal Antelope, "I once fought with an elephant; surprisingly enough I beat him! It is your turn; I am
coming to beat you."

The Water Elephant said to Royal Antelope, "I agree."
Water Elephant was very angry; he said, "Let us fight now by
all means; let us fight now by all means."

Royal Antelope said to him, "No, no, when I fight, I fight
my own way. Now that I have met you face to face, I am not
going to grapple with you; we must set a time when we will
fight."

They agreed on a time.

Water Elephant said, "Then we must fight tomorrow."

Royal Antelope agreed.

As soon as Royal Antelope left Water Elephant, he came to
Bush Elephant.

"Ah, this Bush Elephant," Royal Antelope said, "looks so
very big, but I will beat him in a fight! Just as I beat Water
Elephant some time ago, I will beat Bush Elephant too!"

When Royal Antelope said this to Bush Elephant, he got
very angry.

"Oh," Bush Elephant said, "you are a small creature! You
can stand under my foot to fight! I agree; if you are prepared
to fight me, let us fight!"

Royal Antelope said, "No, no, not that way. Wait for me
tomorrow; you and I will fight then."

Bush Elephant agreed and they agreed to fight at the same
time that Royal Antelope and Water Elephant had agreed to fight.

As soon as the appointed time came, Royal Antelope went
and brought a big twisted iron rope.

Royal Antelope said, "Ah, I will fight my own way. I will
have a tug-of-war with someone; if you can pull me, you are
stronger than I."

Royal Antelope went and tied the rope on Bush Elephant.

Then Royal Antelope went to Water Elephant. He said, "The
time for the fight about which we spoke has arrived. I will
tie this rope on you; I will go to tie it on me. We will have
a tug-of-war. Whoever pulls the other one out is the strongest."

Water Elephant also agreed. Royal Antelope tied the rope
well on Water Elephant and left. The rope was not on Royal

Antelope. As soon as Royal Antelope reached midway between the elephants, Royal Antelope held onto the rope.

Royal Antelope said, "Now you are challenged. Let us pull on the rope now."

Then Water Elephant and Bush Elephant began to pull each other; all day they pulled each other; they continued into the night--neither was able to pull out the other.

Royal Antelope came as they were tugging; he said, "Let us stop now."

Water Elephant slackened the rope; Bush Elephant slackened the rope. Royal Antelope came to one and untied the rope; he came to the other and untied the rope.

Royal Antelope said to each of the elephants, "Recently I spoke about a fight to you, I said I was superior to you."

When evening came, Water Elephant and Bush Elephant knew that something had happened; they were afraid. Then Royal Antelope told them about the trick. He told them that he had not fought them but that they had fought each other; he told them that he had wanted to test them.

That is where we stopped.

Kia wọ Hagbe wulo i nja hele ta ndọgbọ hele hugọni kẹ i ti ngahui gọ ye lọ ngi gbayangọ tewenga ngi mbaẹ ma.

Folo yila gbuai lọ wọ kẹ Hagbe wulo kẹ i hijenga kẹ i ya nja hele gama.

Yẹ "Ah, helei ji kia be ngi wọlọngọ a pele-o-pele kẹ ma ta mu yẹ lapi lọ ngi ngi gula ye ndapi na nya mia wọ ngi leweni ngi ma ngi ngi gulani."

Yẹ "Hi lọọ ngi wama piema a nja helei ji bẹ."

Kẹ nja hele ndea yẹ "Baba yẹpẹi ye ji gbe ndopoi ji ndema" yẹ "bi wulongọ pọting ji mia ba gu bi lapi a hele!"

"Kuo," yẹ "mua hele mu lapinga yila ngi ngi gulanga-e," yẹ "bia bẹ bia mia na bi ndẹ i longa" yẹ "ngi wama piema a bie."

Ta nja hele i ndea ngi ma yẹ "Kulungọi." Hindẹi ji i gbalẹnga ha wa ngi ma. Yẹ "Kẹ mu pie na họ, mu pie na họ."

Kẹ Hagbe ndenga ngi ma yẹ "Mn mn nya nda lapi nga kọ ngi ya lapi lọ, mua numu mu ya lọ ndapi gọma. Kia na ngi wanga

ngama ngamẹi ji ye ngamẹi ji yaa na na ngaa yẹ lima ngi li ngi
gbundẹ bi ma kẹ mua bia mu lapinga ma lọọ lọ gẹ ye lọẹ na
hitinga lọ kẹ mu ndapi gọnga."

Kẹ ti gọlẹnga lọma.

Yẹ "Kẹ sine họ."

Kẹ ta bẹ i lumanga.

Kia leke i gbuani hele gama kẹ i lewenga nja hele gama
"A nja hele ji" yẹ "kia bẹ bi ngi lọma ngi wọlọnga wai ji kẹ
nga ngi gulalọ lọọ ndapi hu" yẹ "hi mia mua hele bẹ mu yẹ
pieni" yẹ "ngi ngi gulai lọ" yẹ "tao nga ji bẹ gula lọ."

Ta bẹ hi lọ i ndeni ngi ma ji gbalẹnga wa ngi ma.

"Kuo" yẹ "bi wulongọ bondẹi ji mia ba gu a lola nya gọ
bu ndapi va;" yẹ "kulungọi na họ na bi ma gbatẹngọi nya va
kẹ mu lapi."

Kẹ i ndea yẹ "Mn mn yo" yẹ "nya mawulo sina" yẹ "ma bia
ma lapi lọ."

Kẹ ta bẹ i lumanga kẹ ti gọlẹnga ye wati na lọọ; ta hele
ti gọlẹni ma kẹ ta nja hele bẹ ti gọlẹnga ma.

Kẹ ngele wonga kia leke ye wati ji hitini kẹ i ya ngeya
limba wa lọ na gbatẹngọ a kọlu kọlu leke yẹ la kẹ i ya wanga
la.

Yẹ "Ang nya nda lapi nga kọ mua numu ma ndalẹi lọ wa,"
yẹ "bi gunga lọ bi nya gbuanga lọ kẹ bi leweni nya ma."

Kẹ i ya i li i kpulọ hele ma.

Kẹ i ya nja hele bẹ gama yẹ "Ndapi ji gẹ ngi ndeni bi ma"
yẹ "ye ndapi lọ hitinga ma" yẹ "na ngi piema" yẹ "ngi ngeyẹi
ji gbulọ ma lọ bi ma. Nya bẹ ngi li ngi gbulọ nya ma." Yẹ
"Mu nda ndaẹ wa numui leke gungalọ nga mba ma" yẹ "kẹ ta mia
ngi gbayangọ."

Kuo kẹ ta bẹ lumanga kẹ i hele yilinga kpaung a ngeyẹi
na kẹ i ya ta kia i gbuani na ta ngeyẹi ji ii ngi ma-o, kẹ
i ya. Kia leke wọ i foni ti luahu ye ndia ndiẹi kẹ i hounga
ngeyẹi na ma.

Kẹ i ndea yẹ "Ngi mbamboya-o mu nda la-o."

Kẹ ti tọtoa a ti nyọnyọ lalala ti wuvailọ wọ ti lalama
kpeing. I lẹ kpindi ma numu gbi ii guni a ngi mba gbua. Kẹ
i wa, ti loni ndalẹi ji wama lọ.

Kẹ i ndea ye na ma yẹ "Mu gbe na."

Kẹ ji ngeyẹi yọkọnga kẹ ji bẹ ngeyẹi yọkọnga. Kẹ i wanga ji gama i ngeyẹi vulo i wa ji bẹ gama i ngeyẹi vulo.

Yẹ "Wu tọnga hiye ndapi gẹ nga nde." Kẹ i ya i ndenga ji ma yẹ "Ngẹ ngi leni gẹ bi ma bia bẹ." Kẹ ngi ndenga "Ngẹ ngi leni gẹ bi ma."

Kia na kpọkọi i wẹni na ti kpẹlẹ ti bọ wiengọ na ti nyọnyọ ti luangọ na na kẹ i hungẹnga a tie kẹ ta tieni ya na ha ta lapi. Kẹ ti nyọnyọ mia ha ngi longọ i ti hungọ. Miando mia mu gẹlẹni na.

------

1. Recorded by young man from Pujehun in Freetown on February 16, 1960.
2. In the mid-nineteenth century, Thompson observed that Hippopotamus (nja hele) "abounds in many of the African rivers. They have their particular places--as much as the natives have their towns--so that we always know just where to go to find them" (Thompson:198).

TALE 60:   THE PALM WINE TAPPER AND THE PALM BIRD[1]

At one time Njagbe tapped palm wine:[2] The palm wine was very strong; if a person drank only one calabash /of wine/, he would not return /for more/ for four days.

At one time a palm bird saw this wine; he said, "I will finish that wine by myself."[3]

The container of wine was very large.

Every time Njagbe and Palm Bird went to the wine place, Palm Bird said, "I will finish this wine by myself."

Then Njagbe made a bet with him; he said, "You will not finish this wine."

Palm Bird said, "I will finish it!"

They made this bet at one time.

Palm Bird wanted to gather all his relatives together. He called them all.

On the day that Palm Bird was going to drink the wine,

Palm Bird gathered all his family. They all came; they all
looked exactly alike. They all came.

When Njagbe stooped over to put wine into a cup to give
to Palm Bird, one palm bird would step behind and another
would step in front. If Njagbe turned, he saw one palm bird;
he did not see any difference. At one time Njagbe kept giving
wine; he thought that he was giving wine to only one palm bird.
In fact, so many palm birds were there that some of them did
not get /any wine/ before the wine container was empty. At
that time Njagbe lost the bet.

That is why making bets is very deceptive; it is bad.

The story is ended.

Njagbe ji mia wọ i ndọi boni ndọi na gbandingọ kẹlẹma
ii ma. Ba kpọli koko yilakpe lọwọ nani ii lini na.

Ndọi ji mia wọ mbakui ji tọilọ wọ yẹ "Ndọi na ta" yẹ
"nya yilakpe kpọyọlọ."

Koto mia ngolọngọ mbu.

Kia wọ ta ta ti li ti ya ndọi ji ya gbele gbi ti ya ta
ta ti ya ndọi ji ya yẹ "Ndọi ji nya yilakpe nga kpọyọlọ ndọi
ji lọ wọ."

Kẹ ta bẹ kẹ ti maliwali hounga ta ta yẹ "Bii ndọi ji
gbọyọ."

Yẹ "Nga kpọyọlọ."

Maliwali ji lọ wọ ti houngọ a yẹma.

Kẹ mbakui ji ngi longọ i li i ngi bonda kpẹlẹ lẹma i wa i
lo kpẹẹ.

Foloi ji wọ ti yẹ lima ndọi ji gama kẹ mbaku ta ta na lima
kpọli ma kẹ mbaku ya i ngi bonda gbi lẹma. Ti gbi ti wa ti
yandọ ti gbi ti yilakpe.

Kia wọ ti wani wọ njagbe mawẹlẹnga yẹ i ndọi ji wui i
fenga ji wẹ i ya yẹ i mawẹlẹ yẹ i pekẹi wui kẹ ji gbua woma
kẹ pekẹi gbua kulọ. Ta i wotenga ta yila gbe mia ẹẹ ti lua
hu gọ i loni wọ ndọi na vema ta yẹ mbaku yilakpei na mia, i
ndọi na vema ngi wẹ. Inge ti wekpẹ bẹ tii sọe kẹ ndọi
gbọyọnga kotoi hu. Maliwali na i gula wọ fọ njagbe ma.

Na va mia maliwali houla ngandẹ ngandẹ ii nyandeni.

Dọmẹi ji ye kẹlẹmẹi mia.

---

1. Recorded by man from Bo in Freetown on January 12, 1960.
2. Palm wine (ndǫ), which also figures in Tale 91, is ex-
tracted from the raffia palm (nduvu).
3. The palm bird (mbaku) or village weaver (Pleiositagra
cucullatus) also appears in Tale 95. The village weaver is
said to be "strongly gregarious, whether feeding, flying,
roosting, or nesting" (Elgood:59).

TALE 61:   A WISE MAN AND A LITTLE CHILD[1]

A very wise man at one time.

    At one time there was a man who thought that his wisdom
/was greater/ than everyone else's in this world. He got up;
he wove a big basket; he put a lot of wisdom into it; he put
it on his back to travel. This man would not take any other
person's advice; he thought that he alone was wise. If anyone else explained anything to him, he would not accept it.
He thought that he was the only person who was wise; he continued to believe that.

    For some time the man was walking on a bush path. He
went until he met a little child sitting on the path; his mother
had gone on another path and left him sitting on the path; the
child sat waiting for his mother. When the man went, the basket of wisdom was set on his back. The man was far away when
he saw the child. (But we all know that on a bush path bushes
overhang where a person walks; branches hang over the center
of the path.) This man with the basket on his back was approaching (the child); a tree branch caught in the basket and
the man was unable to go on; the basket held him and he could
not let the basket fall.

    The little child sitting on the road said, "Bend the bas-
ket down a little; turn aside; the basket will pass."

    The man did not pay attention to the child; he said, "Of
course, child, I am wise. A basket of wisdom is set on my
back, so I am going. I will give some wisdom to anyone. And
you have come; you little one, are you wiser than I?" The
man did not pay attention /to the child/.

    But what happened?

    The man could not pass. He spent the whole day at that
place, although the little child had explained to him that if
he lowered the basket a little, he could pass. As soon as the
man bowed down, the hamper was free; the man was able to pass

easily. As the man turned /back/, he saw a tendril hanging behind him and he knew that the wisdom which the child gave to him had enabled the basket to pass. The man came out from under the basket; he dropped it forever. It happened there at that time that the man promised never to take the basket; the man believed that in this world a person's wisdom is never complete.

For this reason if a little child shows you his wisdom, you should first examine it; you should not say, "Of course, I am older than you; you cannot give me any wisdom."

Nęmahulemǫ wa wǫ.

Kena yila mia wǫ i hiye yę ngi nęmahu lewe ndunyęi ji hu numui gbi ma. Kę i hiyenga i nęmahu lewe ji i kaha wa vę i nęmahu lewe ji i puma kpoto; i pęlę woma a lewe la. Kenęi ji ęę numu gbi ngi nda nęmahu lewe wumbu wǫ yę ta yakpe mia ngi nęmahu lewenga numu gbi le a bie hinda gbi hungę a ngie ęę mbumbu. Yę ta yakpe mia numui ngi nęmahu lewengǫ. I loi lǫ lani.

Lǫwǫi lęnga a yę jiama kę i ya a ndǫgbǫ wele yila kę i ya i male ndopo woi ji i heini pelei ji ma ngi nje i wa pele yeka ma i ngi longa heini pelei ji ma ta heini a ngi nje mawo. Kia i ya nęmahu le gahęi ji lǫ węlę ngi woma. I longa huguhangǫ kę i ndopoi ji lǫnga kę mu kpęlę mu kǫlǫ ndǫgbǫ welei ta numu bi ya jiama la bǫmbǫisia ta wa kę mbękęisia ti hęlę pelei ye ndia ndięi. Kenęi ji i foni kine na kahęi ji lǫ węlę ngi woma kę ngulubękęi ji kę i wilinga kahęi ji hu ęę yaa gu a lewe. I ya i lewe kę kahęi ji gba ii yaa i li kę kahęi ji gba tao ęę gbua kahęi ji bu a gula.

Ndopo woi ji lǫ heini pelei ji ma ndopo woi hi mia kę i ndenga yę "Kahęi na i ye mahuwęlę bi hęlę," ye "kahęi na a lewelǫ."

Ii lalima "Ingę," yę "ndopoi nya nya nęmahu lewengǫ nęmahu le gahan węlęni nya woma. Famia ngi lima numu gbi ngi fe ngi wę ta bi waa bi woi ji bi ma ny nęmahu lewe ma." Ii lalima.

Kę gbǫǫ wieni?

Ii yaa i lewe i luvani hindęi na haa. Sia ji ndopo woi ji hugęni a ngie kę i kahęi ji i gotonga kę i kahęi ji a gulo i lewe. Kia le i gotoni kę kahęi ji i lewenga lo-o i gu i lewe i yaa ngi vawęini gbi. Kia i woteni i ngeyęi ji lǫ na ngi woma kę i konga kę ndopo woi ji nęmahu le ji i fe ngi wę ta mia pieni kahęi ji lewe. I gbuani lǫ kahęi na bu i gula haa. I hiyeni wǫ. Wati na ma i wa i gęlę hi. Kenęi na ii ya kahęi na wumbuni i lani lǫ le la kę ndunyęi ji hu numu ęę nęmahu le gbǫyǫ.

Famia ndopo woi nda nẹmahu le na gẹ i kẹni a bie mahungọ le pẹing bi tọ baa yẹma "Ingẹ, nya nya wovangọ nya lengọ bi ma, bia bẹ gu a nẹmahu le vela mbẹ."

---

1. Recorded by young man from Pujehun in Freetown on May 13, 1960.

Friends

TALE 62: SPIDER, FROGS, AND NIGHTINGALE[1]

Spider got a wife in a certain wife-getting ceremony.

Spider went to Frogs and Nightingale to beg /for help/;
he said that they should go with him to this Sande-leaving
dance.[2] Frogs and Nightingale went and performed at the
Sande dance; Spider received great happiness and respect
there. They all returned happily with the Sande initiate.

After two years passed, Spider received a messenger who
said that his mother-in-law had died.

Spider went to his wife; he said, "A messenger came; he
said that your mother died. But how shall I mourn her, when
my voice is so ugly?"

His wife said to him, "Yes, it is appropriate that you
go to weep for her, because you are her son-in-law. Sit down
and decide how you will arrange to go to mourn her."

Then Spider returned to the house with a troubled heart.
He did not know what to do, because his voice was ugly.

In the afternoon he went down into the swamp; he gathered
all the Frogs; he begged them /to help him/.

Spider said /to the Frogs/, "Let us go to mourn my mother-
in-law."

Spider returned and went to Nightingale. He said, "I beg
you; let us go to mourn my mother-in-law." He said, "Look,
my voice is ugly; do not remain behind lest I be disgraced."

All the creatures agreed to Spider's plan.

In the morning Spider took a bag; he put all the Frogs
in it; he caught Nightingale; he put him in his throat. He
went to weep /for his mother-in-law/. Spider walked and
walked and walked. He walked far until he approached the
town.

Then Spider said to the Frogs who were in the bag and to
Nightingale, "We are approaching the town." He said, "Therefore, assist me now; let us begin to weep."

Then Frogs and Nightingale began to weep:

"Ah, the great one, ah;
"They have tapped a little wine;
"Jami-o, Lusia's mother.

"Ah, the great one, ah;
"They have tapped a little wine;
"Jami-o, Lusia's mother.
"Ah, the great one, ah;
"They have tapped a little wine;
"Jami-o, Lusia's mother."

Then everyone in the town came to the edge of the town to greet Spider: paramount chiefs, women, men. Everyone came to the road, even old people. They all came to the edge of the town to greet Spider. They embraced him joyously and brought him into the town. They went into the paramount chief's compound.

The people consoled Spider. They said, "Your mother-in-law has died."

The chief also ceremoniously gave Spider the news /of his mother-in-law's death/. The chief said, "But I am happy to receive you on this day. Your weeping has pleased all the townspeople. Therefore, I am sending messengers to the other paramount chiefs so that they may come to hear your voice. /I shall call/ the young men in the other towns."

Spider expressed happiness at this declaration.

A large crowd accompanied Spider into the visitor's house. They gave him a lot of food. Spider was trembling greedily for the food; he did not give much rice to Frogs and Nightingale. Spider was given not one houseful of rice but two housefuls of rice. Spider cheated Frogs and Nightingale; he gave them only twelve dishes of rice; they ate them, but they were unsatisfied. Then the people returned with wine and other drinks; Spider cheated Frogs and Nightingale.

When evening came, Frogs got out of the bag and returned to their swamp. Nightingale also got out of Spider's throat and returned to the tree from which he had been taken.

In the morning the paramount chiefs gathered. Spider was still lying down; he had eaten a lot of food and drunk many drinks the day before; he felt very tired. While Spider was lying down, a messenger was sent to him.

The messenger said, "Go there, speak as you did yesterday. The people, whom we told to gather to hear your voice, have come."

The messenger awakened Spider. He arose feeling tired but happy about going to let these local freemen hear his voice. When Spider got up, he took his bag; without looking inside, he put the bag under his arm. Spider did not cough to see if Nightingale was in his throat. Spider left the house.

Spider went into the center of the crowd of people. The paramount chief of the town embraced him; the chief spoke a few words to the paramount chiefs who had come from other chiefdoms. The chief explained that since Spider's mother-in-law had died, Spider had come to weep there. Spider was happy about what the chief said. The paramount chiefs who sat together said that they wanted to hear Spider's voice; Spider agreed.

When Spider wept, his voice was very ugly, for Frogs and Nightingale had revolted against him. Frogs and Nightingale had left; Spider did not check to discover if they were still there. Spider was openly disgraced.

Spider began to weep with his ugly voice: "Nya-a-o, nya-a-o, nya-a-o."

Then some critical young men began to cry: "Ye-i, ye-i, ye-i!" The chief's servants began to catch and beat these young men.

For a short while Spider continued to cry. He could only say "Nya-a-o, nya-a-o, nya-a-o."

The local freemen also became disgusted. They caught Spider and beat him; they kept beating him.

Spider /got away/; he ran up to the eaves and squatted there.

For that reason to this day whenever you enter a house, you will see Spider in the eaves. Even if Spider is on the ground and he sees you, he will run and climb to the edge of the eaves so that you will find him there. To this day Spider is afraid. Whenever you find Spider, you will find him in the eaves.

This story is how at one time Spider came to be stuck up in the eaves until today.

Kasilo nyaha joelo ye nyaha jọ gomẹi ji hu.

I li lọ i kpegbenga manẹnẹ kẹ Sikonde yẹ "Ti li Sande gomẹi ji hu." Kẹ ti ya ti lilọ ti Sande gomẹi ji ga a kohunẹ wa mia mbẹ hou wa mia ndọbla ti feni ngi wẹ. Ti yamailọ a Sande yoi ji a kohunẹ wa.

Fo fele lewengo woma i tomo majọẹ lọ ta ngi Kasilo tẹ
"Ngi yemọi i hanga."

Kẹ i ya ngi nyahẹi gama yẹ "Ngi tomo majọnga tẹ bi nje
i hanga, kẹ ngi ye hindẹi ji wiema, ji nya wo nyamungọ?"

Ke ngi nyahẹi ndenga ngi ma yẹ "Mn, maaa houlọ bi li bi
ngọẹ wie jifa mblamọi mia a bie," yẹ "fale na hugbatẹ le lilẹ
vuli bi hei na gbọọ hugbatẹ le ba pie kọ bi li ngọmẹi ji."

Kasilo pie lọ i yama pẹlẹi bu a ndii mọnẹ. Ii kọ gbọọ
a pie tao ngi wo nyamungọ.

Kpọkọ volei i yei lọ kpetei hu i kpegbenga kpẹlẹ lẹmba
i ti manẹnẹ.

Yẹ "A mu li mu nya yemọi wọ wo."

I yama i li Sikonde bẹ gama. Yẹ "Kọnẹ le a mu li mu nya
yemọi wọ wo" yẹ "kpe nya wo nyamungọi" yẹ "wa lo heini nya ya
a wufe."

Ti kpẹlẹ ti lumailọ ji ma.

Ngele woilọ i li a bẹki i kpegbengẹisia kpẹlẹ wu hu i yama
i Sikonde bẹ hou i ngua ngi bolo hu kẹ i ya ngọmẹi. Ngi lingọi
ji ngọmẹi ji i jia i jia i jia kẹ pelei huguhangọ yẹla kẹ i
fonga tẹi gblanga.

Kẹ i ndenga kpegbengẹi jisia ma ti yẹ bẹki hu. Kẹ Sikonde
bẹ ma yẹ "Mu fonga na tẹi gblanga-o" yẹ "fale" yẹ "kpọmẹi ji wu
wanga fa" yẹ "a pie na" yẹ "a mu ngọẹ ji lọto."

Kẹ ti ngọẹ ji lọtonga a pie la:

"Ya janga mani ya;
"Ti ndọo mbọo ya;
"Jami-o ya Lusia ngi nje.
"Ya janga mani ya;
"Ti ndọo mbọo ya;
"Jami-o ya Lusia ngi nje.
"Ya janga mani ya;
"Ti ndọo mbọo ya;
"Jami-o ya Lusia ngi nje."

Ke tei kpẹlẹ ngonga kẹ ti yeinga pelei wunga Kasilo gulọ
ndọ mahanga le nyahanga le hingale kẹ ti gbi ti yeinga pelei
hu numu wovanga le ti gbi ti yeilọ pelei wunga Kasilo gulọ.
Ti ngi gului lọ a kohunẹ kẹ ti lẹnga tẹi hu ti li ndọmahẹi
gatẹi hu.

Tia bẹ ti ngi lahoi lọ na tẹ "Bi yemọi hanga."

Mahęi bę i konai lǫ ngi ma yę "Kę" yę "nya gohunęngǫ bi
majǫ va a folei ji" yę "tao" yę "ngǫę ji bi piema" yę "ndangǫi
ndǫbla gbi wohu" yę "fale" yę "nya tobla loma ndǫmaha wekęi
nasia gama" yę "kǫ ti wa ti bi woi ji męni" yę "jifa tia vuli"
yę "ta gulǫ ti ma mani wie kǫ nahi bi woi ji męni va" yę "kę
na kǫnga wekęisia ti ta wekęisia hu."

Kasilo bę i gohunęlǫ ji ma.

Faha wa lilǫ a ngie pęlę bu ngi hota welęi bu ti ti gǫilǫ
a męhę gboto ke nahu gbi męhę ma gbęli ji lǫ ngi hu. Kpegbengęi
jisia ta Sikondeni ii ti gǫni a mbęi. Mbęi na ti yę a fe ti
we. Ti mbęi velǫ nasia ti lęngǫ tę "Mba gale-o pęlę yela
kinęi," nya ngii lęni ngę mbęi ti feni ta pęlę fele fendangǫ
ye kalęi leke kę i ti gavai lǫ. I ti gǫ a mbagale pu mahu
felekpe ti męni ii ti goveni. Tia bę ti yama ti wa a ndǫi,
kpǫle hani jisia gboto i ti gavai lǫ hu.

Kpǫkǫ welęi lǫ kę kpegbengęi jisia ti gbuanga bęki hu kę
ti yamanga kpetei hu mia ti gbiani na. Sikonde bę gbuai lǫ
ngi bolo hu kę i yamanga mia i ngi gbuani na.

Kę ngele wonga kę ndǫmahangęi jisia kę ti lęnga ma ta ngi
Kasilo ta taa lani i męhę gboto menga gbuęi i kpole gboto
wienga gbuęi ye kahu gbǫyǫ lǫ ngi ma. Ta lǫ lani kę ti numu
longa na ngi gama pęlęi bu.

Tę "A li na wu nde wuę jisia gbuęi mu yę ti ma muę ta
lęmba na hi ta kenęi ji womęni. Ti wanga."

Kę ti ya ti ngi wu kę i hijenga i hijeilǫ ngi gahu, i
gbuangǫ tao ngi gohunęngǫ yęla li va na hi kǫ nungęi jisia
ndǫblęi jisia ti ngi wo męni. I hijeilǫ i bęki wumbu ii
hugbeni kę i nguanga gbambu ii ngi bolo hu gbuani ina wǫi
Sikonde lǫ na. Kę i gbuanga pęlęi bu kę i ya.

I ya kę i wuanga fahęi jisia lia. Nunga ti vahangǫ
yęla. Kę i longa. Ndǫmahęi ji i ye tęi ji hu i ngi guilǫ.
I hije i lo i njępenga le ndǫmahanga wekęi jisia gama ti yę
gbuani ndǫ gęwęi nasia hu, i yama i kenęi Kasilo hinda huge
yę "Kę ngi yemǫi mia hanga fale ngǫ woma mia i wanga na."
Kasilo bę i gohunę lǫ ji ma, ndǫmahanga ti heilǫ woma yila
tę ti longǫi ti ngi womę ni i lumai lǫ.

Jina wǫ Kasilo i yę ngǫę ji wiema. Ndǫe wǫ na i yę pie.
Wu kǫę lǫ a tǫnya ngi wo nyamungǫ yę la. Wati na kpegbei jisia
ti gbemgbani a ngie. Ti lini kę Sikonde ji bę ti lini kpęlę
na i lini na ii ya hugbatę wieni aa kǫ ina wǫi tia na. Ngi
ya wufei lǫ lǫǫ ngitiiya.

I tatoi lǫ a ngo nyamu yę la "Nya-a-o, nya-a-o, nya-a-o."

Kẹ njia hugbua gọnga ti tọtonga a yele gula la. Ta nde
"Ye-i ye-i ye-i!" Bọilopoisia ti yẹ mahanga woma ti tọtoi
lọ a ti hou la ta ti la ta ti lewe.

Kẹ Kasilo ji wielọ wati huguhangọ wo va a yẹ leke "Nya-
a-o, nya-a-o, nya-a-o." Ndọbla bẹ ji gbalei lọ ti ma. Ti
Kasilo hei lọ ti ndewe. Ti loilọ ndewe ma.

I lẹ kpọgbọungẹi i ya a pimẹ i wẹlẹ na.

Famia a folei ji bẹ pẹlẹ gbi leke bi wani mbu mia leke
bi Kasilo lọ ngalọ na. I yẹ ndọlọ mẹi yo, bi ngi lọngalọ leke
ndọmẹi a lewe a pimẹ lọ. I lẹ kpọgbọungẹi ya kọ na hi bi
wanga lọ bi ngi male kpọgbọungẹi. A lua a folei ji bẹ mia-o-
mia mu Kasilo maleni na ma ngi male kpọgbọungẹi lọ.

Kẹ ji lọ wọ wieni Kasilo gbangọ ha kpọgbọunga.

----

1. Recorded by a man from Bumpe in Bo on April 16, 1960. See
Tale 63 for another version of this tale. I published an
English translation of this tale in "Mende Folktales" (West
African Review, 1960-61).
2. Kpegbe, green frog; Sikonde, "nightingale."

TALE 63: SPIDER AND NIGHTINGALE[1]

Spider and Nightingale.

A long time ago there was a big dance in a town. The
townspeople wanted a singer at this dance. At that time they
did not have a singer who sang well.

Now greedy Spider was there and he went to Nightingale.
He arranged with Nightingale to go to the dance in his throat.
Spider made an agreement with Nightingale.

Spider said, "When we go there, if we receive anything,
we will divide it equally." He said, "Let us go and perform
at this dance."

Nightingale agreed and he got into Spider's throat. They
went together /to the dance/.

Spider went and Nightingale sang the song very sweetly
throughout the day. At night food was brought after they had
left the dancing place.

Then Spider said, "Nightingale, come out of my throat so that I may eat my food."

Nightingale came out of Spider's throat; he sat watching Spider eat. Spider ate all the food; he did not give any food to Nightingale. Spider was the only one to eat. As soon as Spider had eaten the food, it was time to sing.

Spider said, "Nightingale, get back in my throat; let me go to sing my song."

Twice Nightingale did that; twice Nightingale bore the situation. The third time that the rewards of food, money, and clothing were brought Spider took everything; he did not give Nightingale anything. When the time for singing came and the people gathered filling the town, Spider wanted Nightingale to get in his throat.

Nightingale said, "I will not get /into your throat/." As soon as Nightingale said that, he flew away and returned home.

When Spider came outside, his voice was ugly. At that time the townspeople who had given Spider all those things said that they would take away his gifts.

That is why if you cheat your companion when you have made an agreement, it is bad.

Kasilo ta Sikunde.

Wati huguhangọ wa wọ komẹ wa gulailọ ta yila hu. Ye komẹ ji ndọlẹi ti longọ a ngolemọ. Wati na hu ngolemọ gbi ii yẹ na. Numu gbi na wọ a ngole yekpe ya.

Kẹ Kasilo ji jifa i kọlọ leke kẹ mẹhẹ hindei mia kẹ i ya kẹ i ya Sikunde gama kọ ta ta ti li i yẹ ngi bolo hu lia. Kẹ i hugbatẹ wienga a Sikunde.

Yẹ "Mu ya hani gbi le mu kpua ma kọlẹlọ mahẹungọ jọ ma a bie" yẹ "fale mu li mu ndoli ji ga."

Kẹ Sikunde lumaa kẹ i wa ngi bolo hu kẹ ti ya.

I ya i ngolei ji yanga manẹngọ wa i luvani lọ ngolei ji yama kpẹing. Kpindi ji le ti wama a mẹhẹ jisia. Ti vaya na le ngolemẹi ji.

Kẹ i ndea yẹ "Sikunde gbua mbẹ nya bolo hu ngi nya mẹhẹ mẹ."

Sikunde a gbualǫ ngi bolo hu a yę hei lǫ a ngi gbe. I
męhęi na i mę kpęlę ęę Sikunde gǫ. Ta yakpe. Kę ji le i
męhęi na męa ngole gbei na hitea le.

Kę i ndea yę "Sikunde yama nya bolo hu ngi li ngi nya
wolo ya.

Sikunde ti na wie heima fele; Sikunde a ndohu ngi yeya.
Ye sawayęi na na kia na le i li ti męhęi na ti wai la hani
nasia kpęlę mawa hani na-o kǫpǫi nasia-o kulęi nasia-o kpęlę
i mę fo ii Sikunde gǫi. Wati na na ti li ngole gbe ji hiti
na nunga gbi ti wa ti lęi lavea, ngi longǫ na Sikunde i yę
ngi bolo hu.

Sikunde bę kę i ndea yę "Ngęę ya li." Kia le i na leni
kę Sikunde bubua. Kę i yama.

Ji wǫ Kasilo gbia ngitiiya njępęi gbi ti nde ngi wo ii
yę nęi. Nunga ti ndelǫ wǫ tęi na hu ti nde hakęi nasia kpęlę
i kpuai tęi na hu ti kpęlę gbia ngi yeya.

Na va mia kava gula la bi mba ma na wie wa taa le ma
hinda hu ma ii nęni.

---

1. Recorded by young man from Pujehun in Freetown on February
12, 1960.

TALE 64: SPIDER AND BAT[1]

This story is about Spider and Bat.

At one time Spider and Bat were great friends. They arranged to go to visit a friend in another village.

As they were going, Spider said to Bat, "Comrade, let us
take more beautiful names. My name will be 'Strangers' and
yours will be 'Men.' When we are there, if they give us any
food saying, 'Strangers, here is your food,' I will be the
only one to eat. But if they say, 'Men, here is your food,'
you are the only one to eat."

Bat agreed to this plan.

Spider and Bat went on and reached their friend in his
town. When they arrived, the man was very happy to see them.
He told his wife to cook sweet rice for them. When the rice
was given to a little child, she brought it to the visitors'
house and met them there.

The child said, "Strangers, here is your rice."

When the child had gone, Spider said, "Comrade, my name was called. I am the only one to have this rice." Spider ate all the rice; he did not give any to Bat.

Every day that is what Spider continued to do. Bat became emaciated.

In the evening Bat used to go to the rubbish pile to take the scraps of food that were thrown there. Once as he was doing this, the little child, who brought food to them, saw Bat.

She said to him, "Father, why are you doing this? Isn't the food that mother prepares and I bring enough for you? You are thin, and so you come to eat rubbish."

Then Bat said to her, "That is not the problem. I do not eat any of the food that your mother prepares. Recently we took names; Spider said that my name is 'Men' and his name is 'Strangers.' When you bring food, you say, 'Strangers, here is your food'; he is the only one who eats; he does not give me any. But if you came and said, 'Men, here is your rice,' the food would be mine and I would eat it."

The child said, "Now, return and sit down. I am going for food.

When the child brought the food into the house, she met Spider and Bat there.

She said, "Men, here is your food."

Spider jumped up; he said, "Child, are you mad? Have you forgotten? Can't you say, 'Strangers, here is your food?' Instead you say, 'Men'; what type of men?"

The little child said, "Father, I said, 'Men, here is your food.' I did not say anything else." Then the little child left immediately.

Then Bat took the bowl of rice; he put it in a corner; he ate greedily. But there was a lot of rice and it was also very sweet. Then he put away the remainder. Spider was very hungry; he wanted the rice for himself; he wanted to steal the rice, but Bat was in the house.

That night a big dance was held in the town; everyone went to the dance. Spider went; Bat also went to the celebration.

Before Bat went he thought, 'If I leave this rice, Spider will steal it; therefore, I shall make a plan.' Bat took a banana leaf; he cut it and put it on a string; he hung it above the door so that if anyone saw it he would think that Bat was swinging there. So Bat prepared before he went to the dance.

Spider was extremely hungry; he wanted to enter the house to eat the rice. But when he looked at the doorway, he saw the leaf swinging there and thought it was Bat. Then Spider returned to the dance; he stayed for a while; he came again to the house. Every time Spider came to the house, he saw the leaf swinging there and thought that it was Bat. All night Spider kept going and coming. When morning came, Spider had not eaten any rice; he had not found a way /to get it/.

In the morning at the dance, Spider sang: "Bat is not in the house, he is not outside it! Bat is not in the house, he is not outside it!"

Spider kept singing; he was burning with hunger, he hid; he left the town; he returned to his own village.

This is the end of the story.

Dọmẹi ji ndaloni Kasilo ta Ndẹvẹ lọ ma.

Wati yila wọ Kasilo ta Ndẹvẹ ti yẹ lọ ndiamọ ya wahu. Ti hugbatẹilọ li va vama ti ndiamọ yila ma fula weka yila hu.

Kia ti yẹ lima Kasilo ndeilọ Ndẹvẹ ma yẹ "Ndakpẹi mu lapi mu nda nyande nyandenga wumbu i lewe jisia ma. Nya nya la a Hotanga. Bia bi la a Kọnga. Mu ya ti mẹhẹi gbi vengalọ mu wẹ ti ndenga lọ tẹ 'Hotanga wu mẹhẹi gbe' nya yakpe mia lọ nga mẹ kẹ ti ndenga lọ tẹ 'Kọnga wu mẹhẹi gbe' bia yakpe bu wo mia bi mẹ."

Ndẹvẹ lumani lọ ji ma.

Kẹ ti ya ti fo ndiamọi ma ngi ye ta hu. Kia ti foni kenẹi gohunẹngọ wa ye la ti lọva i kahu i gbua gboto wielọ ti ma i nde ngi nyahẹi ma i mba i nenẹ wa yili ti va. Kia ti mbẹi veni ndopo wuloi wẹ i lini la ti hota wẹlẹ bu lọ i ti maleni lọ na.

Kẹ i ndenga yẹ "Hotanga wu bẹi gbe."

Kia ndopo wuloi yamani kẹ Kasilo ndea yẹ "Ndakpẹi, nya lei mia ti lolinga nya yakpe lọ nya wulọ a mbẹi ji." I mbẹi na gbi mẹilọ ii Ndẹvẹ gọni.

Folo gbi hi i yẹ pie ha i lo hu Ndẹvẹ i ganya kọvọ kọvọ kọvọ.

Kpọkọ i wẹlẹngalọ wọ a li kawọẹ ma lọ a mẹhẹ wẹ jisia ye
kọtu kọtui jisia wumbu ta pili kawọẹ ma. Folo yila i loni ji
wiema lọ kẹ ndopo wuloi ji a mẹhẹ belẹ ti wẹ kẹ i ngi lọnga.

Kẹ i ndea ngi ma yẹ "Kẹkẹ, gbẹe bi ji wiema? Mẹhẹ gbi
na baa mẹ? Mẹhẹi ji kpẹlẹ ye a fe nga wa la, ẹẹ bi gove? Bi
ganyangọ hi bi lewema a kawọ ma mẹ."

Kẹ i ndenga ngi ma yẹ "Na ii le mẹhẹi ji kpẹlẹ bi nje a
ngili nya ngii mẹma. Mu ndanga wumbunga ge Kasilo yẹ nya nya
la a Kọnga ta ngi la a Hotanga. Bi wanga a mẹhẹ bẹ 'Hotanga,
wu mẹhẹ gbe.' Ta yakpe mia a mẹ ẹẹ nya gọ, kẹ ina bi walọ
bẹ 'Kọnga, wu bẹi gbe," nya bẹ nya wo a yẹla nga mẹlọ."

Kẹ ndopoi wuloi ndea yẹ "Kẹ yama bi hei nya lima mẹhẹ
woma."

Kia i lini, kẹ i wanga a mẹhẹ i wa la pẹlẹ bu i ti venjọ
kpẹlẹ maleni na lọ.

Yẹ "Kọnga, wu mẹhẹi gbe."

Kasilo i hijelọ sa yẹ "Ndopoi gbẹ e bi gbowangọi bi
lemanga lọ bẹẹ nde ba yẹma 'Hotanga, wu mẹhẹi gbe' kẹ baa
nde bẹ 'Kọnga;' gbẹ gọnga?"

Ndopo wuloi yẹ "Kẹkẹ hi ngi ndeni ngẹ 'Kọnga wu mẹhẹi
gbe' njẹpẹi weka gbii nya la." Kẹ ndopo wuloi i ya a mẹ kpa.

Kẹ Ndẹvẹ i mba galoi ji wumbunga i lewela sọkui hu ta
yakpe i mẹ kpae kẹ mbẹi gbotongọ wa yẹ la tao nẹngọ wa, kẹ
i ya i ye mọni la magbatẹ. Ndọlẹi lewea Kasilo ma i manilọ
ngi ma yẹ i mbẹi na huma kẹ Ndẹvẹ ii ya gbuani.

Kpọkọi na kẹ ti ndoli wa gula tẹ hu kẹ numui gbi ti
ya ndoli ji hu. Kasilo i li Ndẹvẹ bẹ kẹ i ya komẹi hu.

Kia i ye lima i ndeilọ nẹmahu yẹ "Ngi mbẹi ji longa
Kasilo a humà, fale, gbẹ ngi nẹmahu le gbua." I ndawẹi lọ
wumbuni manalaa ji i malewe i ngeyẹi wa hu i hẹlẹ pẹlẹ la
ma a kọ numu gbi bi gomẹnga ma ba ngili lọ la bẹ Ndẹvẹ mia
i vẹmbema la. Hi i hugbatẹni kẹ i ya ndoli hu. Ngi li gẹ
na ndoli hu.

Ndọlẹi ji i Kasilo mọnga seẹ kẹ i wa ngi longa i wa i
wa pẹlẹ bu i mbẹi mẹ kẹ i pẹlẹ la mahu gbenga a tọ ngawẹi
ji a fẹmbẹ na ta i yẹ tọ yẹ "Ndẹvẹ mia." Kẹ i gbọma yama
ndoli hu i lẹmbi seẹ kẹ i gbọma wa i ye wani gbi a male
ndawẹi ji a vẹmbẹ ngi ngilingọ la lọ yẹ "Ndẹvẹ mia." Hi i
yini piema gbuu i lo hu ngele i wo ii mbẹi na mẹ wele gbi
jọni.

Ngele wo hu na ndoli ji hu kẹ i ngolei gula i ngolei
gbua ta yakpe yẹ "Ndẹvẹ ii pẹlẹ bu ii ngitiiya gbegbe kigbe"
yẹ "Ndẹvẹ ii pẹlẹ bu ii ngitiiya gbegbe kigbe."

I ndoli ji lọ gani kakaka, ndọlẹi ji i ngi mọ, kẹ i
lọwunga, i gbua hota wele na hu i yama ngi ye fula hu.

Dọmẹi ngi gẹlẹmẹi mia.

---

1. Recorded by man from Bunumbu in Kailahun on April 12,
1960. See Tale 65 for another version of this proverb tale.
I published an English translation of this tale in West
African Review (1960-61).

TALE 65: SPIDER AND BAT'S VISIT[1]

At one time Spider and Bat went visiting. They went until they came to a big town. They went to the chief.

Before they reached the big town, Spider said to Bat,
"Comrade, when we go into this town, my name will be Strangers.
What will yours be?"

"Oh," said Bat, "my name will be Men."

"Ah," Spider said, "whenever we go anywhere and we are
brought food, if they say, 'Men, here is food,' I will not
eat. But if they say, 'Strangers, here is food, I will be
the only one to eat; you will not eat any food."

Then Bat agreed and they went on.

When food was cooked and brought, the child said,
"Strangers, here is your food." Bat remained sitting and
Spider ate all the food, he finished it completely.

The next morning food was cooked and brought, the child
said, "Strangers, here is your food." Spider was the only
one to eat any food.

Now Bat started to become emaciated. Bat went to the
chickens and ate their lice. As Bat was going to eat some
bananas behind the house, he met the little girl.

She said, "Why, Father, I just now brought food to you.
Have you come so soon to eat a banana?"

"Ah, my child," Bat said, "we recently took names on the road. If you say, 'Strangers,' Mr. Spider is the only one who eats. If you say, 'Men, here is food,' I am the only one who eats. Since we came here, 'Strangers' is the only one who gets food."

"Oh," she said, "is that all?"

He said, "Yes."

Then the child returned. She explained /the agreement/ to her mother and to her family. When an entire cow had been cooked for the visitors, the child brought all the food.

She said, "Father, good afternoon."

Spider and Bat said, "Yes."

She said, "Men, here is the rice."

Spider said, "Kiyee, Child, you have brought this food! What kind of a character do you have? This child has no sense! What did you really say?"

"Oh," she said, "I said, 'Men, here is your food.'"

"Do you know that this one is mad! Speak the truth!"

She said, "I said, 'Men, here is some food.'"

Then Bat alone ate the food. Afterward when the child came, she said, "Men, here is some food." Bat ate the rice; some remained and he kept it.

Spider and Bat went to this dance. Spider thought that when Bat left, he would return to the house. Bat went and split a banana leaf, fixed it well: it looked like his wings, and hung it above the door.

When Spider left Bat at the dance, he said that he was coming into the house. Over the door Spider saw the leaf swinging, he thought that it was Bat; Spider ran back to the dance. He met Bat there; he ran back to the house; he ran back to the dance. He met Bat at the dance; he decided to run back to the house, where the banana leaf hung at the door. When the leaf began to swing, Spider ran back to the dance; he ran to stand near Bat.

Spider began to say this proverb: "Why is Bat standing outside now? Is this one not gbegbe kigbe? Bat is not in the house; he is not outside the house. Is this gbegbe kigbe?"

This is the end of this story: Spider disgraced himself because of greediness.

Ndẹvẹi ji mia wọ ta Kasilo ti li hota wele hu jẹsiamẹi. Ti ya ti fonga ta wa na ji hu. Kẹ ti ya mahẹi gama.

Kẹ pẹing ti fo ti foa ta wama kẹ Kasilo ndenga Ndẹvẹ ma yẹ "Ndakpẹi mu li ma tẹi ji hu" yẹ "nya nya la a Hotanga-yo." Yẹ "Ọ bia bẹ?"

"Kuo" yẹ "nya bẹ nga la a Kọnga."

"A" yẹ "ji mu lima hinda" yẹ "mu ya mẹhẹ gbi ti wa la; ti ndenga tẹ 'Kọnga mẹhẹ gbe'" yẹ "ngẹẹ mẹ-o" yẹ "kẹ ti ndenga tẹ 'Hotanga mẹhẹ gbe'" yẹ "nya yakpe lọ nga mẹ" yẹ "bẹ mẹ."

Kẹ Ndẹvẹ bẹ luma kẹ ti ya.

Kia wọ ta mẹhẹi ji yili ti wa tẹ "Hotanga mẹhẹ gbe." Ndẹvẹ a lo heilọ Kasilo i kpẹlẹ mẹ i kpọyọ sẹng.

Ngele yekei i wo ti mẹhẹi ji yili ti wa la tẹ "Hotanga a mẹhẹ gbe." Kasilo yakpe lọ a mẹ.

Kẹ Ndẹvẹ tọtonga na a ganya la a li na tẹngẹi jisia gama a ti ma mumuli jisia mẹ. I loni wọ lima sẹlẹi ji lọ mẹma pẹlẹi ji woma kẹ ndopo wuloi ji ngi malenga na.

Yẹ "Gbẹi, Kẹkẹ, ngi wa wẹ a mẹhẹi sanga ba wa ba sẹlẹ mẹ?"

"Ah nya loi," yẹ "kẹ mu mbiyẹ lọ gẹ mia pelei hu ye" yẹ "wu ndea wẹ Hotanga kenẹi na ta yakpe mia a mẹ, Kenẹi Kasilo" yẹ "wu ndea we 'Kọnga mẹhẹ gbe,' nya yakpe lọ nga mẹ. Ke sia gẹ gba mu wa Hotanga yakpe mia ta ti gọ."

"Kuo" yẹ "na lele?"

Yẹ "Hn."

Kẹ ndopoi ji yama kẹ i ndenga ngi nje ma kẹ i hungẹnga a ngi bonda. Kia wọ ti mẹhẹ wa yilini le nika gbuha yila ti kpẹlẹ yini kẹ hota mẹhẹi ji. Kia wọ ti li la leke.

Tẹ "Kẹkẹ bi wa."

Tẹ "Hn."

Tẹ "Kọnga mbei gbe."

Kasilo yẹ "Kiye-e-e, ndopoi, bia bi wai a mẹhẹi ji. Bi bi yẹgi yena? Ngi kọ ndopoi ji nẹmahu ii leni. Bi yẹ vui gbẹ?"

"Kuo" yẹ "ngẹ 'Kọnga mẹhẹ gbe.'"

"Hẹ ji kpowamọ lọ, tọnya yia le."

Yẹ "Nge 'Kọnga mẹhẹ gbe.'"

Kẹ Ndẹvẹ mẹhẹi ji mẹa. Foma ye ji ti wa tẹ "Kọnga mẹhẹ gbe." Ndẹvẹ mbẹi ji mẹa i gbuhama i tonga.

Ti ya ndolimẹi ji yẹ i Ndẹvẹ lo na i wa pẹlẹi ji la. Ndẹvẹ bẹ kẹ i ya i mana lawẹi blama i kpatẹ panda. Bi tọa kia ngi gbaki na kẹ i hẹlẹnga pẹlẹi na bu.

Kia Kasilo a Ndẹvẹ lo komẹi hu kia a wa yẹ "I wa pẹlẹi ji bu kẹ i lọnga ngi mahu fẹnẹ-fẹnẹ ta a tọ Ndẹvẹ mia kẹ i yama a pimẹ kẹ i yama ndoli hu. I li i Ndẹvẹ male na yẹ "Gbẹ na ngi yama." Kia i wa a pimẹ kuku manalawẹi ji hẹlẹi pẹlẹi la. Kia i yẹ fẹnẹ-fẹnẹ i yama a pimẹ. I loni wama kẹ i wani na i lo Ndẹvẹ gbla.

A salei ji hei gbẹi na "Ndẹvẹ ta i loi ngitiiya? Gbegbe kigbe ya a ye ji gei ji na? Ndẹvẹ ii pẹlẹ bu na ii ngitiiya gbegbe kigbe ya ji?"

A dọmẹi ji ye kẹlẹmẹi mia: Kasilo i jambo wọ fọ mẹhẹ hindẹi na woma.

---

1. Recorded by man from Bo in Freetown on January 27, 1960. I published an English translation of this tale in West African Review (1960-61).

TALE 66: SPIDER AND MONKEY[1]

At one time Spider and Monkey decided to cut the brush for their farm. They would work at one farm for one week; the next week they would work at the other farm for a week.

They began to work on Spider's farm. When they reached the farm, they cut brush until cooked food was brought to them. When Monkey came, he sat down by the food and he started to put his hand into the food.

"Oh," said Spider, "go, wash your hands! Comrade, you have such black hands! Don't put your hand into this food! Go wash your hands!"

Monkey kept washing his hands; he rubbed his hands smooth

with sand again and again. When he finished, he showed his
hands to Spider.

"Oh," Spider said, "they are not white."

Monkey returned to wash his hands; Spider ate all the
food. Spider continued to behave in this way toward him until Monkey was very disturbed and they had finished working
at Spider's farm.

When they went to work at Monkey's farm, Monkey killed
a bear that day. The food was cooked until it was very sweet.
When the food was brought, Monkey washed his hands and put
them into the food.

When Spider came, Monkey said to him, "Show me your teeth."

Spider showed his teeth to him.

Monkey said, "Comrade, your teeth are black! If you make
them as white as mine, we will put our hands into this dish."

When Spider went to clean his teeth, he kept washing them
until he went away.

That is why tricky cheating is bad.

This story is ended.

Kasilo ji mia wọ ta Kuala. Ti ndeni tẹ gbẹ ti tewe yengẹ
wie. Ti ya wọ ta ngengei ji wie ji ye kpama hoki yila. Hoki
na hitia ti li ji bẹ ye kpama hoki yila.

Ke ngengei ji ti ye wọ piema ti tọtoni Kasilo ye kpama.
Ti ya ti fonga kpalẹi ji hu ti ndowẹi ji wie haa kẹ ti kọndẹi
yilinga ti wa la. Ti kọndẹi ji yilinga ti wa la. Kia Kuala
a wa yẹ i hei kọbu. Kia Kuala a wa yẹ i loko hitẹ hu.

Ye "Li bi bi yeyẹi wua, ndakpẹi, bi yeya lẹlẹi bondẹi ji
mia ba wa ba loko ti tẹ mẹhẹi ji hu. Li bi yeyẹi wua."

A lo lọ ngi yeyẹi wuama i nganyẹi ji wumbu nganyẹi ji
wumbu i ngi yeya gbongo kakakakakaka. Kia a wa a kẹ a ngie.

"O" yẹ "ii ya goleni."

Kẹ i yamanga na i lo piema i mẹhẹi na mẹfo. I loni wọ
piema a ngie haa kuala bẹ ta le hei ngi li longọ kẹ ti kpọyọnga
Kasilo ji gama.

Kia wọ ti lini Kuala ye kpama Kuala ndili lọ wani foloi na.

Ti mẹhẹi na yili yenge-yenge-yenge. Kẹ ti wa la kẹ Kuala i
wa i ngi yeya wua i loko i tenga hu.

Kẹ Kasilo wa yẹ ngi ma yẹ "Bi yọngọli gẹlẹ."

Kẹ i kẹnga.

I nde ngi ma yẹ "Ndakpẹi," yẹ "bi yọngọli lẹlẹi ji lini
baa kole fo a wie, kia nya ndẹi ji na" yẹ "mua bi mue loko
hite kaloi ji hu."

Kia wọ Kasilo li ngi yọngọli hu gole ma i loni wọ hu lọ
fo i li.

Na va mia kava ngandẹ ngandẹ ii nyandeni.

Dọmẹi ji ye kẹlẹma mia.

---

1. Recorded by man from Bo in Freetown on January 27, 1960.

TALE 67: SPIDER AND MAGGOT[1]

At one time Spider and Maggot made farms. They used to
work in their farms in rotation.

One day they went to Maggot's farm, they worked throughout the day; the time for cooking the workers' food came.

Maggot said to his wife, "Throw away all the sauce in the
house."

Then Maggot's wife threw away all the sauce in the house.

Maggot said, "Hayekpenga, cut my side a little."

His wife came and cut his side, only his fat; she put the
fat in the pot; it made a lot of sauce. After the sauce was
cooked, everyone ate until their stomachs were filled; the food
was very sweet to them.

Spider saw what had happened.

Early in the morning they went to Spider's own work place.
As soon as they arrived, they worked for a while and the time
for cooking food came. Spider also told his wife to throw out
all the sweet palm oil in the farmhouse. The woman did just as
her husband had told her to do. When Spider's wife set the food
pot on the fire, she did not have any oil to cook the food in.

Spider's wife called him; she said, "Spider, come here. Today you told me to throw away the oil. Now it is time to cook the food. What will I cook the food with?"

Spider said, "Come, cut my side."

When Spider's wife cut his side, only white water came out; no oil came out.

She said, "Now bring the fat! I want to cook the food now. Your companion has been working all day. I am not so concerned about you, but what about your companion?"

There was no way out. Spider's wife had thrown out the oil; all the oil in the calabashes had been thrown away; the oil bottles were broken.

Then Spider's wife went to Maggot. She said, "Friend Maggot, please I beg you to give me a little oil so that I may cook for you to eat."

As soon as Maggot agreed, Spider's wife cut his side a little; the oil came out; she cooked; they ate the food. That night everyone's stomach was filled.

That is why if you see your companion doing something that you cannot do and you want to do it, don't say that you will do it. At one time Spider cut his side; no oil came out; if his wife had not begged Maggot for oil, they would not have eaten any food that night.

What I heard, I have related.

Kasilo ta Gbawo kpema yila yelo wo na. Kasilo ta Gbawo ji ti ye lo a kpalęi la. Kpalęi ji ti ndani wo ta yenge wo kpalęi ji hu a tei lo.

Folo yila kę ti ya Gbawo ye kpa hu ti li ti luva yengema kpęing. Kondęi yili gbe hitilo kine.

Kę Gbawo ndenga ngi nyahęi ma yę "Hakpęi na kpęlę ha pęlęi na bu kpę wili."

Kę Gbawo ngi nyahęi na hakpęi na kpęlę wilinga i ye kpuęi na bu.

Kę Gbawo ndenga yę "Hayekpenga," yę "ngakahui ji le kulo!"

Kę i wa i ngi ngakahui na le inge ngi wulęi na leke, i puni fęi na hu kpotongo wa yela hakpęi na hu ti ngi ti mę ti gbi ti gohu i ve męhę na nęngo wa yela ti gbi la.

Kasilo ji i na lǫnga.

Kę ngele ye kę wonga kę ti ya na Kasilo nda yengemęi ji. Kia le ti fonga ti ngengei ji wie haa kǫnda yila gbei ji hitilǫ le Kasilo ji kę i ndenga bę ngi nyahęi ji ma yę "I ngulǫ wo wu hani nę gbi le hakpa le" ye "i pili i gbua gbuęi na bu." Kę nyapoi bę kę i pienga kia lo gbǫ ngi hini ndeni ngi ma. Jina i kǫndęi ji i fęi ji heinga na ngulǫ gbi ya na a męhęi ji yili.

Kę i Kasilo lolinga yę "Kasilo wa lę bę ha bę ngi ngulęi jisia wili, męhęi yili gbei lǫ na hitima gbǫ na nga męhęi ji yili la?"

Kę Kasilo i ya yę "Wa le bi nya gakamęi ji huanga."

Kia wǫ Kasilo nyahęi ngi gakamęi na huanga nja golei le lǫ gbuęi ngulǫ gbi ii gbuęi.

Kę i ndenga yę "Kę wa na a ngulęi-o nya longǫ na ngi męhęi yili, bi mba luva yengema bia bi va bę wę i le kę ǫ bi mbaa."

Kuo pele gbi ya na Kasilo a ngulęi gbua la i pienga ha ngulęi ti ye kpulęi gbi wilinga ti ye sani wongǫnga.

Nyapoi na kę i ya Gbawo gama yę "Nyande Gbawo, kǫnę le ngi wa bi ma nęnę ma wa mu li bi nya gǫ a ngulǫ wulo ngi męhęi ji yili wu mę."

Kia le wǫ Gbawo i luma kę i ya i ngi yakamęi kulo huanga. Kę ye ngulęi na i gbua ti ngili ti męhęi na mę la. Kpǫkǫi na numui gbi ti gohu i ve.

Na va mia bi mba bę ba tǫ na le a hinda wie, ye hindęi ji bia bi bęla kę bi maninga ma bę nga pielǫ. Kasilo i ngi ngakęi na leweni wǫ ngulęi yila ii gbuani na, ngi nyahęi na ina wǫ ęę Gbawo manęnę ta wa wǫ ti męhę mę a kpǫkǫi na.

Ngi ji humęni ngi hugę.

---

1. Recorded by young man from Pujehun in Freetown on May 30, 1960. Gbawǫ is a maggot that lives in palm trees. Reverend Stott's manuscript includes a Mende text and English summary of a version of this tale; Migeod's The Mende Language (1908) presents a Mende text and English translation of a version of the tale.

TALE 68: SPIDER AND STAR[1]

At one time a man went and made a fence in the water to catch fish. We all know that such a fencemaker is a fisherman.[2] He caught many fish in this fence.

One day Spider was walking and looking for a woman. Spider met the man just as he was taking fish out of the fence. Spider saw the fish; he wanted the fish very much; he begged the man for a few fishes; the man gave him some fishes. Spider waited for the man to catch more fish; then they went into town together.

As soon as they reached the town, Spider went on and went to Star.

Spider said, "Star, I want to make an arrangement with you. There is a man who has a fence which catches a lot of fish. At midnight tonight I want to go to steal the fish."

Star agreed /to Spider's plan/.

As soon as it was midnight, Spider and Star arose and went. As Star went he gave off light so that Spider could see. They went and stole a great many fishes. Then Spider divided the fish unequally; when he divided the fish, Spider cheated Star a little. Star looked at the fish; his share was very small; Spider's share was very large. Spider's share was larger than Star's. The only thing that Star did was that when it was time to leave, Star ran away. Star had the light; Spider was unable to walk at night and he remained sitting until morning.

When the fisherman came, he found Spider there; he caught Spider; he made a lot of noise. Spider was taken into the town and beaten. At that time everyone knew that Spider was a thief. When they stopped beating Spider, he ran into the thatch. At that time he refused to jump down onto the ground, because he knew that all the townspeople knew that he was a thief.

Lọwọ huguhangọ woma yela wọ kena yila i lilọ i li i kalẹi gonu njẹi hu. Kenẹi ji mu gbi mu kọlọ le kẹ numui na kalẹi-gonu-mọ gbi le nyẹgbẹmọ mia. Kalẹi ji ya i ye a nyẹ gboto gbuama.

Folo yila Kasilo ji i loni nyahẹi gọkọi jẹsia ji ma, kẹ i fonga kenei ji ma i male kine kenẹi ji nyẹi ji gbuama kalẹi ji hu. Kasilo kẹ i nyẹi ji lọnga kẹ i longa wa a nyẹi ji kẹ i kenẹi ji vẹlinga kulo yẹ i ngi gọ nyẹi ji hu kẹ kenẹi ji ngi gọnga kulo nyẹi ji hu; i kenẹi ji mawo na ta ti ngi nyẹi na hou kẹ ti ya tẹi hu.

Kia leke ti foni tẹi hu Kasilo ji kẹ i lewenga bẹ i li Dumbeka gama.

Yẹ "Dumbeka," yẹ "ngi hinda hulanga nya longọ ma bia mu hugbatẹ wie. Kenẹi na mia kalẹi wa ngi yeya ye kalẹi na a wa houlengọ wa. Nya longọ kpọkọi ya la woi a kpindi lia mu li mu nyẹi na huma."

Kuo kẹ Dumbeka bẹ luma.

Kia leke kpindi lia ji hitini kẹ ti venjọ ti hijenga ti li. Dumbekẹi ji a lewe a ngọmbui ji ve a lewe a ngọmbui ji ve ta ti gulọ lọ kẹ ti ya ti li ti nyẹi na huma kpoto wa nyẹi ji. Gomẹi ji lọ na wọ. Kasilo ji i nyẹi ji gọle lọ ii kọlẹni mahẹungọ i kọlẹ lọ kẹ i Dumbeka gava i ngi gọni hou kulo hi. Dumbeka bẹ i nyẹi ji gbe. Ngi ndẹi ji gulongọ wa Kasilo ndẹi ji gbotongọ wa. Tawao Kasilo lenga ngi ma. Ii hinda yeka wie. Ta bẹ kia leke ti li gbele ji hiti le kẹ i lewenga a pimẹ tawao ta taa ngọmbui ngi yeya. Kasilo ji ii guma kpindi hu jia kẹ Kasilo heinga i loni wọ heilọ ngenda.

Kia kenẹi i wani i wani i Kasilo male wọ na kẹ i ngi hounga sale yele mia i pie kaka. Ti li la tẹi hu ti li gbọma tẹi hu ti ndewe na haa numui gbi ti kọ na wọ kẹ Kasilo humamọ le. Kia leke ti gbeni ngi ma wati na mia wọ i le ma ngeleya njasẹi hu a ye wie na ii ya wọ lumani a gbuja ndọma jifa i kọnga numui gbi ti kọ na leke humamọ mia a ngie.

---

1. Recorded by young man from Pujehun in Freetown on May 30, 1960.
2. Fisherman, nyẹgbẹmọ.

TALE 69: SPIDER AND CHAMELEON[1]

Chameleon and Spider.

Once when a big rainy season fell and a big famine fell on the land, Spider and Chameleon went to dig bushyams.

When they had dug out a bushyam, Spider said, "Comrade Chameleon, when we reach our destination, we should boil this bushyam and wash it together. Then let us sit down and eat it."

Chameleon agreed. They took out the bushyam, put it in a basket, put it on their heads, and returned to the town. They were very happy. Then they went and washed the inside of the pot; they split firewood and put it under the pot; the pot boiled; the bushyam cooked; they took it out and put it into a big basket; they took it to the riverside; they put it in a boat; they took it to the middle of the river; they turned it into the water.

Since Chameleon was heavy, he sank but not as far as the bed rock; Spider was very light, he could not sink. Then Chameleon hung stones on his body and threw himself into the water. He went down and reached the yam; he washed it; he ate a lot of the yam until his stomach was very full. He gathered together the scraps of yam; he washed them; he wrapped them up; he came out of the water and took the remainder for his children.

Spider did not get anything to eat; he remained hungry; he returned to the town. When he arrived, he found Chameleon inside the town waiting for him.

Spider said, "Comrade, how did you arrive here without my knowing? I thought that we arranged to wash the bushyam in the water. How did you come here?"

Then Chameleon said to Spider, "Today you thought that you could trick me, but I am sensible. If you want to eat the bushyam, tie a rope around your waist so that you can reach the bushyam under the water."

Then Spider went and made his children tie a big rope around his waist. On one end they hung a stone; they held onto the other end.

Spider said to his children, "When I have been sunk for a short time, pull me out with the rope please."

Then Spider went and sank the stone; he looked for the yam; he looked for it, but he did not see it. Then his children pulled on the rope, but he did not want to come out; he cried out; they stopped pulling. When they pulled the rope again, he came out.

That was how Spider's waist became very slender at one time.[2]

The story is finished. That is why cleverness about food is bad.

Ndoko ta Kasilo.

Hama wa mia wọ gulani. Ndọlẹ wa mia wọ gulani ndọẹ hu kẹ Ndoko ta Kasilo ti ya ngawu gbiamẹi.

Kia ti yẹ a ngawui ji gbua ta ngandọ kẹ Kasilo ndenga yẹ "Ndakpẹi Ndoko, ngawui ji mu yaa wọi ma a houlọ mu ngili hinda yila tao mu ngua hinda yila mu mẹ."

Kẹ Ndoko lumanga kẹ ti ngawui na gbuanga ti pu kahẹing
ma ti nda wumba ti yama tẹi hu; ti gohunẹngọ wa yẹ la. Kẹ
ti ya ti fẹi hu wua ti heinga ti ngawui ji ma wa ti pu fẹi
ji hu ti kọwui bembla ti pu mbu; fẹi na i nẹ; ngawui na i
yili kẹ ti kpuanga, ti pote samba wai hu, kẹ ti yeinga la
njẹi la ti li ti pu ndẹndẹi hu ti li njẹi lia kẹ ti potenga
njẹi hu.

Kia Ndoko ta ngi miningọ yẹ la i lọmbui lọ kẹ ii guni
a fo nja galẹi ma, kẹ Kasilo ta ngi ya powo powo ii guni a
lọmbu . Ndoko bẹ i kọti hẹlẹ hẹlẹi lọ ngi ma kẹ i wilinga
njẹi hu kẹ i yeinga i fo ngawui na ma i ngua i mẹ na
kakakakakaka; ngi go i ve kpang i ye mọnui nasia lẹtẹmba
i mawa i tiwi i gbua njẹi bu i li a ye mọnui ngi lengẹisia
we.

Kasilo ta ii gbẹ-o-gbẹ majọni mẹ va hi wọ ndọlẹi loni
ngi ma kẹ ti yamanga tẹi hu. I lini na i malẹni Ndoko heini
tẹi gohu a ngi gulọ gbe.

Kẹ i ngi mọlinga yẹ "Ndakpẹi, bi ye pieni bi foni beindo
na hi ngii kọni? Nga tọ ma bia mia ha mu hugbatẹni kọ mu
ngawui wa njẹi hu. Bi ye na pienga bi wanga mbei?"

Kẹ Ndoko bẹ ndenga Kasilo ma yẹ "Bi yẹ ha nya gasomalọ
kẹ ngi nẹmahu le jọnga bi ya lọ bẹ bi ngawui na mẹ, ngeya gbulọ
bi lia na lọ a wie bi fo ngawui ma njẹi bu."

Kẹ Kasilo ya i pie ngi lengẹisia ti ngeya wa gbulọ ngii
lia ti kọtu hẹlẹ kaka yila ma ti kakẹi ye pekẹi hou.

Yẹ ti ma "Ngi lọmbunga lọ hu lẹmbinga lọ see vu nya lala
a ngeyẹi, hoe."

Kẹ i ya i lọmbu a kọtui ji i ngawui ji gokọli i kọkọli
ii tọni. Ke ti ngi lalanga tao ii loni gbu kẹ i yele gulanga
kẹ ti gbenga kulo kẹ ti ngi lalanga gbọma kẹ i gbianga.

Na mia wọ wieni Kasilo lia ya wọ lengi lengi.

Dọmẹi gbọyọa, famia mẹhẹ hinda gaso ii nyandeni.

---

1. Recorded by man from Tikonko in Bo on April 16, 1960.
Reverend Stott's manuscript includes a Mende text and English
summary of a version of this tale.
2. See Tale 30 for another tale explaining the slenderness
of Spider's waist.

TALE 70:   SPIDER AND DOG[1]

At one time Spider and Dog were close friends.[2] They
went about together; they liked each other; they ate together.
If one of them made a rice farm, they would eat the food together.

Each time that they helped each other with food, Spider
said to Dog, "Go, eat. Let me go; I will return to eat."

Spider thought that Dog's nose was his whole mouth.

Spider said, "Go, eat; I will return." And Spider went.

As soon as Spider returned, he found the food almost half
eaten.

"Oh," said Spider, "who ate the food that you had?"

"Actually," said Dog, "I was the only one."

Spider said, "I do not believe it."

In the morning when food was cooking, Spider said, "Small
Mouth."

Dog said, "Yes."

Spider said, "Go, eat; I will return; you have a small
mouth."

As soon as Spider returned, he found all the food had been
eaten.

Spider said, "Are you the only one who ate the food?"

Dog said, "Yes."

Spider said, "It can't be you. I do not believe it."

This continued to happen until one day some food was
left, Dog put his mouth into the rice. When Dog opened his
mouth in front of Spider, Spider shouted.

Spider said, "Sene! Oh, Comrade! Your mouth has not
split; your head has split!"

This is the end of this story.

Kasilo mia wọ ta ngila ti yẹ ndoma hu. Ta lewe ti longọ
ma, ta mẹhẹ mẹ luahu ji i kpa la mbẹi ji i bẹ i kpa la mbẹi
ti venjọ kpẹlẹ ta mẹhẹ mẹ hinda yila.

Ke kpele gbi ti gbǫnga mǝhęi ji ma kę Kasilo ndenga ngila ma yę "Ya, mę. Gbę ngi li ngi wa a mǝma."

Ngilęi ji hokpęi ji i tǫnga yę ngi lęi kpęlę mia.

Yę "Ya, mę ngi wa."

Kę i ya.

Kia le a wa a male mǝhęi ji tengǫndia mǝnga.

"Kuo" yę "yǫ a numui ji i mǝhęi ji mǝni yeya."

"Ingę" yę "nya yakpe mia."

Yę "Ngi lai la."

Nge wonga ti mǝhęi ji yilinga yę "La wuloi."

Yę "Aa."

Yę "Ya, mę ngi wa. Bi la woi ji."

Kia leke a wa a male i mǝhęi ji kpęlę mǝa.

Yę "Bia yakpe lǫ bi mǝhęi ji mǝni?"

Yę "Hn."

Yę "Bia ya na," yę "ngii lai la."

Hindęi ji lǫ ti loi piema na haa folo yila ma tia mǝhęi ji ti ya lemangǫ kę ngila mbęi ji i la węlęnga hu. Kia wǫ ngila boi wǫ Kasilo lenga kę Kasilo yele gulama.

Yę "Sęnę, kuo, ndakpęi" yę "bi la ii blai wǫ bi wu lǫ wǫ blani."

Dǫmęi ji hi ye kęlęmęi mia.

---

1. Recorded by man from Bo in Freetown on January 27, 1960.
2. They were close friends, ti yę ndoma hu.

TALE 71: SPIDER AND CHIMPANZEE[1]

Oh, my father, how Spider became broad at one time.

At one time all the young men in the world worked for

Spider; they planted rice for him. Spider's son Buma was the
person who called people to work. Everyone was very happy
planting rice.

Just when all the animals were happy, Spider carried a
big hammer in a bag and went into the middle of the animals.
Suddenly he beat the biggest animal on the head.

Then Spider quieted the rice-planters; he said, "My people,
look what happened. The animals were going to the farm; that
young man came, he fell, he died."

There was a rule that if a death occurred in that country,
Spider was the only one who could bury the corpse.

Spider said, "What can we do?"

The animals said, "Take the corpse; you bury it that is
the only way."

Spider took the corpse and ate it with his children in
the farmhouse.

Within two days Spider said, "Go, plant my rice."

The animals began to do the rice planting again. When
Spider saw a big animal, he killed it.

Spider said, "Oh, look at this! Look it has happened
again."

The animals said, "Go, you bury it."

Spider continued /to behave/ like that for some time
until he angered Chimpanzee.

Chimpanzee said, "We are all going to plant rice."

When they went to plant rice, Spider did not know that
Chimpanzee had noticed that Spider wanted to kill him.
Chimpanzee and the others were planting rice; they were very
happy. Then Spider took out the hammer from the big bag.
When Spider held the hammer upside down and was about to hit
Chimpanzee, Chimpanzee seized Spider. When Chimpanzee struck
Spider heavily with his head, Spider's chest became broad at
that time. That was how Spider became broad at one time.

A nya kẹ, hani na wieni wọ Kasilo yẹ i vẹvẹlẹ.

Kasilo mia wọ kọnga gbi ti ndunya ta yenge ta wẹ. Ti ya
wọ ngengemẹi ji mbawumẹi ji. Ngi loi la a Buma ta mia a toli

wie. Buma ji ya wo toli wiema. Buma ji ya wo toli ji wiema.
Mbawulęi ji nęnga wa.

Kine huanga kpęlę wohu, hama wa lo ngi yeya wango kpafęi
hu hęlęngo ngi ma, i lima ti lia lo. Huęi na vuli ngolongo ti
ma a męi kpoo i ngi wumba lenga.

Kę i mbawublęi nasia bę lalodonga. Yę "Nya bonda, hindęi
gbe kia hu na gbele na" yę "huanga lo lima a kpalęi kę ndakpoi
na i gbua mia i gula i haa."

Ta tę ha gula wo ndoloi na hu gbi haa ta yakpe mia a kpou.

Tę "Kę mua ye pie?"

Tę "Kę li la bi kpou piegi na."

I ya a na i li i mę fo kpu i la ta ngi lenga.

Hu a yįi fele yę "A li wu nya bęi wu."

Ti ya wo mbawumęi ji gboma i hani wa na lo a kę i paa.

Yę "Kuo a kpele ji gbele gboma i gula gboma."

Tę "Li bi kpou."

I loni na ma haa hindęi ji kę i gbalęnga Ngolo ma.

Ngolo bę yę "Mu kpęlę lo mu lima mbavumęi ji."

Kia le ti lini mbawumęi ji męma i ngolo loa ngi yama
wuama ngi longo i pa. Kia wo ti loi ngoloni ti mbęi ji wu.
Mbęi wulęi i nęna wo hu. Kę i gbia kpafa wai ji hu ta mia
kia wo i ngawęi yę i ngolo le a męi kpa ngolo i gbawua. Kia
wo ngolo woteni i ngi wu hu gbolę la wo gbelei ta mia ngi lii
hu ji vęvęlęngoi ji wo. Na mia wo i pie Kasilo yęi wo vęvęlę.

---

1. Recorded by man from Bo in Freetown on January 12, 1960.

TALE 72: BUSHCAT AND COCK[1]

At one time Bushcat was very afraid of Cock. When Bushcat
saw Cock's comb, he thought that it was fire and he ran away.
Every time that Bushcat saw Cock, he ran away.

Cock used to wonder, "Why is it that every time this
handsome young man sees me he runs wui-wui-wui; he never stops?"

One day Cock met Bushcat. Bushcat was about to run away.

Cock said, "Wait a minute."

Bushcat waited.

Cock said, "Why is it that every time you see me, you run away?"

Bushcat said, "Friend, there are all kinds of things of which I am not afraid. But I am afraid of that big fire which is set on your head."

"Oh," Cock said, "there is not any fire there!"

He said, "You are lying."

Cock said, "Come, touch it."

He said, "I will not do that. I would burn myself."

For some time Cock kept saying to Bushcat that there was not any fire on his head. Bushcat had wanted to eat Cock, but he was afraid of the fire. As soon as Bushcat learned that Cock's comb was not fire and that it would not burn him, he bent over and killed Cock. Since that day Bushcat beats Cocks and catches them.

This is the end of the story.

Te hina mia wọ. Nyagbe a luwa tẹi ma kẹlẹma ii ma. Ngi gbẹgbẹi ji ngi wumba i tọa yẹ ngọmbu yatẹngọ mia kẹ i lewea a pimẹ. Kpe gbi ji le Nyagbe a Tẹ lọ kẹ i lewea a pimẹ.

Tẹ nẹmahu a gili yẹ "Gbẹi ba-a-a ndakpao nyandei ji kpe ma gbi i nya lọa a wimẹ lọ wui-wui-wui ngi la ẹẹ ya yẹ ndọma?"

Folo yila kẹ i malenga Nyagbe loi; Nyagbe yẹ i lewe a pimẹ.

Yẹ "Lo lẹ."

Kẹ i loa.

Yẹ "Gbẹi kpele gbi bi nya lọnga" yẹ "ba lewelọ a pimẹ?"

Yẹ "Na hi nyande," yẹ "gbẹ-o-gbẹ ii le nya" yẹ "luwama ma;" yẹ "ngọmbu yatẹngọ wa na hi bi wumba" yẹ "ta mia ngi luwama ma."

"Kuo" yẹ "ngọmbu yaa na-e."

Yẹ "Ndẹ mia."

Yɛ "Wa lɛ bi jala."

Yɛ "Ngɛɛ pie," yɛ "nga nya mɔlɔ."

I loi lɔwɔ njɛpɛi ji lema ngi ma ye ngɔmbu ii ngi wumba.
Kia wɔ Nyagbe a ngi gɔ gbɛi ji ngɔmbu ii le ii ngi mɔi tao ngi
longɔ wɔ i Tɛ mɛ kɛ ngɔmbui ji mia a luwa ma a mɛi vu i wɛlɛa
poma i paa fɔ. Folei na mia wɔ Nyagbe ngi ndea wɔ Tɛnga ma,
kia bɛ na wɛ ta bɛ ta ti houma.

Dɔmɛi ji ye kɛlɛmangɛi mia.

---

1. Recorded by man from Bo in Freetown on January 27, 1960.

TALE 73: FOWL AND BUSHFOWL[1]

My father, there are Fowls in the town and Bushfowls in
the bush. At one time Bushfowl and Fowl used to argue when
they met.

"Ah," Bushfowl said, "you fowls are saved! Imagine, people
catch you; they carry you to town; they give you food; they put
you into the pen at night; they carry you on their backs into
town. You are saved!"

"Yes," Fowl said to him, "Comrade, stop."

Bushfowl said, "Comrade, truly! Don't say that to me!
I am in the bush; people set traps there; hunters hunt me."

Fowl said, "Stop! I am in as much danger in the town as
you are."

"Oh," Bushfowl said, "that is a lie."

"All right," Fowl said, "tonight when they are putting
us into the pen, jump in among us."

"Oh," Bushfowl said, "I agree."

At night when people were catching fowls to put them into
the pen, Bushfowl came; all of them were carried into the town.
When they had just come to the town, visitors came to the man
who owned fowls.

The man asked his wife, "Is there any meat?"

She said, "There isn't anything."

He said, "Isn't there any dried fish?"

She said, "No, there is not."

He said, "Oh, then look in the fowl pen. Catch one fowl and prepare a meal for these visitors."

Bushfowl heard that conversation; he pressed into a corner of the pen. When the woman's hand reached into the pen, it touched near his foot. Bushfowl lifted up one foot; he pressed into the corner. The woman caught a big cock near Bushfowl--kuo kuo kuo; she took him out; she killed him. Bushfowl watched the woman through a loose place in the pen and saw her kill the fowl. Bushfowl was so anxious that he did not sleep that night.

When daybreak came, the people went to their farmhouse. As soon as they arrived and opened the fowl pen, Bushfowl got out immediately; he flew away into the bush.

Even today Bushfowl and Fowl do not meet anywhere.

Nya kẹkẹ, tẹi jisia ti tẹi hu mu yeya kẹ kọkọyẹ ji ndọgbọi hu. Tia mia wọ ti yẹ mawoi hou kọkọyẹ ta tẹnga ji ti ya jẹsiamẹi ti hukpọngalọ.

"Ang" yẹ "tẹnga wua wu baongọi" yẹ "indọo nunga mia ta wu hou ti li a wue tẹi hu tia mia ta mẹhẹ ve wuẹ; kpọkọ wẹngalọ ti wu wa kulii hu ti wu wẹ gọnga kẹ ti ya a wue tẹi hu" yẹ "wua wu baongọi."

"E," tẹ yẹ ngi ma yẹ "Ndakpẹi," yẹ "gbe."

Yẹ "Ndakpẹi mbọ" yẹ "baa njẹpẹi na le nya ma." Yẹ "Engẹ" yẹ "nya ngi ndọgbọ hu" yẹ "maniyatẹbla lọ lema kpandẹwilibla lọ lema nya woma."

Yẹ "Gbe-e," yẹ "kpundẹi na nya ma tẹi hu" yẹ "nyọkọ gbi i bi ma."

"O" yẹ "nde mia."

"Kulungọi" yẹ "kpọkọ hitingalọ wuẹ" yẹ "ti ya lọ mu wama kulii hu" yẹ "bi wili mu lia."

"Kuo" yẹ "ngi kulunga."

Kia wọ kpọkọ wẹlẹni ti yẹ tẹnga hou ma ta ti wa kulii hu kẹ kọkọyẹ wanga na kẹ ti kpẹlẹ ti ya a ti yẹ tẹi hu. Ti fonganga tẹi hu-o ii bẹni bẹ hinda hu guhangọ ma kẹ hotanga ti gbianga ti wa kenẹi ji gọma ngi wo a tẹngẹi jisia. Ti fonga kenẹi.

I ngi nyahẹi humọli yẹ "Hua lọ na?"

Yẹ "Hani gbi ii na."

Yẹ "Nye bẹ bẹ ii na?"

Yẹ "Ii."

"Kuo" yẹ "kẹ tẹ kulii na hu gbe" yẹ "wu tẹ yila hou" yẹ "wu mẹhẹ hinda hugbatẹ hotangẹi jisia wẹ."

Kua bẹ kọkọyẹ humẹninga. A kẹ i yamanga mia kulii i tọhui i li i gbọnda na. Ti yalọ ti loko wa kulii ji hu ti loko jiangalọ ngi gọi ji gblanga kẹ i tẹnga yila i lukpe mia i gbọnda na kẹ ti tẹi ye hinda wai ji hounga ngi gblanga, "Kuokuokuo." Kẹ ti kpianga kẹ ti panga ta lọ na gbema i wukpenga kulii ji ye fulofulomẹi ta lọ na gbema kẹ ti tẹ wanga. Kua kpindi na ii yini na ndi hẹlẹ wa hu lọ.

Kia wọ ngele woni ti lini a ti ye kpuẹla ti fonga leke; kia ti kulii lawoni kia wọ i gbiani kpu i wilini wọ ndọgbọ hu.

Folei ji bẹ ta tẹ tẹ hugbe hinda yila.

---

1. Recorded by man from Bo in Freetown on January 7, 1960.

TALE 74: DOG AND MONITOR LIZARD[1]

At one time Dog had great fame; we all know that to this day wherever Dog goes, people shout at him.

Once Monitor Lizard asked Dog, "Dog, what kind of medicine do you have that you have gotten this sort of fame?"

Dog said, "If you really want my medicine, I will show it to you."

"Oh," Monitor Lizard said, "is that so? Then early tomorrow morning I want you to show me that medicine."

Very early in the morning Monitor Lizard went to Dog; he said, "I have come to have you show me your medicine."

Dog said, "Wait."

After some time Dog said, "Come, lie on my back."

Monitor Lizard lay on Dog's back.

As soon as Monitor Lizard was on Dog's back, they went to the chief's compound. They found the chief's sauce cooking on the fire. Immediately Dog jumped into the pot of sauce. Then a woman beat Monitor Lizard with a stick; Dog did not feel it, but Monitor Lizard was beaten a lot.

Monitor Lizard said, "Put me down."

But Dog said, "No, wait a little while."

Monitor Lizard and Dog came out and set out again on the road for the town. They travelled for some time until they reached a Muslim's prayer mat. As soon as Dog came, he got on the prayer mat; he urinated on it--va va va. Then the Muslim took a big stick; he beat Monitor Lizard lying on Dog's back. Dog did these things, but he did not receive the blows.

When they left, Monitor Lizard implored Dog to let him down; he said, "Dog, I beg you; let me down now; let me go."

Dog said, "No, wait a little. Recently you said that you wanted to know about the medicine that makes me famous; I want to show you my fame now."

Monitor Lizard kept begging Dog until they reached the chief's compound. As soon as Dog jumped onto the veranda of the sheep's house that was being swept, he ran away. When a woman took a stone to strike Dog, she missed Dog and hit Monitor Lizard.

Monitor Lizard said, "Let me down!"

When Dog let Monitor Lizard down, they were no longer friends. At one time Dog did not show Monitor Lizard why he is famous.

Kpe wọ ngila i tọwọ wai majọni wọ. Wati yila i yelọ wọ na ngila lọwọngọ wa tawaò mu kpẹlẹ mu kọlọ kia bẹ hu nà ngilẹi hinda gbi lè i lini na ta jọlẹlọ lọọ a ngie, i loni lọ na hu.

Yila, kẹ pama i ngi mọlinga yẹ "Ngila bia halei ye gbẹ lọ vuli i bi yeya bi tọwọ bondẹi ji majọnga?"

"Ọ" yẹ "halei na bi ya vuli bẹ bi longa lọ la" yẹ "nga kẹ lọ à bie."

"Kuo," yẹ "hi ye?" Yẹ "Kẹ ngele wongalọ sina nga lolọ bi halei na gẹ a nge."

Kẹ ngele wonga ngenda tẹtẹi kẹ pama i ya ngila gama yẹ
"Ngi wa na bi halei gẹ a nge."

Ngila yẹ "Mawulo."

Kia hu lẹ mbini ji kẹ ngila ndenga yẹ "Wa bi wẹlẹ nya
woma."

Kẹ pama i wẹlẹnga ngila woma.

Kia le i hijeni le la nda laa ti lini mahẹi ye kuhu lọ.
Ti maleni ti mahẹi hakpẹi ji heinganga i yilinga panda wanda
ti hanisia gbi wunga hu. Kia leke i lini i wilini ye hakpa
vẹi na hu lọ. Ngulu wai ji ti mbumbuni ti pama lọ leweni ta
i wẹni ngila woma ngila ta ii kọni kẹ pama ndewei ji i wa waa
ngi ma.

Kẹ i ndenga yẹ "Nya gbuja."

Kẹ ngila ndenga ngi ma yẹ "Mn mn mawulo i longa kulo."

Kẹ ti gbuanga mia kẹ ti tẹi hu wele langa gbọma la ma ti
li haa. Kia gbọma ti lini ti foni gbọma kinẹing ti maleni
kinẹing mọlemọi ji jẹli yalẹi ji i lani. Kia leke ngila i
foni ma leke i lẹni hu lọ kẹ i wo wonga na va va va. Kẹ ti
ngulu wai wumbunga gbọma "Gbẹe ngilẹi ji wanga i ji nyọkọ
wienga hmm?" Kia leke ti gawani gbọma ti pama lọ leweni ta
i wẹni ngila woma. Ngila ta ji kpẹlẹ ti piema ẹẹ ti ya ti
gọ. Kẹ ti gbuanga gbọma miando.

Kia na ti lini pama i yẹ lọ na vuli a ngila manẹnẹ yẹ
"Ngila" yẹ "nya gbuja na kọnẹ bẹ le."

Yẹ "Mn mn i longa kulo. Halei ji gẹ bi longa bẹ bi kọ
gbẹva lọ nya lọwọngọ" yẹ "ye tọwọi mia na nya longọ ngi kẹ
a bie."

Pama i ngila manẹnẹ haa kẹ ti gbuanga gboma mia ke ti ya
gbọma. Kia gbọma ti foni mahẹi ye kuhu. Kia leke ti gọwọi
yilini piyassẹi hu mbalanga ti wẹlẹi bu te ti na yela kẹ
ngila wanga na na i ya i lewenga a pime. Kia gbọma ti kọti
wumbuni kẹ ti ngila họwọ ti gbulani ngi ma ti pama lọ howoni.

Kẹ pama ndenga yẹ "Nya gbuja."

Kia wọ ngila i pama gbujani foloi ji bẹ pama ta ngila ti
yaa loni ma. Tawao ii yaa lumani wọ ngila a kẹ a ngie gbẹva
lọ ngi lọwọngọ.

1. Recorded by young man from Pujehun in Freetown on May 13, 1960.

TALE 75: CAT AND LIZARD[1]

Cat and Lizard.

At one time long ago Cat and Lizard liked to visit each other. Whenever they met, they would joke. They enjoyed visiting with each other.

One day Cat was very mocking. Cat went and met Lizard bowing on a tree in the sun.

(But we all know that Cat is a thief; sometimes he steals; sometimes he does not steal and catches fish to eat. But on the day that Cat does not find any fish, he will steal.)

One day Cat met Lizard bowing down in the sun warming himself.

Cat began to mock Lizard; he said, "Lizard, I have come to ask you to show me the road to Scaley-scaley." Knowing that Lizard's skin was very scaley, Cat said, "Show me the road that goes to Scaley-scaley."

Lizard himself looked at Cat for some time; he said, "Sit down."

And Cat sat down.

Lizard said, "To show the road that goes to Scaley-scaley is not easy; it is difficult. But one word that I will tell you now is that there are some people whom you see whose fur is very fine and whose skin is very beautiful, it is very smooth. But some of them if there is any stealing in town, they are responsible. Sometimes if you meet these people who have robbed and who have been beaten very hard, and who have had thief-catching juju put in their eyes, they sit licking their hands. That is how those beautiful people behave."

When Lizard said that, he angered Cat. Cat got up and ran after Lizard. Cat hunted Lizard--koe koe koe, and Lizard hid himself.

At one time that was how it ended. Up to this time Cat and Lizard are not friendly. Speaking the truth destroyed Lizard's and Cat's friendship.

At that time Cat's and Lizard's friendship ended, because Lizard said to Cat, "Cat, whenever I meet you and a friend's pot is set near the fire, you would eat from it, you would be beaten, you would have thief-catching juju put in your eye, you would sit licking your paw."

As soon as Lizard said that, Cat became very angry with him. His friend had spoken the truth to him. That is what happened at one time so that whenever Cat sees Lizard, he gets up and runs after him.

Gọnẹ ta Kolo.

Lọwọ gboto lewengọ ma wọ Gọnẹ ta Kolo ti longọi wọ wama ta jia vuli luahu. Tao ti ti nyọnyọ malenga wọ ta sẹisẹi yẹpẹnga lelọ bẹlingọ yẹpẹnga. Ta tewe a tia yekpe ti enjoi.

Folo yila kẹ Gọnei ji ngi hẹmangọ wa. I lilọ i li i Kolo male wẹ i wẹ ngului ji ma foloi ya.

(Kẹ mu kpẹ mu kọlọ Gọnẹ ta humanọ mia a ngie, wati lẹnga na a humẹi wielọ wati lẹnga lọ na ii humẹi wie a nyẹi jia lọ hou a mẹ. Kẹ foloi na ma ii nyẹi lọilọ a humẹi wielọ.)

Folo yila kẹ i ya i Kolo male wẹ foloi ji ya a nge wo.

Ta yese mia ta ngi Gọnẹ yese mia i hiyeni a hẹmẹi kẹ i Kolo mọlia yẹ "Kolo ngi wa vu bi mọlima bi pelei ji gẹ a nge a li wọyawọyama." I kọlọ Kolo wui woya woya. Yẹ "Pelei ji gẹ a nge a li woya woyama."

Kẹ Kolo bẹ i ngi gbe haa kẹ i ndenga yẹ "Hei lẹ."

Kẹ i heia.

Yẹ "Pelei na i li woya woyama kẹ la ii le bẹ a yẹ gbọwuma" yẹ "kẹ ngi njẹpẹ yila le na bi ma" yẹ "nunga lẹnga lọ na ba ti lọ" yẹ "ti yomboi na nyandengọ wa" yẹ "tao ti nyandengọ wa ti luwima" yẹ "ti luwui na gbogbongọ" yẹ "kẹ ti lẹnga na huma gbi wienga ta hu" yẹ "tia yẹ la." Yẹ "Lọwọi lẹnga lọ na bi ya ba malelọ ti humẹi na wie ti ti lewenga panda-da-da ti ti yamẹi na lọ a kaima ta yẹ hei lọ hi ta ti yeyẹi nasia gọmi ta ti yeyẹi jisia gọmi" yẹ "hi mia numui nasia ti nyandengọ ta pie."

Ji lengọi i gbalẹnga Gọnẹ ma i hiyea i hitẹa Kolo woma i loni kpẹma kọẹ kọẹ kọẹ kẹ Kolo bẹ i loa hu ngi yeya.

I hiye wọ wati na ma i wa i gẹlẹ hi. Kia bẹ hu na Kolo ta Gọnẹ tii loni ma. Tọnya yia le va wọ i wieni Kolo ta Gọnẹ ti ndomaya vayẹi i gbua wọ.

Ye wati na ma i wa i gẹlẹi hi jifa Kolo ndeilọ Gọnẹ ma
yẹ "Gọnẹ bia wati gbi va nga bi malelọ mba ti ve bẹ ya hei
ngọmbui gbla kẹ bi na mẹa kẹ ti bi lewenga ti bi yama wu kai
hu ba yẹma heilọ ba bi yẹisia gọmi."

Kia le i na lei na i gbalẹi lọ ngi ma. Ngi ndiamọi mia
i tọnya yiei na lea ngi ma. I hiyea ma wọ wati na ma i wa i
gẹlẹ hi Kolo ji le Gọnẹ Kolo lọma i hiyema i hitẹ poma.

---

1. Recorded by young man from Pujehun in Freetown on February
16, 1960.

TALE 76: THREE FRIENDS[1]

At one time there were three very close friends: Hen Egg,
Tadpole, and Fly. They went to a place to cut palm nuts. When
they arrived there, who was going to climb up the palm tree?

"Oh," Hen Egg said, "I know how to cut palm nuts, therefore, I will climb up."

Hen Egg climbed up the palm tree; he reached the neck of
the palm nuts; he cut the palm nuts; he finished /cutting7.
When he was coming down the palm tree, Hen Egg fell on the
ground and broke.

When Hen Egg broke, Tadpole shouted, "Ooh!"

Tadpole's mouth split as far as his neck.

Then Fly said, "Behold, I shall go to explain everything
in the town."

Fly ran until he came to the town.

Fly said, "Good afternoon."

The people said, "Comrade, what is it?"

"Oh," Fly said, "wait; let me wipe the sweat from my face."

As soon as Fly wiped his face, his head remained in his
hand.

Of these three people at that time: who was more foolish
than his friends?

Ndiamọnga sawa mia wọ ti hiyeni ti lei loma ti janga kpẹlẹma ii ma, tẹ yawui ji, kputu, kẹ ndili. Kẹ ti ya towu lewemẹi. Ji ti ya towu lewemẹi ji ti ya ti fonga; yelọ na lẹma tọkpọi ji hu?

"Kuo," tẹ yawu yẹ "nya nya bẹngọ a towu leela, fa lọ nya mia nga lẹ hu."

Kẹ tẹ yawu i lẹnga tọkpọi ji hu. Tẹ yawu i lẹlọ wo tọkpọi ji hu na kẹ i fonga towui ji bobu i towui ji le i kpọyọ seng. Ngi hitẹmẹi ji mia wọ i gbuani mbai hu ji lẹ a mẹi kpọ i gula ndọlọmẹi a mẹi gbue kẹ i wolonga le.

Wolongọi ji kẹ kputu yele gula yẹ "Kpo!"

Kẹ ngi lẹi bla i to ngi bobuma.

Kuo kẹ ndili yẹ "Kpẹ ngi li ngi hungẹ tẹi hu."

I lewenga a pimẹ. Kia wọ i lini i foni tẹi hu.

Yẹ "A wama he."

Tẹ "Ndakpẹi gbe?"

"O," yẹ "a nya mawulo ngi fọndọi yila ngi yama."

Yilangọ le kẹ ngi wui loa ngi yeya.

Numu sawẹi jisia yẹ gbẹlọ wọ ngi malamangọ ngi mba ma?

---

1. This riddle tale recorded by man from Bo in Freetown on January 27, 1960.

TALE 77: FIRE AND BUSHCOW[1]

A long time ago Fire and Bushcow were friends.

Every time /they met/ Fire said to Bushcow that he should walk to his house to visit him.

Fire said to Bushcow, "You say that I should go to visit you, but I do not visit you, because I am a bad person." He said, "My behavior is bad, therefore, I do not want to go to your house."

Every time that Bushcow and Fire met, Bushcow said, "What

is the matter? I come to visit you every time; you do not go to me."

Once Fire agreed to visit Bushcow. He said, "When the sun rises, I will go to my friend's house. Before I can go visit you, I must walk on dry leaves and little sticks; I must walk on them. So put them on the road that I will be walking on."

Bushcow went and gathered little sticks and dry leaves and put them on the road.

One day Bushcow was sitting at his house and he saw some smoke coming. Fire was coming slowly to meet him. Bushcow saw that all the animals ran away from the approaching fire. At first Bushcow went into his own house; he did not know what was happening; he came outside and looked. As soon as Bushcow came outside, he saw the smoke and that his friend Fire was coming slowly toward him.

"Oh," said Bushcow, "look my friend is coming."

Bushcow stood there in order to make sure who it was.

When Bushcow had stood for some time, Fire was approaching him; Bushcow began to feel uneasy; Fire started to burn him; the smoke became too much for Bushcow. Bushcow ran into his house; he stayed in the house.

Fire kept walking slowly; he kept walking slowly; he kept walking. Fire reached the door of Bushcow's house; he stood outside the door; he stayed there.

Bushcow was hiding in the house; Fire came and stood outside. Bushcow, who recently had said that his friend should come to visit him, hid from him. Fire came inside the house; he stayed there for some time; he sat on top of the house; he started to burn it.

Bushcow's wife and children were in the house; they all began to burn.

Now everyone complained, "So you intended to kill us with leprosy!"

Bushcow's wife and all his children were in the house. Some of them went to hide in the kitchen; they started to burn; the ones that were able to run, ran away and were saved.

So Bushcow's and Fire's friendship was destroyed at one time; until today Bushcow and Fire are not friends.

Wati lenga lengo woma wo ngombu ta tewu ti ye wo ndomahu.

Kpema gbi va ngombu yelo a nde tewu ma ye "I jia i li i
fo ngi ma wela i va ngi ma."

Ngombu yelo a nde tewu ma ye "Bia lo be ndema be ngi li
ngii va bi ma;" ye "ke" ye "nya hinda nyamungo-o," ye "nya
wiehindei ii nyandeni," ye "fale ngii loni ngi li bi ye pele
bu."

Kpema gbi va tewu tia ngombui ti gomenga lo hi mia a nde
ngi ma ye "Gbee? Nya nga wa bi gama wati gbi va; bia be li
nya gama."

Wati yila ji na ngombu i minini na wa tewu ma ke ngombu
ndenga "Kuo," ye "folo lenga" ye "ngi limalo ha ngi li ngi fo
nya ndiamoi ye pele bu;" ye "ke peing be ngi ya li mbei vama
bi ma nya ge ngi koo lo nya nga jia ndawa bei jisia hu-o ke
kpangba nyanyai jisia" ye "ta mia nga jia hu" ye "fale" ye
"pie bi pu pelei ma nga wa a jia hu."

Ke tewu be i ya i kpangba nyanyai na-o ke ndawa bei nasia
kpele i tema i pu pelei ma.

Ye mbei na folo yila ti ye heini lo ke i ndulii ji longa
a wa, ke ngombui a wa le a wa ngi male ma. Fuhani jisia gbi a
to na ta lewe a pime ji ta wa, ta wela ngombui ji ma. Halei
i ya ngi ye pele bu ii ko gbolo wiema ke i gbuanga ngitiiya i
na gbe. Kia leke i gbuani ke i nduli ji longa ke ngi ndiamoi
ngombui ji a wa, a wa le a wa ngi mahu.

"Kuo," ke i ndenga ye "bi longa lo be nya ndiamoi lo wama."

Ke i longa ko i hugo gbelo panda wanda.

Kia i loni haa ngombui ji ye foma ngi ma ke ndoe ndoe ji
totonga ke ngombui ji totonga a ngi mola ye ndoe ndoe ke ndulii
ji gbowonga ngi la ke i lewenga a pime i li i lowu ngi ye pele
bu i loni pelei na bu lo.

Ngombui na i lo lo jiama le i lo jiama le i lo jiama i
wa i fo pelei na la ke i longa ngitiiya i lo.

Ang na hu na i lowunga. Kia le wo ngombu i wani i loni.
Ngi ndiamoi ji ge ye i li i va ngi ma i lowunga ngi ma. I ya
i wanga pelei bu. Ta be i lo haa ke i heinga pelei na wumba
ke i totonga a mola.

Tewui ji ngi nyahei ji i pelei ji bu ke ti kpele ti totonga
a mola.

Ke numui gbi ti gbonyenga naa, "Kuo le gbokpolu lo ge bi
bi mu wa."

Kę ta ngi lengęisia gbi ti yę na pęlęi na bu ti lęnga kę
ta li ta lǫwu kichin hu-o kę ti lęnga ti tǫtonga a mǫla ye
nasia ta gu pimę ma tia tia lǫ wǫ ti leni a pimę ti gbia hu.

So i ya wǫ na ma haa i wa i gęlę na hi teku ta ngǫmbu
tii yaa loni ma, kia bę hu na.

---

1. Recorded by young man from Pujehun in Freetown on February
12, 1960

TALE 78:   LEOPARD AND DOG[1]

A story about Leopard and Dog.

A very long time ago Leopard and Dog had a very good friendship.[2] At one time they used to arrange things.

Once Leopard and Dog said, "What would be good: let us
initiate into a society all the beasts and all the creatures
in this world."[3]

Then Leopard and Dog initiated them into a society. All
the beasts, all the creatures--even little ones, the very big
ones joined; Leopard and Dog initiated them into a society.[4]
They began this society at one time. Leopard and Dog agreed
at one time.

Every day Leopard and Dog killed one creature and ate it.
They did this for some time; they were doing this for almost
two years. The creatures did not notice, because there were
so very many of them.

One day the beasts in their society went to dig up bushyams.

When they were going, Dog said, "Let me follow them. I
am going to watch over them, because my brother Leopard is
staying behind."

As soon as they had gone, Leopard said, "This Dog's
children are very sweet."

At that time Dog had three children. Then Leopard
caught one of Dog's children and killed it; he cooked it;
he ate it; it was very sweet.

Then Leopard's eye was on Dog; he said, "I am trying to eat
Dog's children; if I eat his children, he will attack me."

When Dog came, he asked Leopard, "Leopard, where are my children that I left with today? I left my three children with you today. I have returned and I see only two. I do not know where the other one went. Now I asm asking you about the third one."

Leopard said, "I do not know about your children's affairs."

The way Leopard answered Dog's questions did not appease Dog. Dog said to the animals that he wanted to hide.

Dog said, "What would be good: we will hide in the town. We are very friendly. Let me go to get fire; we will cook this yam."

As Dog was going, he took his two children. Until this day Leopard calls Dog on their big drum; Leopard taunts Dog. Dog refuses to go to Leopard, because he fears that if he went, Leopard would eat him.

Because of what happened at one time, Dog and Leopard were never friendly again. Dog went to the town. That is why we see Dog in the town and Leopard in the bush.

Dọmẹi na kọloni kọli ta ngilẹi ma.

Lọwọ huguhangọ wa wọ kọli ta ngila ndoma yekpe yekpe yẹilọ ti luahu. Ta ti ta lọ wọ hinda bẹ ta hugbatẹ.

Wati yila i hitilọ na kẹ kọli ta ngila ti ndenga tẹ "Na ma nyandengọ a huangẹisia gbi ọ vuhanisia gbi le ti ndunyẹi ji hu mu ti hale hu.

Kẹ ti ti wa halei ji hu. Ti huangẹi jisia gbi fuhani gbi leke fuhani wẹwẹa-o ye mba mba ngọngu-o kẹ ti ti kpẹlẹ wa halei ji hu. Ta ngila halei ji ti ngua wọ ti wo yila wọ.

Folo gbi va wọ ta fuhani yila ta pa ti mẹ ti ji wie lọwọ hu guhangọ va ti yẹ ji wiema na ngungọ vuli a fo fele kẹ huangẹi jisia tẹ wo heima, gbe jifa ti gbotongọ wa.

Folo yila ye halei ji ti loi lọ ma kẹ huangẹi jisia kẹ ti ya ngawu gbuamẹi ji kẹ ti ya kẹ ti ngawui ji gbua.

Kẹ ti yẹ lima kẹ ngila ta ndenga yẹ "Gbe nya ngi to ngi wama. Ngi li ngi yẹ ti mahu jifa nya ndewe kọli ta i loma."

Kia wọ ti li kia le ti li kẹ kọli ndenga yẹ "Ngilẹi ji" yẹ "ngi lengẹi jisia ti nẹngọ wa le."

Na hu ngila lenga lǫ na sawa. Kę i ngila loi ji hou yila kę i pa i ngili i mę męngǫ wa.

Kuo kę ta bę ngi yamęi i loa ngila ma. "Ye ngilięi ji" yę "ngi lapima ngi ngi lengęisia mę na bę ngi ngi lengęi jisia męa le kę i hiyenga nya woma."

Ye hindęi ji kia ngila i wani kę i kǫli mǫlia la. Ye "Kǫli ǫ nya lengęi jisia ha ngi ti longa a bie? Nya lenga ti sawa ha ngi ti longa a bie. Ngi ya ngi wa kę gbe na ngi wa ngi ti lǫnga le felekpe? Ngii kǫ ye na i ya mindo lǫ nya ha le bi mǫlima ngę nya gǫ a nęmahu lewe yilakpe."

Yę "Bi lengęi nasia ngii ti hinda hungǫ."

Mǫli na kpęlę i kpęmboni ii ngila lilęini kę ta bę i ndea huangęi ye nasia ma yę ngi longǫ i lǫwu.

Yę "Na ma nyandengǫ" yę "nya mua nunga lǫwu tei hu mua ti mu lengǫ wa le ma. A gbę nya ngi li ngi wa a ngǫmbui mu ngawui ji yili."

Kia le wǫ i yę lima ta be i li wǫ a ngi lenga fele nasia. Kia wǫ i lini a tie foloi ji bę kǫli lǫ ngila lolima ti ngili wa na hu wǫ ta ngęli, kę ngila bę ii luma a wa gbamęi i wa i ngi męma

Na va lǫ wǫ kǫli ta ngila ti ya wǫ gbǫma ndoma ya gbi hu tao ngila i ya ta hu. A na va mia ngilęi ta ma tǫ tęi hu kǫli ta i ndǫgbǫi hu.

---

1. Recorded by young man from Pujehun in Freetown on February 12, 1960.
2. Had a very good friendship, ndoma yekpe yekpe yęilǫ.
3. "Initiate into a society," lit., kill in medicine, wa hale hu.
4. In this sentence a differentiation is made between animals (huangęi) and creatures or insects (fuhani).

TALE 79:   TWO FRIENDS[1]

At one time there was a very greedy man named Koli Kpama. There was another young man named Neheli Kpama, who did not work except to invite himself /to others' houses/.

Now Neheli Kpama went to Koli Kpama's farm. When Koli Kpama's wife went to harvest rice, Neheli Kpama sat down and did not go /with her/. The woman cut the rice; she finished

/cutting the rice_7; she returned; she boiled the rice; she
placed it in the sun; she beat the rice; she pounded it; she
finished /beating the rice_7. She cooked the sauce; she finished /cooking the sauce_7. She set the rice on the fire; she
cooked it.

When the time came to serve the rice, Koli Kpama did not
want Neheli Kpama to eat even a little rice. Koli Kpama got
a fever; he pretended to be sick. Before long, just as his
wife was dishing out the rice, Koli Kpama died.

"Oh," Koli Kpama's wife said, "such a thing, Neheli Kpama!
Such a thing!" She said, "Neheli Kpama, go tell them in the
town that Koli Kpama died."

"Oh," Neheli Kpama said, "I certainly shall go to report
/his death_7 in the town. But if people come here soon to mourn,
they will eat the rice. Therefore, give me my rice; I will eat
it. Then I will go to tell about his death."

The person who had just died lifted his head. He said,
"What rice do you mean?"

Neheli Kpama said, "That rice!"

Koli Kpama said, "No, you will not eat that rice!"

Immediately Neheli Kpama and Koli Kpama began to fight in
the farmhouse over the rice. They quarreled and kept fighting
until people came there. At that time neither of them ate any
of that rice at all; they both failed to eat any rice.

The ending of this story was shown thus.

Ndakpoi mia wo kolingo kęlęma gbii ma. Ta toli a Kolima
Kpama. Ndakpoi yila bę lǫ na ta toli a Nęhęli Kpama ta ęę
yenge męhęli mia wǫ a pie.

Kę Nęhęli Kpama ji i ya Koli Kpama ye kpama kę i fonga
na ta ta na ti fongǫ ji le na kę ngi nyahęi ya mbalemęi kę
Nęhęli Kpama heia kę ii yaa. I mbęi ji lewenga i gbǫyǫnga
i wa i fuvu i nda foloi ya mbęi ji i nde i hiya i kpǫyǫ; i
hakpęi yili i kpǫyǫ i mbęi ji heinga i ngili.

Mbęi ji gbua gbe hiti lo wǫ Koli Kpama ji męma ii loni
i Nęhęli Kpama i ngi mbęi ji me kulo bę. Kę kǫlęi wua ngi
ma kǫlęi ji wua ngi ma kę i higbenga a kęwę. Ii guni bę a
hinda hu guhangǫ ngi nyahęi yę mbęi gbua mahu kine kę i ha.

"Kuo," kę ngi nyahęi ndenga yę "hinda bondęi ji" yę
"Nęhęli Kpama," yę "hinda bondęi ji" yę "Nęhęli Kpama," yę
"li bi nde tęi hu" yę "bę Koli Kpama haa."

"Kuo," yẹ "ngi lima vuli ndema tẹi hu" yẹ "kẹ" yẹ "nunga
ti wa na wie ngọmẹi ji" yẹ "mbẹi ji mẹmẹi a yẹ lọ ti ma," yẹ
"fale," yẹ "nya nda mbẹi ve ngi mẹ" yẹ "ngi li na ngi ngi hayẹi
ji le."

Numui ji ha i hanga kẹ i ngi wui wumbunga yẹ "Mbẹi ye gbẹ?"

Yẹ "Mbẹi na."

Yẹ "Mn mn" yẹ "bẹ na mẹ."

A mẹ jega ti hounga kpuẹla mbẹi ji va. Ti yie lọ wọ na ti
lo lapima haa nunga ti wa na na; mbẹi na ti venja tii ya wọ
mẹni fọ ti ba a mbẹi mẹla.

Dọmẹi ji ngi gẹlẹma gẹlọ a ji.

----

1. Recorded by man from Bo in Freetown on January 12, 1960.

TALE 80: THE LAZY MAN AND HIS FRIEND[1]

The lazy man and his friend.

At one time there was a young man who was very lazy; he
refused to do any work. He had a friend who was very strong.

The lazy man said to his friend, "Comrade."

The strong man said, "Yes?"

The lazy man said, "Let us go into the bush. Let us go
to set traps for animals."

The strong man did not refuse; he said, "All right."

As they went, the lazy man smoked his pipe which he enjoyed
more than anything else.

When the lazy man and his companion arrived, his friend
said, "Comrade, now we have arrived.

The lazy man said, "Yes."

The strong man said, "Let us make a hut."

When the lazy man started out, he took his hammock. Now
he hung the hammock and lay down in it.

The lazy man's companion said, "Comrade, let us work."

The lazy man said, "Leave me; I am smoking my pipe."

"Oh, Comrade, you and I came to work. How can you say that you are smoking your pipe?"

The lazy man said, "Leave me; I am smoking my pipe." He lay down /in the hammock/.

Then the strong man made the hut; he finished the hut; he said, "Comrade."

The lazy man said, "Yes?"

The strong man said, "Let us go to set traps now."

The lazy man said, "Leave me; I am smoking my pipe."

Oh, then the strong man went; he set a trap; he caught an animal in the trap.

The strong man returned; he said, "Comrade."

The lazy man said, "Yes?"

The strong man said, "It is about an animal. Get up, we will hold it and bring it."

The lazy man said, "Leave me; I am smoking my pipe."

The lazy man remained smoking his pipe for some time. His companion did all the work by himself. Just as the lazy man turned and looked into the hammock, he saw a diamond--a first-class diamond--there. The lazy man took the diamond; he sold it; he became rich.

A person, therefore, does not become rich, because he is strong.

Hawamọi ta ngi ndiamọi.

Ndakpa yila mia wọ hawangọ kẹlẹma ii ma ẹẹ luma ngenge gbii ma. Kẹ ngi ndiamọi ji ta ta lewema ti lòngọma kpayangọ hulewengọ.

Kẹ i ndea na ngi ma yẹ "Ndakpẹi."

Yẹ "Aa."

Yẹ "Mu li ndọgbọi hu," yẹ "mu li mu ya mani yatẹ huanga gulọ."

Yẹ "Eye." Ii mawani.

Kẹ ti ya kẹ tao a tavẹi gbọle ngi jongọ gbi ma.

Kia wọ ti li ta ngi mba ji foi leke kẹ ngi mba ndea ngi ma yẹ "Ndakpẹi na mu wa."

Yẹ "Hn."

Yẹ "Mu bafa wẹlẹ."

Hindẹi i yẹ lima kẹ i ya a mbomẹi kẹ i mbomẹi hẹlẹa bẹ i la hu i la mbomẹi ji hu.

Kẹ ngi mba ji ndea yẹ "Ndakpẹi mu yenge-o."

Yẹ "Gbe nya ma nya nya tavẹ gbọlema."

"Kuo, ndakpẹi, ma bia mu wa gẹ ngengema ta mia bẹ bia bi tavẹ gbọlema?"

Yẹ "Gbe nya nya tavẹ gbọlema."

Kẹ i la.

Kẹ ndakpẹi ji bafẹi wẹlẹnga i kpọyọa yẹ "Ndakpẹi."

Yẹ "Aa."

Yẹ "Mu li na mu mani yatẹ."

Yẹ "Gbe nya ma nya nya tavẹi gbọlema."

Kuo kẹ ndakpẹi ji ya kẹ i mani ji yatẹa kẹ huẹi ji gọwọa.

Kẹ i wa yẹ "Ndakpẹi."

Yẹ "Aa."

Yẹ "Huẹi le, bẹ" yẹ "hiye mu houma mu waa la."

Yẹ "gbe nya ma," yẹ "nya nya tavẹ gbọlema."

I loi wọ tavẹi ji lọ gbọlema haa. Ngi mba ji yakpe a ngengei ji kpẹlẹ wie. A yẹma i wotea yẹ i mbomẹi ji hugbe kẹ i diamọn ji lọ nga na no one ji kẹ i wumbua i li i majia i gbatẹ fọ.

Famia numu ẹẹ gbatẹ kpaya fa.

1. Recorded by man from Bo in Freetown on January 20, 1960.

TALE 81: A MAN SELLS HIS DEATH[1]

At one time a man who was dying sold his death to his companion; he gave it to his friend. The man was very wealthy: he had a lot of money; he had many boats.

The man remained there with his wealth and he drank wine; he drank such a lot of wine that he had only Ł700 left. The man sat down and thought; he thought about how his money was being used up.

The man went to one bar, he left Ł60 there; then he went to another, he left Ł80 there; then he went to another, he left Ł100 there; then he went away.

The man said, "Now I am leaving this money here."

The barman said, "Yes?"

The man said, "When I come here with my companions to drink liquor, we will drink liquor. When we have drunk as much liquor as the money I have left, take your pencil and raise it. When you raise your pencil, I will know that the money is used up. When I get up, I will take my hat off my head and I will say, 'Good day.' Do not say anything to me."

The barman agreed to that plan.

The wealthy man said the same thing to all the barmen.

Then the man went and gathered all his wealthy friends; he said, "Come, let us eat food."

Before the man gathered his friends, he went to buy a fez; he bought one; he put it on his head.

When the man and his companions went and sat down at one bar, they drank a lot of wine. The man got up. As soon as the barman lifted his pencil, the man took his hat off his head and said, "Good day." The barman did not speak.

The man's friends said, "All right."

They all went out.

One extraordinarily rich young man said to the man, "Comrade, we go and just drink wine; the barman does not ask you /for payment/!"

"Oh," said the man, "you have not seen anything! Let us go to another bar."

Then they went on to the second bar. There they drank wine; they drank and they drank. As soon as they had drunk enough wine, the bar man raised his pencil; the man took his hat off his head and said, "Good day." The bar man did not speak; no one saw the bar man speak.

Then the wealthy young man said to the man, "Comrade, what do you do?"

The man said, "I bought this hat with all the riches that I had at one time. If you own this hat, all your children, your siblings, your relatives will feed on the hat forever. If you go to eat food at any place, you simply take the hat off and say, 'Good day'; the barman will forget to ask you for any payment."

"Oh," the young man said, "sell me that hat!"

The man said, "I have told you that I have put all my riches in this hat. Are you asking me to sell it?"

"Oh," the young man said, "I will give you all my money /for the hat/."

At one time the man went and prepared a paper; the young man signed it and gave all his wealth to the man; the man gave his hat to the young man.

The young man gathered some people and they went to drink; they drank a lot of wine; they got up /to leave/.

When the young man took his hat off his head, he said, "Good day."

The barman said, "Come, sign your bill."

Then the young man signed the bill and went out.

Now the young man acquired an endless number of debts. The young man's heart was destroyed. At one time he went to hang himself; he thought, "My companion was dying some time ago; he sold his death and gave it to me. I will go and say that at one time a man who was dying sold his death and gave it to his friend."

Kena yila mia wọ i yẹ hama kẹ i ngi hei majia i fe ngi mba wẹ i pili ngi wẹ. Kenẹi ji i gbatẹi lọ kẹlẹma gbii ma. Kọpoi ngi yeya kpotongọ ndẹndẹ gbotonga ti ngi yeya.

Kenei ji i longa na kpatei ji hu lo ke tao a ndoe gbole
ngongo i nde ji lo gbole na kakakakaka ke kopoi ji longa ngi
yeya leke pong hondo wofla ta be i hei i hugbe i hugbe ke
kopoi ji wama gboyoma ngi yeya.

I ya bar na ma i pong nu sawa gboyongo lo na ke i lewea i
ya mia i pong nu nani gboyongo lo na ke i lewea i ya mia i pong
hondo yila lo na ke i lewea.

Ye "Ji ngi kopoi ji loma mbei."

Te "Hn."

Ye "Ji mbei ngi wama ndogbolemei ma nya mbanga" ye "mu
ndoe gbolenga i gunga leke a kopoi ji ngi ji kei" ye "bi pensui
wumbu bi te." Ye "Bi tenga" ye "ke ngi konga ke kopoi gboyonga"
ye "ji ngi hijenga boloi na a ye nya wumba ngi kpia ngi ndea
nge 'Ma lo hoe.'" Ye "Ba ya njepe gbi le nya gama-o."

Ke Barmoi na luma.

Hi i pieni a ti kpele.

Ke i ya i ngi mbanga kpele liama numu gbatengoi jia ye
"A wa mu mehe me."

Peing i ti lemba ke i ya sultani boloi ji ma ngeya ke
i ngeya yilakpe ke i pienga wumba.

Kia wo ti li ti ya ti hei mia ti ndoe ji gbolea kaka ti
ndoe gbolea kaka. I hijenga le Bar Master i pensui na lenga
leke ke i boloi ji gbia wumba ye "Ma lo hoe." Na ee ya yepe.

Te "Eye."

Ke ti gbua.

Ndakpao yila kpatengo kelema ii ma kopoi ngi yeya maluwango
ye "Ma li ndakpei ma ndoe ji gbole leke," ye "te bi mali."

"Kuo," ye "bi ya hinda hu loni" ye "mu li bar ye pekei
ma."

Ke ti lewea ke ti ya ti ya bar ye pekei ji ma ti foa na
ti ndoe ji gbole na ti kpole ti kpole. Kia le i guni ke bar
moi ji ngi pensui lenga ke i boloi ji gbia wumba ye "Ma lo hoe."
Tii yepei tii toi a yepe.

Ke i ngi molia ye "Ndakpei gbe le?"

Ye "Kpatei kpele wo ngi hu ngi ngeyani a boloi ji lo.
Boloi ji i ye bi yeya bi lo gbi le bi ndenga-o bi mambla gbi-o

wa lo kunafǫ bǫlǫi ji lǫ hu mema" yę "bi li bi mehę gbi me
hinda bi bǫlǫi ji gbia leke bę 'Ma lǫ hoe,'" yę "kę i lema
ti te nęmahu" yę "tę ya bi mǫli."

"Kuo," yę "bǫlǫi ji majia nya ma."

Yę "Ngi ndea bi ma ngę nya gbatęi kpęlę ngę ngi punga
bǫlǫi ji hu lǫ. Ta mia?"

"Kuo," yę "nga nya navoi kpęlę ve lǫ bue."

Kenęi na li lǫ wǫ ti kǫlǫ gbate i signi kę ngi gbatęi
kpęlę kenęi na mia ngi wo le i fe ngi wę; i bǫlǫi ve ngi wę.

Kenęi li wǫ i nunga lęima ti li wǫ ti ndǫe ji gbǫle lǫ
na kakaka ti ya ti gbua.

Kia i bǫlǫi ji gbua wumba yę "Ma lǫ hoe."

Tę "Wa bi signi."

Tao kę i signinga kę ti lewea.

Hindęi ji wie na kę kpęi gbotonga ngi ma kęlęma ii ma.
Ngi li nyaninga wa hulengǫ. I li lǫ wǫ i ye wǫ ta yakpe
hęlęma i ndeilo wǫ ye "Nya mba na mia gęgę i yę hama ta mia
ngi hęi majia i feni mbę nga li lǫ ngi nde ngę 'Ndakpao yila
i yę wǫ hama i ngi hęi majia i fe ngi mba wę.'"

―――――――――――

1. Recorded by man from Bo in Freetown on January 20, 1960.

TALE 82: THREE HUNTERS[1]

At one time three friends decided to go hunting. The three
friends who prepared to go hunting were named: Shooting Expert,
Sharp Eyes, and Big Jaws.

As they were going, Sharp Eyes saw a deer beyond a big
lake. Immediately Sharp Eyes came and explained to Shooting
Expert who had brought his gun.

Sharp Eyes said, "Shooting Expert, I saw a deer beyond
a big lake."

As soon as Sharp Eyes said that, Shooting Expert asked,
"Where is it?"

Sharp Eyes showed him the place. Shooting Expert shot the animal with his gun and killed it.

"Ah, now how are we going to cross this lake?"

They walked about looking for a boat in which to cross the lake so that they could get the animal.

Then Big Jaws said, "Aha, now the time has come for me to do my own work. Step aside."

They stepped aside.

Big Jaws put the entire lake into one side of his jaw; his jaw was not even filled on that side.

Then they went and took the animal; they brought it back; they took off the animal's skin; they cut it up; they put it in a pot.

Then the others said, "Shooting Expert, go into the town for salt; we will put it in with the meat; it will cook."

Shooting Expert thought that if he turned his back while he went for the salt, his companions would eat the animal in his absence. Shooting Expert walked backwards very slowly; he went until he came to an old hole; he fell into the hole and died.

Now two of them remained with the meat.

Big Jaws said, "Sharp Eyes, go and bring water; we will put it on the meat; it will cook; we will eat."

Then Sharp Eyes also thought that if he turned his back, his companion would eat the meat in his absence. Sharp Eyes kept walking backwards very slowly; he went until he fell into the water and crocodiles ate him.

Now only one person remained there with the meat. The only remaining person was Big Jaws. While Big Jaws was cooking the meat, a leopard was chasing after a deer. When the deer ran near Big Jaws, he stepped into the meat sitting on the fire in a pot. A little soup remained on the deer's foot.

Big Jaws said, "First I will go after that deer to lick the soup from his foot; then I will return to eat the meat."

Then Big Jaws chased after the leopard and drove the leopard away from the deer. As soon as Big Jaws caught the deer's foot and was about to put it in his jaws to lick it, the deer kicked and divided Big Jaws's cheek in half. At that time Big Jaws himself died there.

Now none of the three ate any meat, because they were very greedy. None of them had any sense, so they all died at one time.

That is why excessive greediness is bad.

Ndiamonga sawęi nasia wǫ ti lini tę lima kpandęwilimęi lǫ. Ndiamǫnga sawa gbe le wǫ ti hiyeni ti hugbate tę ti lima kpandewilimęi. Ye nungęi jisia ti le lǫ wǫ a ji ndiamǫ tǫtoma mǫi mia wǫ a ngi la a Kpandęwilikpama ye feleyęi la a Yamangalesaki ye sawayęi la a Gomawugbunję.

Ti loi na lima kę Yamangalesaki kę i ndǫpęi lǫnga mia gboyęi woma kę i wa yakpe kę i hugęnga Kpandęwilikpama. Kę ti ye lima Kpandęwilikpama ta li lǫ a ngi gbandę.

Yę "Kpandęwilikpama" yę "ngi ndǫpęi lǫnga gboyęi woma."

Kia leke i na le kę Kpandęwilikpama ngi mǫlinga yę "Naa mi?"

Kę i na gęnga. Kę Kpandęwilikpama i huęi ji bonga a kpandęi ji kę i panga.

"Ah ma ye naa li mu gboyęi ji lewe?"

Kę tia na lewema a ndęndę gǫi na ta njęi ji lewe ti li ti huęi ji wumbu.

Kę Gomawugbunję ndenga yę "Eh hę" yę "wati hitinga na nya nga nya nda yengei wie;" yę "a lukpele."

Kę ti lukpia.

Gboyęi na kpęlę i pu ngi goma hu kakayęi ji hu ii le kakęi ye na ii ngi gomęi lave le pęing bę ngi goma kakyęi.

Kę ti ya kę ti huęi na wumbu ti wa la ti huęi na gǫlǫ gbua ti tewe ti pu fęi hu.

Kę ti ndenga "Kpandęwilikpama, bia li tęi hu bi li bi wa a kpoloi; mu pu huęi ji hu i yili." Kpandęwilikpama ji yę "A wove węi i yę lima kpoloi ji woma ngi bangęi jisia" yę "kę ti huęi ji męnga ngi woma." I loi lima a woma wę selę kę i ya i ndowa bǫngǫ wova male kę i gula ndowęi na hu kę i ha.

Kę ti longa fele huęi ji ma kę ti venja kę ti hugbatęnga.

Kę ti ndenga "Yamangalesaki" tę "Yamangalesaki, bia li bi li bi wa a njęi na ho mu pu huęi ji ma i yili mu mę."

Ta be i loi lima ye "A womave wei ke a ngi mbaa huei ji
menga ngi woma." I loi lima a ngi woma wei sele sele sele ke
i ya i gula njei hu ke ndambanga ti ngi menga ke huei ji.

Ke numu yilakpe longa na huei ji ma. Numu yakpe longoi
ji huei ji ma na ta a Gomawugbunje. Gomawugbunje ji jina i
loi huei ji yilima ke ndopei ji koli ji loloi ngi woma a wa
a ngi gbe a pime. Ji ke ti wa ke ndopei ji ke i wa a pime
ji ke i wa ke i wilia huei ji hu i heinga ye fei ji hu ke
huwayei ji kulo langa ngi goma.

Gomawugbunje ye Gomawugbunje ye "Ngi ma peing ngi li ngi
ndopei na ngi nya supui na gomei ngi goma; ngi wa ngi ya huei
ji vuli me."

Ke i hitenga koli na woma i wime haa i koli na gbe huei
na ndopei na ma ke i hijenga. Kia leke wo i ndopei na hou
ndopei na gowei na houni le ye i pu gomahu i ngi gowei na
magomi ndopei na i ngi gowei na vai wo i ngi gomei na i koleilo
ndia na fele. Ta be i ha wo mia.

Ti kpele na le tii huei na meni jifa ti mehehindango wa.
Tawao nemahu le gbi tie ti kpele ti halo kpu na i lowo fo.

Na va mia mehei hinda hu lewengo ii nyandeni.

---

1. Recorded by young man from Pujehun in Freetown on May 30,
1960.
2. According to Thompson in the mid-nineteenth century,
crocodiles (ndamba) were found in all African rivers. "They
grow to the length of 20 feet or more, and are very dangerous
animals, frequently killing people, when in the water"
(Thompson:103-104).

TALE 83: TWO STRONG FRIENDS[1]

At one time two strong people were friends.

One day one said, "Comrade, you and I are really friends,
but I am stronger than you."

Then the other said, "Comrade, you are lying. You are
not stronger than I; I am stronger than you."

The first said, "You are not stronger than I."

They kept arguing until one of them took a palm tree which

was there; he caught it; he bent it; he tied it around his waist as a belt.

Then the other said, "Is what you have done a demonstration of your strength?"

He said, "Yes."

The other said, "My demonstration will be greater than that."

Then he went to a huge rock; he hit the rock; it turned into sand.

One of them tied a palm tree around his waist as a belt; when the other hit a rock, it turned into sand. Of the two which one was stronger at one time?

Kpayabla felea gbe wọ ti yẹ na ti venjọ kpẹlẹ ti yẹ ndiamọ ya hu lọ.

Kẹ folo yila i gbua kẹ ye ji ndenga yẹ "Ndakpẹi," yẹ "mua bie mu vuli loma a ndiamọyẹi ji" yẹ "kẹ ngi gbayani bi mà."

Kẹ ye na ndenga yẹ "Ndakpẹi, bi lẹ ni" yẹ "bii gbayani nya ma" yẹ "ngi gbayẹi bi ma."

Yẹ "Bii gbayẹi nya ma."

Ti loi ye mawalei ji houma kẹ ye ngi la i ya tọkpọi i yẹ loni hindẹi kẹ i hounga i kpini kẹ i kpulọnga lia a belti.

Kie kẹ ye na ndenga ngi ma yẹ "Na bi pieni kpaya hindẹi le?"

Yẹ "Mm."

Yẹ "Nya nga hinda wielọ tewengọ na ma."

Kẹ i ya kọtui fawa wa ji hu hu a li polong kẹ i hugbolẹnga kẹ kpẹlẹ na i wotenga a nganyẹi.

Ti venja na ye na i tọkpọi na gulani liama a belti-e. Numui na i fawẹi na huleweni i woteni a nganyẹi-o. Numui felei na ye lọ wọ ngi gbayangọ.

---

1. This riddle tale was recorded by young man from Pujehun in Freetown on February 12, 1960. I published an English translation of this tale in West African Review (1960-61).

TALE 84: A QUARRELSOME MAN[1]

This story is about Ndunyama Hinda.

A young man hated his companion very much. They lived
in the same town. The young man's companion did all sorts
of things for him, but nothing that he did pleased the young
man.

This is what happened.

When the young man and his companion quarrelled, all the
elders condemned the young man. Despite all that, the young
man kept mocking his companion; he said, "You are made clean."
The situation became unbearable.

Now one young man came into the town where he knew that
the two men were quarrelling. When Ndunyama Hinda came at that
time, he went to the quarrelsome man.

Ndunyama Hinda said, "You are full of quarrelling. Let
us quarrel."

The young man said, "What is the matter?"

He said, "My name is Ndunyama Hinda. I do not believe in
God. If I believed in God and you quarrelled with one of your
companions, you would be condemned. Despite all that, there
is a quarrel between us. Therefore, you and I are quarrelling."

At that time they continued to quarrel for forty years.
They did not eat any food; they were constantly hungry; they
kept quarrelling. When at last the quarrel was decided,
Ndunyama Hinda was acquitted.

Therefore, hatred is bad. If any of your companions sur-
pass you, try to pardon him yourself.

Ndunyama Hinda ji ngi ma.

Ndakpao yila mia i loloni a ngi mba i lololo a ngi mba ji
kakakakaka. Ta ta ti heini. I gbe-o-gbe yeka wiema a ngie
ke na hu gbi ngi hinda ii neni ngue.

Hindei ji lo wieni.

Ndobla gbi ngi mba ji ta ta ta yia ti ya ti ngi le kote.
Ke na hu gbi leke ta loi ngi mba ji woma helema. A ye "Bi
kole." Ke i gbowunga.

Ndakpao yila mu li ge le mia ma li na ke i wa tei ji hu

kẹ i nungẹi jisia ti lua hu gọnga kia ti yiama.   Kia wọ
Ndunyama Hinda hijeni wọ i li kenẹi ji gama.

Yẹ "Bi goinga a njia ma bia mu yia."

Yẹ "Gbẹe?"

Yẹ "Nya la a Ndunyama Hinda.   Nya ngi lani a Ngewọ.
Ngi langa a Ngewọ" yẹ "bi mba gbi wa ta wu yia" yẹ "ta bi
lẹlọ" yẹ "na hu gbi njia mu gohu.   Fale nya bẹ ma bie mu
yiama."

Ti loi wọ njie ma fo numu fele gbọyọngọ ta yia tẹ mẹhẹ
gbi mẹ; ndọlẹi ti ma tuu ta yia le.   Ti njiẹi ji lelọ wọ ti
Ndunyama Hinda lemua.

Famia tomaya ii nyandeni numu gbi bi mba lewea bi ma,
lapi bia bẹ bi bi nda lemuma gọi.

---

1.   Recorded by man from Bo in Freetown on January 20, 1960.

TALE 85:   THE MBEMBE DANCE[1]

At one time a big dance was held in a town called Mbembe.

Some years ago in a village there was a man named Kpana.
Kpana was a skillful dancer and he liked dances very much.
Once he held a dance ceremony in Mbembe. When the time for
the ceremony came, a very large crowd attended--many important
people came, many people of high status came to attend this
dance.

Now it happened that eight very virile young men decided
to go to this dance of which they had heard.

One of them was Ngielo. As soon as he went into the bush
to cut the brush, he heard about the dance. When we went to
cut the brush, he cut the brush; he finished cutting; he went
to the dance in Mbembe.

Then the second young man came and found the place where
the brush was cut; it was very dry; it was very beautiful.

He said, "Who is it that has done such beautiful brush
cutting? The time for felling trees has arrived, but he has
not felled the trees."

One man said, "At one time a man came and cut the brush; he left it drying; he went to the dance in Mbembe. Why don't you fell the trees here? Then the farm will become yours."

Then the young man felled the trees; the land was drying; he did not burn the land; he went to the dance in Mbembe.

Then the farm dried; the time to burn the farm came; and a third young man came.

He said, "Who is that who has felled all the trees; he laid such a very beautiful farm, but he did not burn it?"

That man again said, "At one time there was a young man who brushed the farm; he did not fell the trees; he went to the dance in Mbembe. Another came; he felled the trees; he did not burn the farm; he went to the dance in Mbembe. Why don't you burn here; the farm will be yours?"

The third young man came and burned the farm; he did not plant rice; he went to the dance in Mbembe.

Then a fourth man also came.

He said, "Who is it that owns such a very beautiful burned farm? The time for planting rice has come; everything is burned, but he has not planted rice."

That man said again, "At one time there was a young man who brushed that farm; he did not fell the trees; he went to the dance in Mbembe. Another came; he felled the trees; he did not burn the farm; he went to the dance in Mbembe; another burned it. Why don't you plant rice here; the farm will be yours?"

The fourth man planted the rice. When he had planted the rice, he did not wait to weed it, and he went to the dance in Mbembe.

Then a fifth young man came.

He said, "Who is it that planted this rice? Among such very beautiful sprouting rice are weeds that he did not take out!"

That man said, "At one time one young man came; he brushed that farm; he did not fell the trees; he went to the dance in Mbembe. Another came; he felled the trees; he did not burn the farm; he went. Another came; he burned the farm; he did not plant rice. Another came; he planted the rice. That is the story of that rice. Why don't you weed among the rice; the farm will be yours?"

Then the fifth young man weeded the farm. As soon as he had weeded it, he did not want to drive birds away from the rice; he went to the dance in Mbembe.

Then a sixth young man came, he found the rice weeded and the birds sitting there.

He said, "Who is that owns this well-weeded rice and was unable to drive birds away from it?"

This man said, "There was a man who weeded the rice, but he did not drive away the birds. Why don't you drive away the birds; the farm will be yours?"

The sixth young man drove away the birds. As soon as the rice dried, he did not want to cut it; he went to the dance in Mbembe.

Then a seventh young man came; he found that the rice was dry and getting over-ripe.

He said, "Why, who is it that owns such dry rice and he has not cut it at all?"

That man said, "You cut the rice. At one time the person, who owns the dry rice, went to the dance in Mbembe."

The seventh young man cut the rice; he did not take it into the town; he left it there; he went to the dance in Mbembe.

Then an eighth young man came.

He said, "Why, who is that owns this rice which he did not take into the town; he left it to sprout in the bush?"

Then the man said, "If you carry the rice, it will be yours."

The eighth young man carried the rice into the town. When he took the rice into the town, he did not make a granary for the rice; he left it standing outside; he went to the dance in Mbembe.

And a ninth young man now went.

He said, "Why who is it that owns such rice; he put it here so; he did not build a granary to put it in?"

The man said, "At one time one young man began that work; he did it for some time; he left the work; they all went to the dance in Mbembe. If you build a granary here and put the rice in it, the rice will be yours."

As soon as the ninth young man built the granary and put
the rice in it, the dance ended and all the young men came
there. Each person, who now came to finish his work, found
his work finished: brushing, felling, burning, rice planting;
everything was finished. When all of them came, they met one
another there. Who was the person who would eat the rice?
They began to fight about it. At that time long ago they
started to fight. They called it war.

That was the time long ago that war began. And before
that time our grandfathers did not have war; war was not in
the world at one time. That is how at one time war began.

Komẹ wa wọ i gulani ta yila hu ta na loli a Mbẹmbẹ.

Folo lẹnga woma wọ fula yila hu ye lọ wọ na ye fulẹi ji
hu kena yila yẹlọ na, ye kenẹi ji ngi lẹi mia wọ a Kpana.
Kenẹi ji ngi bẹngọ wa a ndoli tao ngi longọ wa ndoli hindẹi.
Kẹ wati yila kẹ i halei wa ndoli halei ji kẹ i ngua Mbẹmbẹ.
Halei ji wangọi ji na na faha gboto gboto wa, nunga wa gboto
wa, tobla gboto wa, ti yẹ lọ a li ye ndoli ji hu."

Kẹ i loa hu kẹ nunga ti hijia ndakpaonga wunduwundua ti
ye wayakpa ti hijia tẹ ti lima ndoli ji hu lọ ti ndoli ji kẹ
ti ye tọ mẹninga.

Kẹ ye ngla lọ na i yẹ kinẹi Ngielo. Kia le i li ndọgbọi
ji hu kọ i ndoi wie kẹ i ndoi ji ma lo mẹninga. Kia i ndoi
na hoe i ndoi na wie a kpọyọ kẹ i wa i li Mbẹmbẹ komẹi ji hu.

Kẹ pekẹi ji wa i ndoikẹi ji malea i benga na panda hu
nyandengọ wa hu.

"Yọ i ndoi nyande nyande ji wiea? Pọ kpe hitingọ ii pọe
ji wie."

Kẹ kena yila ndea ye "Kena yila mia wọ i wa i ndoi ji
hoa i piea i gbiama i bema i ya wọ Mbẹmbẹ komẹi hu bẹ bi
mbe wọ i ya bi wo?"

Kẹ i pọi na wiea pọi na i ndọe bema ii mọni kẹ ta bẹ
ya Mbẹmbẹ komẹi hu.

Kẹ kpa na i be na i be na kẹ kpa mọ gbe ji hitea kẹ pekẹi
wa.

"Yọ ngi wo fọ a pọ kpa nyande nyande wa na i lani ii
mọni?"

Kẹ kenẹi na ndea gbọma ngi ma ye "Kena yila mia wọ i kpa
na loinga ii pọi i ya Mbẹmbẹ komẹi hu; pekẹi wa i pọa ii mọni
i ya Mbẹmbẹ komẹi hu. Bẹ bi mbe mọ họ i ya bi wo?"

Kẹ ye na wa kẹ i mọe ta bẹ ii pui hiyia i ya Mbẹmbẹ komẹi
hu.

Kẹ pekẹi bẹ wa.

"A ye yọ ngi wo a mọtu nyande nyande mbondẹi ji i mọa.
Mba wu kpe hitingọ na hu kpẹlẹ mọngọ ẹẹ pu."

Kẹ kenẹi na ndea gbọma yẹ "Kena yila mia wọ i wa i kpa na
loinga ii pọi i ya Mbẹmbẹ komẹi hu, peka wa i pọnga i mọi i ya
Mbẹmbẹ komẹi hu, peka mọa. Bẹ bi mbe wu họ i wotea a bi wo?"
Kẹ ta bẹ i mbẹi ji wua ta bẹ kia i mbẹi ji wuni ii mawoi a
ngului ji gbua kẹ i ya Mbẹmbẹ komẹi ji hu. Kẹ pekẹi wa. A
yẹ yọ i mbei ji wua? Mba value nyande nyande bondẹi ji" yẹ
"ngului ji wungọ na hu ẹẹ ya kpua." Ye "Kena yila mia wọ i
wa i kpa na loinga ii pọi i ya Mbẹmbẹ komẹi hu, pekẹi wa i
poa ii mọi i ya na wa i mọa ii pui, pekẹi wa i pua. Ta mia
hi ye mbẹi na hu." Yẹ "Bẹ bi mbẹi hu gbua họ i wotea bi wo?"

Kẹ ta bẹ hu gbia kia le i hugbua ii mawoi mbẹi ji a magbẹ
kẹ i ya Mbẹmbẹ komẹi hu.

Pekẹi i wa i male mbẹi ji gbuangọ hu ngọningẹisia ti
heinga.

"A yọ ngi wo lọ a mba gbua hu nyandei ji kẹ ẹẹ gu a magbẹ
la?"

Kenẹi ji ndea yẹ "Kena yila mia ngi gbua a mbẹi na kẹ ẹẹ
magbẹ. Bẹ bi mbe magbẹ họ i wotea a bi wo?"

Ta bẹ i magbẹ. Kia le mbẹi bei ii teni kẹ i ya Mbẹmbẹ
komẹi hu.

Kẹ pekẹi i wa i mbẹi ji male mbengọ ta na galima.

Tẹ "Gbẹi yọ ngi wolọ a mba be bondẹi ji gẹ ẹẹ ya teye-e?"

Kẹ kenẹi na ndea "Bi mbẹi lewe numui na wọ ngi wo mia a
mba bei na i ya Mbẹmbẹ komẹi hu." Ta bẹ i mbẹi na lewe i li
la tẹi hu kẹ ta bẹ i ndea na kẹ i ya Mbẹmbẹ komẹi hu.

Kẹ pekẹi i wa.

"A gbẹi yọ ngi wo a mbẹi ji ẹẹ ya li la ta hu i wui hi
ndọgbọ hu mavalema?"

Kẹ ta bẹ kẹ kenẹi na ndea yẹ "Bi mbẹi belẹ bi wo mia."

Kẹ i ya la tẹi hu. Ngi lingọi ji la tẹi ji hu ii kpu
loni mbẹi ji va i ndoni le wini ngitiiya kẹ i ya Mbẹmbẹ komẹi
hu.

Kɛ peka na i ya.

"A gbɛi yo ngi wo lo a mba bondɛi ji i pua mbei hi ee kpui
lo a tɛ nda lo?"

I ndea yɛ "Kena yila mia wo i ngenge na totonga i pie haa"
yɛ "hi lo ngenge na longa wiema ti ya wo kpɛlɛ Mbɛmbɛ komɛi hu.
Bi mbe kpuwui lo bi tɛ nda i wotea bi wo."

Kia le wo i kpuwui loni i mbɛi na lɛnda. Hu ii guhani kɛ
komɛi na vaya kɛ ti kpɛlɛ na kɛ ti wa na. Numui ji ta na wama
ngi loi ji gboyoma i wani i malei ndoi ji gboyongo pongo mongo
ye mbɛi ji kpɛlɛ i wa i gboyoa. Kɛ le na mba womɛi i malei ye
pekɛi ji bɛ wo i ngi woi ji wie ti wama noma i wai i malei na
kpɛlɛ gboyongo. Ti kpɛlɛ ji na ti wai kɛ ti wa na ti gome na.
Yo na a mbɛi ji mɛ? Kɛ ti totonga a lapila. Tao wati na hu
wo ti ndapi na totoi ye wati mia wo ti yɛ toli a koi.

Kpemɛi na mia wo ko totoni kɛ wati na hu wo maada ti nda
hindɛi wo ko ii ndo hu wo. Na mia wo koi ya gbua-e.

---

1. Recorded by young man from Pujehun in Freetown on February
12, 1960. The various stages involved in making a rice farm
are clearly delineated in this tale.

TALE 86: DOG AND FLY[1]

Why Dog and Fly are not friendly.

At one time there was an important chief who had many
messengers, many servants, many dogs, and many creatures.
Dog and Fly lived with this chief. Every time that the chief
wanted Dog, Dog had to be called first; each time that the
chief wanted Dog, they first had to call Dog. Calling Dog
annoyed all the servants and all the sick people.

One day the people said to the chief, "Chief, we are all
tired of calling Dog. Even if food is given for him, we have
to call Dog first; he comes then we can eat the food. When
the food is eaten, Dog goes out. If you say that you want
Dog, we have to call him first. What is he catching here?"

Then the man went to Dog; he called Dog. He said, "Dog,
do you understand that I have made you the leader of all
these people, these servants, these sick people. You yourself
stand over all these people. Now I am telling you the rule:
when the time for eating food comes, everyone must be here.
If you are not here, the others will eat the food; they will

not give you any food. In addition to this, I am making another rule now: when you come, all the others will laugh at
you and mock you; you will not do anything to them. I have
made the rule that you will not do anything to them. Therefore, do not leave this place so that you will not miss the
time for eating food."

Dog said, "It is agreed."

The evening of the day that the law was made came; they
cooked the food; all Dog's companions came for the food. When
they came, they asked for Dog. Dog was not there.

The chief said, "Where is Dog?"

"Oh," they said, "Dog is not here."

"Oh," the chief said, "eat the food."

The people said, "This demonstrates /what/ we were saying."

Then the people ate this food; they all ate the food; it
was sweet to them; they ate; they were laughing.

As soon as the people had just finished this food and
were washing their hands, Dog approached--yaoun yaoun--he was
very breathless; he approached. As soon as the people saw Dog,
Fly began to mock Dog.

Flies arose and went over to Dog, "Ho--o, we have eaten
the rice; we have not given Dog any rice."

Just now Dog turned around, he said, "This is my own share,"
and he caught a fly and swallowed it. He said, "This is my own
share."

Up to this time, therefore, Flies mock Dog as at one time
the chief said that they should do to Dog. Up to this time,
therefore, as soon as Fly passes, he keeps going around Dog;
he is mocking Dog.

Fly says, "Ho--o, they have eaten the rice and they have
not given Dog any."

Dog himself turns; he says, "This is my own share!" And
he catches Fly.

That is why today Dog and Fly are not friendly, because
Fly mocks Dog.

Gbeva ngila ta ndili tii loni ma.

Wati yila ye wọ na maha wa yila yẹ lo na. Mahẹi ji
mẹssẹn jisia ti ngi yeya gboto wa ti yẹ lọ na ta bọilopoisia
kẹ ta ngilani kpẹlẹ mia ti ye na ngila-o ndili-o kẹ na fuhanisia
gboto ma ti yelọ mahẹi ji ngi gama. Mahẹi ji kpema gbi wọ i
gbenga ngila va kẹ ta ngi loli pẹing kpema gbi va i longa i
ngila lo kẹ ta ngi loli pẹing. Ji i wie toli ji i gbọwo
bọilopoisia kpẹlẹ la i gbọwo higbebla ti kpẹlẹ la.

Kẹ tia bẹ ti ndea folo yila tẹ "Mahẹi, ngila ta mu kpẹlẹ
mua mu gbahanga na ngi loli le ta ngi ma mẹhẹi bẹ-o i ve na
kẹ mua ngila loli pẹing i wa mu ya mẹhẹi ji mẹ. Mẹhẹi mẹngọ-o
kẹ i gbua. Bi lọ bẹ-o a ngila longọ kẹ ma ngi loli pẹing. Kẹ
i mbei hou gbọva?"

Kọwọi kenẹi ji i pie ngila i li kẹ i ngila lolinga yẹ
"Ngila, hẹi bi ya ngi bi wotea a tokulọ nungẹi jisia kpẹlẹ
mahu bọilopoi jisia-o higbebla-o ti kpẹlẹ ji bia bia bia bi
loni ti mahu kẹ na sawa le ngi kẹ na mẹhẹi mẹ wati ta i hitinga
numu gbi le ba yẹ mbei; bii yẹlọ mbei. Ta mẹhẹi na mẹ tẹ bi
gọ. Poma ji bi wama ti kpẹlẹ ji nya nga pielọ ngi sawa la na
ti kpẹlẹ ji to bi yẹlẹ lọ ta hẹlẹlọ bi ma bẹ gbẹ-o-gbẹ wie a
tie. Na leke nya nya jawa la gọ le bẹ gbẹ-o-gbẹ wie a tie."

Yẹ "Fale ba ya gbua mbei jifa baa gbula mẹhẹi mẹ wati ji
ma."

Ngila yẹ "Kulungọi."

Foloi na ti sawẹi lani kẹ ye kpọkọi na hitia ke ti mẹhẹi
ji yilinga; ngi mbangẹi nasia gbi kẹ ti wa mẹhẹi ji gama ti
wa wati ji na ti ngila mọlima. Ngila ii ya na.

Kẹ mahẹi ndenga yẹ "Ọ ngila?"

"Kuo," tẹ "ngila ii mbei yẹ."

"Kuo," yẹ "a mẹhẹi mẹ."

Tẹ "Ji gẹ mu ndema."

Kẹ ti mẹhẹi ji mẹnga ti gbi ti mẹhẹi ji mẹ manẹngọ wa ti
wẹ ta mẹ ta yẹlẹ.

Kia le ti mẹhẹi ji gbọyọi le ti yẹ na ti yeya wama ke
Ngila gbuanga yaoun-yaoun ta wama ngi vondengọ wa kẹ i gbuanga.
Kia le ti ngi loni ndili ji-o ngi hẹlẹmangọ.

Ke ti hijenga ti ya ngi mahu "Ho-o mu mbei mẹa muii ngila
gọni-o."

A wotelọ na le yẹ "Nya ngi ndẹi." Kẹ i na hounga i kpọle "Nya ngi ndẹi."

Famia hẹlẹmẹi na va ndilini kia bẹ hu na hẹmẹi na wọ mahẹi na i ndea yẹ "Ti ya pie ngila ma." Kia bẹ hu na famia ndili ji le ta teni ti loma i ya bembẹma le numui na hẹlẹmẹi na mia a pie.

Yẹ "Ho-o ti mbẹi mẹa tii ngila gọni."

Ta bẹ i wotea na le yẹ "Nya ngi ndẹi," kẹ i na hounga.

Na va mia foloi ji bẹ ngila ta ndili tii loni ma jifa a hẹlẹ ngi ma.

---

1. Recorded by young man from Pujehun in Freetown on May 30, 1960.

TALE 87: CAT, RATS, AND MICE[1]

Why Cat and Rat are not friendly.

At one time Cat and Rats were friendly; they ate food together; they played together.[2] Then at one time famine occurred in their country and remained there.

Then the old woman who was the leader of the Sande society went to her husband Cat. She said, "Mr. Man, since this famine has come, I want to make this big Sande ceremony, then we will be able to eat food this year. I want to have this Sande ceremony; we will eat these Rats."

Her husband agreed to this plan.

Then this old woman, the chief's wife, called all the Rat women. She put this plan before them; she said, "I want to initiate you into Sande."

The Rats agreed.

She said, "That initiation will enable you to bear children."

The Rats came and entered the Sande bush. They made a big ceremony in the town. The time for leaving Sande was announced.

When the Sande leaving time was announced, the old woman said, "Now before I bring this Sande group out, I have a message to give to you. Before I bring you out of the Sande bush, I will put you in groups. The tondo rats will be in one place; the fologbeteni rats will be in one place; the lende rats will be in one place; all the ndonde rats will be in one place."2

The rats agreed to this plan.

The time to leave the Sande bush came; the rats were taken to the riverside; they were dressed in Sande clothes; they wore head-dresses; they were put in groups; they waited for a long time.

When they were taking these Sande initiates into the town, the Sande leader sang a song. She thought: during this song I wish to kill the rats according to my plan. When the rats were arranged, she sang the song. All the Sande initiates came out; they all of them sang the chorus of the song. There was a big gathering /of rats/ in the bush. As they were taking them into the town, they sang:

"Gbegbeto gbegbeto, Rats,
"Gbegbeto gbegbeto, Rats,
"Gbegbeto gbegbeto, Rats,
"Rats, your water is boiling.
"Gbeto we are sitting on your life, Rats.
"Gbegbeto gbegbeto, Rats,
"Gbegbeto gbegbeto, Rats,
"Gbegbeto gbegbeto, Rats,
"Gbegbeto gbegbeto, Rats,
"Gbegbeto gbegbeto, Rats,
"Rats, your water is boiling.
"Gbeto, we are sitting on your life, Rats.
"Gbegbeto gbegbeto, Rats,
"Gbegbeto gbegbeto, Rats,
"Gbegbeto gbegbeto, Rats."

As the old woman sang, 'We are sitting on your life,' she squeezed the neck of a Tondo Rat; she laid it down; she had killed that Rat.

"Gbegbeto gbegbeto, Rats,
"Gbegbeto gbegbeto, Rats,
"Gbegbeto gbegbeto, Rats,
"Rats, your water is boiling.
"Gbeto we are sitting on your life, Rats.
"Gbegbeto gbegbeto, Rats,
"Gbegbeto gbegbeto, Rats,
"Gbegbeto gbegbeto, Rats."

Everytime the old woman said, 'Your water is boiling,' she squeezed a Rat's neck with her claw; she killed the Rat; she put it down. Thus for some time the old Cat was killing Rats. She killed all the fologbeteni rats; she killed all the tondo rats; she returned and killed the ndonde rats. She came to the lende rats.

When the old Cat reached the lende, one Rat was clever-- though they are small. A lende stood up, she looked back; she saw that all her companions were dead. When before the song had been sung noisily, it was no longer sung loudly; now only a few were singing.

Then Rat cried out to her companions, she said, "Let us go, they have trapped us."

And Lende Rats went and climbed into the bush. They gave a name to that Rat girl, they said that her name is Lende (i.e., Jumper). So today that Rat is named Lende.

The incident that happened at that time made Rats and Cats unfriendly. If Rats see Cat, they run away; they go and hide. This was what happened at one time to separate Rat and Cat.

Gbọ na wie gọnẹi ta nyina tii loi ma.

Gọnẹi ta Nyinani ti yẹ wọ ngo yila hu tao ta mẹhẹi mẹ wọ hinda yila ta loli hinda yila. Kẹ wati yila ma ndọlẹi wie lọ ndọlọi hu ti lọlọi na hu kẹ i longa hu.

Kẹ mamẹi na na hi Sande jowo yẹ la a ngie kẹ i ya ngi hini gama gọnẹi kẹ i ndea yẹ "Kenẹi nya lọngọi ji ndọlẹi ji wa nya longọi ngi Sande wa ji lọ a wie mu gu mẹhẹ mẹ foi ji. Nya longọi ngi Sande wa mu nyinangẹi jisia mẹ."

Ngi hini i lumai lọ hindẹi ji ma.

Kẹ mamẹi mahẹi nyahẹi ji kẹ i nyahangẹi jisia kpẹlẹ lolinga nyina nyahangẹi jisia kẹ i hindẹi ji wunga ti gulọ yẹ "Nya longọi ngi wu wa Sande hu."

Tia bẹ ti lumailọ ma.

Yẹ "Na a wie wu ndenga le."

Ti wai lọ na kẹ ti Sande ji wanga. Ti komẹ wa wie lọ tẹi hu kẹ i longa hu. Kẹ ti Sande gbia lọẹi ji venga.

Sande gbia lọẹi ji vengai ji hu i ndeilọ yẹ "Na" yẹ "pẹing ngi ya Sande ji gbua," yẹ "ngo lọ nya la" yẹ "nga nde wuma." Tia bẹ ti lumai lọ ye ngoi ji ma. Yẹ "Pẹing ngi ya wu gbia Sande ji hu nga wu heilọ a kunga. Tọndọni kinẹi ta yẹlọ kaka

yila ma fologbeteni kpęlę ta yęlo kaka yila ma, lendeni bę
ta yę lǫ kaka yila ma, ndondę nyinęi ti kpęlę ta yęlǫ kaka
yila ma."

Ti gui lǫ ti luma ji ma.

Sande gbia lǫi ji hitilǫ ti li a tie njei la ti Sande
ti ti mayii kę ti ti heinga na a ku ti lembęi wę ti wumba.

Ji na ti yę lęma a Sande ji tęi hu ngole lǫ wǫ na Sande
jowoi kpuani yę ngole lǫ a ji ngi longǫ yęla i ti kpęlę wa
vui kia ngi gili yęi i ndei ta tao kia ti hugbatęi i na ji
na i ngole ji gbuani ti kpęlę Sandebla kpęlę mbǫgbęi jisia
ti ti gbuani ti kpęlę ti yę ngole ji houlǫ kumavui. Komę wa
yę ndǫgbǫi na hu ti yę lema a tie tęi hu tę

"Gbęgbęto gbęgbęto ma, nyina-ee,
"Gbęgbęto gbęgbęto ma, nyina-ee,
"Gbęgbęto gbęgbęto ma, nyina-ee,
"Ma nyina tǫndǫ bi njęi;
"Ma nyina tǫndǫ bi njęi.
"A gbuyę gbuyę.
"Gbęto mua hei bi bi lewui ma nyina-ee.
"Gbęgbęto gbęgbęto ma, nyina-ee,
"Gbęgbęto gbęgbęto ma, nyina-ee,
"Gbęgbęto gbęgbęto ma, nyina-ee,

"Gbęgbęto gbęgbęto ma, nyina-ee,
"Gbęgbęto gbęgbęto ma, nyina-ee,
"Gbęgbęto gbęgbęto ma, nyina-ee,
"Ma nyina tǫndǫ bi njęi;
"Ma nyina tǫndǫ bi njęi;
"A gbuyę gbuye.
"Gbęto mua hei bi bi levui ma, nyina-ee,
"Gbęgbęto gbęgbęto ma, nyina-ee,
"Gbęgbęto gbęgbęto ma, nyina-ee,
"Gbęgbęto gbęgbęto ma, nyina-ee."

Mua hei bi bi levui ma kę i tǫndǫi na bole ligba kę i
nda kę i na wa.

Yę

"Gbęgbęto gbęgbęto ma, nyina-ee,
"Gbęgbęto gbęgbęto ma, nyina-ee,
"Gbęgbęto gbęgbęto ma, nyina-ee,
"Ma nyina tǫndǫ bi njęi;
"Ma nyina tǫndǫ bi njęi;
"A gbuyę gbuyę.
"Gbęto mua hei bi bi levui ma, nyina-ee,
"Gbęgbęto gbęgbęto ma, nyina-ee,
"Gbęgbęto gbęgbęto ma, nyina-ee,
"Gbęgbęto gbęgbęto ma, nyina-ee."

'A gbuyẹ gbuyẹ gbẹtoi' na i ye gbi ndeni a ye ngila bo
ligba a ngi ye ngawui na i pa kẹ i nda hi haa loi i ti wama.
I fologbeteni kpẹlẹ wa i lendeni kpẹlẹ wa i yama i ndondẹ
nyinẹi nasia wa kẹ i fonga na lende tia ti ma. Ngi fongọi
ji lendẹi ma kẹ nyina mia kavangọ.

Kia bẹ ti gulọngọ yẹla lende loilọ i wohu gbe kẹ i tọa
yẹ kẹ ngi mbangẹisia gbi ti wangọi tia landai. Kia ha ngole
i houa la kuma ii ya houma la hi ngla ngla mia na le na ti
wole ma.

Kẹ i yelei gula ngi mbanga ma yẹ "A mu li ti mu gbenga."

Kẹ ti ya ti lẹma ndọgbọi hu kẹ ti ndẹi venga nyina loi na
wẹ tẹ "Ngi la lende." Fale foloi ji bẹ nyinẹi na la a lende.

I hije foloi ji ma i hije wati na ma hindẹi ji wie nyinanga
ta gọnẹisia tii loi ma. Ti tọnga le ta lewe a pimẹ lọ ti li ti
lọwu kẹ ji lọwọ wienga nyina ta gọnẹ ti lua hu kọlẹnga.

---

1. Recorded by young man from Mano in Bo on April 16, 1960.
2. They were friendly, lit., they were in one voice, <u>ti yẹ
wọ ngo yila hu</u>.

TALE 88: THE MAN AND THE BUSH SPIRIT[1]

At one time a man met a bush spirit.

There was a house in the bush belonging to a bush spirit who used to take people there. Every time that a person went on that road, the bush spirit would catch him and take him to the house.

One day the bush spirit met a man.

The bush spirit said to the man, "Come, let us go to my house."

But the man was afraid.

The bush spirit said, "Do not be afraid, I will not do anything to you. I will take you."

Then they went and slept in the house for the entire night.

When morning came, the man said, "I should like to return now. Now that I have come /to your house/; we have slept here; I would like to return."

The bush spirit said, "As I truly love you, I will do something for you. If you go, I will give you all the things which I have taken from people. If I keep these things, I do not have any use for them. Therefore, I want to give them to you; take them into town. When you go, be sure not to tell /anyone/ in the town what has happened."

The man said, "Yes."

The bush spirit said, "Be certain not to tell anyone in the town."

The man said, "Yes."

Then the man went into the town. Before the man was poor. Now when he returned, he was very rich.

Then people began to ask him /about his wealth/. People on the right questioned him and people on the left questioned him.

"Ah, Comrade, how is it? We heard that you were such a very poor man before. How have you become such a rich man?"

At first the man refused to explain; he said, "So it is. Great God has given me riches. I was walking about; God has given me riches."

The people kept questioning him.

One day the man got up; he went; he drank a little wine. The wine went to his head.

The man began to say, "Of course, when I missed my way some time ago..."

As soon as the man said, 'When I missed my way some time ago,' the spirit yonder in the bush sang a little message that he had shown to the man before so that he would not explain his secret. The spirit said to the man,

"Ki jenge jenge jenge jenge-ei.
"It is a violation!
"Ngombu, do not tell jenge;
"If you say it, you will surely die.
"Ki jenge jenge jenge jenge je."

The man did not notice; he did not realize that it was the little message that the spirit was showing him so that he would not explain his secret. The man did not listen to that message.

The man said again, "As soon as I went, I reached a big town and I met a spirit."

And again the spirit said, "Jenge jenge jenge jenge je."

"Then the spirit gave me a place to sit."

The spirit kept saying that little message to the man.

The man was telling the secret. As soon as the man finished explaining exactly how the spirit gave him those riches, those valuable things, the man fell backward; he died at that time.

The spirit came for every one of those things. He took back all those things. At that time the people remained in their poverty yonder.

The story is finished now.

Kenei wo i ndogbo yosoi maleni.

Pele lo wo na i ye ndogboi hu. Ndogbo yosoi ji ye na wo

a li a nungẹi jisia. Kpẹlẹma gbi va wọ bi lewenga a pelei
na a bi houlọ a li lọ a nunga pẹlẹi ji bu.

Lọ yila ma kẹ ta kena yila ti gomẹnga.

Yẹ kenẹi ma "Wa mu li nya ye pẹlẹ bu."

Kẹ kenẹi luanga.

Kẹ ndọgbọ yosoi ndea yẹ "Baa lua ngii gbẹ-o-gbẹ wiema a
bie. Ngi lima lọ a bie."

Kẹ ti ya ti yi na gbu.

Kẹ ngele wonga kẹ i ndea yẹ "Nya longọi họ ngi yama na.
Na na ngi wanga ma bia mu yinga mbeindo kẹ nga lolọ na sina
ngi yama."

Yẹ "Kia vuli nya longọ a bie ngi ye hindẹi lọ wiema a bie,"
yẹ "kẹ na leke nga nde bi ma yẹ bi ya lọ" yẹ "hakẹi ji kpẹlẹ"
yẹ "nya longọ ngi fe bi wẹ, hakẹi ji wọ a hou nunga yeya," yẹ
"jifa ti lo bẹ nya yeya ye nguama gbii nya yeya." Yẹ "Fale
nya longọ ngi fe bi wẹ. Bia bi li la tẹi hu." Yẹ "Kẹ bi yaa"
yẹ "hinda gbi wieni" yẹ "baa hungẹ tẹi hu-o."

Yẹ "Mn."

Yẹ "Baa hungẹ tẹi hu-o."

Yẹ "Mn."

Kẹ i ya tẹi hu. Kenẹi ji wọ ngi nyaningọ i lini na kpatẹmọ
wa yẹla a ngie.

Kẹ nunga ti tọtoa a ngi mọlila. Ta ngi gbua ngeje hu ta
kpua kọwọ hu.

"Ah, Ndakpẹi, gbẹe, bia mua woini mu na wọ bi nyaningọ
wai ji i wanga na i wienga bi wotenga hi a kpatẹmọ?"

Ta bẹ ii lumani halẹi hu aa hungẹ. Kẹ i ndea yẹ "Hi mia
na" yẹ "Ngewọ wa mia nya gọnga. Ngi longa lewetewema lọ Ngewọ
nya gọnga."

Ti nọọ hang ngi ma.

Folo yila i hijeilọ leke i ya i ndọ wule gbọlenga leke.
Kẹ ndọi ji lẹnga ngi yama.

Kẹ i tọtoa a ndela. "Ingẹ ji gẹgẹ ngi yakani."

Ngamẹi ji kia leke i ndeni yẹ "Ji gẹgẹ ngi yakani, kẹ
hani wai na longa miando ngafẹi na kẹ i lọnga ndọgbọi na hu

ke i ndenga njẹpẹ wo lọ wọ na a kẹ a ngie kọ i kọ kẹ aa njẹpẹi
na hungẹ. Kẹ i ndea ngi ma.

    "Ki jenge jenge jenge jenge-ei
    "Ka ka mia!
    "Ngọmbu, baa nde-o jenge;
    "Ba nde ba ha lọ-o.
    "Ki jenge jenge jenge jenge je."

    Ii lalini ma i kọma njẹpẹi wo mia kenẹi na kẹma a ngie
kọwọi a hindẹi na hungẹ ii wo loni hindẹi na ma.

    Kẹ i gbọma pienga. "Kia leke ngi lini kẹ ngi fonga ta
wai hu kẹ ngi hani wa malenga."

    Kẹ i gbọma ndea yẹ "Jenge jenge jenge jenge je."

    Kẹ i heima venga mbẹ.

    I loni haa njẹpẹ woi na lema lọ ngi ma haa.

    A njẹpẹi na hungẹ. A njẹpẹi na hungẹ. Kia leke wọ i
ndeni i kpọyọni leke kia kenẹi na kpatẹ hakẹi nasia veni ngi
wẹ haka yekpei nasia. Kia leke wọ i kpọyọni a nde la kẹ i
gulanga a woma wie. I ha wọfọ.

    Kpatei nasia gbi leke hani na gbi ta bẹ kpẹlẹ i wa wọ ngi
hakẹi nasia woma gbi i yama la. Ti lo wọ heini a ti nyani. Na
miando mia.

    I gẹlẹni na.

---

1. Recorded by young man from Pujehun in Freetown on
February 16, 1960. In this tale the bush spirit is referred to as "ndọgbọ yosoi" and "hani wa."

TALE 89: KPANA AND THE BUSH SPIRIT[1]

    At one time Kpana married a woman. He went to his wife's
town. When Kpana went there, he said that they should give
him some bush to cut brush /for a farm/. The people gave him
all the bush; he did not cut brush. He said that he would
cut brush in the bush near the town.

    The people said that they had failed; they said, "We
agree. You are our brother-in-law. You have come here; you
have said that you will cut brush in this bush; we agree."

And the people gave him this bush.

At one time Kpana came into the bush to cut the brush; he was busy throughout the day. His wife cooked some food and brought it to him.

As soon as his wife brought the cooked food, Kpana said, "Put the food down. When you go now, it is time for you to go fishing."

The woman put the food down.

As soon as the woman left, a bush spirit came out. As the bush spirit approached Kpana, he changed into a man; he approached Kpana.

The young man said, "Father, come; we will eat the food."

They ate the food.

As soon as they had finished, the bush spirit said to the young man, "Give me water." He said to Kpana, "Give me water."

Kpana gave water to him.

When the spirit washed his mouth--chuku, chuku, he dropped eight bags of money /on the ground/.

The spirit said, "The money is yours. But be certain not to explain to your wife how I am giving this money to you."

As soon as Kpana went into the town, his wife persistently questioned him for some time. She persistently questioned him until Kpana explained.

Kpana said, "How I have gotten this money: when I go to cut brush, there is a man whom I ask to eat food; as soon as he washes his mouth with water, the money comes out of his mouth--first the eight bags of money, then the ten bags of money. He took the eight bags of money and the ten bags of money out of his mouth."

"Oh!" She said, "Kpana you are crazy! A person washes his mouth and money comes out; now how much more would you get, if you killed him and split his stomach. Don't you believe that you would get more money?"

Kpana listened to his wife's words.

At one time Kpana went; he sharpened his cutlass on a stone. His wife brought the food; she put it down. As soon as she left, the man approached; Kpana invited him to eat.

They ate the food; they finished /eating/. When the spirit
said to give him some water to wash out his mouth, he turned
away. Kpana bent back his cutlass; he thought that he would
fall on the man, but he split his knee in half.

Then the spirit turned to Kpana; he said, "Ah, Kpana,
you have injured yourself, /because of/ a woman's words."

This is the end of this story.

Kpana mia wǫ. I nyahẹi ji jǫni kẹ i ya ngi nyaha welei
ji hu kẹ i ya na yẹ "Ti ngi gǫ a ndǫgbǫ i ndoli." Ti ndǫgbǫi
gbi veilǫ ngi wẹ ẹẹ ndoli yẹ "Kẹ ndǫgbǫi na le tẹi na gblanga,
ta mia a ndoi."

Nunga ti nde ti gbahang tia bẹ tẹ "Mu loko lǫ ma mu mbelẹi
mia a bie na na bi wanga bẹ ndǫgbǫi ji lǫ ba ndoi mu kulunga."

Kẹ ti ndǫgbǫi ji venga ngi wẹ.

Ndǫgbǫi lǫ wǫ i wani hu foloi na i lini ndoimẹi i luvani
kpẹing. Kẹ ngi nyahẹi kǫndẹi ji yilinga kẹ i ya la ngi woma.

Kǫndẹi ji yilingǫ i ya la leke-o yẹ ngi ma yẹ "Mẹhẹ lo"
yẹ "bi ya lǫ na kpe bi lima nyẹ gbẹmẹi lǫ."

Mẹhẹi ji longǫ-o.

Ji leke nyapoi lini kẹ ndǫgbǫ yosoi ji gbianga. Ndǫgbǫ
yosoi ji gbianganga kẹ i maluvenga a kena yila i gbianganga.

Kẹ ndakpaloi bẹ ngi mǫlinga yẹ "Kẹkẹ," yẹ "wa mu mẹhẹ
mẹ."

Ta ta ti mẹhẹi ji mẹnga.

Ti kpǫyǫnga leke yẹ ndakpaloi ma "Nya gǫ njẹi hu." Yẹ
Kpana ma "Nya gǫ njẹi hu."

Kẹ Kpana njẹi venga ngi wẹ.

Kia wǫ i ngi la wani chuku chuku i kulani kǫpǫ bẹgi
wayakpa mia i kulani.

"Kuo," yẹ ngi ma "bi wo mia."

Kẹ i na wumbunga kẹ i ya la.

Kia ngi nyahẹi kǫpǫi ji lǫni yẹ "Kuo," yẹ "mindolǫ bi
gbianga na a kǫpǫ bondẹi ji?"

"Ah, Nyande, mbǫ baa loko wili nya ma hinda hu."

Kę ti na la ma gbatęnga.

Ngele wekęi i wo kę i wanga. Kia wǫ ngi nyahęi wani i
męhę loni gbǫma i yę yama ma lǫ kinęng kę kenęi ji gbianganga
gbǫma kę i ngi mǫlinga gbǫma męhęi ji ma kę ti męnga kę i ngi
la wanga chuku chuku gbǫma kę i kǫpǫ bęgii pu gulanga.

Yę "Bi womia," yę "kę ji ngi fema hi bi wę" yę "baa hugę
a bi nyahęi yo."

I lini lǫ wǫ tęi hu leke ngi nyahęi ji gbǫndailǫ ngi ma
ha i gbǫnda ngi ma haa kę i hugęnga.

Yę "Ba kpatęi ji ngi piengǫ" yę "kena yila mia nga ngi
mǫli męhę ma ji nga li ndoimęi" yę "ta mia a ngi lęi hu waa
leke" yę "i ye njęi ji wungalǫ ta mia kǫpǫi ji a gbia ngi la
kǫpǫ bęgii na wayakpęi gęgę kę i bę pu" yę "ta mia i gbiani
kę ji bę pu" yę "ta mia i gbiani ngi la i gulani."

"Kuo," yę "Kpana bi wuhu! Numu i ngi lahu wa kǫpǫ i
gbia na hęi kę lę a bi pa bi ko bla. Bii lani la ba kǫpǫ
jǫlǫ i lewe na ma?"

Kpana bę kę i wolonga ngi nyahęi layięi ma.

I lini lǫ wǫ leke i mbogbęi ji yakpa kakakaka. Ngi nyahęi
li lǫ a kǫndęi i ndo leke. Ngi yamangǫ leke kę kenęi ji
gbianganga kę i ngi mǫlinga męhęi ji ma. Ti męhęi ji mę ti
kpǫyǫ. Kia wǫ kenęi ndeni yę "Njęi ve," kenęi ji yę i ngi
la wa i wote miande. I gawanga a mbogbęi ji yę i kenęi yo na
i gulanga kenęi ma i ngi wombi lǫ wǫ blani i ndia fa.

Kę kenęi wotenga ngi mahu yę "O ya" yę "Kpana" yę "bi bi
nęmunga" yę "nyaha layia lǫ."

Dǫmęi ji ye kęlęmangęi mia.

---

1. Recorded by man from Bo in Freetown on January 12, 1960.
Tale 5 is a more elaborate version of this story; Tale 90 is
a similar tale.

TALE 90: KPANA AND THE BUSH SPIRIT'S POT[1]

This story is about Kpana and the bush spirit.

Kpana and the bush spirit were friends.

The bush spirit said to Kpana, "Tomorrow I will come with a lot of money; I will fill a pot completely with money. If I do that, you must sacrifice a living person to me every year.

Then the bush spirit began to bring money to Kpana and his wife.

They said, "Let us play a trick on this bush spirit so that he will not be able to make us give a person."

Then they punctured the pot.

When the bush spirit came with the money, he would put it in the pot; the money would enter the pot and fall to the ground. The bush spirit did not know what was happening. For some time the bush spirit came with money; the pot did not get full.

When Kpana and his wife observed that the bush spirit took the money out of his belly to put in the pot, Kpana's wife said to him, "Kpana, when the bush spirit comes, let us split his stomach open and take out all the money inside. Then we will be rich forever."

And Kpana agreed /to her plan/.

When the bush spirit came one day with the money to put into the pot, Kpana took a very sharp ax to split the bush spirit's stomach in order to take the money out of his stomach. When Kpana did this, he missed the bush spirit with the ax and split the front of his own leg. Then the bush spirit understood the trick; the bush spirit left.

The money, which the bush spirit had brought at different times, Kpana and his wife spent on various things. They did not get any more money. They were very poor.

This is the end of the story.

Dǫmęi ji ndalongǫ Kpana ma ta ndǫgbǫ yosoi.

Kpana ta ndǫgbǫ yosoi ti ndiamǫya lǫ gbatęni.

Kę ndǫgbǫi yosoi ndenga Kpana ma yę "Nga wa lǫ sina a navo gboto ngi fę yila venda kpang kę ngi na wienga lǫ ba gulǫ bi sa gbia nya gama fo gbi a numu vulu.

Kę ndǫgbǫ yosoi ji i tǫtonga a wala a navoi ji Kpana wę ta Kpana nyahęi.

Kẹ ti ndenga tẹ "Gbẹ mu kaso gula na hi ndọgbọ yosoi ji
ma aa gu mu ma numui ji ve va." Kẹ ti fẹi gbutanga.

Ndọgbọ yosoi wangalọ na a navoi ji i ya puma fẹi ji hu
navoi a fẹi volo i gula ndọlọmẹi. Ndọgbọ yosoi ta ii hugọ.
Ji lọ wieni haa ndọgbọ yosoi a wa le a navoi fẹi yo ẹẹ venda.

Kia na ti mabẹni kẹ ndọgbọ yosoi ji a navoi ji gbua ngi
goi hu lọ a pu fẹi ji hu, kẹ Kpana nyahẹi ndenga na ngi ma
yẹ "Kpana, ndọgbọ yosoi ji wa mu ngi goi ji hu bla kẹ mu
navoi ji kpẹlẹ gbianga na kẹ mu gbatẹnga ku na fọ va."

Kẹ Kpana kulunga.

Kia ndọgbọ yosoi wani lọ yila ma a navoi ji i ye puma
fẹi hu kẹ Kpana konu yandingọ wa wumbunga kọ i ndọgbọ yosoi
ji bla ndia fa i navoi ji gbia ngi gohu. I loni na lọ wiema
kẹ i gbulanga ndọgbọ yosoi ma a konui ji kẹ ta ngi Kpana kẹ
i ngi haka yamẹi bla ta kẹ ndọgbọ yosoi gasonga ti yeya kẹ
i ya.

Navoi na gẹgẹ na ndọgbọ yosoi wani la ti loni na
nguanguama lọ ti ma hinda hu hani kẹ kpẹlẹ gbọyọnga. Tii
yaa navo weka majọni kẹ ti longa fẹli hu.

Dọmẹi gẹlẹmẹi mia.

---

1. Recorded by young man from Tikonko in Bo on April 18,
1960. I published an English translation of this tale in
Sierra Leone Bulletin of Religion (1961).

TALE 91: THE PALM WINE TAPPER AND THE SPIRIT[1]

   This story is about a palm wine tapper who was not afraid
of spirits.

   Once he was told, "You see that big raffia palm grove.
Do you understand that there is a spirit there who has eaten
many people? Therefore, do not go to tap palms there."

   The man who was unafraid of spirits said that he would
go to the raffia palm farm. He went there; he started to tap
wine. Once the man met a big man there; they greeted each
other; the tapper took out some of the wine and set it down;
they drank it; the tapper returned /to the town/. The next
morning the tapper went again /to the grove/. Every time
the tapper went looking for wine, he met the big man and
they would drink wine /together/.

Once the tapper dreamed that the man came to him.

The man said, "I am the owner of that raffia palm farm /where/ you were tapping /wine/. I am the spirit there. But do not be afraid. You will get a cat. I will make you rich; when you take the cat into your compound, whatever you tell the cat that you wish, the cat will give it to you."

Then the tapper awakened from his dream. He went and he got a cat. He brought this cat into his compound.

As soon as it was morning, the man said to the cat, "Cat, I want a very plump baby."

Immediately a plump baby appeared shouting and crying very sweetly. The palm wine tapper took the plump baby and gave it to his wife. The woman rejoiced greatly, because they had not had a child for a long time.

The next day the tapper said to the cat, "Cat, I want £500."

Immediately £500 appeared in the house. The tapper collected all the money. He gave a big party. He called all his friends; they spent the entire day at the party. They drank palm wine; everyone was drunk.

When night came, the tapper's wife said to him, "Oh, Wine Tapper, how did you happen to get such money?"

Then the tapper explained to her how he had gotten the cat in a dream; he told her everything.

The woman said, "Oh, yes; I have been wondering where you got this money."

As soon as morning came, the wine tapper met the old man.

The man spoke to him a lot; he said, "Comrade, Wine Tapper, look; recently I said to you, 'Do not explain our conversation to your wife. Do not tell anyone.' Look now you have explained everything. You will no longer have that cat."

The tapper said, "I accept your decision. I will give you my decision, but let us wait a while. Here is a little thing."

The remainder of the wine were there: the especially strong ones--whiskey, gin, and very strong stout. The tapper took out /these drinks/.

The tapper said, "First we will drink."

Oh, the spirit began to argue and argue. Then the spirit began to sing and to turn summersaults; he fell down. When morning came, all the drinks were inside the spirit and he began to tell everything that he had hidden from the palm wine tapper. When the spirit's head cleared, the palm wine tapper began to recount some of the spirit's secrets.

"Oh, yes," the spirit said, "Comrade, you have not explained this conversation vainly. I am not going to be angry with you. Take the cat. You and it will live together forever."

So at one time that happened: the spirit did not remain angry with the palm wine tapper, because wine will make a person tell secrets that he did not want to tell before.

Dọmẹi ji ndalongọ ndọbọ lọma na hi ẹẹ luwa ngafanga gbi ma.

Lọ yila ma kẹ ti ndenga ngi ma tẹ "Nduvugba wai ji bi tọma hẹi ngafa lọ na na hi nunga gbotȯ mẹnga ta luwama, fale baa li na nduvulọ bọma."

Kenẹi ji ta ẹẹ luva ngafa ma yẹ "Fale a li lọ na nduvu gbaẹ na hu." I li i ndọi bọ kẹ i ya na kẹ i tọtonga a ndọi ji bọla. Lọ yila ma kẹ i kenẹi jẹmbẹ yila malenga kẹ ti vanga ma kẹ i ndọi ji tẹnga gbuanga kẹ i tonga kẹ ti kpọlenga kẹ i yamanga. Ngele i wo gbọma kẹ i ya wati-o-wati i ye gbi lini ndọi ji gama gbema a kenẹi ji malelọ kẹ ta ta ti ndọi gbọlenga.

Lọ yila ma kẹ i henganga kẹ kenẹi ji wanga ngi gama.

Yẹ "Nya mia nya wo mia a nduvu kpaẹ na bi mbọma" yẹ "nya mia ngafẹi a nge na. Kẹ baa luwa." Yẹ "Bi gọnẹi ji majọngalọ." Yẹ "Nga gbekpelọ a bie" yẹ "gbamaile ve gọnẹi na bi va lọ la bi ye kulu hu gbọlọ leke kpẹlẹ bi ndeni gọnẹi na ma bẹ bi maningọ ma gọnẹi na a felọ bi wẹ."

Kẹ kenẹi ji kẹ i wunga hengẹi ji hu kẹ i ya kẹ i gọnẹi majọnga kẹ i yala ngi ye kuluhu.

Nge woi lọ leke kẹ i ndenga gọnẹi ma yẹ "Gọnẹi," yẹ "nya longọ a ndola gbọvọngọ wa."

A mẹ fia kẹ ndola gbọyọngọi ji gbianganga a yele a wọ manengọ wa. Kẹ kenẹi ji ndọbọmọi ji kẹ i ndola gbọvọngọi ji wumbunga kẹ i fenga ngi nyahẹi wẹ kẹ nyapoi gonẹnga ma kẹlẹma gbii ma gbmaile ndo ii ti yeya wọ.

Lọi ye pekẹi kẹ i ndenga gọnẹi ma yẹ "Gọnẹi," yẹ "nya longọ a pọng họndọ lọọlu."

Kia hu na hu gbandi na kẹ pọng họndọ lọọ lu na kẹ i
gẹnga pẹlẹi na bu. Kẹ i ti kpẹlẹ yandọnga kẹ i komẹ wa
gulanga kẹ i ngi mbanga gbi lolinga ti luvani komẹ hu lọ
kpẹing ndọgbọengọ wọ yaa ha ti ndọi bọi hani numu-o-numu
ndọi houngọi na.

Kpindi wẹi lọ leke kẹ ngi nyahẹi ndenga ngi ma yẹ "Kuo,"
yẹ "Ndọgbọ," yẹ "gbẹe na bi ye hijenga a navo gbotoi ji
bonda-e?"

Kẹ ngi hungẹnga a ngie gbọọ i gọnẹi ji majọni ye hengẹi
ji hu kẹ i hugẹnga kpẹlẹ kẹ i gbọyọnga.

Kẹ nyapoi bẹ yẹ "Eh hẹ, nya gẹ nya nẹmahu ngi lima ngẹ
'mindo lọ ba hijenga a navoi ji?'"

Ngele woi lọ leke kẹ ndọbọmọi ta kena wovẹi ti gomẹnga.

Kenẹi i yia ngi ma kaka yẹ "Ndakpẹi ndọbọ" yẹ "gbe na ngi
ndenga gẹ bi ma ngẹ 'Baa njẹpẹi ji hugẹ a nyaha. Baa hugẹ
a numu-o-numu.' Gbe na bi hugẹnga. Gọnẹi na bẹ bẹ yaa lila."

Ọ ta bẹ yẹ "Kungọi" yẹ "nga yialọma," yẹ "kẹ mawulọ lẹ"
yẹ "hani wulo lọ mbei."

Hi ndọi ji ye mọni jisia ti loni kenẹing ye kpaya-kpayangọi
ji wiski ji kẹ jin ji kẹ stouti wa wai jisia kpẹlẹ kẹ i kpuanga.

Yẹ "Mu ji gbọle lẹ pẹing."

O, kena wovẹi ji ngafẹi ji kẹ ti tọtonga na tikpọi tikpọi,
o kẹ ngafẹi tọtonga a wolela bẹ a windẹ ngi wumahu a gula.
Ngele wo ya na gbọ na kpẹlẹ gẹ ngi gohu kẹ i tọtonga a ndela
ge kpẹlẹ na i ndọwunga ndọbọmọ kẹ i kpẹlẹ hungẹnga. Kia na
ndọi ji leweni ngi yama kẹ ndọbọ tọtonga a tẹnga hugẹla.

"Kuo e" yẹ "ndakpẹi," yẹ "bii njẹpẹi ji hugẹni gbama."
Yẹ "Nge ya lile bi ma;" yẹ "li a gọnẹi ji" yẹ "kuna fọ i wata"
yẹ "wa yalọ a hei."

Hi wọ hindẹi ji wie na aah, ngafẹi ji ii yaa wọ fọ lileni
ndọbọma gbamai ndọ ta a pielọ numu bi bi li hu yẹpẹi gbi hungẹ
na bẹ wọ hugẹmani ii bi ma a ngeva.

---

1. Recorded by man from Bo in Bo on April 16, 1960.

TALE 92: THE SPIRIT'S GOLDEN CUP[1]

At one time a spirit dug a well and placed a gold cup in it.

At one time there was a very long road on which a great many people used to walk. This big road opened the heart of the country; it went past the spirit's town. The spirit dug a well /by a road/. The water that came from the well was very clean.

What happened?

The spirit put a gold cup near the water. He placed it by the edge of the water so that anyone who came could drink with it. The rule that he made was: if a person drank the water, he should not take away the gold cup. The spirit would not drink water from any cup except his gold cup.

Everyone used to travel on that road. When they came, they drank water in the gold cup, they thought that it was very beautiful.

Once a nursing mother came on this road. Her child was sitting on her back. As soon as she came, she saw the cup; she drank water in the cup; her child cried for the cup. The woman should have returned the cup, but she took it, she threw it into her bundle, she tied it up tightly, and she carried it away. She took the cup and hid it in the ceiling of her own house.

The spirit had been busy all day; he came in the afternoon. He had been busy eating food all day; he was thirsty. He searched for the cup; he searched; he searched; he searched; he searched; he searched; he did not see it; he searched for it; he did not see it. By morning he /still/ had not seen the cup; he looked into the distant sky, he did not see the cup, he went.

At one time the spirit had a big bell. If the cup was somewhere and the spirit rang the bell, the bell would dis- cover the location of the cup. Then the spirit went; he struck the bell--ki; the spirit heard /the cup/ very far away; the bell traced /the location of/ the cup to the town. Then the spirit started on the road; he went for a while; then he rang the bell which traced the cup again; now he was not far from the cup.

As soon as people /heard the bell/, they said that some- thing dangerous was about to happen. They all left the town. Only the woman and her son remained /in the town/; everyone else went.

The spirit came and arrived in the town. He looked until
he saw his cup in that house. He went there and found only
the woman and her son. As soon as the spirit took the cup
/by that time he was very thirsty/, he did not bother that
woman and her son; he /just/ killed them; he swallowed them;
he took his cup; he returned; he drank some water.

That is why extreme greed is bad. At one time that woman
was greedy; she and her child died, because she saw the gold
cup and decided to carry it away because she had never seen
such a beautiful cup. She and her son took the cup that she
had wanted at one time. That spirit killed them. In the
evening when the people came there, they did not find a single
person; they did not find the woman and her son; they saw only
their blood there; they did not see the spirit who had eaten
them for his cup. For that reason excessive greed is bad.

Hani wai na wọ i ndowei bọni i kani gbolu kọpui gulanga.

Pele wa yila i yẹ wọ na. Ye pelei ji huguhango wa. Nunga
ta jia la faha gboto wa mia ye jia a ye pelei na. Pele wa mia
ndawọngọ ndọlọ lima ye wa yela. I yẹ na na hani wai ji ke i
ya hani wai ji ngi tei ji i yẹ na gbalanga kẹ i ndowei bọnga.
Ye ndowei na ye njẹi na a gbua na kọlengọ wa.

I ye wie?

Kẹ i kani gbolui ji gula njẹi ji mia. Tawei ji gbatẹngọ
yela a kani gbolu kọpui ji-o; kẹ i kulanga njẹi na ya numui
gbi wa le kọ bi longa la bi kpọle. Kẹ sawei le wọ i kẹni numui
bi njẹi gbọlenga bẹ kani gbolui lawẹi ji gbua na. Hani wai ji
ẹẹ nja gbọle tawa yeka gbi hu kẹ lọ-o ngi kani lawẹi ji.

Numui gbi ti yẹ na le a pelei na ta wa ta njẹi na gbọle
kọpui na. Tao ti kọpui na lọnga vui nyandengọ wa a yela tie.

Wati yila kẹ koima yila kẹ i wa a pelei ji. Ngi loi ji
heingọ na i ngi yeya kẹ i wa. Kia le i wani i kọpui ji lọni
le i njẹi ji gbọleni hu kẹ ngi loi wọnga kọpui ji va ta bẹ i
yẹma i kọpui ji yama kẹ i kọpui ji wumbunga kẹ i pilinga bọntii
hu i ngi kpaung kẹ i ya la. I li i ndọwu hu ti ye pẹlẹ bu mia
ye ngelei ya.

Jina hani wai ji i luva hu kpeing kẹ i wa. Kpọkọ voloi
ji i wa i luva mẹhei ji mẹma kpẹing. Nja gbọle mai ji lọ na
ngi ma. I kọpui ji gọkọi. I kọkọi i kọkọi i kọkọi i kọkọi ii
tọni i kọkọi ii tọni. Nge wongo gbẹ ii kọpui ji lọni; i nge
gbundọ hu gbe ii kọpui ji lọni kẹ i ya.

Bamande wa lọ wọ ngi yeya ye bamandei ji kọpui ji ya
hinda-o-hinda i ndenga bamandei ji a ndahoulọ. Kẹ i ya i ye
bamandei ji lewe kẹ kọ kẹ i mẹninga huguhangọ wa kẹ kọpui

ji i bamandei ji lahoua tẹ hu kẹ ta bẹ i ye pelei ji hounga; i li haa kẹ i ya gbọma kẹ i bamandei ji lewenga kẹ kọpui ji i ndahounga gbọma. Na hu na hu ii yaa guhani na hu.

Kia le nunga bẹ ti humẹni le ye "Kabauakọ hindẹi na i yẹ wiema," kẹ ti kpẹlẹ ti gbua tẹ hu ti nyapoi ta ngi loi na le lo kẹ ti ya.

Hani wai ji i wa i wa kẹ i fonga tẹi ji hu. I kpe wa haa kẹ i ngi kọpui na lọnga pẹlẹi na bu. I li i nyapoi ji ta ngi loi ji felekpe lọ male lọ na. Ta bẹ kia le i ngi kọpui na gbuani na hu na njabọlemani gbongọ wa le na ngi la-e ta bẹ ii mọnẹ nyapoi na ta ngi loi na venja kpẹlẹ mia i ti wani i ti gbọi i ngi kọpui le i wa i njẹi gbọle.

Na va mia Hani mai ye hulengọ wa ii nyandeni. Nyapoi na mani wọ hani mai ma tao ta ngi loi na i ti venja kpe jukuilọ jifa i kọpui na lọnga kpatẹngọ a kani gbolui aa ye i lima la jifa wọ gba ii ya kọpu nyande bondẹi na lọni. Ta ngi loi ti lima kọpui i yẹma ti yeya i mai wọ na ma. Hani wai na i ti wa wọfọ. Kpọkọi ji nunga ti wana na ti wani tii numu yakpe bẹ male ti maleni nyapoi na-o ngi loi na-o. Ke le ti ngamẹi na ti tọni na tii tọni hani wai na i ti mẹ wọ fọ ngi kọpui na va. Na va hani mai hulengọ wa ma ii nẹni.

---

1. Recorded by young man from Pujehun in Freetown on May 13, 1960.

TALE 93: THE BUSH SPIRITS' GIFTS[1]

If a hump is on a person's back, it is sickness, but if a hump is on your chest, you bought it with a big colored country cloth.[2]

In a town there were a man with a hump on his back and his companions. The man was walking about; he was walking about with one of his companions.

The hunchback said, "Let me go onto the path to urinate."

The hunchback went onto the path.

As soon as the man went onto the path, some spirits saw him; they said, "If a thing is on a thing, let us take it off, or if it is not on, let us put it back immediately--gbu."

Then the spirits put the hunchback inside the dancing ring. A big hump tree was standing there; the humps hung

everywhere. The spirits danced around /the tree/ and they
sang:

> "Round and round,
> "If people meet you in the dance, they will
>   beat you.
> "Round and round,
> "Let us hang it there, they will beat you."

The spirits said, "If a thing is on a thing, let us take
it off, or if it is not on, let us put it back on."

Then they took the hump off the man's back--whoosh; they
hung it /on the tree/; they shoved him away--whoosh. Then the
man went on his way.

When the man came out of the path and into the town, his
companion asked, "Comrade, recently we were in the town; we
saw a hump on your back; now your back is flat." He said,
"How can that be? What have you done so that your back is
flat?"

The man said, "When I go there, I will show you."

"When will you do it?"

The man said, "We will go there tomorrow morning." The
man spoke to the town chief's son, even though he should not
have said anything. He said, "We will go there tomorrow
morning."

In the morning they went there.

When they had just reached the place, the man said, "Enter
that place, let me see."

Then the chief's son entered the place with a big hump on
his back.

The man said, "Enter there."

The chief's son entered.

As soon as the spirits saw him, they began to dance; they
said, "If a thing is on a thing, let us take it off, or if it
is not on, let us put it back on."

> "Round and round,
> "If people meet you in the dance, they will
>   beat you.
> "Round and round,
> "Let us hang it there, they will beat you."

They said, "If a thing is on a thing, let us take it off, or if it is not on, then let us put it back on."

And they took the hump off--whoosh; they hung it yonder /on the hump tree/; they shoved him away--whoosh.

Then the chief's son went in the town; he said /to his companion/, "Your father is poor; if the spirits take the hump off your back, you do not give them anything."

But a person should not speak that way to the spirits. If you say that to them, you will hurt them a lot. A person should not say that to them at all; they do not want anything. If you say that to them, you will hurt them a lot. If you have a hump on your back and the spirits have taken it off, you do not give them anything.

Then the chief's son took a big colored country cloth; he placed it on his back. Then he went and entered that particular place; he stood there.

As soon as the chief's son arrived, he said, "Be quiet."

Then the spirits became quiet.

The chief's son said, "Recently the spirits took a hump off the back of a person whose father is poor; that person did not give anything. I have come to give you something because you took my hump from my back and my father is rich."

The chief's son hurt the spirits. They put him back inside the dancing ring.

The spirits said, "If a thing is on a thing,

"Round and round,
"If people meet you in the dance, they will
        beat you.
"Round and round,
"Let us hang it there, they will beat you."

The spirits said, "If a thing is on a thing, let us take it off, or if it is not on, let us put it back on."

Then the spirits took the bundle from the chief's son; he remained there; they took it from him and they set a hump forcefully on his chest; they took off the bundle and they put a hump on his chest.

The spirits said, "The hump on his chest--he bought it with the big colored country-cloth; that is why we put it on his chest." They said, "A person should not reward us for

this act. If we take the hump off your back, you should leave,
you should go quietly, but you should not make a reward. As
he gave us this reward, we put that hump on his chest. He
bought his chest hump with this big colored country-cloth.
That is the proverb."

Ngaungauẹ ya numu woma higbe le kẹ i ya bi gohu kẹ bi
ngeyani a kula nyẹi gbali lọ.

Ndakpẹi ji mia ngaungauẹ ngi woma ti tẹi hu ta ngi mbanga.
Kẹ i longa jẹjiama kẹ i ya i lewenga kẹ ta ngi mbaẹ ti wama.

Yẹ "Gbẹ ngi wua pele hu."

Ngaungauẹ ji ngi woma kẹ i wuanga pelei ji hu.

Kia i wuani leke kẹ ti ngi lọnga tẹ "Hinda a yẹ hinda ma,
mu kpiama ọ ẹẹ yẹẹ ma mu ngama ma a mẹ gbu."

Kẹ ti ngi wunga ngitiwaiya ngaungauẹ wulu wai loni,
ngaungauẹ hẹlẹni hu gbi. Ta mbembe kẹ ti ngolei gbianga:

"Tutumbembe tumbembe,
"Numui ta male ti ndewe.
"Tutumbembe tumbembe,
"A mu hẹlẹ mia ti ndewe."

Tẹ "Hinda a yẹ hinda ma mu gbi mu kpiama ọ ẹẹ yẹẹ ma mu
ngama ma."

Kẹ ti kpia ngi womẹi na vẹlọ kẹ ti hẹlẹnga kẹ ti tukpenga
vẹing. Kẹ i ya ngi lingọi.

Jina i gbiani na i wani tẹi hu na. Kẹ ngi mbaẹ ngi mọlinga
yẹ "Ndakpẹi mua woini mu tẹi ji hu gẹ ngaungauẹ ji bi woma mu
tọnga; na bi woma ya sahẹing." Yẹ "Gbẹe na? Bi ye pienga na
na hi bi womẹi ji ya sahẹing?"

Ta bẹ yẹ yẹ "Ji wọi nga li nga na gẹ wọi a bie."

"Ba ye pie?"

Ye "Ma lilọ na sina a ngenda." I ndenga ta mahẹi loi ma
na. Yẹ "Ma lilọ na sina a ngenda."

Kẹ ngele wonga kẹ ti ya na.

Kia ti lini ti foni leke hindẹi na, yẹ "Wua hindẹi na lẹ."

Kẹ i wuanga na inge ngaungauẹ waẹ wẹni ngi woma kuyọ.

Ye "Wua na."

Kẹ i wuanga na.

Kia leke ti ngi lọni kẹ ti ndoli gulanga tẹ "Hinda a yẹ hinda ma mu kpiama ọ ẹẹ yẹ ma mu ngama ma.

"Tutumbembe tumbembe,
"Numui ta male ti ndewe.
"Tutumbembe tumbembe,
"A mu hẹlẹ mia ti ndewe."

Tẹ "Hinda a yẹ hinda ma mu kpiama ọ ẹẹ yẹ ma kẹ mu ngama ma."

Kẹ ti kpianga ma vẹ lọ kẹ ti hẹlẹnga mia kẹ ti tukpenga vẹing.

Kẹ i ya i ya tẹi hu ngi lingọi ji tei ji hu kẹ i ya na. Yẹ "Wua wu kẹni ti nyaningọ, ngaungauẹ ti gbianga lọ wu woma wu hani ve."

Kẹ numu ẹẹ na le ngafanga ma bi ndenga lọ ti ma a gbalẹ lọ ti ma wa. Numu ẹẹ na le ti ma keing; tii lọni a hani gbi, bi ndenga lọ ti ma a gbalẹlọ ti ma wa. Yẹ "Ngaungauẹ ji i nya woma nya ndẹi." Ti wu ndẹi gbianga lọ gẹ wẹ hani ve.

"Nya ngi lima lọ." Kẹ i kula nyẹi gbali ji wumbua kẹ i nda mbei kẹ i ji be wumbunga kẹ i nda mbei. Kẹ i ya kẹ i longa kẹ i wua ye hindẹi na i lọni na.

Kia leke i foni na yẹ "A londo."

Kẹ ti hu yẹnga gili.

Yẹ "Nasia gẹ ti kẹkẹni ti nyaningọ ta ngaungauẹ gbia ti woma tẹ hani ve. Nya ngi wanga ngẹ ngi hani ve wu wẹ gbamani nya wu nya ndẹi gbianga nya woma, nya kẹkẹ gbatẹngọi."

Kẹ i gbalẹnga ngafanga ma kẹ ti ngamanga ndoli hu.

Tẹ "Hinda a yẹ hinda ma,

"Tutumbembe tumbembe,
"Numui ta male ti ndewe.
"Tutumbembe tumbembe,
"A mu hẹlẹ mia ti ndewe."

Tẹ "Hinda a yẹ hinda ma mu kpiama ọ ẹẹ yẹ ma kẹ mu ngama ma."

Kẹ ti kpianga ma kẹ i longa mia kẹ ti kpianga kẹ ti heinga ngi lima vi kẹ ti na gbianga kẹ ti punga ngi woma.

Te "Ji ngi limei ji" te "i ngeyani a kula nyẹi gbali lọ
famia mu puni ngi lima," te "gbamai numu ẹe mu pawa beindo
hindẹi ji va mu hindẹi ji wienga lọ ba gbialọ na bi li bi wẹ
yẹlẹng kẹ numu ẹe pawa wie. Kia i pawẹi ji wienga famia mu
ngaungauẹ na wẹlẹnga ngi limẹi ji. Ngi lima ngaungauẹ ji i
ngeyani a kula nyẹi gbali wai ji lọ. Ye salei mia."

---

1. This proverb tale was recorded by man from Mattru Jong
in Freetown on September 6, 1960.
2. Cloth made from fine indigenous cotton has long been made
in Mendeland (See T. J. Alldridge, The Sherbro and Its Hinterland (London:1901:96-99).

TALE 94: THE SPIRITS AND THE YOUNG WOMEN[1]

At one time there was a big dance in a big town, please.

As soon as some spirits in heaven heard of the dance,
four young men arranged to go down to earth. These four spirits
were named Nyandebo, Hawudui, Seigulajembe, and Ndamawa.[2] As
soon as the day that they had arranged to go to earth came,
they got up and put all their things in one place. They tied
their things in a big bundle. The only road that the spirits
were able to come down to earth on was a big rope which hung
so that the spirits could come out of heaven and climb down
to earth. When the time that they had arranged came, the
spirits hung the rope; they climbed on it; they jumped down;
they untied the rope and hid it in a big forest. Then the
spirits dressed themselves handsomely; they went to the dance.

When the spirits arrived at the dance, four young women
liked them a lot. The dance was performed for four days. As
soon as the dance was finished, the youths said goodbye and
that they wanted to return /home7. When the young women
heard this, they said that the young men should not go and
leave them. The young women said that they should all go.
Throughout the night no one slept; the young women were begging to go throughout the night until morning. The young men
pointed out all the disadvantages; the young women refused to
accept them.

As soon as the time that they had arranged to leave came,
the young women dressed themselves finely; they arranged their
bundles; they went to say goodbye to their families. They
spent the entire day walking. As soon as they were approaching
where the young men had hidden the rope, they all stopped. When

they stopped, the young men said that each person go with his own young woman into the bush to beg her /not to go with him/.

As soon as they went into the bush, Seigbulajembe and Ndamawa entered with their young women who agreed to remain.

But before they would leave them, the young women asked, "When will you return to us? Tell us where and when you will return here."

The young men said to them, "Whenever any big dance is performed in this town, we will come here. You call us; we will come."

When the young men said this, the young women agreed.

At that time Nyandebo and Hawudui were completely unsuccessful with their own young women. When the young men saw that night was coming, they explained all about themselves to the young women.

As soon as they had explained everything to them, the young women said, "If you died, we would die. Even if you were beasts, we would to turn into beasts today."

This was said, and Hawudui said to Nyandebo, "Night is covering; our companions will be waiting."

As soon as he had spoken, Nyandebo also said to the young women, "We have begged for some time; we are unable to convince you to remain. Whatever we do, we now know that you will not agree to remain; I want to give you some advice. When we arrive, you will see trembling people, people with sore feet, lepers; when we are there, all the sick people will come to greet you. If they come to you, do not shun them. If they invite you to eat food, eat it."

When this was said, Nyandebo's young woman agreed. Hawudui's young woman said that she did not agree; because her skin was very fine, she would not lower herself anywhere for anyone.

As soon as they arrived, these trembling people--all these sick people--came joyfully to them. When a sick man came to greet Hawudui's young woman, she pushed him away. She told him that he should not touch her and that she had not come there to lower herself. When these sick people cooked food, she refused to eat it.

Nyandebo's own young woman used to go and tell proverbs with these sick people.[3] When they cooked food, she would sit and eat it. In the morning she went with very hot water to wash their sores. So she kept doing for some time until the time for them to return came.

As soon as they arranged to say goodbye to their young men, Nyandebo's friends began to advise her. They said, "When you leave here, examine the boxes before you; make your choice. Go there; do not take a new box--a shiney one. The one which you see is old and dirty, that is the one for you." They repeated everything; they said to her, "The box that is new and the one that has gold on it are boxes with bad-tempered creatures inside them. But the one that you see is old, that box has rich things in it."

One night the young women called their lovers; they said to them, "We want to return now."

And the young men asked them, "When do you want to journey?"

The young women said that they wanted to leave the next day.

When this was said, Nyandebo and Hawudi said, "Yes, we agree, but first let us tell our chief."

The young men went and explained everything to the chief who agreed to it.

That night the chief gathered all his messengers; he said to them, "Early tomorrow morning put all the boxes outside. When the boxes are in place, go to call these women."

As soon as morning came, the messengers put all the boxes outside. When they had finished, they went and told the chief. And the chief called one bearer to go to call the young women.

As soon as the women arrived, the chief said that they should choose a box.

Hawudui's young woman was the first at that time to go there. As soon as she looked at the boxes and she came to the one that was the shinest of all the boxes, she stood; she looked at it; she looked at it.

She said to the chief, "This is the one that I want."

Then the chief himself told his messengers that they should take it to her young man's own house. While the messengers were taking the box, the chief said to Nyandebo's young woman that she should look for her own choice.

Nyandebo's young woman was not hasty about making a selection. She looked at all the boxes; returned; she walked

past all the boxes four times. As soon as she came to the
older box, she stood; she looked at it; she looked at it; she
turned to the chief.

She said to him, "This is the one that I want."

When this was said, the chief called one of the messengers
and told him to take the box.

When the time to leave heaven arrived, a big rope was hung.
The rope was hung until the young women jumped down /to the
earth/. The young women spent the day returning /home/; they
arrived in the afternoon. When the arrived, Hawudui's young
woman sent someone to call all her family to say that she had
come with great wealth that she wanted to present to them.

Now at this time Nyandebo's young woman called her mother
and her father; she gave the box to them. They opened the box;
they took out all the rich things. They divided all the things
among the entire family; afterward there was still a surplus
/of rich things/. They began to trade, because the box con-
tained more items than there were family members; they gave
things to all the dancers in the town, there was still more.

While they were preparing for this feast, Hawudui's young
woman collected all her relatives. She gathered them /together/
in one large house. She told her father that he should open
the box. As soon as her father opened the box, a leopard jumped
out and killed her father. A lion jumped out also and all kinds
of other bad creatures filled the house; they ate all the
people. As soon as the animals had eaten the people, they began
to fight in the house; they continued to fight until they broke
a window; they came out of the house and went into the bush.

At one time this young woman's stubbornness caused all
the bad-tempered creatures to be in the bush today. Her companion caused wealth to be in the world today. Therefore, it
is inappropriate for a person to defy her husband's advice.

Komę waa yila i gulailǫ wǫ ta wa yila hu hoe.

Kia le ngafangęi nasia ti ngelegohu ti humęnini, kę ye
ndakpaonga nani ti hugbatęnga yeiva ngelebu. Ye ngafa nani
jisia ti lęi mia wǫ a ji: Nyandebo, Hawudui, Sęigulajęmbę
kę Ndamawa. Kia le foloi na ma ti hugbatęni yeiva ngele bu
ti hitini, kę ti ti hakęisia kpęlę wunga hinda yila. Ti gili
bundu wa hu. Kę pelei na le wǫ ngafanga ta gu a yeila ngelebu
ta lǫ a ji, ngeya wa mia wǫ ta hę, nahi ta gbua ngelegohu a
yei ngelebu. Ye ngeyęi ji mia wǫ ta hęlęma haa ti yei. Ji
wati na ti hugbatęni i hitini, kę ti ye ngeyęi ji hęlęnga.
Ti yei wǫ a ma wielǫ kę ti gbujanga. Ti gbujanga kę ti

fulonga ti nduwu ngola wa hu. Kẹ ti ti mayinga panda. Ti
fongọ-o kẹ ti hitia komẹi hu.

Ti hitẹngọi ji komẹi ji hu-o kẹ nyapo nasia ti longa a
tie gbong. Ye komẹi ji i gani wa nji nani valọ. Kia le ye
gomẹi ji i ye gbọwọma, kẹ kọngẹi jisia ti vẹinga tẹ ti longọ
ti yama. Kia le wọ nyahangẹi jisia ti ji humẹnini, kẹ ti
ndenga ti ma tẹ tẹ li ta ti lo. Tẹ ta ti kpẹlẹ mia ta li.
Kpindi na pii nji ye gila bẹ ii yena. Tii yini nyahangẹi
nasia manẹnẹma pii ngele ii wo. Ti kabande gbi gbualọ ti
ma gẹ tii guni ti ma ti lova.

Kia le wọ wati na ti hugbatẹni i hitini kẹ nyapoi jisia
ti ti mayinga panda ti ti hakẹi kpẹlẹ hugbatẹ kẹ ti ya ti
vẹli ti bondẹisia ma. Ti luvani wọ jiama kpẹing. Kia le
wọ ti ye foma mia wọ ti ngeyẹi ji lọwuni na, kẹ ti kpẹlẹ ti
longa. Ti longọi ji hu-o ke kọngẹi jisia ti ndenga, tẹ,
numu gbi ta ngi nda nyapoi ti li a ngila ngila ndọgbọi hu
kọti ti manẹnẹ.

Kia le ti wani ndọgbọi ji hu kẹ sẹigula jẹmbẹ ta Ndamawa
ti ngua ti nda nyapoi jisia ma, kẹ ti lumaa yama va.

Kẹ pẹing ta ya gu ti ma, kẹ nyapoi jisia ti ti mọlia, tẹ
"Jina wa mu yama, kẹ a hugẹ a mue migbe mia na wa yama mbeindo?"

Ke kọngẹi jisia be ti ndenga ti ma tẹ "Wati na le gomẹ
wa gbi i gulanga leke tẹi ji hu wa mbei, wu mu la loli, ma wa."

Ji lengọi ji-o kẹ ti lumanga.

Nyandebo ta Hawadui tii guni wọ fọ ti nda nyapoisia ma.
Kia ti tọni kẹ gbindi lọ wẹma, kẹ tia bẹ ti hugẹnga a tie
kpẹlẹ kọloni ti ma.

Kia le ti gbọyọni a hugẹla a tie kẹ nyahangẹi jisia ti
ndenga ti ma tẹ "Wu hama mu hama. Kia bẹ huanga mia a wue
mua bẹ ma luma woteva a huanga a foloi ji."

Ji lengọ-o kẹ Hawudui ndenga Nyandebo ma yẹ "Kpindi lọ
wẹma taa ti mbanga lọ ti mawuloma."

Kia leke i gbọyọni kẹ Nyandebo bẹ i ndenga ti ma yẹ "Mu
wu manẹnẹnga haa mu guni wu ma. Gbọ na le mua pie ta lọ. Mu
kọlọ na kẹ wu luma lova. Ndahi na le nya longọ ngi fe wu wẹ
ta lọ. Mu fonga, wa tọlọ kpẹlibla-o, ngelebla-o, kpọkpọbla-o
kẹ naa ma yẹ mi ma higbẹbla gbi ta wa ta va wuma. Ti waa wu
gama, wua ti jasi. Ti wu lolinga mẹhẹ ma, wu mẹ."

Ji ji lengọ-o kẹ Nyandebo nda nyapoi ji i lumanga ma.
Hawudui nda nyapoi ta kẹ i ndenga ye ẹẹ luma jifa ngi luwui
yekpengọ wa ii ngi ma maye mi hinda wueva.

Kia le wo ti foni, ke kpelingei jisia-o kena Higbebleisia gbele ke ti waa a gohune ti mahu. Kia higbemoi ji i wani ye i va Hawudui nda nyapoi ji ma ke i ngi lugbenge. Ke i ndenga ngi ma ye a foo ngi ma ii lini mia wuava mayemi hu. Higbeblei jisia ti mehei ji yiinga wo ee luma a mela.

Nyandebo nda nyapoi ji ta a lilo wo ta ti ti hei ta salei gula. Ti mehe yiinga wo ta ti mia ta hei ti me. Ngele wonga wo a ngendei i ya a njei gbandi kolo i wa i ti gbalemeisia wua fo. Hi mia haa i loi piema ti yama gbei a ya hiti.

Kia le wo ti hugbateni veliva ti lakpoi jisia ma, ke Nyandebo nda ndiamoi jisia ti tatonga a ndela ngi ma te "Bi yaa mbei hakei nasia hugbema ta to ko bi bi limei ye ndia, bi yaa na, baa kanga nina wumbu, taa ma ye mavogoyei. Ye na ba to magbulingo kpi kpi taa bo ngi we." Ti jiama kpele ti nde ngi ma te "Kanga ye na ninango-o ke ye na kani gboIui na ii ma ii yeni a haka lo nahi ndimavula vuheinga le mia ti hu. Ke ye na ba to magbulingo i yeni a kanga lo nahi kpatehaninga lee mia ti hu."

Kpindi yila ma ke nyapoi jisia ti ti lakpoi jisia lolinga ti nde ti ma te "Mu longo naa mu yama."

Ke ti lakpoi jisia ti ti molia te "Migbe mia naa ti longo ti jeijinga?"

Ke tia be ti ndenga ti ma te "Ti longo ti lii sina."

Ji lengo-o ke Nyandebo ke Hawudui ti ndenga te "Mn, mua, mu lumaa, ke gbe peing mu huge a mu mahei."

Ke ti ya ti huge gbele a mahei ji ke ta be i lumanga ma.

Kpindi na ke mahei i ngi lobla gbele legama i nde ti ma ye "A ngenda tete sina ti hakeisia gbele lekpe ngitiiya. Ti kpoyonga a ti legbela, ti li nyahangei jisia gama ti ti loli."

Ngele woi lo le wo ke ti hakei jisia kpele lekpenga ngitiiya. Kpoyongo-o ke ti ya ti huge a mahei. Ke mahei be i tombumo yila lolinga ye "I li i nyapoi jisia loli."

Kia le wo ti foni ke mahei i ndenga ti ma ye "Ti ti limei ye hakei nasia lia."

Hawudui nda nyahei ji yese mia wo i lini na. Kia le wo i ye hakei jisia hugbema ke i fonga ye ngila ma nahi i ye a volo i le hakeisia gbelema. I lo, i kpele, i kpele.

Ke i ndenga mahei ma ye "Ta mia ngi longo la."

Ke mahei be i ndenga ngi bublei jisia ma ye "Ti ngi we ti lila ngi lakpoi ye pele bu." Ti ye lima a hakei ji ke mahei ndenga Nyandebo nda nyapoi ji ma ye i ngi nda limei gokoi.

Ta ii magbẹli bẹ wueni. I kpẹlẹ gbeleilọ, i yama i jia ti
mahu nahi tengọ heima nani ma. Kia le wọ i foni kanga ye
ngova ngova wa yilama kẹ i longa, i kpele, i kpele, kẹ i
wotenga mahẹi gama.

I nde ngi ma yẹ "Ta mia ngi longọ la."

Ji lengọ-o kẹ mahẹi i ngi bumọ yila gbuanga i nde ngi
ma yẹ i lila.

Ji ti gbua gbe na ngelegohu i hitini, kẹ ti ngeya wa
hẹlẹnga. Ta mia wọ ti hẹlẹni la haa ti gbuja. Ti luvani
wọ yama kpẹing ta ya a foo a kpọkọ voloi. Ti fongọi ji hu-o
kẹ Hawudui nda nyapoi ji i numu longa ngi bondẹisia gbi lolima
yẹ "I wa a kpatẹ wa nahi longọ i majọna ti ma."

Na ye kpemẹi ji, Nyandebo nda nyapoi ji kẹ i ngi nje
lolinga ke ngi kẹkẹ i hakẹi ji majọ na ti ma. Ti ye kanga ji
lawo ti yẹ kpatẹhani jisia kpẹlẹ gbua hu. Ti kọle kọlẹ kpẹlẹ
mbondẹisia kpẹlẹma i mọnu. Ti felengọ wẹ lawo nahi tengọ mu
lọlu gbọyọngọ ma, hakẹi i mọnu mbondẹisia ma. Ti fe gomẹngablẹi
jisia gbi wẹ ti yẹ ye tẹi ji hu i mọnu lọ gbọma ti ma.

Ti yẹ ye kpatẹ gomẹi ji lọ gama kẹ Hawudui nda nyapoi ji
gunga ngi nda bondẹi jisia kpẹlẹ ma. I ti yandọ pẹlẹ wa yila
bu. Kẹ i ndenga ngi kẹkẹ ma yẹ "I hakẹi ji lawo." Kia le wọ
ngi kẹkẹ i hakẹi ji lawoni, kẹ kolui ji i gbuja kẹ i ngi wanga.
Kẹ sugbui ji bẹ i gbuja, kẹ naa fula vuhẹinga gbi le ti gbua
ti pẹlei na nave kpang ti ti kpẹlẹ me. Kia le ti kpọyọni a ti
mẹla kẹ ti tatoa a lapila pẹlẹi ji bu. Ti loima haa kẹ ti
kanyamẹi ji wonga. Ti gbua wọ ti li ndọgboi hu.

Nyapoi ji wohu gbunda mia wọ i pienga fula vuhẹinga ti
ndọgboi hu a foloi ji. Ngi mba ji ta ta mia wọi pienga
kpatẹi ndunya a foloi ji. Faa ma ii houni numu i ngi hini
layia gbuahu.

---

1. Recorded by young man from Bunumbu in Freetown on February
12, 1960.
2. Nyandebo, Too Handsome; Hawudui, Death Prone; Seigulajembe,
Rattle-rattle; Ndamawa, Great Sleeper.
3. Proverbs (sale) mark the speech of culturally sophisticated
Mende (see discussion in Chapter 2).

TALE 95: KPAULA AND THE SPIRITS[1]

The story that I am going to tell is about Mr. Kpaula
and the spirits.

At one time there was a man whose name was Kpaula. He
was a farmer. Not very far from the town in which he lived
was an old sacred place where no one would work. If anyone
said that he was going to work there, people would warn him.

They would say, "Do not work there, because if you do,
something bad will happen."

Kpaula was annoyed by that rule and he was also very
stubborn. He was determined that he would go to work in
that bush.

One day Kpaula sharpened his matchet--kene kene. He
went saying that he was going to mark his farm in that bush.

As soon as Kpaula started to cut the brush, he heard a
person asking,

"Who is it; who is it in this deserted place?
"Who is it; who is it in this deserted place?"

Kpaula said,

"It is I; Kpaula is in this deserted place."

Then someone asked him again,

"What is Kpaula doing in this deserted place?"

Kpaula said,

"Kpaula is cutting brush in this deserted place."

Then the voice from the tree burst out singing,

"Oh, men, women,
"Let us go; let us help Kpaula."

As soon as that was said, all the bush began to move--
gbele, gbele, gbele, gbele, gbele, gbele; at once the brush
was cut: a tree fell--bi--here; a tree fell--bi--there.
Before long, the bush had been cut; everything was cut, and
no one was there.

After one week Kpaula said to himself, "I will start to
fell trees."

Kpaula took his ax which was very sharp--kene kene.

As soon as Kpaula went /to the farm/ and had cut down
two trees, the third tree asked,

"Who is it; who is it in this deserted place?
"Who is it; who is it in this deserted place?"

"It is I; Kpaula is in this deserted place."

"What is Kpaula doing in this deserted place?"

"Kpaula is felling trees in this deserted place."

The voice said,

"O, men, women,
"Let us go; let us help Kpaula."

As soon as this was said, you immediately saw that some one had felled a tree--ngǫnǫ; the smell of trees was everywhere, everywhere; the smell of tree filled the entire farm. All the trees were lying on the ground as if a person had trampled a half-grown forest completely.

When the farm had finished drying, Kpaula said, "Tomorrow I will go to burn my farm. Perhaps the rainy season is not far off."

When morning came, Kpaula took one bundle of kindling and went /to the farm/; he laid a little fire; he lit the fire.

As soon as the smoke rose to the sky, a voice in a tree said to him,

"Who is it; who is it in this deserted place?
"Who is it; who is it in this deserted place?"

Kpaula said,

"It is I; Kpaula is in this deserted place."

"What is Kpaula doing in this deserted place?"

Kpaula said,

"Kpaula is burning a farm in this deserted place."

"O, men, women,
"Let us go; let us help Kpaula."

Of course, a person could not see the source of the smoke; he simply saw everywhere, everywhere that the fire was. Even Kpaula himself, if he were not careful, would have been trapped in the fire. Quickly the farm was burned completely. Then Kpaula stooped over in the bush to work; nothing was in the burned farm.

So it was and time passed. Kpaula had sat for some time waiting; he had the money for all the rice seed and he sharpened all the hoes. Kpaula sat there waiting for the first rains in order to plant the rice.

When the rain came, Kpaula said, "Tomorrow I will go to plant /the rice/."

Kpaula went to the farm to plant the rice. Then he sowed the rice; he did not scatter it playfully, he sowed it carefully; he remained working alone, he sowed all the rice carefully. Of course, Kpaula knew that he was not making the farm alone; he stubbornly continued to farm at that time. The situation was approaching a climax (lit., head). When all the sowing of the farm was finished well, Kpaula took a hoe.

As he was about to plow /the rice under the ground/, the voice in the tree asked him,

"Who is it; who is it in this deserted place?
"Who is it; who is it in this deserted place?"

Kpaula said,

"It is I; Kpaula is in this deserted place."

"What is Kpaula doing in this deserted place?"

"Kpuala is plowing rice in this deserted place."

"O, men, women,
"Let us go; let us help Kpaula."

Very quickly--Kpaula did not see anyone--but there were an endless number of hoes ploughing the farm; all the farm work was finished in less than two hours. Then Kpaula went away. Thus they kept doing the farm work together for some time; the rice dried.

At that time Kpaula sent his little child to watch the rice. Of course, but would a bird sit there? If you saw the farm, you would think that people were filling the entire farm--that there were more people than stumps in the farm! No bird's mouth got even one grain of rice; the rice dried.

The morning when Kpaula was going to cut just three /rice plants/--he was going to cut a little of the rice, Kpaula sent his son /to the farm/ first. When the little child went /to the farm/, he met a palm bird with a bell on his foot sitting there.

"Oh," the boy said, "haa-haa!"

And the palm bird turned to him, it said, "As you said 'haa,' as you said 'haa;' what rice eating bird would have a bell on his foot? Lai wa a wa lai. With a bell on his foot?"

Instruments began to play. The child did not know the source of the sound; Gbang, drum, drum, shake-shake--all the instruments were playing, and the child started to dance. /As he danced/, he broke the rice.

In all that area the people who had remained in the town heard the sound of dancing; they said, "Kpaula, Comrade, are you sitting down? Go to your own farm; a little noise is coming from there. We warned you at one time; go there quickly to see /what is happening/."

Kpaula ran down the road--kibi kibi kibi kibi; he arrived /at the farm/. When he arrived, he was about to beat the child.

"Why, Child, you came to drive away birds! Why are you making noise? Did you come to dance this way? Look, the rice is broken."

"Father, wait; go; see the bird over there," the boy said. "That bird caused all this."

And Kpaula pursued the bird, "Haa-haa!"

The bird turned to Kpaula; at that time everything was quiet; the bird said, "As you said, 'haa,' as you said, 'haa;' what rice-eating bird has a bell on his foot? Lai wa a wa lai."

The instruments started to play: kpo gbungu gbungu gbungu gbungu; Kpaula started to dance. /Kpaula danced so vigorously that/ perspiration poured here, perspiration poured there. Kpaula kept dancing. He and his son did not notice anyone cutting the rice, but all the rice was cut, all the rice dropped off, and all the rice was taken from the farm. Not a single bundle /of rice/ remained in the farm.

Oh, Kpaula put his hands on his head; he entered the town with an /anguished/ cry.

Some people said, "What is it?"

"Ah," Kpaula said, "trouble has fallen. I did not get even a single bundle of rice; the spirits took all the rice."

"Ah, I myself warned you long ago."

"In any case," Kpaula said, "I am a man. I know what I will do."

Then Kpaula went to a diviner.

The diviner said to Kpaula, "What I see is that it is the spirits. /It was their land/ where you cut that farm, where the child was when the ripening time was coming and you had told him to watch the rice carefully. You should take a lot of pepper to smoke out the spirits. When you smoke them out, they will give you your rice, and they will not do anything else to you." The diviner said, "But you saw at brush cutting time, at tree felling time, at rice planting time, and at bird driving time that as soon as you began to work, the job was done. Ah, it was the spirits who were doing the work; that was why at one time we warned you not to work at that place. And now the only thing for you to do is to smoke them out; they will give you your rice."

Kpaula said that he understood.

Kpaula bought some pepper; he bought the number of bags that the diviner instructed; Kpaula carried all the bags to the mouth of a cave. When Kpaula was going there, a big crowd /of people/ came with him. Kpaula said that the people should help him; they saw what he was doing. Kpaula came and laid a fire; he put the pepper at the mouth of the cave and laid a fire on it; he began to smoke out the spirits.

Of course, before long the spirits began to suffocate inside; they were coughing and sneezing. Kpaula was oppressing them. Although they were truly spirits, they could not overcome this situation even with their strength as spirits. Before afternoon (lit., the sun swung sideways), the heat had overcome the spirits: children were fainting; women were fainting.

Then the spirits' chief said, "What would be good: let us give /Kpaula/ this rice. At one time we labored for the rice, but we did not expect the course of action that our companion has started against us. Let us give him this rice."

The spirits started to put the rice in baskets.

As Kpaula was breathlessly doing his work, he saw the cave spirit--vu. A man came out of the cave to Kpaula; he was carrying rice on his back.

The spirit said, "Father, look /here is/ your rice; father, look /here is/ your rice."

Very quickly in unending succession the spirits brought all the rice and gave it to Kpaula. When the spirits brought the rice so, the people carried it into the town; so they continued /to do/ until the spirits had given Kpaula all his rice. Kpaula took it into the town.

So that was what at one time Kpaula's stubbornness caused, but Kpaula's heart was strong--he was always bold in heart; he achieved success (lit., sweetness) in the end.

The story is finished.

Dọmẹi ye ji ngi kpuama kọloni kenẹi Kpaula lọma ta ngafanga.

Kena yila mia wo ye na ngi la a Kpaula. Kpayengemọ yẹla a ngie. Tei na i ye hu hẹma wova yila yẹlọ na maguhangọ kulo a tẹi. Numu gbi ee yenge na. Numu gbi bi longa wọ bi yenge na, nunga ta bi lahi lọ.

Tẹ "Baa yenge na jifa bi peinga hinda nyamu a gbua lọ."

Kpaula ji ngi lilengọ yẹla tao ngi wohu gbundangọ i ndei lọ huleng yẹ 'i yengema ndọgbọi na hu.'

Folo yila kẹ i ngi bogbẹi yakpa kẹ nẹkẹ nẹ i li yẹ 'Ndọgbọi na hu' yẹ 'ta tifa gulama.'

Kia le i tọtoni a ndoe ji wiela kẹ numu kẹ i mẹninga numu yila a ngi mọli

"Ye le ye le tomboi ya?
"Ye le ye le tomboi ya?"

Ta bẹ yẹ "Nya le Kpaula le tomboi ya."

Kẹ numui ngi mọlia gbọma yẹ

"Kpaula a gbọ wie tomboi ya?"

Ta bẹ yẹ "Kpaula a ndoe wie tomboi ya."

Kẹ ngului ji ngi wo gbiama yẹ

"O hingẹisia-o, nyahangẹisia-o,
"A mu li, mu gbọ Kpaula ma-o."

Njẹpẹi na lengọ leke ndọgboi gbi a hije gbẹlẹ-gbẹlẹ-gbẹlẹ-gbẹlẹ a ndoe wie le ngului a gula bi nga ji lewe le bi nga ji lewe bei kẹ hu ii guhani kẹ ti ndọgboi na loinga ti kpọyọ hu gbi ya wakali o ya numu gbi ii hu.

Kẹ Kpaula yakpe wuki yila woma kẹ i ndea yẹ ngi ma gbọma "Ngi pọi tọto."

Kẹ i koni ji wumbua ta bẹ nyakpangọ kẹnẹkẹnẹ.

Kia le i ndei ngului ma fele ya sawẹi na kẹ ngui ngi mọlia

"Ye le ye le tomboi ya?
"Ye le ye le tomboi ya?"

"Nya le Kpaula le tomboi ya."

"Kpaula a gbǫ wie tomboi ya?"

"Kpaula a pǫi wie tomboi ya."

Yẹ

"Kuo hingẹisia-o, nyahangẹisia-o,
"A mu li mu gbǫ Kpaula ma-o."

O ya njẹpẹi ji lengǫ leke bi yẹ tǫ le numui ye na ngonǫ
pǫ wui gungǫ hu gbi hu gbi kpa na gbi ngi gui gunga na a-mẹi
pǫponde pǫi gbǫyǫa mia. Kpẹlẹ ndangǫ ndǫma kia numu a njǫpǫ
nẹmgbẹ yẹ ngeya wuai gbi.

Ji na kpa ji benga i gbǫyǫa kẹ Kpaula ndea yẹ "Nga lilǫ
sina ngi nya kpa hu mǫ tẹnga hamẹi ma ii yaa guhani."

Ngele woi lǫ kẹ i hẹmui ji gbua ngili yakpe kẹ i ya i
ngǫmbui woi la kẹ i toanga.

Kia le ndului ji lẹni ngele ma, ngului ngi mǫlia

"Ye le ye le tomboi ya?
"Ye le ye le tomboi ya?"

Yẹ

"Nya le Kpaula le tomboi ya."

"Kpaula a gbǫ wie tomboi ya?"

Yẹ

"Kpaula a kpa mǫ tomboi ya."

"Kuo, hingẹisia-o, nyahangẹisia-o,
"A mu li mu gbǫ Kpaula ma-o."

Ingẹ na ta numu ii yaa yẹ ndului hiye wele lǫ ta tǫ le
hu gbi hu gbi hu gbi hu gbi ngǫmbui ta hu gẹlẹnga ii le yela
vuli ta ngi Kpaula vuli ii yẹ ngi mahugbẹ i yẹ loma ngǫmbui
hu. Folo kẹ kpa na i mǫa i gbǫyǫa kẹ Kpaula wẹlẹ a ndǫgboi
hu a pie gbẹ-o-gbẹ ii yẹni mǫtui ma.

Hingǫ wati lengǫ ji na i heinga haa i mawonga mba gbalẹi
gbi sǫngǫi na ngi yeya kẹ i kali gbi ngakpanga i heini na a
hamayẹi ye haleyẹi mawoa kǫ i mbẹ i wu.

Ye njẹi na i wa kẹ i ndea yẹ "Nga lilọ sina ngi ngukpẹi magole."

I ya na ngukpẹi magọlemẹi ji lọ. Kia le i mbẹi ji fai ta bẹ ii faini a saisaiyo i fai i lo vuli venge le i gbi lo lẹpẹu vaini. Ingẹ i kọlọ na kẹ ta yakpe ii le a yẹ kpa lama kẹ i pie na wọa ngoli hu gbonda. Hinda gbi a folọ pẹing ye ngui ma. Kẹ kpa gbi panda gbọyọa i kali wumbua.

Kia le i yẹ putu kẹ ngului ngi mọlia

"Ye le ye le tomboi ya?
"Ye le ye le tomboi ya?"

Yẹ

"Nya le Kpaula le tomboi ya."

"Kpaula a gbọ wie tomboi ya?"

"Kpaula a mbẹi wu tomboi ya."

"O hingẹisia-o, nyahangẹisia-o,
"A mu li mu gbọ Kpaula ma-o."

Hu gutungọ gutu gutu gutu ii yẹ nunga lọ kẹ kali ta ngu gẹlẹngọ ii le yẹla vuli ti kpalẹi na wu ti kpọyọ gbẹlẹng ii gui bẹ a hawa fele kẹ ti kpa gbọyọa. Kẹ Kpaula i ya ngue. Hi ti loi kpa ji wiema a ngo yila haa i lo hu mbẹi i be.

Ngi lo woi lọ wọ a li mba magbẹimẹi. Ingẹ kẹngọni a heilọ na bi tonga bẹ nunga ti gungọi kpa hu gbi nunga ti yẹ vahani ngukpei ma i yẹ kpa hu. Ngọni gbi lahei mbẹi ye ngila bẹ ma kẹ mbẹi benga.

Ngendẹi ji na i lima haa i jala le sawa hu i mbẹi kulo lewe i ngi loi yoso loni. Ndopo woi lini i male mbakui heini kpowe ji ngi gọma.

"Kpo-o," yẹ "ha--ha!"

Kẹ mbakui wotenga ngi mahu yẹ "Kia bi kẹi 'ha' kia bi kei 'ha,' mba mẹ ngọni gbọ kenjei kọma-o? Laiwa a wa la. Kenjei kọma-o?"

Ti ngaihai wunga hu. Ye ngaihai hijemẹi ji ndopoi hẹ ii kọ gbang sanggba kelei segbula ti gbi wua hu kẹ ndopoi ngua bu a lolila i mbẹi wongọi lọ.

Kẹ na hui na gbi nunga ti loi tẹi hu lọ kẹ ti ndoli woi ji mẹninga tẹ "Kpaula, ndakpẹi, bia hei? Kẹ bi li bi nda luvamẹi na hu, sọlẹ wolọ gbuama na. Mu ndea wọ bi ma humba a folẹ na bi na gbe."

Ta bẹ kẹ i pele hou a pimẹ kibi kibi kibi kibi kẹ i fonga i
yẹ ndopoi lema vuli ji i foni.

"Gbẹi, Ndopoi, bi wa ngọni gbẹma gbọ bi ye sọlẹ bi wa
ndoli bondẹi ji gama? Mbẹi ji wongọ-wongọ yẹi ji gbe lẹ!"

"Kẹkẹ mawolẹ li bi ngọni na lọ mia" yẹ "Ngọni na lọ wa
a ji gbi" yẹ "kpẹlẹ fọ."

Kẹ ta ngi Kpaula kpẹnga "Ha--ha!"

Kẹ ngọni wotenga ngi mahu na hu ya lonyo yẹ "Kia bi kẹi
'ha' kia bi kẹi 'ha,' mba mẹi ngọni gbọ kenjei kọma-o laiwa
a walai?"

Ngaihai wunga hu kpọ gbungu gbungu gbungu gbungu gbungu
kẹ Kpaula i jọsua lolila ndoli fọndẹi a mbla mbei a mbla mbei.
I loi wọ ndoli na gama ta ngi loi mbẹi na tii nu gbi lọi kẹ
mbẹi gbi lewei lọ i gbole i gbua kpa hu sahẹng. Ngili yila
kpe bẹ ii loi na.

O kẹ Kpaula loko la wumba a ngọ i gbuanga tẹi hu.

Nunga tẹ "Gbei?"

"A," yẹ "tamaa gula mbẹi ye ngla bẹ ngili yakpe bẹ" yẹ
"ngii majọni. Ngafanga ti ya gbi."

"Ah! nga ngi ndei lọ wọ bi ma."

"Na hu gbi" yẹ "hindo lọ a nge nga kọlọ na nga pie."

Kẹ i ya tọtọgbẹmọ yila gama.

Kẹ tọtọgbẹmọi ndea ngi ma a yẹ "Na ngi tọma," yẹ "ngafanga
mia" yẹ "ndolẹi na bi tẹnga lenga wọ bi kpa na la-a na" yẹ
"ndopoi lọ na kpe ndakpangọ wa bi ndea bẹ mbẹi na i majọ" yẹ
"kẹ na le a wie kẹ ba pujẹ ta vui ngi gbua i gboto bi li la
bi ti lulu." Yẹ "Bi ti lulua ta bi mbẹi na velọ kẹ gbẹ-o-gbẹ
yeka ii na ta pie a bie," yẹ "kẹ bi tọilọ ndoikpe, pọkpe,
mbawukpe, ngọnigbẹkpe ji le ba li ba la gẹ a ngengei kẹ bi
tọnga i wiea i gbọyọa. Ah," yẹ "tia mia wọ ti ngenge na wiema
na va wọ mu bi lahima muẹ 'Baa yenge hindẹi na.' Kẹ na ta pele
le ba jia le ta mia a na bi ti lulua ta bi mbẹi velọ."

Ta bẹ yẹ i kọlọ.

I pujẹi ji yeya ye bẹki ta ngi ye kpawangọ gọ i wa i gbi
belẹ pui ji la. I yẹ na wama na ta fahang wa lọ ti wani yẹ
"Nunga ti to ngi ma." Ti tọ gbọi wiema i wani lọ i ngọmbui
ji la i pujẹi wu kpui na la i ngọmbui gula ma i tọto a ti lulu
la.

Ingẹ hu ii guhani ti vondea miando kohu kẹ tohẹn-o ndiso-o i gunga hu gbi ta bẹ i nikpanga ngafanga lọ a tie a pele-o-pele kẹ ye ji ta ti guni tẹ ndo a ngafa bẹ a yẹ ma. Foloi kulọ i lẹkpẹ ndondoi gbọwunga na ti la ndenga ta wuma nyahanga ta wuma.

Kẹ ti mahẹi ndenga na ti ma yẹ "Na nyandengọ" yẹ "a mu mbẹi ji ve. Mu mọnia wọ kẹ ndakpẹi ji pelei ye ji i hounga a mue mu lii ii yẹma. A mu mbẹi ji ve."

Ti tọtoi lọ a ngi mbẹi ti wu la kahanga ma.

Ngi hindẹi, ta ta le piema ngi vondengọ ma kẹ i tọnga kpui i blanga kakama wiema vu. Kena yila i gbua ngi ma fa ngi mbẹi na ngi gbaki ma.

Yẹ "Kẹkẹ, bi mbẹi gbe; kẹkẹ, bi mbẹi gbe."

Yẹ ndawei hu ii yaa yẹ lewe fulo fulo fulo ngi mbẹi na gbi ti wa ti fe. Kia ti yẹ wala hi nunga ti yẹ belẹ tẹi hu i lo hu ti ngi mbẹi na kpẹlẹ ve, i yama la tẹi hu.

A hi wo ta i ngi nda wohugbondẹi na wie kẹ ji ta bẹ ngi lii longọ hinda gbi a tolọ le ndii ma i nẹnẹ majọi lọ kẹlẹmẹi.

Dọmẹi gbọyọa.

---

1. Recorded by man from Bunumbu in Kailahun on April 12, 1960. In this tale, the various phases in rice farming are clearly delineated. Reverend Stott's manuscript includes a Mende text and English summary of a version of this tale; summaries of versions of the tale have been published by Innes (1965):58 and Winch (1971):29-33.

TALE 96: THE TWIN AND THE SPIRIT[1]

How at one time a little child killed a spirit.[2]

There was a spirit who used to sit on a big road. If anyone came and fell into a big hole under the hammock in which he lay, he would eat the person. Now this situation troubled the country.

There were twins who were children.[3]

One twin said to his mother, "Mother, I am going to kill the spirit who is killing people."

His mother said, "Oh!" She took a whip and flogged the child; she said, "Do not do that!"

"Oh, Mother," the child said, "I am going."

The twin went.

When the twin was a mile away from the spirit, he changed into a very little child who was so small that he was unable to talk; he was just like a child who begins to walk, like a two-year old. And the twin went on.

When the twin came, the spirit was lying in the hammock. The spirit saw someone passing under him, and he saw the little child.

"Oh," the spirit turned to the child. He said, "Oh, little child."

The twin said, "Yes."

"Where is your mother?"

The twin said, "Yes."

"Oh," the spirit said, "good! I have found my child. Come, lie in the hammock. I will go; I will bring a ripe banana for you."

As soon as the twin lay in the hammock, the spirit got up; he turned his back to the twin. Then the little child turned into a big young man behind the spirit; he pushed the spirit into his very own hole. The spirit fell in the hole; he broke his arm. The spirit tried and tried before he was able to get out of the hole. The twin returned to childhood just as he was before; he lay down in the hammock where before he had been lying.

When the spirit got out of the hole, he slapped the twin; the spirit said, "Was it you who pushed me? Was it you who pushed me?"

The twin wept.

The spirit sat and looked at the twin. Such a small child would not be able to push him that strongly.

The spirit said, "Oh, I accused you falsely. You are my child."

The spirit took the twin; he again laid him in the hammock; he said, "Lie down; I will go; I will bring a ripe banana for you."

As soon as the spirit turned his back, the twin again turned into a big young man. The twin pushed the spirit, and the spirit fell. When the twin pushed the spirit and the spirit fell, the spirit's neck broke and he died.

Then the twin went into the town; he said, "I have killed the spirit."

When the twin killed that spirit at one time, all the people there were saved. Now there was not any spirit there, no spirit was disturbing the people at that time.

Na wọ wieni ndopo woi i ngafẹi wani.

Ngafẹi ji mia i yẹ heini pele wai ma. Kẹ numu gbi leke bi wanga ndowa wa mia mbọngọ i lani mbomẹi bi gula ndowẹi ji hu kẹ i bi mẹnga. Kẹ hindẹi ji lọ na gbọwoni ndọẹ kpẹlẹ ti pelei gbule, hindẹi na i gbọwu na i gbọwu na ndọẹ hu.

Filagẹi jisia ti ti lenga.

Kẹ ye yila ndenga ngi nje ma yẹ "Ye," yẹ "ngafẹi ji nunga wama ngi lima lọ ngi pa."

Yẹ "Kuo!" Kẹ i foma wumbunga i fogba. Yẹ "Baa na wie."

"Kuo, ye," yẹ "ngi limalọ."

Kẹ i ya.

Kia wọ i lini i loni pele bolo yila kẹ i wotenga a ndopo wa hẹ, kulongo ẹẹ gu a yẹpẹla. Kia leke ndo a jia a nina fo fele toni, kẹ i ya.

Kia wo i lini hani wai ji loni lani mbomẹi hu lọ a tọ numui ji a lewe ngi bu a yẹ ma i tọnga ndopo woi.

"Kuo!" Kẹ i wotenga ngi mahu, "Kuo," yẹ "ndopoi woi."

Yẹ "Ii."

"O bi nje?"

Yẹ "Ii."

"O bi kẹkẹ?"

Yẹ "Ii."

"Kuo," yẹ "kọkọkọ!" Yẹ "Ngi nya lo gọkọnga." Yẹ "Wa bi la mbomẹi hu. Ngi li ngi wa a sẹlẹ gbọli bi wẹ."

Kia i lani leke mbomęi na hu i hitęni i woveni, ndopo woi na kę i wotenga a ndakpalo wa ngi woma kę i tukpenga ngi gbǫgbǫ lowęi na kę i gulanga hu kę ngi lokoi yalenga. I lapi, i lapi, i lapi, pęing yę i gbua ndowęi ji hu kę ndopoi i yamanga ndopoya hu. Kia haa na, kę i langa mbomęi ji hu mia ha i yę lani na.

Kia i lęni kę i kpolęnga, "Bia bi nya lukpeni, bia lǫ bi nya lukpeni?"

Kę ndopoi ji ngǫę wienga.

I hei i kpe kę ndopoi bonda ęę gu i ngi lukpe a tukpei na bonda.

Yę "O ya" yę "ngi banga ba nya loi ma."

Kę i mbumbunga i nda gbǫma mbomęi hu. Yę "La," yę "ngi li ngi wa a sęlę gbǫli bi wę."

Ngi wovengǫi ji leke kę i wotenga gbǫma a ndakpalo wa kę i tukpenga kę i gulanga. Kia wǫ i tukpeni i gulai wǫ kę ngi bolęi tenga hu kę i hanga.

Kę i ya tęi hu i li i nde yę "Ngi hani wai wanga fǫ."

I hani wai na wa wǫ nunga gbi ti bao na. Na yę hani wa weka ii yaa na a yę wǫ nunga vawǫlima.

---

1. Recorded by man from Bo in Freetown on January 12, 1960. I published an English translation of this tale in "Supernatural Beings in Mende Domęisia."
2. In this tale, the malevolent spirit is called ngafa and hani wa.
3. In Mende culture twins (felanga) derive powers from their unusual birth and are the object of a cult. Mende villagers say that Ngewǫ gives twins their powers. The eldest twin is named Sao and the junior Jina irrespective of sex. Moreover, twins are associated with termites and their mounds. I was told that at the birth of twins, termites would leave their mound and come to visit the newborn babies. A ceremony must be performed when twins are born lest they die and each pair of twins observes special food taboos. Since twins can see and do things that ordinary mortals cannot, people consult them for various purposes such as obtaining wealth, gaining employment, and getting relief from a troublesome situation. In Tale 97 a twin also figures.

TALE 97: THE TWIN, THE MUSLIM, AND THE SPIRIT[1]

At one time there was a spirit who was very big, who behaved very badly, and who was very bad. This spirit put his
town beside a big road that went through the country.

If someone were going into the spirit's town, at one
time he made a law. He had a very big hammer which was very
heavy. He would give the traveller the hammer and say, "Hit
my head ten times with this hammer; I will hit your head only
once with it." I tell you that you would not be able to lift
that hammer; even if the spirit put it on your hand you hit
him--kose kose--two or three times, your shoulders would begin
to hurt. Then the spirit would ask, "Have you finished?" If
you agreed, he would come and take the hammer; he would hit
you on the head; he would eat you. The spirit destroyed many
people's lives that way.

One time there was a small child who was a twin.

The twin went and said to his family, "I am going to kill
that spirit that is killing people."

His family said, "Do not do that. In fact, do not say
that."

His family was angry with him; they beat him for some
time; they left him.

The twin said, "Even if you do all that to me, I am going
to kill that spirit."

Then the twin got up and went to a Muslim; he said,
"Learned man, I have come to have you work for me."

What kind of work is that?"

The twin said, "I want you to prepare holy water and a
charm for me.[2] I want to fight the spirit that has killed
those people."

Then the Muslim said, "When you go, tie the charm on this
hammer."

The Muslim gave the child a hammer; he said, "Tie the
charm on the handle of the hammer and sprinkle a little holy
water on it." He said, "Do not agree to hit the spirit with
his own hammer; hit him with this hammer."

The child said, "It is agreed."

Very early in the morning the child got up and started on the road. He spent the whole day walking. It was just afternoon when the child arrived joyfully before the spirit.

Then the spirit explained the entire situation to the child; he said, "If anyone comes as a stranger, he cannot sleep here. I have a little law: you hit my head ten times with my big hammer; I hit your head with it only once." He said, "When I have just done that, you may pass."

And the child said, "But Grandfather, /must I do that even/ when I am a small child?"

"Oh," the spirit said, "it is the law here."

The child said, "Then it is agreed."

And the little child decided to put his hand into his bag to take out his hammer; he sprinkled holy water on it; he tied the charm on it tightly; he said, "Then prepare yourself."

The spirit went and sat down. When the little child hit the spirit's head only once, the spirit became deaf.

"Oh," the spirit said, "small child, you have hit me ten times."

"No," the twin said, "Grandfather, I have only hit you once."

Then the spirit said, "Continue."

When the child hit the spirit's head again, both the spirit's eyes became dark (i.e., blind). As soon as the small child hit the spirit's head a third time, the spirit's head divided in half; he fell; he died.

The only thing that the child did was that he came, he took a knife out of his small bag, he cut the spirit's neck--fiaa, he took his head and hid it. Then he left.

Before five minutes had passed, a professional hunter approached and found the spirit lying /on the ground/. The hunter shot his gun /at the spirit's corpse/ ten times; then he immediately went into the center of town.

The hunter said, "I have killed the spirit who was making people afraid recently."

Then the little child also arrived; he said, "Did you really kill that spirit?"

The hunter said, "Yes."

The child said, "No, you are lying. You are not the one who killed the spirit; I killed him."

Then everyone rushed to see the place where the spirit had died. When they came, they found the dead spirit. When the professional hunter said that he had killed the spirit, everyone believed him, because he was an important person and he had a gun. When the little child said /that he had killed the spirit/, no one believed him.

Then the people said, "Little child, did you say that you killed this spirit?"

The child said, "Yes."

"What will you show us to prove that you killed this spirit?"

The child said that they should ask the man, because the man said that he killed this spirit; he should show them something /to prove/ that he killed this spirit.

Then the people asked the professional hunter, "Hunter, did you say that you killed this spirit?"

He said, "Yes."

"It is agreed; we have seen that this spirit is dead, but he does not have a head. Go and bring his head."

The hunter went and tied an ant hill; he brought it. The people set it on the spirit's neck, it did not fit. When the hunter tied and brought a boat, it did not fit.

When the people asked the little child, they said, "Little child, you said that you killed the spirit. Go and bring his head."

As soon as the little child went and brought the spirit's head, the people set it /on the spirit's neck/; it fitted perfectly. Then they put the little child on their shoulders.

At one time that little child brought happiness into the world. The child became a happy person.

The people said to the professional hunter who had lied, "You are a liar. In vain you went there. You did not kill this spirit. You just wanted to claim /that you had killed/ it."

At one time the people made that little child chief in
that country; they drove away that professional hunter, because he lied to them.

Hani wa yila i yẹlọ wọ na. Ye hani wai ji gọlọngọ wa tao
i pie nyọmungọ wa tao ngi nyamungọ wa yẹla. Hani wai ji i li
i ngi lẹi ji la le kinii pele wa ma. Ye pelei na i ma ndọlọ
lima.

Bi ya wọ pẹing bi ya li hani wai ji tẹi ji hu, sawa yila
mia wọ i nde. Hama wa ngi yeya ye hamẹi na ngọlọngọ wa tao
miningọ wa. Ta mia wọ a fe bi wẹ yẹ "Nya wumba le a hamẹi
ji pu" yẹ "nya nga bi wumba le la le yakpe." Ngẹ bia bẹ gu
bẹ pẹing ba hamẹi na wumbu kẹ inge i ngua ye bi yeya kẹ bi le
ngi ma kọsẹ heima fele ye sawẹi na na kẹ bi gbakisia ti tatonga
a gbalẹ la kẹ i ndenga yẹ "Bi kpọyọa?" Bi luma le ta wa le i
mbumnua a bi le vuli wu ma kẹ i bi mẹa. I numu gboto ti levui
nyanilọ na hu.

Wati yila ndopo wo hi kẹ ndopoi ji felai yela.

Kẹ i ya i nde ngi bonda ma yẹ "Hani wai na i na wiema kẹ
ngi ngi paa."

Ngi bonda tẹ "Baa na wie." Tẹ "Ba yẹ bi la lẹ pẹing
njẹpẹi na ma."

Ti jọlẹ ngi ma ti ngi lewe haa ti gbe ngi ma.

Yẹ "Wu na bẹ kpẹ wie" yẹ "ngi ma ngi hani wai na wa."

Kẹ i hiyea kẹ i ya mọimọ yila gama yẹ "Kamọ" yẹ "ngi wa
bi yenge mbẹ."

"Gbẹ ngengei la lọ a gbẹ?"

Kẹ i ndenga yẹ "Nya longọ bi nẹsi gbua mbe kẹ lasimọ."
Yẹ "Hani wai na a nungei nasia wa ta mia nya longọ ngi ngi lapi
a ngie."

Ke mọimọi ji bẹ ke i ndenga i ngi gọ a navo wulo ke i
fenga. Kẹ i lasimọi ji wienga panda kẹ i fenga ndopoi ji we
kẹ nẹsi.

Yẹ "Lasamọi ji bi mala" yẹ "bi ya" yẹ "bi ngili hamẹi
ji."

Mọimọi i ngi gọ a hamẹ. Yẹ "Bi ngili hamẹi ji ye nguima
kẹ bi nẹsi ji kulo vaifaima." Yẹ "Baa luma baa hani wai na
lewe a ngi nda hamẹi na-o," yẹ "hamẹi ji ba ngi lewe la."

Ta bẹ yẹ "Kulungọi."

Kẹ ngele wonga ngenda tẹtẹ kẹ ndopo woi ji i hiyenga i pelei ji hou. I luva jiama kpẹing. Gbọkọ voloi mia kinii kẹ i fonga. Kia le i foni hani wai ji gulọi kẹ i ya ngi gulọ a kohunẹ.

Kẹ i hindei ji kpe hungẹa a ngie yẹ "Numu gbi bi wa hota ya a bie yi mbëi." Yẹ "Sawa wulolọ nya yeya" yẹ "hamẹi ji nya yeya nya hama wai ji mia ba nya wumba le la pu" yẹ "nya ngi bi wumba le la yilakpe." Yẹ "Ngi na wiea le kẹ bi lewenga."

Kẹ ndopoi ndenga yẹ "Kẹ maada jina ndopo wulo a nge?"

"Kuo," yẹ "sawẹi mia mbei."

Yẹ "Kẹ kulungọi."

Kẹ ndopo wuloi bẹ ke i ndenga kẹ i loko wa ngi bọlọi na hu kẹ i ngi hamẹi na wumbua i nẹsi na vaifaima lasimọi na yingọi lọma kpa yẹ "Kẹ bi magbatẹ-o."

Kẹ hani wai na ya i hei. Ji ndopo woi na i hani wai wumba lewe yakpe kẹ ngi woli hu gbọkpọnga.

"Kpo," yẹ "ndopo wuloi" yẹ "i ye pu."

"Ọọ" yẹ "maada," yẹ "nyakpe mia le ngi fea."

Kẹ i ndenga yẹ "Ngamanga-o."

Kia gbọma i ngi wumba lewe la kẹ ngi yamẹi kpẹ gbindinga kẹ sawa ye na kia le ba ndopo wuloi na i hani wai na wumba lewe kẹ ngi wui na kọlẹ ndia kẹ i gula i ha.

Ndopo wuloi bẹ ii gbe-o-gbe wie kẹ i wa i ngi bowẹi na gbualọ ngi bọ wuloi na hu kẹ i hani wai na bolo lewenga fiaa kẹ i ngi wui na gbuanga i li i ndọwu. I gbua na hi.

Ii hitini bẹ minut lọlu, kpandẹwilimọ gbuanganga kẹ i hani wai ji malenga lani kẹ i kpandẹi ji wunga ma puu i pie kẹ i ya tẹ hu. I yẹ lima ndopo wuloi bẹ a li kẹ i ya ndia bẹ tẹ hu kaka.

Yẹ "Hani wai ji gẹ a nunga huluwa" yẹ "ngi pa."

Kẹ ndopoi wuloi ji bẹ i fonga. "Inge" yẹ "bia bi hani wai na wa?"

Yẹ "Mn."

Yẹ "Mn, mn," yẹ "bi ndẹ gula;" yẹ "bia yaa na ba hani wai na wa" yẹ "nya ngi pa."

Kẹ nunga gbi ti gai gama ti wa ti ti hani wai ji wamẹi ji lọ. Kẹ ti walọ ti hani wai ji male hangọ. Eh, numui gbi ji kpandẹwilimọi ji i ndeni yẹ ta hani wai ji wa ti gbi ti lani a ta jifa ta kpako a ngie ta a kpandẹ ngi yeya. Ji ndopo wuloi ji ta ndeni tii lai la.

Kẹ ti ndea tẹ "Ndopo wuloi ji bẹ bia bi hani wai ji wa?"

Yẹ "Mn."

"A gbọ vuli ba kẹ a mue kẹ bia bi hani wai ji wa?"

"Kuo," yẹ "a kenẹi na ta ngi mọli jifa kenẹi na ndenga yẹ ta hani wai ji wa ta i kẹ gbọ a tie, kẹ ta hani wai ji wa."

Kẹ ti kpandẹwilimọ mọlinga, "Kpandẹwilimọi bia bẹ bi hani wai ji wa?"

Yẹ "Ọ."

"Kulungoi. Mu tọa hani wai ji hangọi kẹ ngi wui ii yaa, li le họ bi li bi wa a ngi wui."

Kpandẹwilimọi na a li lọ i kọkọi ye na ma yili a wa ti hei hani wai wu ya ẹẹ bẹnga ii ye na ma. Ji i ndẹndẹi ye na ma nyi ẹẹ bẹnga.

Kia ti ndopo wuloi ji mọli tẹ "Ndopo wuloi na họ bẹ bia bi hani wai ji wa kẹ li le bi li bi wa a ngi wui."

Ndopo wuloi na kia le i li i wani a hani wai na wui ti heininga i bẹ lọga ja. Kẹ ti ndopo wuloi na wumbunga ti gbaki ma.

Ndopo wuloi na wo i wani a kohunẹ ma hinda ndunya. Ndopoi na i wote wọ a kohunẹmọ.

Kpandẹwilimọi na ta i ndẹlọ gulani tia bẹ ti ndelo ngi ma tẹ "Bia ndẹ gulamọ gbama lọ a bie bia ya na baa hani wai ji wa. Bi longọi le bi wẹma."

Ti ye ndopo wuloi na wote wo a mahei ndọlọi na hu, kpandẹ-wilimọi na ti kpẹ tẹ "Kia bi ndẹ gula mu wẹ."

---

1. Recorded by young man from Pujehun in Freetown on May 13, 1960.
2. Lasimọ, charm consisting of a paper with Arabic writing sealed in a leather pouch.

TALE 98:   THE NORTHERN MAN AND THE SPIRIT[1]

The young man and Josogbakui.

At one time Josogbakui was frightening people on a road; he frightened people. If anyone came with a bundle, he would take it away from him. So it happened there. Everyone in the country was upset.

One young man who was very wild came out of the North. He came. He put a lot of small bits of crushed rice in a basket; he wrapped a country-cloth around it; he came.

The young man said, "Father."

The man said, "Yes."

The young man said, "I am going to that town."

He said, "But now the sun has gone down a lot."

The young man said, "I will go; if I want, I will sleep on the road."

"Oh," he said, "Comrade, do not go. Josoi frightens people a lot on this road."

"Oh," the young man said, "but I am going now whatever may happen."

Later the young man came into a compound; he lay down there; he slept and God watched /over him/.

The young man's companion changed into Josoi. He ran after the young man; he chased him kibi kibi kibi kibi. He walked ten miles; he did not see the young man. "Oh, how can the young man walk in this kind of night with such a load?" And Josoi returned. Just as Josoi reached the door, just as he bowed down and entered the house, the young man came out quickly and he beat the door kokoko.

Josoi said, "Who is there?"

The young man said, "It is I, Father."

Josoi said, "Oh, Comrade, what is the matter? What is the matter, Comrade?"

The young man said, "Oh, I went today, but the night is long and the forest is dark. I do not have any fire; give me some fire."

Then Josoi gave him some fire; he said, "Take that fire-wood yonder."

The young man took the firewood.

As soon as the young man went, he returned to his previous place; he lay down there; he lay down again and he slept.

Josoi again followed after him; he pursued him kibi kibi kibi kibi; he did not see him. Josoi walked for twenty miles; he did not see the young man. Oh, then he returned. When finally Josoi had just entered his house, the young man came again and beat on the door ko ko ko ko.

Josoi said, "Who is there?"

"Comrade," the young man said, "It is I, Jo Kpau."

He said, "What is the matter, Comrade? What is the matter, Comrade? Comrade, what is the matter?"

The young man said, "The firebrand that you gave me has gone out in my hand; I have come for you to give me another."

Josoi said, "Eh, there is a firebrand yonder; take it."

The young man took it and left again.

When the young man had just gone, Josoi went again /to the place/ where he used to eat many people. He did not get the young man at all.

When morning came, the young man met Josoi standing on the road. Immediately the young man caught Josoi and took him off that road.

Ah, the little tale that I heard I have now related.

Josogbakui mia wọ. Ndakpoi ta Josoi ji.

A nunga huluwa pelei hu a nunga huluwa. Numu gbi wa haka gbi ya bi yeya a kpua bi yeya. Hindẹi ji wie lọ na ndọlọi kpẹlẹ ti yẹ yẹngẹlẹ.

Ndakpao yila ta bẹ njukpang lọ wa kẹlẹma ii ma, kẹ i gbua mia kọọ kẹ i wanga kẹ i mba gbẹnyẹi ji wụnga kaka kahẹi ji ma i kọndi gulẹi bembema kẹ i wa.

Yẹ "Kẹkẹ."

Yẹ "Ẹẹ."

Yẹ "Ngi lima mbeindo lọ tẹi ji hu."

Yẹ "Kẹ" yẹ "foloi yeingọ wa na."

Yẹ "Nya wao ngi loni ngi yii pele hu."

"Kuo," yẹ "ndakpẹi," yẹ "baa li," yẹ "Josoi a nunga huluwa pelei ji hu ngọlọngọ."

"Kuo," yẹ "kẹ ngi lima na" yẹ "kẹ i ye gbi leni."

Kẹ i wama na kului hu i laa na ndakpaloi ji kẹ i la kẹ i yia. Kẹ Ngewọ pienga.

Ndakpẹi ji i maluvea a Josoi ji i lewenga a pimẹ i tonga ngi woma i kpẹ kibi kibi kibi i jia maili pu ii ngi lọni. "Kuo ye gbẹe ndakpaoi ji jia bondẹi ji kpindi ji hu a haka." Kẹ i yamanga. Ngi yamangọi ji hu i wanga i fonga pẹlẹ la ji le i mawẹlẹni le yẹ i wa pẹlẹ bu kẹ ndakpaloi ji gbu ka ta kẹ i wa kẹ i pẹlẹi ji la lewenga kọkọkọkọ.

Yẹ "Ye mia?"

Yẹ "Nya mia;" yẹ "kẹkẹ."

Yẹ "Kuo," yẹ "ndakpẹi, gbẹe? Gbẹe ndakpẹi?"

Yẹ "Kuo, ngi ya ha." Yẹ "Kẹ kpindi ji wọlọngọ tawao ngolẹi hu gbindingọ nya ma" yẹ "ngọmbui gbi ii nya yeya" yẹ "nya gọ a ngọmbu."

Kẹ i ngi gọnga yẹ "Koba yọmbui na mia," yẹ "mbumbua."

Kẹ i wumbua.

Kia leke i lini kẹ i wa gbọma ngi lomẹi ji ha kẹ i la na kẹ i langa gbọma kẹ i yinga.

I tonga gbọma ngi woma i kpẹ kibi kibi kibi kibi ii ngi lọni. Maili numu gboyọngọ i jia ii ngi lọni. Kuo kẹ i yama. Ngi lengoi ji hu ngi wa pẹlẹ bu leke-o kẹlẹma mia kẹ i wanga gbọma kẹ i pẹlẹ la lewenga kọkọkọkọ.

Yẹ "Ye mia?"

"Ndakpẹi," yẹ "nya mia Jo Kpau."

Yẹ "Gbẹe ndakpẹi? Gbẹe ndakpẹi? Ndakpẹi gbẹe?"

Yẹ "Kọtui ji ha bi feni mbẹ" yẹ "i lufẹnga nya yeya" yẹ "ta mia" yẹ "ngi wa bi nya gọ."

Yẹ "Hẹ," yẹ "ti jọ kọtui na mia" yẹ "mbumbu."

Kẹ i wumbua kẹ i ya gbọma.

Ngi lingọ leke kẹ i lewenga gbọma kẹ i ya ha mia i yẹ la na Josogbakui ji loni wọ wie mẹma kakakakakaka. Ii ndakpaloi ji yaa sọni kpaung.

Ngendei na wama i ngi maleni loi pele ma a mẹi kpa i houa i Josoi na hou wọ fọ i gbia pele ma.

Aa ngi na woi na mẹni ngi hunge.

----

1. Recorded by man from Bo in Freetown on January 20, 1960.

TALE 99: THE NORTHERNER, THE SPIRIT, AND HIS BROTHER[1]

My father, at one time there was a spirit who used to sit on a road and his brother. If they saw a person, the spirit would fight with him at one time. If the person knocked the spirit to the ground, he would die; if the spirit knocked the person to the ground, he would kill and eat the person. While the spirit and the person were fighting, the spirit's brother's duty was to say, "Comrade, knock this foolish person on the ground; we will eat him." Each time there was a fight, the brother said, "Comrade, knock this foolish person on the ground; we will eat him." The spirit killed a lot of people at one time.

Then a man arose in the North who did not lose fights. He came; he said that he was going to fight that spirit now.

"Oh," people said, "do not go there."

The man said that he was going; he went.

When the man arrived there, the spirit immediately said, "Ah, if you want to pass, we must fight before you pass."

The man and the spirit fought; they fought; they fought.

The spirit's brother was worried, he said, "Comrade, knock this foolish person on the ground; we will eat him."

They fought. Then the spirit fell and injured his hand.

His brother said, "Comrade, knock this foolish person on the ground..."

The spirit said, "Do not say, 'Comrade, knock this foolish person on the ground'; do not say, 'Comrade, knock this foolish person on the ground'; my hand is injured."

They fought; they fought; they fought; they fought. Then the young man lifted this spirit and dropped him; the spirit injured his leg.

The spirit's brother remained sitting there; he said, "Comrade, knock this foolish person on the ground."

The spirit said, "In fact, do not say to me, 'Comrade, knock this foolish person on the ground'; that gboi you heard was my hand being injured; this motor you heard was it not my leg that was injured?"

At that time they continued fighting. The young man knocked the spirit down on the ground; he killed the spirit at one time.

This is the end of this story.

Nya kɛ, hani wai yila mia wɔ i yɛ hei pele ma ta ngi nde. Ta ti gbenga bi ma wa ta wu lapima wɔ. Bi ngi gula a halɔ ta bɛ i bi gula i bi wa i bi mɛ. Kɛ wu ya ndapi ji gɔma ngi nde yila lɔ loni ta ngi ndɛi le mia yɛ "Ndakpɛi i babamɔi ji gula mu ngi mɛ." Ti ye gbi yɛ ndapi ji gɔma yɛ "Ndakpɛi i babamɔi ji gula mu ngi mɛ." I nungɛi jisia lɔ wɔ wa kaka.

Kɛ ndakpa-o yila ta bɛ hiyea kɔɔ ta bɛ ngi lapi ɛɛ gɔ kɛ i wa. Yɛ "Hani wai na ngi lima na."

"O," tɛ "baa li na."

Yɛ "Ngi lima." Kɛ i ya.

Kia wɔ i li i foni vaya "A" yɛ "bi longa bi le kɛ mua lapi pɛing bi yá a le."

Ta bɛ kɛ ti ngilinga ma hei. Ti ndapi ji gɔ ti ndapi ji gɔ ti ndapi ji gɔ.

Ngi li a hɛlɛ yɛ "Ndakpɛi i babamɔi ji gula mu ngi mɛ."

Ti ndapi ji gɔ kɛ hani wai ji ya i gula kɛ i tokoi yɛlinga.

Yɛ "Ndakpɛi i babamɔi gula."

Yɛ "Baa yɛ la 'ndakpɛi i babamɔi gula,'" yɛ "baa yɛ le 'ndakpɛi i babamɔi gula'" yɛ "nya lokoi yɛlia."

Ti ndapi ji gọ ti ndapi ji gọ ti ndapi ji gọ ti ndapi ji
gọ kẹ i hani wai ji wumbunga kẹ i kula kẹ ngi gbalẹi yẹlinga.

Kẹ ngi ndei loa hei mia yẹ "Ndakpẹi, i babamọi gula."

Yẹ "Ingẹ baa yẹ nya ma bẹ 'ndakpẹi, i babamọi gula!'"
Yẹ "Gboi na bi mẹnini" yẹ "nya lokoi mia i ngẹlini"; yẹ "mọtoi
ji bi mẹnia" yẹ "nya gbalẹi ya na i ngẹlinga?"

Ti loi wọ ndapi na gọma ndakpoi na i hani wai na gula
i pa wọ fọ.

Dọmẹi ji ngi gẹlẹma ye lọ a ji.

---

1. Recorded by man from Bo in Freetown on January 12, 1960

TALE 100: THE YOUNG MAN AND THE SPIRIT[1]

At one time a spirit was on the road; he built a big town
in which he lived. If anyone walked on that road and he just
reached the spirit, the spirit said, "Come, beat me ten times;
I will beat you once." My father, if you beat him ten times,
he would beat you only once, but you would die and he would
eat you. At one time he killed people there; the situation
was oppressive; he killed people in that country; he killed
many people; the situation oppressed the people of the country.

There was an extremely strong young man and he had a very
large hammer. Then man went; he said, "I am going to kill
that spirit."

People said, "Do not go."

But the man started on the road; he hid the hammer behind
him in a big bag.

When he had just reached the spirit, he said, "Sir, good
morning."

The spirit said, "Yes."

He said, "Thank you."

The spirit said, "Where are you going?"

He said, "I am going to this place."

The spirit said, "Before you pass, there is a little law here."

He said, "What is the law?"

The spirit said, "You hit me ten times; I hit you once."

"Oh," he said, "is that all?"

The spirit said, "Yes."

He said, "Oh, then I agree. Bend over."

When the spirit bent over, the young man hit him once.

Immediately the spirit said, "That was nine times, nine times!"

"Oh," he said, "Father, I hit you just once."

The spirit said, "That is what you say, but it is nine."

Then the spirit bent over again.

When the young man hit him, the spirit said, "Oh, that was ten times, that was ten times!"

The young man continued beating the spirit until he killed him.

At one time the young man killed that spirit; he removed him from that road. People continued walking on that road; no spirit killed them there.

Now I have related the little story that I heard.

Hani wai mia wọ i yẹ pelei ma; i li lọ i ta wa lo i na. Numu gbi bi jia wọ a pelei na bi foa wọ ngi gama leke yẹ "Wa bi nya lewe puu ngi bi lewe yila." Nya kẹ, bi ngi lenga pu a bi lewe yakpe kẹ bi haa kẹ i bi mẹa. I nunga wai lọ na wọ i nunga wa ndolei na hu. Numu gboto mia i ti wani. Hindẹi ji i gbọu na ndọbla na.

Ndakpao yila kpayangọ kẹlẹma ii ma kẹ i ya kẹ i hama wa le mia hamẹi ngọngọ kẹ i luvea kẹ i luvea yẹ "Ngi lima hani wai na wama."

Tẹ "Baa li."

Kẹ i pelei hou bẹ kẹ i ndọwua sọ ngi woma kpava wai ji hu.

Kia wọ le i foi ngi ma yẹ "Kenẹi bi wa-e."

Yẹ "Hn."

Yẹ "Bi sie."

Yẹ "Bi ye lima?"

Yẹ "Ngi lima hindẹi ji lọ."

Yẹ "Pẹing bi lewe yẹ sawa wulo lọ mbei."

Yẹ "Sawẹi la a gbẹ?"

Yẹ "Ba nya lewe pu ngi bi lewe yila."

"Kuo," yẹ "na le le?"

Yẹ "Hn."

"Kuo," yẹ "kẹ ngi kulunga."

Yẹ "Kẹ mawẹ."

Kia ji i mawẹ ji ndakpẹi i hu gbolẹi yila.

A mẹi gbu yẹ "I ya tawu tawu."

"Kuo," yẹ "kẹkẹ" yẹ "ngi lewea le yilakpe."

Yẹ "Ta mia bẹ" yẹ "kẹ tawu."

Kẹ i mawẹa gbọma.

Ji i hu gbolẹi, "Kpuu," yẹ "i ya pu i pu."

"Kuo," yẹ "kẹkẹ ba felekpe mia-e."

I loi wọ ndema haa kẹ i paa.

I hani wa na wa wọ fo; i gbia pelei na ma. Nunga ti lo wọ jiama a pelei na. Hani wa ẹẹ yaa ti wa na.

Ngi na wuloi na mẹni ngi hungẹ.

---

1. Recorded by man from Bo in Freetown on January 27, 1960.

SELECTED BIBLIOGRAPHY

Aginsky, E. G., A Grammar of the Mende Language (Language
    Dissertations, Supplement to Language, no. 20 /1935/).
Anonymous, Mu Jaleisia Lẹẹnga (Bo: Bunumbu Press, 1955).

Beidelman, T. O., "Kaguru Folklore and the Concept of Reciprocity,"
    Zeitschrift fur Ethnologie 92 (1967) 74-88.
Berry, J., Spoken Art in West Africa (London: University of
    London, 1961).

Crosby, K. H., "Polygamy in Mende Country," Africa 10 (1937)
    249-264.
----- and I. C. Ward, An Introduction to the Study of Mende
    (Cambridge: Cambridge University Press, 1944).

Eberl-Elber, Ralph, "Two Mende Tales," Bulletin of the School
    of Oriental and African Studies 10 (1940) 223-234.

Fenton, J. S., "Characters in Mende Stories," Sierra Leone Studies
    15 (1929) 34-41.
Finnegan, Ruth, Oral Literature in Africa (Oxford: Clarendon
    Press, 1970).

Georges, R. A., "Structure in Folktales: A Generative-
    Transformational Approach," Conch 2 (1970) 4-17.

Harnetty, E., "Some Native Proverbs Revised," Sierra Leone
    Studies 9 (1927) 55-60.
Harris, W. T., "Ceremonies and Stories Connected with Trees,
    Rivers, and Hills in the Protectorate of Sierra Leone,"
    Sierra Leone Studies n.s. 2 (1954) 91-97.
----- "Ngewo and Leve," Sierra Leone Bulletin of Religion 1
    (1963) 34-36; 2 (1963), 64-65.
----- "How the Mende People First Started to Pray to Ngewo,"
    Sierra Leone Bulletin of Religion 2 (1963) 61-63.
----- and E. G. Parrinder, The Christian Approach to the
    Animist (London: Edinburgh House Press, 1960).
----- and Harry Sawyerr, The Springs of Mende Belief and
    Conduct (Freetown: Sierra Leone University Press, 1968).
Herskovits, M. J. and F. S., Dahomean Narrative: A Cross-
    Cultural Analysis (Evanston: Northwestern University Press,
    1958).
Hofstra, Sjoerd, "The Ancestral Spirits of the Mendi,"
    Internationales Archiv fur Ethnographie 39 (1941) 177-196.
Hommel, W. L., Art of the Mende (College Park: University of
    Maryland, 1974).

Innes, Gordon, "Some Features of Theme and Style in Mende Folk-
tales," Sierra Leone Language Review 3 (1964) 6-19.
----- "The Function of Song in Mende Folktales," Sierra Leone
Language Review 4 (1965) 54-63.
----- A Mende-English Dictionary (Cambridge: Cambridge
University Press, 1969).

Jedrej, M. C., "An Analytical Note on the Land and Spirits of
the Sewa Mende," Africa 44 (1974) 38-45.

Kilson, Marion, "Mende Folk Tales," West African Review
(December 1960) 87-91; (January-February 1961) 45-48.
----- "Supernatural Beings in Mende Domeisia," Sierra Leone
Bulletin of Religion 3 (1961) 1-11.
----- "Social Relationships in Mende Domeisia," Sierra Leone
Studies n.s. 15 (December 1961) 169-172.
Kilson, Martin, Political Change in a West African State
(Cambridge: Harvard University Press, 1966).

Little, K. L., "A Mende Musician Sings of His Adventures,"
Man 48 (1948) 27-28.
----- The Mende of Sierra Leone: A West African People in Tran-
sition (London: Routledge and Kegan Paul, 1951; 1967).
Luke, H. C., A Bibliography of Sierra Leone (Oxford, 1925).

McCulloch, M., Peoples of Sierra Leone Protectorate (London:
International African Institute, 1950).
Migeod, F. W. H., The Mende Language (London: Kegan Paul, 1908).
----- "Mende Songs," Man 16 (1916) 184-191.
----- "A Mende Dance," Man 17 (1917) 153-156.
----- "A View of Sierra Leone (London: Kegan Paul, 1926).

Ndanema, Isaac, "The Rationale of Mende 'Swears,'" Sierra Leone
Bulletin of Religion 6 (1964) 21-25.

Propp, V., Morphology of the Folktale (Austin: University of
Texas Press, 1970).

Senior, M. M., "Some Mende Proverbs," Africa 17 (1947) 202-205.
Stott, A., "Mende Storytellers and Stories," (ms., n.d.).
Sumner, A. T., A Handbook of the Mende Language (Freetown:
Government Printing Office, 1917).

Williams, G. J., A Bibliography of Sierra Leone 1925-1967
(New York: Africana Publishing Corporation, 1970).
Winch, J. M., "Religious Attitudes of the Mende Towards Land,"
Africana Research Bulletin (Institute of African Studies,
Fourah Bay College) 2 (1971) 17-36.

INDEX OF TALE TITLES

ROYAL ANTELOPE AND SPIDER
West African Mende Tales

Royal Antelope and Spider, with friends and relations—Chimpanzee, Cat, Rat, Leopard, Lizard, and Bush Spirit—figure very actively in this collection of 100 Mende tales. They are a lively part of the oral tradition of the Mende people in Sierra Leone and West Africa.

Marion Kilson has recorded the Mende tales in their original language and translated them into English. Various storytellers recounted their favorites and talked about the occasions on which each tale is most often told. The texts are given in both Mende and English.

The tales themselves are enormously engaging and informative.
Mrs. Kilson's introduction provides a comprehensive discussion of literary values and ideas in Mende society, of interest to all students of oral literature and those social scientists who explore the complex relations between a society and its literature. Her analysis of tale structure and content presents a novel model for generating Mende tale patterns and an intriguing exploration of tale content in relation to Mende social relations and values.

Marion Kilson, Director of Research at the Radcliffe Institute, has taught at the University of Massachusetts in Boston, Simmons College, and Newton College. She is the author of *Kpele Lala: Ga Religious Songs and Symbols* (Cambridge, Mass.: Harvard University Press, 1971) and *African Urban Kinsmen* (London: C. Hurst & Company, 1974; New York: St. Martin's Press, 1974).

$10 (U.S.A. only)
Limited Paperback Edition
ISBN 0-916704-01-7
Cover design by Emily G. Dusser de Barenne

The Press of The Langdon Associates
41 Langdon Street
Cambridge, Massachusetts 02138